W9-ANY-060

Mary Lincoln

Ruth Painter Randall

BIOGRAPHY OF A MARRIAGE

A DELL BOOK

Published by
DELL PUBLISHING CO., INC.
750 Third Avenue
New York 17, N.Y.

Reprinted by arrangement with
Little, Brown and Company
Boston, Mass.

Designed and produced by
Western Printing and Lithographing Company

DEDICATION: For Jim

First Dell printing—February, 1961

Printed in U.S.A.

FOREWORD

Several years before his *Lincoln the President* (volumes I and II) was published in 1945, my husband, J. G. Randall, asked me to collaborate with him in two of its chapters: "The House on Eighth Street" and "Sifting the Ann Rutledge Evidence." As a result of this request I spent many months working in old letters and documents, getting as close to the Lincoln marriage as possible. The Herndon-Weik manuscripts had finally been opened to the public in 1942 and it was thus possible at last to investigate these private papers of William H. Herndon, whose account of Mrs. Lincoln had been largely impressed upon the public mind.

In preparing a biography, as in a court trial, one examines all available evidence and weighs the reliability of those who give testimony. To find out about the Lincoln marriage it was necessary to go deeply into a study of Herndon, the most featured witness in the case of Mary Lincoln. It was my good fortune that, at the time I was working with Mr. Randall, his research assistant was David Donald, who was then engaged in the study which led later to the publication of his *Lincoln's Herndon.*

The long-end result of my collaboration with Mr. Randall in those two chapters (and in no other) was our conviction that Mary Lincoln needed a new trial before the court of historical investigation, that in view of much new material and new means of checking on some of the old "evidence" which had been accepted, judgment should be appealed.

This book is that new hearing in the case of Mary Lincoln. Its aim, however imperfectly accomplished, has been to go over the evidence, old and new, pro and con, to consider it afresh, and to come nearer the truth about Abraham Lincoln's wife.

But a biography should be more than a court trial; it should include portrayal of character. As far as lies within my power I have tried to restore, from tested historical material, the personality of Mary Lincoln. In treating her various qualities, desirable and undesirable, one runs into a vicious circle. Because her failings have been overstated, a biographer has to deal with that distortion to clear the subject of what is false. This involves a repetition of the falsehoods in order to refute them, and the result is a further overemphasis of her failings, which is especially unfortunate since reputations are affected by a Gresham's law: bad report drives out good.

Never has an author encountered more interest and encouragement. Widely separated safe-deposit boxes have been opened to give me unused and unsuspected letters throwing new light on some settled notions. Mrs. Lincoln fortunately wrote many letters; several hundred of them have been studied in the preparation of this book. Lincoln scholars over the country also have constantly been on the alert for references or clues that would be helpful.

This volume is the biography of a marriage. Marriage involves two individuals and their relation to each other. It is impossible fully to understand a wife without knowledge of the husband. I have therefore planned the treatment as a double biography. It has been my purpose to present the personality and intimate life of Abraham Lincoln along with a full-length biography of his wife.

R. P. R.

Urbana, Illinois

edge to help me in understanding Mrs. Lincoln's unstable temperament.

David Rankin Barbee, with signal courtesy and generosity, has shared with me material about Mrs. Lincoln, the fruit of extensive research on his part. Professor Charles H. Coleman has permitted me to use the manuscript of his scholarly study of Lincoln's Coles County relatives. Willard L. King has generously opened the way to my use of Mrs. Lincoln's letters to David Davis. That dear and inspiring lady, Madame Dorothy Lamon Teillard, has conferred a special feeling of closeness to the Lincolns in telling of her father's recollections.

Professor Allan Nevins out of his crowded life has still taken time to send notes and clues uncovered in his own research. Back of many a brief sentence is a pleasant story of a friend who pointed the way to material or otherwise rendered special aid. Among those who have given assistance in various helpful ways are Professor Sleeter Bull, Professor Robert G. Bone, Mr. Lloyd Dunlap, Mrs. James J. Doland, Professor Frank Freidel, Dr. Theodore Fisch, Dr. Lavern Hamand, Professor Arthur Hogue, Mr. J. Walter Hosier, Mr. Frank B. Howard, Professor Jay B. Hubbell, Miss Margaret Norton, Mr. C. Norton Owen, Mr. Thomas I. Starr, Dr. Milton Shutes, Mr. Claude E. Simmonds, Mr. Wayne C. Temple, Professor T. Harry Williams, Miss Lucy C. Williams and Professor J. Harvey Young.

The editors of the New York *Times Magazine* have kindly given permission to use portions of two articles which I published in their pages. Likewise the editor of the *Abraham Lincoln Quarterly* has allowed me to use parts of an article published in its pages.

Like so many others in Lincoln writing, I owe much gratitude to Frederick H. Meserve for letting me draw on his great collection of pictures. Lida E. Voight has by dint of high skill plus woman's intuition deciphered my handwriting to type the entire manuscript.

Finally I wish to record the cherished words of a great and beloved personality. In moments of doubt and groping for expression I have remembered with affection and gratitude Carl Sandburg's advice to me about this book: "Write it in your own way and write it as a woman."

To all these dear benefactors I am profoundly grateful. For errors that remain I alone am to blame. A writer's reach must always exceed his grasp.

R. P. R.

chapter 1

YOUNG MARY IN YOUNG SPRINGFIELD

Springfield, Illinois, January 4, 1840. It was a cold, snowy evening as the stagecoach pulled into town, bearing among its passengers from St. Louis a young couple, Mr. and Mrs. Benjamin S. Edwards, who had decided to make the new state capital their home. The young wife looked with apprehensive eyes upon the raw little town with "No street lights, no sidewalks, and the mud so thick it was hard for the stage to pull through." After depositing some of its passengers at the American House, the old coach went lumbering up through the dark to a large, stately house on the hill where the Centennial Building now stands.

It was the home of Benjamin's brother, Ninian Wirt Edwards, with whom the couple were to stay until their own home was ready. Years later Benjamin's wife described their arrival: "My heart was heavy at the thought of meeting strangers, but O! what a haven of rest it appeared to me when we entered that bright hospitable home and how quickly my fears were dispersed by the cordial welcome we received from all of the family."

The opened door led into a richly furnished interior ablaze with candles, oil lamps, and cheerful open fires. Across that illumination there came to meet her a young woman whose face was aglow with friendliness and welcome. She was a small, pretty, plump girl with vivid coloring of blue eyes, white skin, and light chestnut hair, but what the bride noted was not a catalogue of features but the joyousness of her responsive spirit. "I was attracted toward her at once," said Mrs. Edwards. "The sunshine in her heart was reflected in her face. She greeted me with such warmth of manner that I was made to feel perfectly at home and ... she insisted upon my calling her by her first name, saying she knew we would be great friends and I must call her Mary." So our spotlight comes to rest on Mary Todd as she was when Abraham Lincoln, her future husband, first knew her.

Mary Todd had come to Springfield in the fall of 1839 to make her home with her sister, Mrs. Ninian Wirt Edwards. It was a sensible arrangement for a number of reasons. Mary's fine old home in Lexington, Kentucky, was presided over by a stepmother burdened with many children. Marriage was about the only career open to women in that Victorian era, and unmarried girls were at a premium in Springfield. Mary's cousin, John J. Hardin, once playfully suggested that some enterprising person bring out "a cargo of the ladies" to Illinois, just as a shipload of prospective wives had been taken to colonial Virginia and disposed of at so many pounds of tobacco per head. He felt sure that if such a cargo were landed in Illinois, the entrepreneur would receive "at least several head of cattle apiece."

There was no cargo, but the matter was being well attended to by relatives. Unattached females were being imported into many homes for a "visit," and that word was liberally interpreted in those days of difficult transportation. The same autumn that Mary Todd came to the Edwards mansion, Mercy Levering, an attractive girl from Baltimore, arrived next door to visit her brother until the following spring. A devoted friendship developed between the two girls and they had a companionable winter together.

After Mercy left, Mary was delighted when, in the fall of 1840, another visitor came to the Edwards home, Matilda Edwards from Alton, a cousin of Ninian. Matilda's letters indicate she had greatly looked forward to a visit in the state capital but found the rawness of Springfield quite disillusioning. To use her own words in a letter to her brother: "... this garden of Eden is fast losing the charms with which my fancy decked it. The ... dazling mantle woven by your imaginative sister finds not the wearer in the fascinations of Springfield." Like the young bride of the stagecoach, Matilda quickly formed an affectionate and lasting friendship with Mary Todd, whom she described in the same letter as "a very lovely and sprightly girl."

A more strategic location for matrimonial alliances than Ninian's home could hardly have been found. Frances Todd, an older sister of Mary's, had already "visited" there successfully, and was now the wife of Dr. William S. Wallace, a well-to-do physician and druggist of Springfield.

Ninian Wirt Edwards, son of Governor Ninian Edwards, was prominent and influential, as were the various family connections both of himself and his wife, Elizabeth Todd Edwards. His home was the center of the aristocratic "Edwards clique" and all distinguished visitors to the town, especially when the legislature was in session, found their way up the gentle slope to the house on the hill where hospitality was on a lavish, old-fashioned scale. There pretty girls, dressed as nearly as possible like the fashion plates in the latest *Godey's Lady's Book,* were ready to make life interesting with Victorian coquetry.

The younger set who gathered at the Edwards mansion called themselves "the coterie." It was a remarkable selection of vivid, individual personalities and a number of its names were to be written down in the nation's history. The group seethed with interest in politics, literature, romance, parties, and the perennial fun of youth. Some of its members, like Matilda Edwards, were good letter writers, and with the aid of these faded letters they can be made to describe each other while revealing their own personalities.

Shortly after Mercy Levering's arrival at her brother's home there were signs that her visit was going to be successful. A young lawyer, James C. Conkling, gay and delightful in his epistles, promptly began to court her. When Mercy returned to Baltimore in the spring of 1840, both young Conkling and Mary wrote her long letters. James Conkling obligingly and accurately describes Mary Todd in a letter written in September: "She is the very creature of excitement you know and never enjoys herself more than when in society and surrounded by a company of merry friends." He and Mary (who had just returned from a visit to an uncle) had taken part in a wedding. He playfully referred to her increased plumpness: "But my official capacity on that occasion [the wedding] reminds me of my blooming partner who has just returned from Missouri. Verily, I believe the further West a young lady goes the better her health becomes. If she comes here she is sure to grow—if she visits Missouri she will soon grow out of your recollection and if she should visit the Rocky Mountains I know not what would become of her."

There is a delightful story that gives, for a moment, a flash-back to this lively coterie of young people. Some time during the winter of 1839-1840 there was a rainy period which made the famous Springfield mud even worse than usual. Mud must have been a topic as perennial as the weather judging by old manuscripts of those days; men could hardly pull their feet out of it and carriages mired down around the square.

With unpaved streets Mary Todd and Mercy Levering had been housebound for days in their homes on the hill, and Mary wanted to go downtown. Finally she had a prankish inspiration and sent word to Mercy that she would like her company in an adventure. The two girls took a bundle of shingles as they went to town, dropping them one by one and jumping from shingle to shingle to keep out of the mud. Perhaps the shingles gave out, or perhaps it was not as much fun as it had seemed at first. Anyway, Mary hailed a two-wheeled dray driven by a little drayman named Ellis Hart and rode home in it, to the great shaking of Springfield's Victorian heads. Tut, tut, was the attitude, no lady should make herself conspicuous like that! What is this young generation coming to? Mercy, with more propriety, refused to ride in the dray and the story leaves her stuck in the mud.

A friend of the girls, Dr. Elias H. Merryman, saw what happened. True to his delightful name, he wrote a gay jingle that circulated among the young people. Eight lines will illustrate the tenor of the verse:

> *Up flew windows, out popped heads,*
> *To see this Lady gay*
> *In silken cloak and feathers white*
>   *A riding on a dray.*
> *At length arrived at Edwards' gate*
> *Hart backed the usual way*
> *And taking out the iron pin*
>   *He rolled her off the dray.*

The last line is another case of jesting about Mary's plumpness. She good-naturedly referred to it herself in one of her letters: "I still am the same ruddy *pineknot*, only not quite so great an exuberance of flesh, as it once was my lot to contend with, although quite a sufficiency." She gives here indirectly a glimpse of her rosy cheeks (often mentioned by others), and a suggestion of her abounding health and vitality.

The nearest one can get to a personality of the past is

through letters written by the person. What does one find in Mary Todd's letters to Mercy Levering in 1840? Two have been preserved, one written in July and one in December. The first, which came from Missouri where Mary was visiting leaves no doubt that she was, as is so often stated, a fluent and entertaining conversationalist. No wonder she gained weight on her visit. She was having a wonderful time with dances, excursions, parties, and new friends, all described with vivid interest. Her letters had rhythm and sparkle. Her quotations and aptly turned phrases show a feeling for language, an instinct for the right word. If the sentences are long or involved, a bit ornate or oversentimental, that was the literary style of the age. Although she had an unusually good education, she occasionally (like her future husband and the majority of humanity) slipped up on the spelling of a word.

Every new experience was a delight to Mary. She wrote Mercy of her visit to Boonville, "situated immediately on the river and a charming place." She almost wished she could live there: "A life on the river to me has always had a charm, so much excitement, and this *you* have deemed necessary to my well being; every day experience impresses me more fully with the belief." She described herself as "on the wing of expectation."

There is a trace of guilty feeling because she was having such a good time. In the eighteen-forties innocent enjoyment of life was apt to be considered wicked frivolity. The conscientious Matilda was to refuse to go to a ball even though Cousin Ninian urged her by pointing out that she would appear to great advantage. "No my brother," wrote eighteen-year-old Matilda, "however inconsistant my life may be as a christian I hope I shall ever have strength to resist those worldly fascinations which if indulged in bring a reproach upon the cause of religion." Mary Todd was a devoted church member but saw nothing wrong in having a good time, an attitude which brought her criticism then and later. Apparently Mercy had already made some remarks on the subject, for Mary's letter continues: "Would it were in my power to follow your kind advice, my ever dear Merce and turn my thoughts from earthly vanities, to one higher than us all." But neither did parties and gaiety fully satisfy her: "Every day proves the fallacy of our enjoyments, & that we are living for pleasures that do not recompense us for the pursuit."

Mary's letter contains overflowing affection for her friend, and a suggestion of her sensitiveness: "How much I wish you were near, ever have I found yours a congenial heart. In your presence I have almost *thought aloud,* and the thought that paineth most is, that such may never be again, yet, I trust that a happier day will dawn, near you, I would be most happy to sojourn in our earthly pilgrimmage." The following is really a description of her own sunny spirit: "Cousin [Ann Todd] & myself take the world easy, as usual with me, you know, allow but few of its cares, to mar *our serenity.* We regularly take our afternoon *siestas,* and soon find our spirits wafted to the land of dreams. Then will I think of thee."

Mary's gaiety, blue eyes, and dimples had found an admirer in Missouri. One can almost see a wry smile and grimace as she wrote: "There is *one* being here, who cannot brook the mention of my return, an agreeable lawyer & grandson of *Patrick Henry—what an honor!* I shall never survive it—I wish you could see him, the most perfect original I ever met. My beaux have *always* been *hard bargains* at any rate."

The letter of December 1840 is in more somber mood. Mary in this month had emotional experiences which she does not mention here directly, but certain words of hers are significant. "Why is it," she asked, "that married folks always become so serious?" She noted of a friend after her marriage: "Her *silver tones,* the other evening were not quite so captain like as was their wont in former times." It will be seen later that about this time Mary was pondering what she lightly here called "the *crime* of *matrimony.*" Perhaps she ironically used the word "crime" because her family were opposed to the particular matrimony she was then contemplating.

She mentioned the rejoicing in the recent election of General Harrison, and added: "This fall I became quite a *politician,* rather an unlady like profession . . ." She was aware that any female whose interest strayed from the purely domestic was thought either strong-minded or queer. Not for the world would Mary have laid herself open to such a charge. In a later letter she referred to her "weak woman's heart"; if it sounds affected today, it was then becomingly feminine.

Saddened by the changes of time and probably by family

wishes that were contrary to her own she gave to Mercy a poetic expression of her mood: "The icy hand of winter has set its seal upon the waters, the winds of Heaven visit the spot but roughly, the same stars shine down, yet not with the same liquid, mellow light as in the olden time."

Young affairs went briskly on in the coterie. We have Mary in her turn describing Matilda, who had made quite an impression on Joshua Speed, a personable and susceptible young Kentuckian who kept a store in Springfield. Mercy, of course, had left Springfield before Matilda arrived. Mary's letter continued: "On my return from Missouri, my time passed most heavily. I feel quite made up in my present companion, a congenial spirit I assure you. I know you would be pleased with Matilda Edwards, a lovelier girl I never saw. *Mr. Speed's* ever changing heart I suspect is about offering *its young* affections at her shrine, with some others. There is considerable acquisition in our society of *marriageable gentlemen,* unfortunately only 'birds of passage.' *Mr. Webb,* a widower of modest merit, last winter, is our *principal lion,* dances attendance very frequently."

It might have been added that Edwin B. Webb had two children and was earnestly wooing Mary for their second mother. Perhaps he recognized in her that maternal tenderness, that passionate love of children, which was her characteristic throughout life. But it was enough that she was good-looking, attractive, and had the best possible family connections. No more eligible girl could have been found.

Mary's thoughts, however, were elsewhere. Mr. Webb's efforts were in vain. She confided later to Mercy that she "deeply regretted that his constant visits, attentions &c should have given room for remarks, which were to me unpleasant." He was much older than she was; she did not find him congenial; she would not marry him even though he were "far too worthy for me, with his two *sweet little objections.*"

Mr. Webb was a small man. Another short gentleman came to the Edwards drawing room—a man of massive head and aggressive personality—the "Little Giant," Stephen A. Douglas. His handsome face, neatness of dress, and persuasiveness of voice marked him as a person of influence and promise. He was a young man of power who meant to get ahead in the world. Rumor had it that he too was courting the vivacious Miss Todd; at all events he was frequently present and conversation between two such positive personalities must have had its points.

A gay story about Mary and Douglas gives an amusing picture of the pair on the streets of Springfield. Mary, according to this account, was sitting on the porch weaving a wreath of roses (perhaps as decoration for some coming party) when Douglas appeared and asked her to walk with him. Mary delighted to tease, so she agreed upon condition that he would wear the wreath of roses on his head. Douglas was game, put on the wreath, and so they walked off together, to the probable accompaniment of girlish giggles.

There is no doubt that Springfield gossip coupled the names of the two together. Years later one of her relatives remarked to Mary, "I used to think Mr. Douglas would be your choice." "No," was the emphatic reply, "I liked him well enough, but that was all."

The coterie was like the little town itself, merry, young, and vigorous. Youth was the prevailing quality; it was a new state capital in a growing part of the country, full of young people with their enthusiasms, teasings, and love affairs. If living conditions were a bit raw, it has been said that raw things have more flavor and more vitamins. The town was intensely alive. Intellectual curiosity was seething; lectures on all kinds of weighty subjects were eagerly attended. Politics was a fierce wind always blowing, pushing people into little groups on one side or the other, then redistributing them as the wind changed its direction. Turning the pages of old manuscripts one can recover only imperfectly the vibrant emotions that swept over the men and women of the politically minded and culturally ambitious capital in that period.

They were intensely sociable, these people of Springfield. Parties with entire families attending were so large they were sometimes referred to as "squeezes." Such a modern term as "baby sitters" had not been dreamed of. Mothers took their babies with them to gatherings and parked them on the bed reserved for infants. Dances, balls, sleigh rides or picnics were the order of the day. In all these activities Mary Todd took a keen and joyous interest. Her heart was young and gay.

chapter 2

JOSHUA SPEED'S FRIEND

Mary had not exaggerated when she wrote of Joshua
Speed's "ever changing heart." Along with the handsome
Byronic face that looks out from his picture as a young
man went a Byronic tendency to fall in love. A friend, in
writing to him, mentioned two girls Joshua had been interested in, then added: "and at least twenty others of
whom you can think . . ."

The friend's name was Abraham Lincoln. Between the
two young men was a rare congeniality and understanding. This twenty-eight-year-old Lincoln in April, 1837, had
ridden into Springfield on a borrowed horse with all his
possessions in two saddlebags, and the knowledge in his
mind that he was in debt. He had no money for lodging,
and Speed, liking the young man, offered to share with
him the sleeping room above the Speed store. They were
to share that room for four years.

The newcomer had been a member of the state legislature in Vandalia. One who saw him there described him
as "a raw tall very countrified looking man yet who
spoke with such force and vigor that he held the close
attention of all." More than any other person he was responsible for the removal of the state capital from Vandalia to Springfield. This meant everything to the future
of the little town and there was wild rejoicing over the
news with "a huge bonfire built around the whipping post
on the east side of the square." People were talking about
this young man, especially since he promptly became the
junior law partner of John Todd Stuart, an influential and
prominent citizen and a cousin of Mary Todd.

Major Stuart had met Captain Lincoln when both were
serving in the Black Hawk War; he had liked him and
advised him to study law. Young Lincoln even then had
that magnetism which was to draw people to him all his
life, a quality compounded of whimsical humor, kindness,
interest in people, fundamental goodness, and intellectual
power.

The new arrival soon proved intensely interested in politics. In January 1838 he made a speech on "The Perpetuation of Our Political Institutions" which showed profound thinking on the problems of the day. He addressed it to the Young Men's Lyceum, an organization for the intellectual improvement of Springfield's earnest citizens. Young Lincoln's appearance showed he gave more thought to human problems than to his dress, but meditation did not take cash and new clothes did. He was always companionable with men. His stories, racy and down-to-earth, were superbly told.

With Springfield's well-dressed and educated ladies (when he finally met them) he was shy and uncertain of himself. In fact there is evidence that he felt keenly his lack of family background, social training, and formal education, when he was gradually accepted by the bright young set who had had these advantages. Getting acquainted was hard at first. Mary Todd apparently did not meet him when she visited her sister in the summer of 1837. He was probably not then in Springfield's social whirl.

We find him in May of that year writing to Mary Owens, whom he was courting in a lukewarm fashion: "This thing of living in Springfield is rather a dull business, after all; at least it is so to me. I am quite as lonesome here as ever was anywhere in my life. I have been spoken to by but one woman since I've been here, and should not have been by her if she could have avoided it. I've never been to church yet, nor probably shall not be soon. I stay away because I am conscious I should not know how to behave myself."

Lincoln's courtship of Mary Owens, as related in his own letters, tells a great deal about the young man and his attitude toward marriage. Miss Owens in 1833 had come from Kentucky to the New Salem community to visit her sister Mrs. Bennett Abell. There young Lincoln met her, found her attractive and, as he later wrote, "saw no good objection to plodding through life hand in hand with her."

Mrs. Abell was a "great friend" of Lincoln's when he lived in New Salem; between them was that playful banter in which he always delighted. When she in 1836 started to Kentucky to visit her family, as Lincoln later related it, she "proposed to me, that on her return she would bring a sister of hers with her upon condition that I would engage to become her brother-in-law with all convenient dispatch." Lincoln continued: "I, of course, accepted the proposal; for you know I could not have done otherwise, had I really been averse to it; but privately between you and me, I was most confoundedly well pleased with the project. I had seen the said sister some three years before, thought her intelligent and agreeable . . ."

Lincoln had a young man's natural interest in girls and Mary Owens was as well-educated and cultured a woman as he had met up to that time. He was intellectually lonely and was reaching out for things of the mind. He admitted later that he liked her mental qualities better than her physical: "I also tried to convince myself, that the mind was much more to be valued than the person; and in this, she was not inferior, as I could discover, to any with whom I had been acquainted." He was forced to think of her worthy mind, for, when Miss Owens returned with Mrs. Abell to the latter's home near New Salem, three years had wrought changes very devastating to romance. The lady looked positively "weather-beaten"; she had lost some teeth and gotten fat! As Lincoln wrote two years later: ". . . a kind of notion . . . ran in my head that nothing could have commenced at the size of infancy and reached her present bulk in less than thirty-five or forty years." (In justice to the lady, it must be stated that she was twenty-eight in 1836 and less than a year older than Lincoln.)

He felt bound to keep his part of the bargain but it could hardly be called an ardent wooing. He wrote Miss Owens from Springfield in 1837: "I am often thinking about what we said of your coming to live at Springfield. I am afraid you would not be satisfied. There is a great deal of flourishing about in carriages here, which it would be your doom to see without sharing in it. You would have to be poor without the means of hiding your poverty. Do you believe you could bear that patiently? Whatever woman may cast her lot with mine should any ever do so, it is my intention to do all in my power to make her happy and contented; and there is nothing I can immagine, that would make me more unhappy than to fail in the effort. I know I should be much happier with you than the way I am, provided I saw no signs of discontent in you. . . . My opinion is that you had better not do it."

As if that did not make the matter sufficiently plain, we find him writing her three months later: "I want in all cases to do right; and most particularly so, in all cases with women. I want, at this particular time, more than any thing else, to do right with you, and if I *knew* it would be doing right, as I rather suspect it would, to let you alone, I would do it."

The scrupulously truthful Lincoln was to tell Mary Todd, both before and after he married her, that she was the only woman he had ever really loved. These cautious and tepid letters to "Friend Mary" present no impassioned appeals to contradict that statement. It is hardly to be wondered at that Miss Owens declined Lincoln's proposal of marriage. This hurt his pride a little, as such things do, though it was a relief. By his own words he had never had an involvement from which he "so much desired to be free." Yet he admitted that he was "a little in love with her," which about covers the situation.

Lincoln was consistent as to the type of woman he admired. Many years later, the son of Mary Owens Vineyard wrote a description of his mother as a young woman which can be applied almost word for word to Mary Todd. Miss Owens, he wrote, had a "good education," was "good looking," and "polished in her manners, pleasing in her address, and attractive in society." He went on: "She had a little dash of coquetry in her intercourse with that class of young men, who arrogated to themselves claims of superiority." Mary Todd was an artist at that sort of thing. Miss Owens, according to this filial description, was "a good conversationist and a splendid reader—but very few persons being found to equal her in this accomplishment. She was light-hearted and cheery in her disposition. She was kind . . ."

His mother, the son stated, "admired" Lincoln but "did not love him." That was the difference between these two Marys. Miss Owens had not responded to the unconscious expression of lifelong loneliness in Lincoln's letters. The warmhearted Mary Todd did. Miss Owens failed to meet his taste as to appearance; she seems to have stirred without satisfying his longing for feminine companionship. He had never known a daintier or more companionable girl than Mary Todd. Miss Owens did not care to marry a man who was, as she said "deficient in those little links which make up the great chain of womans happiness."

Mary Todd was to know even more of that absent-mind-edness. It was to irk her too, but because she did love him she was willing to accept that deficiency, teaching him small social courtesies and becoming adjusted (often with lively protest) where it proved impossible to domesticate him.

Above all, Lincoln's letters to Miss Owens laid bare his sensitiveness to the fact that he could offer a wife so little. He had a torturing conscience about it. He would even take himself out of a girl's life for her own good rather than have her risk unhappiness with him in poverty. His unsuitability as a husband for a girl used to luxury was like an aching nerve, and that vulnerable spot was destined to be jabbed by the opposition of the family of the girl with whom he was soon to fall in love. These letters throw great light on events to follow.

Lincoln commenced seeing Mary Todd in the winter of 1839-1840. We have evidence that by the end of 1839 he had been accepted by Springfield society. A printed invitation quaintly headed "Cotillion Party" which "respectfully" solicits the pleasure of the company of the fortunate recipient has been preserved. The invitation patriotically bears the picture of an eagle with an *e pluribus unum* issuing from its beak; it is dated December 16, 1839, and is signed by the sixteen "managers." We find acquaintances in this list: S. A. Douglass (who was spelling his name with an extra *s* at this time), N. W. Edwards, J. F. Speed, and E. H. Merryman. A gentleman destined to come into this story later, J. Shields, is there; and the last name is A. Lincoln. Just how a festive occasion like this impressed young Lincoln from the backwoods flashes out in an old description: "He would burst into a ball with his big heavy Conestoga boots on, and exclaim aloud—'Oh—boys, how clean those girls look.'" Women in remote cabins carrying water from springs and cooking over open fires could not achieve the beruffled daintiness of the girls who belonged to the coterie.

Katherine Helm, daughter of Mary's half sister, Emilie Todd Helm, states in her book, *The True Story of Mary, Wife of Lincoln,* that Mary Todd met Lincoln at a cotillion. To recover that meeting—to bring back the scene, the words—required a bit of dramatization, which she supplied. She gives a pretty picture of the glowing girl whose neat little figure dressed in the latest feminine finery was followed by the eyes of the tall young lawyer. When presented to her, according to this illustrative story, he said: "Miss Todd, I want to dance with you the worst way." Mary after the party (no doubt with her damaged slippers in mind) bubbled with laughter to her cousin Elizabeth Todd, "And he certainly did."

It has been seen that Mary visited Todd relatives in Columbia, Missouri, in the summer of 1840 and wrote a newsy letter about the gay events there. According to a definite tradition handed down in the Todd family at Columbia, Lincoln had occasion to come up the Missouri River to Rocheport and from there made a trip to nearby Columbia to see Mary. Katherine Helm, who had access to inside family stories, gives a full account of that visit. It was a political gathering that brought Lincoln to Rocheport, according to Miss Helm, and when Lincoln came to Columbia, he and Mary, one Sunday morning, occupied the Todd pew in the Presbyterian church. She even gives the circumstantial detail that Lincoln's boat went aground on a sand bar and he was so late he missed the political rally. While one does not take literary dramatization, including conversations, too literally, this well-defined family tradition deserves careful consideration.

Mary did not mention Lincoln in her letter to Mercy Levering from Columbia, though she does put in a cryptic passage which conceivably could have relation to such a visit, on the supposition that Lincoln had written her about his coming: "When I mention *some letters* I have received since leaving S—— you will be somewhat surprised, as I *must confess* they are entirely *unlooked for.* This is *between ourselves,* my dearest, but of this more anon. Every day I am convinced this is a stranger world we live in, the *past* as the future is to me a mystery." Whether this refers to the dawning love affair between herself and Lincoln cannot be determined, but sometime during the months of 1839 or 1840 such a dawning, always mysterious to young hearts, was taking place. If Mary, when at Columbia, was already thinking seriously of Lincoln as a possible future husband, it makes certain other statements in her letter take on new significance. She says she will not accept a certain local suitor because she does not love him and she will never marry anyone she does not love. She also remarks that she fancies her lot will be a quiet one (which certainly seemed at that

time to be the prospect for the bride of Abraham Lincoln)
and adds that she will nevertheless be happy if she is with
those she loves. And she speaks of her beaux as "*hard
bargains.*"

By December 1840 Lincoln's name does appear in a
letter of Mary's. She refers gaily but obscurely to "*Lincoln's lincoln green.*" She tells how a group of young people including Lincoln and herself are planning a "jaunt"
to Jacksonville to spend a day or two, and adds: "We are
watching the clouds most anxiously trusting it may snow,
so we may have a sleigh ride.—Will it not be pleasant?"

James Conkling gave a description of the long-legged
young man in the gaiety of Springfield society: "He used
to remind me sometimes of the pictures I formerly saw
of old Father Jupiter, bending down from the clouds, to
see what was going on below. And as an agreeable smile
of satisfaction graced the countenance of the old heathen
god, as he perceived the incense rising up—so the face
of L. was occasionally distorted into a grin as he succeeded in eliciting applause from some of the fair votaries
by whom he was surrounded." It was a hard thing for the
young man, so lately from the backwoods, to be thrown
into these bright assemblies, to want approval so much,
and yet be handicapped by the lack of early social training. Did his need of a woman's help appeal to Mary Todd's
warm and maternal heart?

At some point the coterie had realized that Lincoln was
paying what was called "particular court" to Miss Todd.
They could notice he was calling her by her nickname,
"Molly." He had joined the other young hopefuls who sat
on the slippery horsehair surface of the Edwardses' sofas
or strolled along Springfield's cowpaths, mud permitting,
with a lady in the twilight. Twilight with lilac haze on
prairie horizon can be almost as potent as moonlight.

There is reason to believe that Lincoln in proper Victorian fashion wrote a letter to Robert Todd at Lexington,
Kentucky, asking the father's permission to pay his ad-
dresses to the daughter, Miss Mary Todd. For years the
descendants of the Edwardses kept the letter which "Robert Todd addressed to his son-in-law Ninian W. Edwards,
asking for information as to the character, ability etc.
of Abraham Lincoln, as a proposed husband of his (Mr.
Todd's) daughter Mary." It cannot now be proved that
Lincoln wrote Mr. Todd, but to Ninian's descendants the

"recollection throughout all these years is that his [Mr. Todd's] request of Mr. Edwards, *was* because of such a letter [from Lincoln]."

We have Mrs. Ninian W. Edwards's description of the two young people as they sat talking together. The older sister noticed how Lincoln "was charmed with Mary's wit and fascinated with her quick sagacity—her will—her nature—and culture. I have happened in the room where they were sitting often & often and Mary led the conversation. Lincoln would listen & gaze on her as if drawn by some superior power, irresistibly so: he listened—never scarcely said a word." It is a convincing picture. Mary was famous among her friends as a "pretty talker." With vivid face which dimpled or frowned in tune with the needs of her story, with a rare gift of mimicry, with enthusiasm that brought out all the color in what she was telling, she could hold a roomful of people in rapt attention. She loved people, was intensely sociable. Young Mary has left a most attractive picture in the record, this "merry, companionable girl with a smile for everybody." Many years later a gentleman described her qualities in words that apply here: "I found her sympathetic, cordial, sensible, intelligent, and brimming with that bonhomie so fascinating in the women of . . . [the] South . . . She was simply a bright, wholesome, attractive woman."

Her popularity was made evident by the flood of mail from various beaux which followed her on her visit to Columbia. Her friendly responsiveness, her cheerful disposition, her gift of making small events glow with color and drama were all qualities to attract a slow-speaking young man given at times to somber moods.

Mrs. Edwards had a poor opinion of Lincoln's contribution to the conversations. She thought he "could not hold a lengthy conversation with a lady—was not sufficiently educated & intelligent in the female line to do so." If that interesting expression "female line" meant conversation about clothes, domestic matters, and the frills of society, she was right: such things were never to register with Lincoln. But this statement, perhaps, means only that conversation did not flow easily between Mrs. Edwards and the young man. Elizabeth Todd had become Mrs. Ninian W. Edwards at the age of sixteen and from that time on, domesticity and society had absorbed her. She was a charming woman with a fine conscientiousness in doing her duty as she saw it, but she apparently did not have Mary's literary interests and her buoyancy.

It will shortly be seen that Mrs. Edwards and Mary differed also in their ideas as to what constituted a suitable marriage. The older sister had married an aristocrat. Mary said (and she usually spoke emphatically): "I would rather marry a good man—a man of mind—with a hope and bright prospects ahead for position—fame & power than to marry all the houses—gold . . . in the world."

Mary's attitude toward her marriage, which was entirely free from snobbishness, has been largely overlooked. Chiefly emphasized have been her remarks that she intended to marry a future President. Most of these statements can be accounted for as an expression of gaiety, optimism and youth's belief in a rosy and glorious future. It is true that she was ambitious for her husband and deeply concerned with his political future, but young Mary wrote her "Dearest Merce" in the summer of 1840: ". . . mine I fancy is to be a quiet lot, and happy indeed will I be, if it is, only cast near those, I *so dearly love*." Love was the factor that would determine her marriage, not ambition. She had declined the descendant of Patrick Henry who lived at Columbia, Missouri, because "I love him not, & my hand will never be given, where my heart is not." She declined the proposal of the widower, Mr. Webb, because she did not have with him the congeniality "without which I should never feel justifiable in resigning my happiness into the safe keeping of another . . ." By the time she wrote this (and probably by the time she wrote the other two statements) she had found out how real was the congeniality between herself and Lincoln. Katherine Helm concluded that Mary found in the young lawyer "the most congenial mind she had ever met." This girl was determined to marry the man she loved even though he came from hardscrabble beginnings and was, as one of her sisters put it, "the plainest looking man in Springfield."

Springfield was quite sure about his homeliness. The conventional taste of the age did not appreciate ruggedness in appearance and then too the young lawyer's early hardships had left their mark on his features. "His face and forehead were wrinkled even in his youth." Lincoln himself once touched upon his appearance in a down-to-earth whimsy: "In my poor, lean, lank face nobody has ever seen that any cabbages were sprouting out." But to Mary that rugged face with its earnest eyes and tender mouth had become more and more dear, and to Lincoln she had become the girl whose presence clothed a moment or an event in iridescence.

So it came about that at the end of the year 1840 they were engaged and, according to Mrs. Edwards, making definite plans to be married. They had plighted their troth for the same reason other young people do—because they were in love with each other and could not be happy apart. A girl who was sister-in-law to Springfield's top aristocrat hardly seemed the logical choice for the impecunious young lawyer, but Lincoln was soon to write Joshua Speed (who by this time was in love with Fanny Henning) that logic has very little to do with courtships; it was not a question of listing the girl's suitable qualities. "Say candidly," he wrote, "were not . . . [Fanny's] heavenly *black eyes,* the whole basis of your early *reasoning* on the subject?" Lincoln had looked into a pair of vivacious blue eyes and was in a state of mind (not by way of reason but by the usual path of normal emotion) to find them "heavenly."

chapter 3

"MIND—EDUCATION—RAISING"

Mrs. Ninian W. Edwards once spoke of the differences in "natures, mind—education—raising &c." between Mary and Mr. Lincoln. At this point it may be well to go back and examine the events and influences that went into the minds and natures of this couple up to the time they planned to merge their lives in marriage. These two had come into the world endowed with qualities of personality and temperament singularly opposite. In family background and environment up to the time of their meeting there was violent contrast.

Mary Ann Todd was born in Lexington, Kentucky, on December 13, 1818. Her father and mother, Robert Smith Todd and Eliza Parker Todd, were cousins. The family was a prominent and influential one, with ancestors of distinguished record in the American Revolution. The Todds were of strong-willed Scottish Covenanter stock, and in this country had followed the pioneer's dream into the "Dark and Bloody Ground" of Kentucky. They had the qualities that go well into the building of a nation: strong courage and character, grit, convictions, resourcefulness, and high ideals in education and government.

The pioneer's fight with the wilderness was over for the Todd family when Mary was born. She came into the kind of home where there was a fan-shaped window above the entrance, the gleam of silver on the sideboard, and rich furnishings reflected in gold-framed mirrors. There were dainty clothes, the gentle brown hands of a Negro "mammy" to receive her, and an imposing circle of relatives to exclaim over the new baby.

Only fate knew there was a connection between this wellborn newcomer and a nine-year-old boy named Abraham Lincoln who was living in a dirt-floor cabin in the Indiana wilderness. There his father and his cousin Dennis Hanks hunted for food, while his sister Sarah, two years older than he, struggled with primitive cooking over the cabin fireplace. The faces of both children must often have been pinched with cold, hunger, and grief. Two months before, in October 1818, they had seen their mother's body placed in a homemade coffin and lowered laboriously into a lonely grave in the backwoods. There was no religious service that day to comfort a sensitive boy who was in the future to mention the painfulness of the "death scenes of those we love." Ever after, a death plunged him into a depression that was more than normal. Life for him, at the time Mary was born, had been reduced to a raw struggle for mere existence, with small chance for things of the mind and spirit, for learning and beauty.

Mary too lost her mother. She was a bright-faced little girl going on seven when her mother died at the birth of the seventh child. The memory of Eliza Parker Todd glows faintly with the tradition of a sunny and sprightly temperament, contrasting with the impetuous, high-strung, sensitive nature of her husband. Mary inherited all these qualities.

William H. Townsend, in his scholarly and delightful book, *Lincoln and His Wife's Home Town*, tells how, when Mrs. Todd died, Nelson, the old body servant and coachman, hitched up the family barouche and drove around to the homes of friends leaving black-bordered "funeral tickets." These cards "respectfully invited" the recipient to attend the funeral of Mr. Todd's "Consort" at his residence on Short Street. Such dignified ceremonial was far removed from the burial of Nancy Lincoln on a lonely knoll in the Pigeon Creek backwoods.

Much is written these days about the effect of childhood experiences on the development of the individual. The sensitive young spirits of Abraham Lincoln and Mary Todd were emotionally scarred by the same tragedy. The death of Abraham's mother left desolation in the wilderness cabin; it removed the essential element of a woman's care. One can only surmise what effect the death of her mother left upon Mary's personality. She could remember the strangeness of a household hushed by the passing of its guardian spirit; perhaps she had gazed at the pale still face in the coffin. In later life the sight of a loved dead face almost threw her into convulsions.

During the interval before Mr. Todd married again the

motherless household got along with the help of Mary's aunt and Grandmother Parker, who lived next door. This difficult interval could do much to create a sense of insecurity in a sensitive seven-year-old girl, and perhaps a feeling of being an unwanted complication. But when Mary's father remarried, the situation became worse. Grandmother Parker and the rest of Mary's maternal relatives furiously resented the stepmother. Mrs. Parker never got over her disapproval. Living next door to the Todd family, she was in a position to foster in Mary a conviction that a great wrong had been done to her. The natural result of this would be that Mary would combat any attempt on the part of her stepmother to discipline her or teach her self-control. At all events, Mary grew up without learning the essential lesson of self-restraint, and this had far-reaching results.

One learns from those who have lost a parent in childhood that the shock is sometimes followed by a feeling that happiness is impermanent and cannot be depended upon. A child so bereaved has a sense of being cheated: other children have two parents; it is not fair to have only one. Mary, looking back, called her childhood "desolate"; ". . . my early home," she wrote, "was truly at a *boarding* school."

All these factors could lead to maladjustment. Certain traits of Mary's in mature life may well have relation to the death of her mother. The resulting lack of discipline left emotional immaturity. In some ways she never grew up. When she married nothing pleased her more than having her husband pet and humor her, and call her his "child-wife." If we find Mary in adult life resentful of criticism and always struggling with a fundamental sense of insecurity, such maladjustment may well have had its beginning in the tragedy of her childhood.

The child at Lexington may be described in the same terms that apply to young Mary in Springfield. She was sprightly, tenderhearted, sympathetic, headstrong, intellectually precocious, and intensely feminine. This lively little girl liked to have her own way. In a medical study of Mary Lincoln's personality, a valuable book, Dr. W. A. Evans writes: "It is a pretty good guess that Mary Todd as a child was subject to temper tantrums." Such explosions were probably no novelty in the Todd family of individualists. He suggests, with a physician's understanding of a nervous temperament, that she may have had "night-terrors."

A young girl who dearly loved the First Lady in 1861 was to find out that Mrs. Lincoln "wanted what she wanted when she wanted it and no substitute!" It is easy to see why there was an inevitable conflict between Mary and her conventional and conscientious stepmother, especially with Grandmother Parker in the background ready to see Mary's side of it and take her part.

The second Mrs. Todd was having babies with what was deemed "becoming regularity" in those days. There was an overabundance of children in the household. Much light on the situation is given in what Mary Lincoln later wrote to her husband when visiting her old Lexington home. She said of her stepmother: ". . . she is very obliging & accomodating, but if she thought any of us, were on her hands again, I believe she would be *worse* than ever."

When Mary was about eight years old, she entered the Academy of Dr. John Ward, a scholarly, benevolent, but strict Episcopal minister who, ahead of his time, believed in coeducation and conducted a school for over a hundred boys and girls from the best families in Lexington. Mary grew up in an atmosphere in which that term "best families" loomed large. Dr. Ward believed in recitations at dawn. There was a current idea that the brain worked better when the body was undernourished, that early rising and study were most desirable. So Mary had to get up by candlelight and trudge several blocks to school, sometimes in winter sleet and snow. This was cheerfully done, for neither then nor later was she one to complain or magnify physical discomfort.

Mr. Townsend gives a sparkling story of a new and overzealous night watchman named Flannigan, who one morning saw a girl with a bundle under her arm hurrying up the street in the early dawn. His Hibernian nose sniffed an elopement and he gave hot pursuit. Girl and policeman arrived at the schoolroom breathless, to the great giggling of the other scholars, and the indignation of the dignified Dr. Ward.

There was another schoolgirl in the Todd household. Elizabeth Humphreys, niece of the second Mrs. Todd, came to Lexington to attend Dr. Ward's, share Mary's room, and, as always, Mary's warm affection. Elizabeth later recalled these school days. Mary, she wrote, was a studious little girl who had "a retentive memory and a mind that enabled her to grasp & thoroughly understand the lessons she was required to learn." She usually finished her homework before Elizabeth, and was soon clicking her knitting needles with the ten rounds of "cotton stocking" that both girls were required to knit each evening. "Mary was always quick in her movements..."

Elizabeth's description of her cousin as a girl ties up with later pen pictures of the young woman: "Her features were not regularly beautiful, but she was certainly very pretty with her clear blue eyes, lovely complexion, and soft brown hair, with a bright intelligent face, that having once seen you could not easily forget. Her form was fine, and no old master ever modeled a more perfect arm and hand."

Elizabeth Humphreys had only the pleasantest memories of Mary and in all the months she roomed with her at the Todd home she had seen no display of temper. But the cousin recognized that Mary said what she thought and that her tongue could be sharp. "Without designing to wound she now & then indulged in sarcastic, witty remarks that cut ... but there was no malice in it— She was impulsive & made no attempt to conceal her feeling, indeed it would have been an impossibility had she desired to do so for her face was an index to every passing emotion."

Elizabeth also described another very important person in the Todd home: "Dear Old Mammy Sally," "a jewel of a black mammy," who spoiled and tyrannized over the Todd "chil'en." They loved her and never dared question her authority. Attending "white folks' church" by sitting in the gallery reserved for Negroes, she learned Bible stories which she recounted to the little Todds with all the flavor and embroidery of *The Green Pastures*. "Ole man Satan" really had horns and hoofs to Mammy Sally and without question he possessed a pea-green tail. Mammy Sally firmly impressed upon her charges the dire fact that jay birds went to hell every Friday night and told the devil all the doings of bad children during the week.

We have, through Elizabeth Humphreys, the story of ten-year-old Mary's scheme to wear hoop skirts. Grown ladies wore them and Mary always wanted her clothes to be the latest thing in style. She and Elizabeth secretly obtained some long willow switches and sewed them inside the skirts of their narrow little muslin frocks, a proceeding which certainly bulged out the skirts but in a manner that only a ten-year-old could consider desirable. When the two little girls appeared in this grotesque attire on Sunday morning before the amazed stepmother, ready to go to Sunday school, Mrs. Todd promptly sent them upstairs to dress properly. Mary burst into tears. As another cousin who knew her in Lexington days said: "She was very highly strung, nervous, impulsive, excitable, having an emotional temperament much like an April day, sunning all over with laughter one moment, the next crying as if her heart would break."

What was happening to young Lincoln in Indiana about the time Mary was concerned with nothing weightier than the wearing of hoop skirts? At nineteen he knew the bitterness and sorrow of the death of his only sister Sarah in the primitive childbirth of the backwoods. It was not only the raw cruelty of such a death which hurt him. He was deeply resentful toward the family into which Sarah had married; he thought their neglect had contributed to her dying. Here was another profound hurt that added to the sadness in young Lincoln's deep-set eyes.

Mary finished the preparatory course at Dr. Ward's, and when about fourteen entered the select boarding school of Madame Victorie Charlotte Leclere Mentelle on the Richmond Pike. Here, according to the announcement in the *Lexington Intelligencer* in 1838, "Young Ladies" could receive "a truly useful & 'solid' English Education in all its branches. *French taught if desired.* Boarding, Washing & Tuition $120.00 per year, paid quarterly in advance." It was a finishing school where they taught, along with other social graces, letter writing and conversation. In these Mary learned full well, for she became an artist at both.

Mary Todd "desired" French. She made the statement years afterwards that the scholars at Madame Mentelle's were not allowed to speak anything else; at all events she learned to speak and write French and retained that knowledge in her later life. It was to serve her well in the White House when she had distinguished foreign guests and in later life when living in France. In 1877 she was to write from Pau: "I have been here sufficiently, not to allow them, to take advantage of me, as is so frequently done, with strangers who do not understand their language. Happily I am not in the latter category."

There were four rich years at Madame Mentelle's for the eager girl to whom each new experience had its charm. Every Monday morning Nelson, the impressive coachman, would bring the Todd carriage to drive her in state down a long avenue to Madame Mentelle's "opposite Mr. Clay's," to use Mary's words of many years later. On Friday Nelson would call again to take her home for the week end. Mary received along with other things instruction in dancing, which she loved, for Madame, like a true Frenchwoman, took great pains with the graces and manners of the young ladies in her care.

Graces, manners, and domesticity were supposed to compass a woman's world. One finds the prevailing view in a discourse on "Female Education" by Reverend Samuel W. Fisher in *Godey's Lady's Book*. Even as late as 1850 we find this pontifical gentleman saying: "There has been a long standing dispute respecting the intellectual powers of the two sexes . . ." He graciously and elaborately concedes that woman may be capable of education but she must not leave her own sphere. She should share "with man the sceptre of influence . . . without presuming to wrest from him a visible authority . . ." The clergyman then points out: "When she forsakes the household and the gentler duties of domestic life for the labors of the field, the pulpit, the rostrum, the court-room, she always descends from her own bright station, and invariably fails to ascend that of man." He gazed in oratorical horror on such an unclassified creature.

The year Mary entered the Mentelle school, 1832, was an important one in other ways. On February 18 her oldest sister Elizabeth was married to a junior at Transylvania University. This student-husband had come of distinguished family. He was Ninian Wirt Edwards; his father, Ninian Edwards, had been territorial governor of Illinois, United States senator, and later state governor. Socially and politically there was at that time no more prominent family in Illinois. In 1833 this couple moved to Springfield to live, thus forming a steppingstone on the path that was to lead Mary to the meeting with young Lincoln.

What was happening to him in 1832? We find him moved to Illinois, where he was living in a village of log

cabins called New Salem. He served a little less than
three months as captain (and, on re-enlistment, private)
of volunteer militia in the Black Hawk War that year; in
that service he met John Todd Stuart and John J. Hardin,
both cousins of Mary. In New Salem he was boarding at
the Rutledge Tavern and was in daily association with
the Rutledge family including Ann, the young daughter,
who about this time was engaged to a friend of his, John
McNamar, whom he called Mack.

The Rutledges were a family of more refined type than
most of those Lincoln had been associated with up to that
time. James Rutledge, the father, was fairly well educated
and is thought to have had a library of twenty-five or
thirty volumes, an almost irresistible attraction to a young
man who walked eight miles from New Salem to borrow
a grammar. Friendship with the Rutledge family meant
much to one who called himself a "friendless, uneducated,
penniless boy." When Ann died in 1835 with her fiancé far
away, Lincoln was naturally deeply distressed. His spirit
was still scarred with the pitiful deaths of his mother and
sister. The tradition of this grief was to be unearthed after
Lincoln's death, and was to become the starting point for
an almost invincible legendary romance.

Young Lincoln in New Salem was not a romantic figure. According to one friend of his there: "There was one
half foot space between bottom of pants and top of socks."
Another friend added details: "His pants were made of
flax and tow, cut tight at the ankle—*his knees were both
out*. Was the toughest looking man I ever saw—poor boy,
but welcomed to every body's house." He *"had nothing
only plenty of friends."*

We turn from the ruggedness of log cabin life to all the
color that glows around the words "Old Kentucky Home."
It was also in 1832 that Robert Todd moved his family to
a more spacious house on Main Street in Lexington. Those
ever-arriving babies had made the Short Street house too
crowded. The new home had all the rich elements that
went into the Southern aristocrat's way of living: large-
scale hospitality, devoted family servants, picturesque
and distinguished visitors, mint juleps, family portraits,
and the soft tones of rich furnishings by candlelight.

The grounds contained coachhouse, stable, servants'
quarters, and a beautiful flower garden. Toward the back
of the lot ran a little stream where the Todd children

played and chased minnows. The boys dubbed it the "blabbing brook" when their wet clothes betrayed them into a spanking for forbidden wading. They were bright and interesting—these Todd children. Mary had the experience of growing up in a large family. Its uninhibited give and take was part of her training, which possibly contributed to the later facility and frankness of her speech. To her cousin Elizabeth Humphreys, her appearance suggested a tea rose; her sharp little tongue, pricking the shortcomings of others, could at times be like a thorn. There was no deep malice in the kind-hearted girl; she saw her own point of view so strongly, it shut out the viewpoint of the other person. Her occasional feeling of spitefulness or resentment was not rooted in a callous nature.

Mary Lincoln herself in 1866 dictated briefly and reluctantly some significant facts about her early life. "I came to Illinois in 1837," she said. "Was in Illinois three months. Went back to Kentucky. Went to school two years after I first came to Illinois." Elsewhere in the same statement, after telling of her attendance at Madame Mentelle's, she added: "Finished my education at Ward's Academy."

These brief sentences contain much. Mary visited Mrs. Ninian W. Edwards in Springfield the summer of 1837, though she probably did not meet Lincoln at that time. Then this girl, approaching nineteen—in age when, according to standards of the time, she might well be getting married—went back to Kentucky and took a sort of post-graduate course.

One wishes for more details about this. Dr. Ward was a most cultured gentleman with much to give an eager student who so delighted in poetry and literature. Mary Todd's period of study far exceeded that of most gentlewomen of her day. This unusual education accounts for the rich literary allusions and quotations in her truly fine letters. There were probably those who thought of her as "highbrow" or "blue-stocking." The Reverend Samuel W. Fisher might have raised a disapproving eyebrow at this excursion outside woman's sphere.

Between 1837 and 1839 then, the paths of Lincoln and Mary were turning toward their meeting. Both were building up knowledge and training for the future: he as a young lawyer in Springfield absorbing the ways and interests of a more cultured society than he had known in youth; she in Lexington following Dr. Ward's guidance in the mental kingdom of books and ideas that was so congenial to her. It was a time of growth and development for both.

The year 1839 brought them together in Springfield. By and by Mr. and Mrs. Ninian W. Edwards realized that Mary was heading toward what seemed to them a very unsuitable marriage. "Lincoln and Mary ... had no congeniality—no feelings &c. alike," said Mrs. Edwards later. There is no doubt she sincerely believed this but it meant only that Lincoln had no real congeniality with Mrs. Edwards. Mary was a better authority on the young lawyer's companionship than her sister, and by her own statement she did not intend to marry a man unless he was congenial. She and Lincoln had a world of things to talk about and some of these topics had significance down the years ahead of them. To survey their interests is to become better acquainted with both.

They loved politics and they had the same political idol, always a strong bond. Lincoln had admired Henry Clay tremendously at a distance, but Mary had known and loved him as a personal friend in Lexington. She perhaps told Lincoln the pretty story of herself as a thirteen-year-old girl with sunbonnet and flying curls riding out to Ashland, the home of Henry Clay, to show him her new white pony. Ashland was opposite the boarding school she attended; she had seen the gallant figure going in and out of his home, and he often came to her father's house.

So did Senator Crittenden and other prominent men of the day whose names meant much to the politically minded young lawyer. She had loved to listen to their conversations, even though she knew it was not considered becoming for young girls to be interested in public affairs. This brings up the scene so delightfully told by Mr. Townsend: When distinguished visitors came, old Nelson, "clad in his blue swallow-tail coat with big brass buttons," would perform the solemn ritual of making mint juleps in the presence of the thirsty admiring guests.

Henry Clay was the leader of the Whig party and both Lincoln and Mary were enthusiastic Whigs. Even in those days when woman's place was strictly in the home, it was well for an engaged couple to agree politically, lest the

peace of that future home be marred. Mary usually gave
strong expression to her views. At fourteen she had had
a sharp clash with one of her little friends who was an
admirer of General Andrew Jackson. Mary referred to
General Jackson as "ugly" and said Mr. Clay was "the
handsomest man in town" with "the best manners" of
anyone except her father. There was violent dissent from
the little Democrat; both small tongues employed hot
words and a lasting estrangement followed. Mary's beau
would have enjoyed that story; he liked spunkiness.

She was always ready to listen to talk of politics and
when it came to that subject the young lawyer was in his
element. He may have had a certain social awkwardness
but when he had given in Springfield his Lyceum address
on political institutions the year before he met Mary, it
had been no commonplace speech. Rather it was notable
for its penetrating knowledge of conditions and distinguished use of language. No one can read that statement
of the democratic ideal of orderly society under law, so
finished in its wording, so eloquent yet so free from trite-
ness or politician-like superficiality, and still think of
Lincoln at the age of twenty-nine as a mere railsplitter
or backwoodsman. John Todd Stuart, one of Springfield's
most cultured gentlemen, had not taken Lincoln into his
law office without reason; the young man had intellectual
power. Mary had found the "good man," the "man of
mind" whom she preferred, she said, to one with all the
houses and gold in the world. By the end of 1840 Lincoln
was serving his fourth term in the state legislature, so
she had basis for believing (as she did) that he had "a
hope and bright prospects ahead for position—fame &
power."

Among the elements the lovers had in common was
Kentucky, the state where both were born, and grew
through childhood. There is a fundamental attachment
which one feels for the state of his birth. As a poet was
to write a few years later, childhood memories

> *Seem hallowed, pure, and bright,*
> *Like scenes in some enchanted isle,*
> *All bathed in liquid light.*

The title of this poem is "My Childhood Home I See
Again," and it should be good authority, for the poet was

Abraham Lincoln himself! Kentucky was not something on a map for Lincoln; it was the memory of his mother, boyish adventure, and the long evening shadows of the Kentucky hills at the cabin on Knob Creek.

Out of this feeling began his understanding of the South. Emerging into national prominence in 1859, Lincoln was to make a speech at Cincinnati in which he appealed to his "brother Kentuckians" across the river, a speech that is like a gesture of outstretched pleading hands. Deploring division between North and South, he said, "We mean to remember that you are as good as we; that there is no difference between us other than the difference of circumstances." Then he mentioned his marriage to a Kentucky girl as a bond: "We mean to marry your girls when we have a chance—" he said, and added, "I have the honor to inform you that I once did have a chance in that way." Lincoln's marriage into the Todd family and his subsequent visits to Lexington made him well acquainted with the views of the ruling Southern class. When the crisis came, he knew how to keep Kentucky in the Union.

The young lawyer could have asked Mary questions about another subject, later to become entangled with politics. "The one vital question that already held Lincoln's interest was slavery," writes Mr. Townsend, "and it is no exaggeration to say that Mary Todd possessed more first-hand information on this subject than any other person with whom he had yet come in contact." She knew the gentle relation between her family and its devoted (and sometimes tyrannical) house servants; she loved old Nelson and Mammy Sally and the others who served in the Todd home. Her stepmother would have punished her if she had used the word "nigger"; the best type of Southern lady did not use that term. Mary throughout her life had a kind, understanding and sympathetic attitude toward colored people.

But the girl had been acquainted too with the hideous aspect of slavery. In one corner of the public square at Lexington stood the slave auction block; in another corner the whipping post, a thing of horror with its floggings and screams. Past the Todd home on Main Street gangs of herded Negroes trudged their way to the slave markets of the South, lines of weary, hopeless men, women and children manacled and bound together by heavy chains.

Lincoln was shortly to write a description of such a line of slaves, "strung together precisely like so many fish upon a trot-line," and later to speak of what a "continual torment" the sight was to him. Mary too was tenderhearted and quick with sympathy for suffering or injustice.

Elizabeth Humphreys recorded the effect upon Mary and herself as young girls in Lexington when news came of a revolting case of cruelty to certain slaves in New Orleans. "We were horrified and talked of nothing else for days. If one such case could happen, it damned the whole institution . . ." Mary's stepmother was a Humphreys, and all the Humphreys clan believed, like Henry Clay (and Abraham Lincoln) in the gradual emancipation of slaves. Of her loved and admired stepgrandmother (who left a will emancipating her own slaves), Mary said to Elizabeth: "If I can only be, when I am grown up, just like Grandmother Humphreys, I will be perfectly satisfied with myself." It is thought that Grandmother Humphreys, who was an emancipationist, had great influence in forming Mary's views on the subject.

Elizabeth Humphreys's recollections also include mention of runaway Negroes. Mammy Sally told the two young girls that she had put a mark on the back fence of the Todd home to show runaway Negroes they could get "vittles" there. Thrilled with this knowledge and full of zeal to help, Elizabeth and Mary gladly kept the secret. A notorious case of brutality toward a slave occurred at a home only a short distance from the Todds' in 1837. Truly, Mary was able to tell young Lincoln things about slavery which he could not have known of his own experience; these two kind people felt and thought alike in their abhorrence of slavery's cruelty.

The engaged couple almost certainly talked of poetry; it was dear to the minds of both. Another of Mary's indispensable cousins wrote that her "love for poetry, which she was forever reciting, was the cause of many a jest among her friends. Page after page of classic poetry she could recite and liked nothing better." Lincoln, too, quoted verses constantly, and even more than Mary was gifted with a remarkable memory.

There is a special congeniality between minds that share a feeling for literary expression, minds that can meet in mutual enjoyment of the same jeweled phrase or the music of a rhythmic line. Lincoln and Mary both would have known what was meant in these rare words of Carl Sandburg: "There are certain old poems ... And we learn them by heart; ... and put them away in the chests and attics of our memories, keeping them as keepsakes, taking them out and handling them, reciting their feel and rhythm, scanning their lines, and then putting them back till the next time they will be wanted, for they will always be wanted again."

Both, of course, wrote verses. We shall see later that a certain too clever jingle of Mary's caused considerable trouble. "My Childhood Home I See Again," already quoted, with its sentiment applied to Lincoln's memories of Kentucky, was actually inspired, as he himself explained, by a visit to his old Indiana haunts and the graves of his mother and sister in the fall of 1844. He did not think that "spot of the earth" poetical, "but still," he said thoughtfully, "seeing it and its objects and inhabitants aroused feelings in me which were certainly poetry; though whether my expression of those feelings is poetry is quite another question." Lincoln and Mary both took poetry seriously. When either wrote, there was a guiding cadence in the mind, an inner testing of the flow of their sentences, but their rhythms were very different.

"The Bear Hunt" by the "poet" Abraham Lincoln is a vivid ballad. The remembered terror of a pioneer boy comes alive in the second stanza:

> *When first my father settled here,*
> *'Twas then the frontier line:*
> *The panther's scream, filled night with fear*
> *And bears preyed on the swine.*

A hunt is organized and the dogs pursue the fleeing bear:

> *With instant cry away they dash,*
> *And men as fast pursue;*
> *O'er logs they leap, through water splash,*
> *And shout the brisk halloo.*

> . . . . . .

> *The tall fleet cur, with deep-mouthed voice,*
> *Now speeds him, as the wind;*
> *While half-grown pup, and short-legged fice,*
> *Are yelping far behind.*

. . . . . .

> *At top of speed, the horse-men come,*
> *All screaming in a row.*
> *'Whoop! Take him Tiger—Seize him Drum'—*
> *Bang,—Bang—the rifles go.*

The bear was slain with vivid detail, suggesting that Lincoln had once attended a bear hunt. The story ends in a humorous twist where the "fice," left far behind in the chase, emerges from the wood, seizes the dead bear ferociously "and swears, as plain as dog can swear, that he has won the skin."

The young engaged couple loved books of various kinds. Mary could have introduced the hungry-minded Lincoln to favorites of hers, for when growing up she had, in addition to her studies, her father's well-filled library always at hand. A pathetic contrast was this to a leggy youth's borrowing of Weems's *Washington* and having to "pull fodder" to pay for it when it was accidentally damaged by rain. In their married life in Springfield we will find Mary reading books and reviewing them to her husband.

Meeting on this broad ground of their love for literature, they looked in different directions, according to their differing temperaments. Lincoln saw life in philosophical grays and the shadows of human injustice; Mary viewed it in Technicolor, all the details made interesting by her zest for living. He loved the poems that appealed "to his tender sympathy with humanity, its hopes and its sorrows." Mary's cheerful nature turned to less profound verse, with cleverly turned phrases that were like the curves of a frill adorning the dresses she loved so well.

Lincoln's delight in Shakespeare and his remarkable memory for long passages is well known; also his love of the theater. We shall find Mary quoting Shakespeare, and the Lincolns attending plays whenever possible. Perhaps Mary told him of the play given in French at the Mentelle school, where she took the principal part. Both loved the verses of Bobby Burns. The Scots poet in his young manhood had also experienced poverty, hard physical labor, and an aching hunger for books. Lincoln had these things in common with Burns; also his sympathy for lowly people.

Mary's feeling for Burns together with her appreciation

of beauty and literature in general is unconsciously expressed in a letter she wrote later in life, after making a pilgrimage to the poet's birthplace: "It does appear to me, that Scotland has spoilt me for seeing any other place in Europe. Edinburgh is a beautiful city—no nook & corner of interest did I leave unvisited, as I now think. We were at Abbotsford—all through the Rob Roy Country—visited all the lovely locks lock Lomond lock Catherine & *all*—all saw the great mountains—castles—visited Burns' birthplace & sighed over poor 'Highland Mary's' grave. And greater than all—went down into the deep & entered 'Fingal's Cave,' not equal to our Niagara—yet it is *wonderful.* The old hundred sung in that vaulted region, by about two hundred people—on *that* day—will ever sound in my ears. It is only in visiting such a spot, that we can fully realize the greatness & power of the Creator." The woman who wrote those lines had a sensitivity which Lincoln must have found appealing in the girl.

She thrilled to the "charm" and "excitement" of life on the river. Lincoln knew all about that charm and even more about the excitement. He could have told her of his trip down the Mississippi to New Orleans and the effect upon a nineteen-year-old boy, fresh from the backwoods, when a new world opened up before him, a picture-book world of a bright-colored city with men of strange race and tongue, and foreign ships outlined against a Southern sky.

Mary knew steamboat travel and loved it as she loved always the joy of going places and seeing new scenes. But Lincoln had twice taken a loaded flatboat to New Orleans, a much more rugged experience. Perhaps he told her too of the mounting excitement and thrill when the *Talisman* puffed up the Sangamon River past New Salem in 1832 and the spectators on the banks cheered wildly with visions of flourishing trade now that a steamboat could reach them, rosy anticipations that were not to be realized. So there was the common topic of river-boat travel between them, a topic that comes alive with drama to the imaginative.

They shared a genuine fostering love of children and a gift for warm affectionate friendships. They knew the language of playful imagining. He could be whimsical and humorous; she could be teasing and gay. Yet a listing of congenial topics seems lifeless against the vitality of young love, just as a description of features gives no impression of glowing personality, of the tenderness in meeting eyes, the charm of a gesture, the pressure of lips. The most important topics between them were those perennial to two people in love with each other and engaged to be married.

But while we have been exploring the evidence of their congeniality in its far-reaching effect, we have been brought up short by a broken engagement.

chapter 4

BROKEN ENGAGEMENT

It becomes necessary in this chapter to deal with the most
tangled aspect of the courtship of Lincoln and Mary Todd
—the broken engagement. It is known that a severe and
crushing emotional crisis in Lincoln's life was associated
with the wretched day which he himself called "that fatal
first of Jan'y. '41," but to spell out the details of this
crisis, to harmonize conflicting explanations given long
after the event, and to reconstruct this bit of personal history from imperfect fragments of evidence, is a task similar
to putting together a jigsaw puzzle with many of the pieces
missing. If there is a broken engagement in one's circle
of friends, details of what happened are usually not
known, though there is apt to be much rumor and conjecture. To uncover what occurred over a century ago
between two young people in the matter of emotions is
an even greater problem, especially when the incident has
been overlaid with a fabricated story of a wedding occasion at which the bridegroom failed to appear. Like the
archaeologist, one has to clear away the dirt and debris
before one can get at the genuine historical material.

The story of Lincoln as a defaulting bridegroom was the
work of William H. Herndon, who became Lincoln's junior
law partner in 1844, and his biographer with the publication of *Herndon's Lincoln* forty-five years later. In telling Mary Lincoln's life story it is necessary to take Herndon along as excess baggage. More than any other he
painted her portrait for posterity, and because of his eccentricities and personal feeling the portrait is a caricature. Since he has distorted and beclouded the account of
the broken engagement in the popular mind, he must be
introduced here. We are forced to suspend the narrative
of two young people in order to hold court, as it were, and
to consider a framed-up account before we can go ahead
with our examination of what happened as a matter of
historical finding.

When we look at a personality of the past, we necessarily do so through the eyes and minds of those then living. A fair appraisal requires the testimony of many contemporaries and an evaluation of each as witness. Herndon's estimate of Mary Lincoln has received the most attention; how trustworthy were the views that came through the refraction of his mind?

This roughhewn man, when he began to collect material for his Lincoln biography after the President's death, was a very different individual from the bright-minded young person whom Lincoln in 1844 took into his office to be his man Friday and do the legal chores. With lively intellectual curiosity Herndon had dabbled in New England transcendentalism and had absorbed from it the idea that truth can be found by introspection. That is, all men operate under the same laws of human behavior; if you wish to understand a man's actions, look into your own soul, where the same motives and laws prevail.

Transcendentalism as understood by New England's philosophers was one thing; Herndon's untutored interpretation of it was another. The man came to believe sincerely that he was possessed of clairvoyant vision. He was self-convinced that he could read people's minds and discover truths that were a closed book to others. With his "mud instinct" and "dog sagacity" he could see, as he said, "to the gizzard" of a question, could read a secret in a face and then interpret that secret and psychoanalyze the personality behind that face by what he called "the lines of human conduct." The man who firmly believes he can perceive truth by his own power of intuition is apt to end by believing what he wants to believe, and Herndon wanted to believe the worst about Mrs. Lincoln.

From the first meeting there had been a mutual dislike. He was antagonistic to the aristocratic group to which she belonged (a group which did not accept him socially) and very much opposed to Lincoln's marriage into that group. She disapproved of him as a partner for her husband because of his drinking habits and for other reasons which will be treated later. She naturally wanted Lincoln to have a partner of more prominence and better standing in the community. Herndon was never invited to a meal at the Lincoln home and actually saw very little of his partner's wife. His sizing up of the Lincoln marriage as unhappy was the result of a mental process, a theorizing about it, not of firsthand observation. Explaining Herndon's line of reasoning, David Donald, his biographer, has said: "Herndon could never quite figure Lincoln out. He behaved queerly—i.e., differently from Herndon; ... his gusty outbreaks of humor would alternate with fits of deep depression. There must be something the matter with this man." Just what was wrong the junior partner did not know but that was where his psychoanalysis, with himself as diagnostician and interpreter, would come in handy.

Antagonistic to Mrs. Lincoln with a dislike that in the end became violent hatred, he developed the theory that an unhappy marriage was to blame for Lincoln's melancholy moods. The story of Lincoln as a defaulting bridegroom was a part of his elaborate building up of that theory in his book. The story proved untrue but it must be remembered that in his busy, weathercock mind Herndon always sincerely believed in whatever notion possessed him at the moment.

This honesty of intention makes his direct record of what was said in his presence valuable. Many of his reported interviews are used herein, but it is never safe to use his recordings, much less his pen-swinging passages of Herndonian comment, without the needful checking. When interviewing, he often, perhaps unconsciously, slanted his questions and jottings toward proving his theories, but that is human nature and especially the tendency of a lawyer. Herndon meant to tell the truth as he saw it. There were also times when a sense of justice caused him to mention Mrs. Lincoln's good qualities, to call her "a highly cultured woman—witty—dashing—pleasant and a lady," and to give her credit for being "a keen observer of human nature—an excellent judge of it —none better." Herndon's shifting mind and rampant expression of his momentary thought make it possible to quote him on all sides of a question.

It has taken long decades to arrive at an appraisal of this man, to give him the particular niche which he deserves—that much and no more—in Lincoln biography. For years he was accepted with but little questioning and with grateful recognition of two services which he performed: collecting a vast, if uneven, body of personal memories and of source material concerning Lincoln's life; and, as Lord Charnwood has said, "substituting for Lincoln's aureole the battered tall hat, with valuable papers stuck in its lining, which he had long contemplated with reverent irritation." Herndon made Lincoln come alive, brought him down to earth, and supplied those picturesque, everyday "close-up" touches without which the great statesman might have remained somewhat of a lay figure.

Any researcher must be sympathetic toward his prodigious efforts in collecting his material and grateful for the resulting Herndon-Weik manuscripts, even while recognizing that their contents must be rigidly checked with established facts for accuracy. The collection is a vast scrap basket of letters, statements, jottings and fragments, the unsifted raw material for a biography. Herndon had to get a literary collaborator, Jesse Weik, a young journalist, to put this conglomeration into something which could be published as a book. Studying these manuscripts, one finds that Herndon submitted his records already processed by his psychoanalysis. Without conscious deception he was capable of skipping over essential facts which he had himself recorded because those facts interfered with his theory of what had occurred and why. Weik had to use not only Herndon's assembled material but also a kind of mulling over—that is, scores of his letters and monographic passages giving the ex-partner's mental pattern of what it all meant. Not even the records were consistent. Those records plus Herndon's voluminous and uninhibited cogitations were less so.

Numerous biographers—notably Albert J. Beveridge—followed the Herndon line, thus crystallizing and perpetuating his portrait of Mary Lincoln. Before other scholars could get access to the Herndon-Weik manuscripts, Beveridge obtained that privilege. In his two-volume *Abraham Lincoln: 1809-1858* he gave briefly the story of the defaulting bridegroom and accepted Herndon's estimate of Mrs. Lincoln. Beveridge was a careful writer, drafting his chapters and revising them many times. He had not completed his revision of his work when he died. Two months before that tragic event, he wrote Jesse Weik that he felt it indispensable for him to restudy the Weik manuscripts (Herndon-Weik manuscripts) as he was not satisfied with the product of his first study of them. Perhaps Herndon's obvious inconsistencies troubled him. It is unfortunate that Beveridge did not live to make this second study of those papers, and to revise and complete the fine work he

was doing. In following Herndon's line, he too presented a
distorted picture of Lincoln's wife. It should be added that
much new historical material by which to check Herndon's
accounts has come to light since Beveridge's biography of
Lincoln was published in 1928.

The Herndon-Weik manuscripts, now in the Library of
Congress, did not become available to the public until
1942. These manuscripts were necessary before we could
have an acceptable biography of Herndon. When that
much-needed study appeared in 1948, it came in full
measure. In David Donald's *Lincoln's Herndon* one has
a competent, readable treatment based on a thorough and
critical study of the sources, a sympathetic treatment
which does justice to Herndon's strivings and at many
points enlists the reader's sympathy, but which—as a
necessity for any critical study—lays bare the eccentricities and distortions, the frustrations and contradictions,
that characterized him as a biographer.

The importance of this for our study of Mary Lincoln is
obvious. If the long-prevailing concept of her has been
mainly of Herndon's fashioning, it is only now, with our
first adequate appraisal of Herndon, that this concept can
be fully re-examined for what it is worth. If the treatment
of him here seems severe, it is because in his relation to
Mary Lincoln we are dealing with him at his worst. In
the twisted image of her which he impressed upon the
public mind, Herndon, self-convinced of his righteousness
and omniscience, committed a terrible wrong. He was a
lawyer and he "framed" her with a lawyer's skill. The
greatest problem in telling Mary Lincoln's story is to remove the encrustations with which he has overlaid it.

Such an encrustation is the account of the wedding at
which Lincoln as bridegroom failed to appear. Herndon
had the fact of the broken engagement to begin with, and
a possible starting point, as we shall see, in Mrs. Edwards's
mention of wedding preparations; his glowing imagination and fluent pen did the rest. It is a prize passage in
his biography of Lincoln. Details were piled high: the furniture arrangement, the decorations, the supper, the
guests, the expectant pleasure, the bride's veil and silken
gown, her flowers, the humiliation when no groom appeared, the messengers sent about town, the departing
guests, the darkness settling over all for the night. Herndon, as he himself said, wrote "in a gallop—with a

whoop." His prose is made up of broken bits of color, like the pattern of a kaleidoscope, and his ideas were as subject to change under a slight new stimulus. Historians have shown conclusively that the incident of the defaulting bridegroom was a fabrication.

Herndon, having made up the story of the wedding occasion out of his "intuitive" knowledge, then produced one of his masterpieces of psycho-invention; he suggested that the (imaginary) blow to her pride which Mary had received at this (fictitious) wedding occasion made her act out "in her conduct toward her husband the laws of human revenge." "Love fled at the approach of revenge," he wrote. This gratuitous suggestion, a product of Herndon's mental gymnastics and nothing more, has so colored the impression of Mary Lincoln that even today one hears the question as to whether she married Lincoln for spite. Once the idea that she married him to make him miserable was created in the public mind, the case was "fixed" against her, and an objective attitude became well nigh impossible. Herndon's theorizings have gone far toward killing the American public's natural fairmindedness as far as Mrs. Lincoln is concerned.

What did happen? Of contemporary evidence—that is, statements made in the early eighteen-forties, none of which is of Herndon's finding—we have scattered bits in letters of the time. These are valuable, but are too few to enable us to recapture all that occurred. There are several accounts given in the eighteen-sixties or later, when memories had had long years to become dim and blurred. One must assemble the available evidence, evaluate it, find out the points of agreement and put the resulting product —meager as it is—in its rightful setting of known facts.

We will consider first the accounts given after 1860, and then follow with the contemporary evidence. Mary's family would naturally know most about the affair, though there we get into the intricacies of antagonistic opinions within the family plus the front of family pride before the outside world. Herndon, questioning Ninian W. Edwards in September 1865, was told that "Lincoln fell in love" with Matilda Edwards, and that was the cause of the estrangement, a statement somewhat invalidated by the comment which immediately follows that Lincoln "did not ever by act or deed directly or indirectly hint or speak of it to Miss Edwards." The Ninian Edwards record continues: "Miss Todd released Lincoln from the contract, leaving Lincoln the privilege of resuming it . . . if he wished." Ninian added that in consequence of the break, Lincoln went "crazy as a *Loon* . . ."

The rupture in the love affair of two people so much in the public eye as Mary and Lincoln resulted, of course, in a buzz of gossip in the town, and the presence of the lovely Matilda at the Edwards home seemed to offer, in the absence of facts, a plausible theory that Lincoln's affections had strayed to her. A letter written by an entertaining lady in Springfield, January 27, 1841, enables one to listen in (as by a sort of time machine) to the wagging tongues. We hear that Miss Todd, who "has a great many Beaus," is "flourishing," but Mr. Lincoln, poor fellow, is in a "bad way." He was out "for the first time for a month" on Monday, runs this letter, and "They say he don't look like the same person." He was "perfectly crazy" for a time, for he is "dying with love they say." His falling so desperately in love with Miss Edwards of Alton has caused him to break off with Miss Todd. He thinks Miss Edwards "so perfect," he says he would not have "one feature of her face altered," and he cannot bear to leave her side in company, "so the story goes." If one may be so bold as to question that mighty authority "They say," it may be mildly remarked that Mrs. Edwards asked Matilda if Lincoln ever spoke of love to her and the emphatic reply was, "On my word, he never mentioned such a subject to me; he never even stooped to pay me a compliment." The "month" of illness will also dwindle, as we will see, to a week, with better-informed evidence.

It has been seen that Mary mentioned Matilda in terms of deep affection in a letter written in December 1840, the very time when she was becoming, or had become, engaged to Lincoln. Lincoln himself, writing to his wife in 1848, spoke of Matilda, then Mrs. Newton Deming Strong, in terms indicating warm continuing friendship. If Matilda had been a factor in the broken engagement, one so quick to resentment as Mary would not have written of her so amiably.

Now with new-found letters of Matilda's it is a delight to present crowning proof that she had no part in the broken engagement. Matilda, writing her brother Nelson in May 1842 said: "I received a letter from dear Molly [Mary's nickname] this eve pressing me much to visit her but ... I think I have duties which demand my time at home and unless something I know not of transpires here I shall remain. She spoke of your being absent, condoled with me upon the loss of 'such a brother' and sent kind particular remembrances to you. Cannot you steal time to write her one of your best letters? It would be a gratification to both her and myself."

As will be seen shortly, Mary's love for Lincoln remained unchanged through the estrangement and she was anxious to renew the engagement. At the time of this letter the renewal was not far off. If Matilda had been a rival, if the engagement had been broken because of Lincoln's supposed love for her, the last thing Mary would have done would have been to invite Matilda back to Springfield for a visit. The very idea would have filled her with dismay. Nor would there have been the affectionate relationship between the two girls indicated in this passage. The discovery of Matilda's letter has given the *coup de grâce* to the theory that she had anything to do with the break between Lincoln and Mary.

With Ninian's statement as authority, Herndon naturally wove the Matilda Edwards explanation, a detached thread of rumor, into the tangled knot of his story. Working on his pet theory that the Lincoln marriage was unhappy, he eagerly grasped every opportunity to involve Lincoln in love affairs with other girls. To take Herndon seriously in this respect is to make Lincoln positively weak-minded in regard to women. A better authority is Lincoln's own repeated statement to his wife that she was the only woman he had ever really loved. "It was always," wrote Mary when she was forty-seven, "music in my ears, both before & after our marriage, when my husband, told me, that I was the only one, he had ever thought of, or cared for."

Mrs. Ninian W. Edwards made two statements to Herndon, the first undated but between 1865 and 1872, the second in 1887. In her first statement, according to the jotting in Herndon's handwriting, she said: "Lincoln & Mary were engaged—every thing was ready & prepared for the marriage—even to the supper &c. Mr. L. failed to meet his engagement—cause: insanity." This was probably the starting point of Herndon's defaulting bridegroom story (he required something which he considered evidence to start with), but, as David Donald points out:

"Most Lincoln experts now tend, with justice, to discount Mrs. Edwards's statements very heavily." Donald points out that her evidence is fragmentary and indirect, a long delayed reminiscence in direct contradiction to the recollections of others, and that there is no contemporary support for her testimony. "But even if one accepted Mrs. Edwards's memory as absolutely veracious," continues Mr. Donald, "the only story that could justifiably be drawn from her facts would be that of a planned wedding and a broken engagement. Around these two fragmentary facts Herndon was able to spin a magnificent cobweb of detail."

Mrs. Edwards also mentioned to Jesse Weik in 1883, forty-two years after the event, that the cakes were baked and arrangements made for the wedding of Mary and Lincoln. Her memory included preparations for the weddings of three sisters which had all occurred many years before, and confusion between these weddings would have been easy. In her second statement to Herndon in 1887, she said nothing of wedding preparations but stated: "Lincoln's & Mary's engagement &c. were broken off by her flirtations with Douglas"—quite a different interpretation. She discarded here the Matilda Edwards theory advanced by her husband; their explanations are not the same, a matter of which more will be said later.

One ounce of contemporary evidence is worth a pound of reminiscence. Turning for a moment to a record written at the time, we search Mary Todd's long, confidential letter to Mercy Levering written in mid-December 1840, approximately two weeks before the date of the alleged wedding occasion. It is significant that there is no mention of wedding preparations in that letter, though it is filled with all the sentimental matters occupying Mary's mind at the time. But, of course, much could have happened between the time that letter was written and the first of January.

Another account comes from Emilie Todd Helm, Mary's half sister, who said she had received it from Mrs. Edwards. The flirtation-with-Douglas theory (which Ninian did not even mention in 1865) has become full-fledged in this version, and is dramatized in Katherine Helm's *Mary, Wife of Lincoln*. If we follow this Helm account, Lincoln, in modern phrase, forgot a "date" with Mary. He was to take her to a party and, when he failed to call for her, she went to the party without him. Belatedly remembering the engagement, he rushed first to the Edwards home and then to the house where festivity was in full swing. There Mary paid him back in true feminine coin by flirting ostentatiously with Stephen A. Douglas, a beau with whose name hers had frequently been coupled. (But aside from Lincoln, the man whose courtship of Mary at this time is most substantiated by evidence was Edwin B. Webb.)

Herndon, more than a score of years after the event, questioned Joshua Speed, and recorded what he said about the break in the love affair. Speed was in such a confidential relationship to Lincoln, and his advice so affected events, that his testimony is especially important. It shows that Lincoln took the initiative in breaking the engagement. According to Herndon's hasty jotting of this conversation with Speed, Lincoln wrote Mary a letter telling her "he did not love her." The reason given for the change of heart was: "Lincoln did love Miss Edwards—" (How the innocent and conscientious Matilda would have resented the way her name was dragged into the affair.)

Herndon's record continues: Lincoln asked Joshua to deliver the letter to Mary. Joshua talked Lincoln out of sending the letter, telling him it was a more manly thing to go and see Mary and explain in person. Lincoln followed this advice, whereupon the girl burst into tears, rose and exclaimed ". . . the deceiver shall be deceived wo is me." Like any other tenderhearted young man seeing the girl he cared for in such deep distress, Lincoln could not endure it. He took her in his arms, drew her down upon his knees, kissed and comforted her. But the record goes on to say that they "parted—he going one way & she an other." Speed made no mention of any wedding default or wedding planned with date set. But his statement included Mary's releasing of Lincoln from the engagement, a most important link in the chain of events that Herndon chose to ignore at this point, putting it in later when it would not interfere with his theoretical story. In Herndon's biography of Lincoln the testimony of Speed is used up to the point where Lincoln drew Mary into his arms, kissed and comforted her; this is taken as a renewal of the engagement and (omitting any mention here of a release) the biography launches into the dramatic account of a wedding at which the bridegroom failed to appear. Then the Herndon biography has Mary, after Lincoln's al-

leged conduct had amounted to deserting her at the altar,
write him a letter releasing him from the engagement.

Speed also said (and Herndon wrote it down) that after
Lincoln called on Mary to break the engagement, he "did
not go to see her for months." The Herndon biography, ig-
noring the words that they "parted—he going one way
& she an other" and the statement that she released him
from the engagement, says that after that call, "Lincoln
continued his visits, and things moved on smoothly as before." One misstatement led to another.

Had Herndon not been riding his theory so hard, he
might have remembered that his home was in Springfield
at the time Lincoln was supposed to have deserted Mary
at the altar, and he certainly would have heard of such
a sensational event as he describes. He makes no mention
of such recollection. If he questioned relatives and friends
in Springfield about the wedding default (as he had opportunity to do and should have done) he received no
confirmation of his theory. Ida Tarbell, when she made
such a canvass in the eighteen-nineties, questioning people who had every reason to know the truth (Mary's relatives, Elizabeth Todd Grimsley, Mrs. John Todd Stuart,
Mrs. Benjamin S. Edwards; also Mary's two sisters then
living, Mrs. Frances Todd Wallace and Mrs. Emilie Todd
Helm; and others), received but one answer: no such
wedding occasion with missing bridegroom had ever happened. Nobody "ever heard of this wedding party until
Mr. Herndon gave his material to the public."

A little later, Octavia Roberts, who had grown up in
Springfield's Lincoln tradition, asked the old-timers the
same question and reported: "I never found anyone who
believed that he [Lincoln] deserted Mary Todd at the altar, except Herndon . . . Everyone knew, however, that the
engagement had been broken." Evidence against his theories did not shake this man's faith in his own intuitive
powers. On the contrary, it was apt to put him on the defensive. As his biographer has remarked: "Nothing so in-
furiated Herndon as a challenge to his omniscience." With
him it came to be a case of conclusions upon which he
based his facts.

Another version of the estrangement should be mentioned—that given by Mrs. Elizabeth Keckley, Mrs. Lincoln's colored seamstress in Washington. Mrs. Keckley's
book, *Behind the Scenes,* is ghostwritten, which leads one

to be wary in using it, checking with known facts as far as possible. Mrs. Keckley claimed to have obtained her version from Mrs. Lincoln and Dr. Anson G. Henry, whose role in this record is that of go-between for the lovers. (We must note well this Dr. Henry, trusted physician and beloved intimate friend of both the Lincolns. He went through deep emotional experiences with each of them, so that his direct testimony about Mary much later in our story is important.)

Mrs. Keckley had opportunity to observe directly what took place in the White House. Her record even though written by another hand will be used in these pages for the White House period and will be found to agree largely with more direct evidence. But when Mrs. Keckley tells her recollection of what Mrs. Lincoln and Dr. Henry told her in reminiscence (perhaps filling in and piecing their items together) and when all this in turn passes through the mind of the one or ones who were writing the story for Mrs. Keckley we have something far less trustworthy. Anyone who has played the game of "gossip" knows how statements change and grow as they pass from person to person.

There is no mention of a broken engagement in Mrs. Keckley's version—only an estrangement brought on by Mary's flirtation with Douglas, and her leading Lincoln on to propose marriage only to refuse him. This was not because she did not love him; her refusal came from a coquettish desire to test his love; also she did not wish to be won too easily. According to this account she meant to accept him later but her rejection of him at first threw him into his great depression.

Dr. Henry, as Lincoln's physician, according to the Keckley story, sought Mary out and explained that Lincoln was physically ill and deeply depressed. Whereupon the girl, regretting what she had done, allowed Dr. Henry to carry back to Lincoln assurance of her love. This ties up with Mrs. Edwards's statement that Dr. Henry, "who admired and loved Mr. Lincoln, had much to do with getting Mary and Lincoln together again." In this respect the Keckley account has verification. Otherwise one feels inclined to discount this highly dramatized version. What Mrs. Lincoln and Dr. Henry really said could have been accurate as far as it went, but Mrs. Keckley or her ghost writer or writers could have drawn inferences to fill out the story. This version omits the basic fact which is confirmed by contemporary evidence, the broken engagement.

We now come to an explanation of the breaking of the engagement which seems to fit more of the curves and angles of the jigsaw puzzle than any other. It is an explanation that has been little considered, but it is worthy of careful study.

Albert S. Edwards, son of Mr. and Mrs. Ninian W. Edwards, years later said that the cause of the break in the engagement was the opposition and disapproval of his parents. They had nothing against Lincoln except his poverty and lack of prospects, but they thought he could not support Mary in a manner which they felt to be essential. When, therefore, he assumed the role of suitor, they gave him the cold shoulder. "During 1841 and 1842," said Albert S. Edwards, "my mother did what she could to break up the match." After the marriage, he said, normal social relations were resumed, but "Mrs. Lincoln, I think, always was a little cool toward my mother for the course she had taken to discourage the engagement."

There is indirect evidence that Mrs. John Todd Stuart gave the same account, saying that Mary herself told her that the Edwardses forced the breaking of the engagement by their opposition.

Herndon's jottings of what Mr. and Mrs. Edwards said to him do not give the impression that their opposition caused the breaking of the engagement, but personalities and attitudes must be considered here. The social ideals of the Edwardses differed radically from Lincoln's. Ninian W. Edwards "was naturally and constitutionally an aristocrat," wrote one of his colleagues in the state legislature, "and he hated democracy . . . as the devil is said to hate holy water." There could be no meeting of minds between him and the man who was to become the embodiment of American democracy. The statements of Mr. and Mrs. Edwards were made after years of association in which there had been the friction and clashes of differing viewpoints and interests. Mrs. Edwards naturally viewed matters as her husband did. Her resentment and lack of understanding of Lincoln crop out in the record of her interviews: Lincoln "was a cold man—had no affection—was not social." She admitted "he was a great man—a good man & an honest one," but then follows a grievance: "He was a little ungrateful, I think, for the want of recollection." Ninian also described young Lincoln in unflattering terms; he was a "mighty rough man," and "was not a warm hearted man." Mrs. Edwards interrupted her first statement to tell of an irrelevant and petty quarrel between herself and Mary in which sharp things were said on both sides.

There was a great deal of class consciousness at the time and Lincoln undoubtedly came from hardscrabble beginnings. The Edwardses and other relatives sincerely believed that in marrying Lincoln Mary was marrying beneath her. (The friendly girl herself was not snobbish as to class. She could be snobbish, however, to people she disliked or disapproved of.) The aristocratic flavor of the Edwardses' attitude was evident later in the remark of another member of the family: ". . . when he [Lincoln] was nominated it seemed impossible that this should ever be. There were so many others that we could name who seemed so much better fitted for this position than he."

A letter which came to light in 1947 shows that Ninian was opposed to Lincoln's re-election and incidentally brings the aristocratic gentleman to life in a description, "a tall lank man dressed in black broad cloth with a cane in his hand." When questioned casually about his attitude toward Lincoln's re-election, Mr. Edwards said, "I am opposed to him on principle." Upon further question as to what principle, he gave the disdainful reply: "I never talk politics in the street." The letter further states that Ninian talked Lincoln down as "not capable."

All these background factors must be considered in assessing the statements of Mr. and Mrs. Ninian Edwards which were given so many years after the event. They would have been considerably embarrassed to admit, after Lincoln had become a great President and a martyr, that they had once opposed their sister's marriage to him on the ground he had no prospects! To admit this to Herndon, a man they regarded with much the same disapproval as Mrs. Lincoln's, would have been hard to take. They played down their opposition and emphasized other factors that come into the story. Mr. Edwards, in his interview, did not mention their opposition at all, but stressed his undoubted early kindness and friendship to Lincoln. There was certainly gossip that Lincoln had fallen in love with Matilda Edwards; Ninian gave that as the cause of the estrangement.

Mrs. Edwards admitted their opposition but gave as the reason the unsuitability of the natures of the two lovers, not the fact that he was poor and had no apparent future. She was a bit vague as to when the opposition began, saying after her description of the two young people together, "I did not in a little time think that Mr L. & Mary were suitable to each other & said so to Mary." She stated that she and her husband encouraged the match in the beginning, then opposed it. "Mr. Edwards & myself after the first crush of things told Mary & Lincoln that they had better not ever marry—that their natures, mind—education—raising &c. were so different they could not live happy as husband and wife . . ." The expression "first crush of things" is ambiguous; it has been taken to mean the broken engagement, but it could conceivably refer to some episode at the point where the Edwardses decided to reverse their position and oppose the match, and try to break off the engagement.

Certain phrases in letters take on new meaning with the possibility that the Edwardses were opposing the match late in 1840 before the breaking of the engagement. In October 1840 young Conkling had noted that Mary "did not appear as merry and joyous as usual." Her letter to Mercy Levering in December shows signs of a troubled spirit; she has lost weight and is pensive. She mentions Lincoln but does not speak of any plans for them to be married. She talks around the subject, which could well be the case if she was at the time combating family opposition. She playfully speaks of matrimony as a crime, which is suggestive.

Herndon quotes Mrs. Edwards as saying in her second statement: "Mr Edwards & myself told Lincoln and Mary not to marry . . . We never opposed Lincolns marriage with Mary." There could perhaps be some qualification explaining the contradiction that has been lost in Herndon's jottings which, as he honestly states, were in this particular case made after the conversation ended. (It must be constantly borne in mind that all these delayed rememberings have come down indirectly.) Mrs. Edwards's second statement was made at least fifteen years after her first, and by this time the family version was that the cause of the broken engagement was Mary's flirtation with Douglas. It could be stated with truth that she flirted with Douglas; she flirted with all her beaux, and it is possible there was

some episode of her coquetry that hurt Lincoln. This flirtation explanation was so useful and romantic that it
grew through the years.

Katherine Helm, niece of Mrs. Lincoln, stresses the family opposition to the match. She had the great advantage
of having the inside family account. She expands on the
"incongruity of such a marriage" and says, with a nice
choosing of the word, that they regarded Lincoln's future
as "nebulous." She places this family opposition *before*
her pretty dramatization of the break between Lincoln
and Mary, supposed to be caused by Mary's flirtation.
That timing ties in with the statement of the son of Ninian
Edwards that the disapproval of the family came before
and was the cause of the rupture.

Albert S. Edwards makes it very clear when the opposition began. He said when his mother "saw that things
were becoming serious between Lincoln and Mary, she
treated him rather coldly. The invitations to call were
not pressed." There were many ways in which Ninian
could directly or indirectly have made it evident to the
sensitive Lincoln that he did not qualify as Mary's suitor.
The Edwardses had welcomed him into their home as a
friend, but when it became apparent that he was falling
in love with Mary, they changed and showed him he was
not wanted as a brother-in-law. Perhaps at that point they
had learned that he was in debt and accepting much free
board and lodging from friends. Possibly some clash or incident revealed how his standards differed from theirs.

From Lincoln's letters to Mary Owens we know how
keenly he felt his limitations of social training and poverty, how humbly he regarded himself, and how conscientiously he felt that any woman "who would be blockhead enough to have" him should understand what she
was getting into. If the Edwardses had made known to
him their disapproval because of those very factors which
were already troubling him, it would have cut the introspective and self-doubting young man to the quick. He
was placed in a position he found intolerable. He had
made love to Mary and won her love in return; he was
bound to her by a sort of contract. Yet her family thought
he was not the right husband and could not take adequate
care of her, and the worst of it was that he agreed with
them.

The one thing on which Lincoln prided himself was his

integrity. He was caught in a dilemma in which no course of action he could take would leave him satisfied that he had done the right thing. Ninian stood as Mary's guardian in Springfield and had certain rights. Fathers and guardians had much to say about a girl's marriage in those Victorian years.

Lincoln had written Miss Owens, ". . . if I *knew* it would be doing right . . . to let you alone, I would do it." The tormented young lawyer decided to ask for a release from the engagement, to count himself out of Mary Todd's life in spite of his feeling for her. This feeling has been questioned because of a sentence in Speed's testimony. Herndon's record of his interview with Speed is one of the hastiest, most disjointed and illegible of his jottings. According to this record Lincoln told Mary "he did not love her." This could be merely what either Speed or Herndon had inferred from the fact that Lincoln moved to break the engagement. Certainly the remark connected with this statement—"Lincoln did love Miss Edwards"—was pure inference or conjecture and was false. It will be seen that such an alleged statement by Lincoln does not jibe with Mary's attitude later.

The opposition of the Edwardses as a cause of the breaking of the engagement presents a new interpretation of Lincoln's great despondency which followed. He was forced to choose between two lines of conduct, neither of which he considered entirely honorable, and this decision was in the supercharged realm of a man's emotion for the girl he had chosen. It was the old dramatic situation of a sensitive human being with a conscience being faced with a cruel conflict as to what he should do. We will find that the Edwardses' opposition throws light on a number of things, and especially on Mary's complete lack of resentment at Lincoln's asking for a release.

chapter 5

"I AWFULLY FOREBODE"

Mrs. Edwards's statement of Mary's releasing Lincoln ran as follows: "The world had it that Mr L backed out, and this placed Mary in a peculiar situation & to set herself right and to free Mr Lincoln's mind she wrote a letter to Mr L stating that she would release him from his engagement."

According to one piece of very indirect evidence Mary later said that the Edwardses forced her to write such a letter. Joshua Speed had told of an interview between the lovers in which Lincoln expressed his doubts about the wisdom of their marriage and then, when the girl burst into tears, took her into his arms to kiss and comfort her. It is possible that the Edwardses, to forestall a reconciliation, worked on Mary's pride (saying that people believed Lincoln had backed out) to get her to write the letter of release. And according to Victorian standards, if an engagement was broken, the lady, not the gentleman, must do the breaking. At least we know that Mary's love for Lincoln remained unchanged.

Lincoln's mind was unquestionably in a state where it needed "freeing" or relief of some kind. Mrs. Edwards and Joshua Speed referred to his insanity following the broken engagement, and Mr. Edwards said bluntly that he "went as crazy as a *Loon.*" These words to Herndon with his psychoanalyzing propensity were like a trumpet call to a war horse. The Herndon biography, following the dramatic account of the imaginary wedding default, gallops off into a vivid description of Lincoln's friends searching for him in the night and finding him at daybreak so "miserable, desperate" that they had to remove knives and razors and all instruments of self-destruction from his reach. His friends "watched him closely in their rooms day and night," says Herndon, which does not jibe very well with the proven fact that Lincoln attended the legislature on January 2, the day after the supposed wedding occasion, and that he made at least a brief appearance there every day except one (January 4) until January 13. He was then confined to the house for a week with a physical illness; between January 13 and January 21 he answered his name only once—on January 19. In this record of attendance and of voting several times on questions in which he was interested there can be the picture of a man deeply depressed and "coming down" with an illness, but not of a man "crazy as a *Loon*," watched closely in the rooms of his friends "day and night."

We can now pick up references to the situation in contemporary letters. Lincoln's physical illness left him pitifully thin and weak. Such physical depletion when he was distressed over the broken engagement increased his deep and torturing depression. Writing John Todd Stuart on January 20, 1841, in behalf of Dr. Anson G. Henry for postmaster in Springfield, he said: "I have within the last few days, been making a most discreditable exhibition of myself in the way of hypochondriaism and thereby got an impression that Dr. Henry is necessary to my existence. Unless he gets that place he leaves Springfield. You therefore see how much I am interested in the matter. . . . I have not sufficient composure to write a long letter." The "last few days" refers to the period when he was shut in by illness; there is a touch here of young masculinity's humiliation at being sick, and having such a "discreditable" type of ailment.

Dr. Henry had evidently concluded that Lincoln had hypochondriasm or hypochrondriasis. The term, as used by physicians then, meant a condition characterized by low vitality, apprehensiveness, and extreme depression. Prolonged worry was often a contributing cause. Excessive morbidity was its most marked feature and that is exactly the quality shown in a letter which Lincoln wrote, again to Stuart, on January 23: "I am now the most miserable man living. If what I feel were equally distributed to the whole human family there would not be one cheerful face on the earth. Whether I shall ever be better, I can not tell; I awfully forebode I shall not. To remain as I am is impossible; I must die or be better, it appears to me. The matter you speak of on my account, you may attend to as you say, unless you shall hear of my condition forbidding it. I say this, because I fear I shall be unable to attend to any bussiness here; and a change of scene might help me."

We have seen the reasons for Lincoln's depression. According to his own dismal appraisal of what his wife must endure, he had fallen in love with the very girl with whom he should not have fallen in love. He had made love to her and then failed her, asked to be released from a contract, and made her unhappy. Yet how could he do otherwise? The expressed disapproval of Ninian Edwards as Mary's guardian had intensified all his doubts and misgivings as to whether he was the right man for the lighthearted girl who was accustomed to so much he could not give her. He had written to Miss Owens that, if he married, he would do all in his power to make his wife happy and contented, and nothing would make him more miserable than to fail in the effort. Mrs. Edwards summed up his trouble very neatly: "Mr. Lincoln loved Mary—he went crazy in my own opinion . . . because he wanted to marry and doubted his ability & capacity to please and support a wife."

Lincoln wanted Mary but it is extremely doubtful if he wanted the in-laws he would get by marrying her. He was deeply hurt by the opposition of Mary's family. Ninian Edwards had been his friend. They had both been members of the "Long Nine" in the legislature at Vandalia. Now this aristocratic gentleman was making it clear he looked down on Lincoln.

Lincoln knew there were many fundamental matters in which he could never see eye to eye with the Edwardses. Marrying into the Edwards clique had political complications. Lincoln was distinctly a man of the people, and it was a political hazard, as well as doing violence to his own nature, to ally himself with aristocracy. It gave his political opponents a chance to accuse him of marrying for politic reasons—to get the backing of an influential group. Less than five months after his marriage he was defending himself in a letter to a friend: "It would astonish if not amuse, the older citizens . . . who twelve years ago knew me a strange, friendless, uneducated, penniless boy, working on a flat boat—at ten dollars per month to learn that I have been put down here as the candidate of pride, wealth, and aristocratic family distinction." It is true that the Whigs were something of an upper-class party, but Lincoln's concept of leadership and his own contribution to the party were in terms of a more popular appeal.

Lincoln was missing Mary. Up to the first of January, 1841, he had been enjoying her sparkle, her femininity, and her interest in him. Throughout the record of their married life run little evidences that he liked to have her with him and missed her when she was away. He was to write her a few years after their marriage that when she was absent, and he had "nothing but business—no variety—" it was "exceedingly tasteless" to him. He was in that situation here. He was also deprived of that social life in which he was just beginning to feel at home, where there was wit, repartee (in which he always delighted) and discussion of topics of absorbing interest. The Edwardses were at the top of Springfield society; it was a heavy thing to be frowned upon by so influential a family with all its prominent connections.

All this came at a time when he had lost faith in himself, when he had got himself into a situation from which he saw no honorable way out. We find him writing Joshua Speed toward the end of the estrangement, "I must regain my confidence in my own ability to keep my resolves when they are made. In that ability you know, I once prided myself as the only or at least the chief gem of my character; that gem I lost . . . I have not yet regained it; and until I do, I can not trust myself in any matter of much importance."

It is no wonder that in the shock following the rupture, he became ill with what sounds very much like a severe case of the "flu." Here is the way James Conkling described him in a letter to Mercy Levering on January 24, 1841: "Poor L! how are the mighty fallen! He was confined about a week, but though he now appears again he is reduced and emaciated in appearance and seems scarcely to possess strength enough to speak above a whisper. His case at present is truly deplorable but what prospect there may be for ultimate relief I cannot pretend to say. I doubt not but he can declare 'That loving is a painful thrill, And not to love more painful still' but would not like to intimate that he has experienced 'That surely 'tis the worst of pain To love and not be loved again.'"

This is an important item in the proof that there was no wedding occasion at which the bridegroom failed to appear. Such a public and sensational event as Herndon described would have set the town on fire with gossip. An aristocratic group like the Edwards clique always has many persons outside the pale who would delight in any humiliation visited upon a member of it. Lincoln's political opponents would have had a field day ridiculing the craven bridegroom, for Herndon's fabricated wedding default turns the scrupulously honorable Lincoln into a cad. The truth was that it was Lincoln's extreme conscientiousness that caused him to move toward the breaking of the engagement. In Conkling's letter we have a person intimate in Mary's circle (who would certainly have been invited to such a wedding occasion as the one Herndon pictured) who thought she had rejected Lincoln.

The answer of Mercy Levering on February 7 is based on the same idea. Of "Abraham" she says: "Poor A—— I fear his is a blighted heart! Perhaps if he was as persevering as Mr. W he might finally be successful." "Mr. W" is, of course, Mr. Edwin B. Webb, the widower who was courting Mary in the winter of 1840-1841.

Conkling returned to the subject in his letter to his fiancée on March 7. "And L, poor hapless simple swain who loved most true but was not loved again—I suppose he will now endeavor to drown his cares among the intricacies and perplexities of the law. No more will the merry peal of laughter ascend *high in the air,* to greet his listening and delightful ears. . . . I fear his shrine will now be deserted and that he will withdraw himself from the society of us inferior mortals."

It is time for Mary herself to throw more light upon the situation and this she does in a letter to Mercy Levering in the June following the estrangement. We find her, like Lincoln, in low spirits. She had not written lately because she felt her letters would be "flat, stale & unprofitable." She wished "Merce" would write oftener; she needed the letters to "cheer" her "sad spirit." "The last two or three months," she confessed, "have been of *interminable* length." She had *"lingering regrets* over the past, which time can alone overshadow with its healing balm." "Summer in all its beauty has again come," she continued, "the prairie land looks as beautiful as it did in the olden time, when we strolled together & derived so much of happiness from each other's society—this is past & more than this."

If the "more than this" had been the Herndon incident of the defaulting bridegroom, how would she have referred to the man who had publicly humiliated her, this girl who was so proud? If Herndon's story had been true, she would either not have mentioned Lincoln at all, or in terms of resentment. What do we have instead in this letter of Mary's?

There is understanding and sympathy for Lincoln and a beautifully expressed wistfulness that she might see him again and that he might once more be his old cheerful self. Shyly avoiding the use of Lincoln's name, Mary in this same letter to Mercy mentioned Joshua Speed and then continued: *"His* worthy friend, deems me unworthy of notice, as I have not met *him* in the gay world for months. With the usual comfort of misery, [I] imagine that others were as seldom gladdened by his presence as my humble self, yet I would that the case were different, that he would once more resume his station in Society, that 'Richard should be himself again,' much, much happiness would it afford me." It is a rarely appealing passage in its delicate wording and its revelation of Mary's heart.

She was anxious to have the engagement renewed. Mrs. Edwards said that Mary got word to Lincoln "that though she had released him in the letter spoken of— yet she said that she would hold the question an open one—that is that she had not changed her mind, but felt as always." The evidence throughout her life shows that Mary gave Lincoln her unbroken love from the time they were first engaged until her grieving widowhood was ended by death. As far as is known he was the only man to whom she ever gave her heart. Her power of affection was summed up by Dr. Henry when he wrote: ". . . she loved him as women of her nervous sanguine temperament, only can love . . ."

During the estrangement she showed constancy and strength of character. She was later, under strain, to develop an emotional instability, but there were no signs of it at this time. Under a difficult situation she was holding up much better than the introspective Lincoln. Spirited as she was, she was not too proud to let Lincoln know she still loved him, a remarkable concession for a Victorian maiden, and a far cry indeed from Herndon's invented theory of revenge.

Her attitude makes it plain that Lincoln's doubts about their marriage were of a nature that she could understand without being personally offended. Had he told her he did not love her, as Herndon gave it in his record of the

Speed interview and in his life of Lincoln, she would have bitten her tongue off before she would have confessed that she still loved him. Likewise, had he told her he loved another (Matilda Edwards as Herndon's record has it), she would have kept a proud silence. But she understood that Lincoln's reason grew out of consideration for her, that he felt he could not give her all the things she had a right to expect. The Edwardses had made that clear to him, and he was self-doubting and deeply hurt.

She was having her own feelings wounded by the family attitude. Her sisters, according to Katherine Helm, had showered her with objections to the marriage, and had plainly given her "that piece of mind" which "never impoverishes the giver nor enriches the receiver." She had been reminded that Lincoln's family was "on a different social plane," that she had eligible suitors, and could make an appropriate or even brilliant marriage. She had to hear Lincoln's rough edges made fun of. Ridicule of the man of her choice is an intolerable thing to any woman.

Those long months of estrangement were a hard test for Mary. Since she did not put down on paper that she was the "most miserable" woman living, her "sad spirit" has been generally lost sight of. But she came through that test beautifully. Hearing her unaristocratic lover talked down by her family, she did not sway in loyalty to him. She kept her head, and family objectors could not influence her against the man she loved. But she learned the advisability of keeping secret from the Edwardses any further developments.

In a letter that has just come to light, we can see Mary as she appeared to Sarah Edwards, a visiting relative from Alton, in the late spring of 1842. It was very "quiet" at "Cousin Ninian's," wrote Sarah, and there was very little company, "& since Cousin Elizabeth, united with the church they have given up parties entirely." We must remember Mrs. Edwards's conviction at this time that parties were inconsistent with religion; it throws light on her later statement that Mary was "frivolous." Mary's love of society, her joy of living, her seeing of life in glowing colors made up one of her greatest attractions, but it was a quality not appreciated by the pious of the time.

Against this partyless background Sarah found Molly (Mary) "as lonesome as a gay company loving, girl,

could be so situated . . ." Kindly extending an invitation
to the girl to visit her in Alton, she was perhaps puzzled
that Molly would not take this easy way out of her lone-
someness; ". . . we cannot induce her to come down to
see us," wrote Sarah. We shall see later what Sarah did
not know, that Molly had secret and romantic reasons
for not leaving Springfield just then. Without telling all
she knew or what was afoot, she made her excuses to
Sarah for not coming to Alton. This letter of Sarah Edwards to her cousin Nelson, brother of Matilda, here used
for the first time, gives another glimpse of Mary Todd's
animation and affection: ". . . she spoke often of you
[Nelson] & told me to give you much love when I wrote
with all kinds of pretty messages which I cannot recollect."

Turning from this close-up view of Mary during the
estrangement to consider Lincoln's further thoughts and
feelings of that period, we find a rich source of the best
evidence possible. Joshua Speed left Springfield early in
1841; the companionship as roommates came to an end,
though he and Lincoln remained close friends for life.
They had been confidential with each other to a rare degree and had evidently talked over matters of deep concern
to young men, including that important subject, marriage.
Lincoln wrote Joshua a series of letters which have been
preserved, and in them may be traced the young lawyer's
changing emotions from June 1841 to October 1842,
which was shortly before his marriage.

Time lightened Lincoln's deep melancholy of January,
though he was distressed by the broken engagement until
his reconciliation with Mary. Still he was soon leading his
normal life again and attending to business as before. He
wrote John Todd Stuart on February 5, 1841, discussing
political details with his usual keenness and clarity and
showing a hearty interest in a certain appointment.

In a letter recently unearthed we find a report of Lincoln's condition in May. The letter was written by Joshua
Speed to William Butler, a friend of both Speed and Lincoln in Springfield, and it brings out the interesting fact
that Joshua too was a victim of melancholia. "I am glad
to hear from Mrs. Butler that Lincoln is on the mend,"
wrote Speed. "Say to her that I have had one attack since I
left Springfield . . . I am not as happy as I could be and yet
so much happier than I deserve to be that I think I ought

to be satisfied." There was a plan on foot for Lincoln to visit Joshua in Kentucky; the letter continued: "Say to Lincoln that I will keep my promise about going back with him."

Just what good company Lincoln was a month later is revealed in his cheerful letter to Speed on June 19, 1841. It is a delightful "whodunit," skillfully told, involving the disappearance of one Archibald Fisher, thought by the Springfield community to have been murdered. Lincoln would have made a good writer of detective stories. There are thrilling details of the hunt for the body, including the tearing up of Hickox's milldam to drain water from the pond, a performance enthusiastically entered into by everyone except Mr. Hickox. There were clues of "scuffle-ground, drag-trail, whiskers, and carriage tracks." In short the whole town was "agog" and thoroughly enjoying itself, when a doctor appeared with the information that Fisher, owing to a head injury, would at times wander off in a state of derangement. The doctor further said he had seen the "murderee"—to use Lincoln's word—on the very day that one of the suspects had been arrested for the supposed murder. This testimony caused complete deflation of the zealous investigators. The account concludes: "Langford, who had taken the lead in cutting down Hickoxes mill dam, and wanted to hang Hickox for objecting, looked most awfully wo-begone; he seemed the *'wictim of hunrequited haffection'* as represented in the comic almanac we used to laugh over; and Hart, the little drayman that hauled Molly home once, said it was too *damned* bad, to have so much trouble, and no hanging after all." Here is Lincoln using the intimate nickname "Molly," and the reference is, of course, to the much-talked-of dray ride mentioned in the first chapter. We find "my Molly" also in one of the Lincoln letters to Speed the year after his marriage.

Following the account of the fictitious wedding default with Lincoln's supposed resulting insanity, Herndon's biography says that Speed "induced Lincoln to accompany him to Kentucky." This is not true. Speed went home by himself and Lincoln remained in Springfield attending to his usual business. We know there were plans for him to visit Joshua later, and in June we find him writing his friend, "I stick to my promise to come to Louisville." Mistakenly stating that Speed took Lincoln home with him,

the Herndon biography goes on to picture the young lawyer as "living under the cloud of melancholia," and suggests he was contemplating suicide. Joshua's mother bestowed "motherly care and delicate attention" upon him,
according to Herndon, with the result that he "improved
gradually day by day gaining strength and confidence in
himself, until at last the great cloud lifted and passed
away." We have seen Lincoln's gay letter to Joshua in
June. It was late in the summer of 1841 before he went
to his friend's home in Kentucky, and his melancholia
had been brought under control by February 5 of that
year. By September 27 he had returned to Illinois from
his visit, and was writing Joshua's sister Mary the most
delightful of thank-you letters. He wrote to her, he said,
because they had been "something of cronies" while he
was there, and because he did not have "the express permission" to write her mother or any of them. Apparently
the stately courtesy of the time required a lady's permission to write to her, though it is a little hard to understand
why he should have been so formal toward a lady who had
bestowed "motherly" care upon him.

There was no formality toward Mary Speed, however;
we catch a flash of young Lincoln's teasing and gay
romping with the girl as he wrote her: "I remembered . . .
that, while there, I once was under the necessity of shutting you up in a room to prevent your committing an as-
sault and battery upon me . . ." This is rather lively behavior in a man "living under the cloud of melancholia."
Where is the woebegone figure dripping with gloom pictured by Herndon?

This brings up a notable failing in the Herndon biography. One of Lincoln's outstanding traits was his great
American humor, akin to that of Mark Twain, but the
humorless Herndon was puzzled and bored by his partner's jokes and "queer stories." Herndon's book overem-
phasizes Lincoln's sad moodiness and abstraction while
his playfulness and merry laugh are usually lost sight of.
This defect becomes more clear when one reads what is
back of the biography—that is, the lengthy effusions of
amateur psychology in the Herndon papers. One of the
most amusing of these (it is the sort of funniness that is
unsuspected by the one writing it) is the passage in which
he works out a labored explanation that Lincoln indulged

in humor as a sort of setting-up exercise to increase the sluggish circulation of his blood.

Very apparent in Lincoln's letters to Speed is the warmness of his affection for his friend. He missed Joshua so much, and regretted that he was not coming back to Illinois. "How miserably things seem to be arranged in this world," he wrote. "If we have no friends, we have no pleasure; and if we have them, we are sure to lose them, and be doubly pained by the loss." What a similarity of feeling is here to what Mary wrote Mercy Levering in regard to her leaving Springfield. "To me it has ever appeared that those whose presence was the sunlight of my heart have departed—separated—far and wide, to meet when?" To both Lincoln and Mary warm, affectionate friendships constituted one of life's true values.

In Lincoln's letter to Speed on January 3, 1842, we get further details of Joshua's terrible case of the "blues." He was courting Fanny Henning and was not sure he loved her enough to marry her. (To the long-married, these introspective, marriage-shy young men are at times a bit amusing. They were dubious about the institution of marriage itself.) Lincoln was most understanding and sympathetic as he naturally would be in the unhappy state of his own love affairs. But their cases were not completely parallel; there is more of Joshua here than of Abraham. Lincoln was bolstering Speed up throughout the experience, not the reverse. And how Joshua needed bolstering! Lincoln wrote of his friend's "nervous temperament," "twinge of the soul," "present affliction," "melancholly bodings," and "agony of despondency." Joshua had told Lincoln that "something indescribably horrible and alarming" haunted him, and Lincoln believed that under this "immense suffering" Joshua could not live unless he got better. These expressions should not, by careless association of ideas, be taken as describing Lincoln, though Lincoln did mention that he considered his own nerves "defective."

Joshua, who had courted twenty-odd girls, could well wonder if what he felt was the real thing. He apparently had a flirtation on his conscience. It has been concluded that Lincoln's reference to Sarah Rickard indicates that Joshua had been Sarah's beau, and he was worried for fear he had left her unhappy. Early in February of '42 Lincoln reassured Joshua on this point; he had seen Sarah, he said, and she "seemed very cheerful." Several weeks later his letter to Joshua said: "One thing I can tell you which I know you will be glad to hear, and that is, that I have seen Sarah, and scrutinized her feelings as well as I could, and am fully convinced, she is far happier now, than she has been for the last fifteen months past."

In addition to the complications of a poor man without social background marrying a girl of wealthy and aristocratic family against the wishes of that family, Lincoln probably also recognized that Mary's excitable and impetuous temperament needed, and would always need, protection from her own impulsive acts. Each young man seemed to question whether marriage was the ideal state depicted in the good old-fashioned ending, "They lived happily ever after." Lincoln expressed this thought in one of these letters: "I now have no doubt that it is the peculiar misfortune of both you and me, to dream dreams of Elysium far exceeding all that any thing earthly can realize."

The self-questioning Mr. Speed was married February 15, 1842. In justice to Fanny of the "heavenly black eyes" and to Joshua whom Lincoln loved, it should be stated that the marriage turned out to be a singularly happy one. We have been forced here to deal with only one side of a correspondence; we do not have the letters Joshua was writing Lincoln during this period, more's the pity. That Joshua wrote letters of rich quality and that he gave complete devotion to Fanny are facts both illustrated by the following passage from a letter he sent her many years after they were married. "I wrote to you yesterday, and to-day, having some leisure, I will write again upon the principle, I suppose, that where your treasure is there will your heart go. My earthly treasure is in you; not like the treasures only valuable in possession; not like other valuables acquiring increased value from increased quantity; but, satisfied with each other, we will go down the hill of life together as we have risen."

Returning to the year 1842, it is not surprising to find Joshua writing Lincoln shortly after his marriage that he is "far happier" than he ever expected to be. The news "thrills" Lincoln "with joy." He thinks he should be "entirely happy, but for the never-absent idea, that there is *one* still unhappy whom I have contributed to make so.

That still kills my soul," he continues in an agony of remorse. "I can not but reproach myself, for even wishing
to be happy while she is otherwise. She accompanied a
large party on the Rail Road cars, to Jacksonville last monday; and on her return, spoke, so that I heard of it, of
having enjoyed the trip exceedingly. God be praised for
that."

These words furnish further proof that Lincoln took the
initiative in breaking the engagement: at the same time
they give evidence of his love for Mary. He could not endure her unhappiness; it was torture to him. We have
seen that the sight of her tears resulted in his embracing
her with kisses and holding her on his lap to comfort her.
He reacted as a young man in love normally does.

His tender attitude, revealed in the above words, was at
war with his consciousness of poverty. "I am so poor, and
make so little headway in the world, that I drop back in a
month of idleness, as much as I gain in a year's rowing,"
ran his letter of July 4, 1842, in which he declined to visit
Joshua again because he could not afford it. The poverty
was true enough, but just as Molly had declined an invitation to leave Springfield shortly before, Lincoln was
making an excuse; he had secret romantic reasons for re-
remaining in town.

A new note was showing up in his letters now, a vital,
more confident note. In February he had written: "I tell
you, Speed, our *forebodings*, for which you and I are
rather peculiar, are all the worst sort of nonsense." "Richard" was becoming himself again. What has been called
his "infallible monitor of common sense" had come to
his rescue. By July he was writing that he believed "God
made me one of the instruments of bringing your Fanny
and you to together, which union, I have no doubt He had
fore-ordained. Whatever he designs, he will do for *me* yet.
'Stand *still* and see the salvation of the Lord' is my text
just now." Something was happening to cause this new
erectness of spirit. Certain mutual friends were volun-
teering to be "instruments" of Providence for the unhappy lovers in Springfield.

We have seen that Dr. Henry had some part in bringing
Lincoln and Mary to an understanding of each other's real
feelings. A most important instrument was Mrs. Simeon
Francis, wife of the editor of the *Sangamo Journal*. Both
Mr. and Mrs. Francis were warm friends of the young

Whig lawyer. She contrived to bring Lincoln and Mary face to face at her home without either expecting it. The details of that kindly plotting are lost. Nor can one recover from scattered comments on cold pages the magnetism of personality and the force of attraction which were in operation when the girl's expressive blue eyes once more met the deep-set gray of Lincoln's. He had reached that state where weary souls have so often gone for comfort; his mind was standing still to await revelation of God's design for him. This was more than a gesture on the part of Providence; it was a positive shove!

That meeting was followed by further secret meetings at the Francis home, though just when they took place is not revealed. There is romance in this story, though there is no record to give details of those stolen trysts, the excitement, the plannings, the help of friends in carrying messages before the day of telephones, the care to keep all secret from the disapproving Edwardses. We do have an account of how other girls would tease Mary about her "tall beau," and how she "bore their jokes and teasings good naturedly but would give them no satisfaction, neither affirming nor denying the report of her engagement to Mr. Lincoln." She was keeping her own counsel and her poise.

Mary, who had declared she would marry only for love, who said she preferred a good man, a man of mind, to all the wealth in the world, was showing that she meant it. This girl had courage and conviction. Lincoln found her ready to give up the pampered existence at the Edwards mansion, with its tie-up with prominence, to live with him in one room of an economical boardinghouse. It is an appealing love story that has been lost to sight because Herndon covered it up with his belittling distortions and fabrications. Yet the nation can well be proud of this American romance, this actual case where a girl of the aristocracy remained loyal to her lover of log-cabin origin, meeting him secretly and defying family opposition to her marrying a man "on a different social plane."

It is a dramatic story. There entered into it a sensational event, one that makes us realize how long ago this all happened; Lincoln, as his lady's champion, was challenged to a duel!

chapter 6

A DUEL PREVENTED BUT NOT
A WEDDING

The rampant politics of Springfield was always a matter in which Lincoln was deeply involved. A tense political situation became entangled with the love affair. James Shields, state auditor and a Democrat, was among those who had come to the Edwardses' parties. He had been born in Ireland and from all the evidence must have kissed the Blarney stone at least twice. His exaggerated gallantry combined with a rather pompous manner seems to have caused much merriment among the young ladies who received his compliments. Lincoln as a Whig differed with the handsome Irishman politically, especially in certain matters pertaining to banking and taxes.

On September 2, 1842, the Whig newspaper of which Lincoln's friend Simeon Francis was editor, the *Sangamo Journal,* published a picturesque and humorous letter (written by Lincoln but signed "Rebecca") which ridiculed Shields at considerable length. In this letter Rebecca, a backwoods character of the "Lost Townships," relates how she stepped over to the house of her neighbor Jeff "to see if his wife Peggy was as well as mought be expected, and hear what they called the baby." She found Jeff "setting" on the doorstep of his log cabin reading a newspaper. To quote "Rebecca's" words: " 'How are you, Jeff?' says I,—he sorter started when he heard me, for he hadn't seen me before. 'Why,' says he, 'I'm mad as the devil, aunt Becca!' 'What about,' says I, 'ain't its hair the right color? None of that nonsense, Jeff—there aint an honester woman in the Lost Townships than—' 'Than who?' says he, 'what the mischief are you about?' I began to see I was running the wrong trail, and so says I, 'O nothing, I guess I was mistaken a little, that's all. But what is it you're mad about?' "

What Jeff was mad about, of course, was the current situation in regard to state bank paper and taxes, in which Lincoln's views were opposed to Shields's. An engaging discussion between Jeff and Rebecca followed, and finally Jeff burst out: "Shields is a fool as well as a liar. With him truth is out of the question, and as for getting a good bright passable lie out of him, you might as well try to strike fire from a cake of tallow."

Jeff, in Lincoln's droll storytelling, continued: "I seed him [Shields] when I was down in Springfield last winter. They had a sort of a gatherin there one night, among the grandees, they called a fair. All the galls [gals] about town was there, and all the handsome widows, and married women, finickin about trying to look like galls, tied as tight in the middle, and puffed out at both ends, like bundles of fodder that hadn't been stacked yet, but wanted stackin pretty bad. Shields was floating from one lady to another and on his very features could be read his thoughts: 'Dear girls, *it is distressing,* but I cannot marry you all. Too well I know how much you suffer; but do, *do* remember, it is not my fault that I am *so* handsome and *so* interesting.' "

Lincoln's was the second of four "Rebecca" letters which were published in the *Sangamo Journal.* The first and third do not concern us here; they were mild and dealt with the political situation in general rather than with Shields in particular, and their authorship is a matter of conjecture, with Simeon Francis himself being suspect.

But the fourth, dated September 8, 1842, is important to this story. Lincoln's "Rebecca" letter had used the discussion of two backwoods characters as a device to bring out points and objections in the political dispute; the fourth serves little purpose but personal ridicule of Shields. Women, it must be admitted, often view matters personally; this was the work of Mary Todd and her friend Julia Jayne. In this letter Rebecca had heard that Mr. Shields was so angry over the anonymous letter (written by Lincoln) that he was threatening to demand satisfaction of the writer. "I was so skart," she says, "that I tho't I should quill-wheel right where I was." Coyly admitting that "Mr. S." was "rather good-looking than otherwise," with blushes and hesitating "widowed modesty," she suggests as compromise a matrimonial alliance with Shields. "And I don't think, upon the whole, that I'd be sich a bad match neither—I'm not over sixty, and am just four feet three in my bare feet, and not much more around the girth . . ." And ". . . isn't marrying better than fightin, though it does sometimes run into it?" One can almost hear the giggles of the two girls as they concocted this letter.

The unfortunate Mr. Shields continued to be a target. On September 16 the *Journal* printed a saucy jingle signed "Cathleen," a mock serious effusion celebrating the marriage. "Rebecca, the widow, has gained Erin's son."

> *The combat's relinquished, old loves all forgot,*
> *To the widow he's bound, oh! bright be his lot!*
>
> . . . . . .
>
> *The footsteps of time tread lightly on flowers—*
> *May the cares of this world ne'er darken their hours.*

All the girls with whose hearts the groom had wrought havoc in the past were left with only the *"soft blarnied store"* of their wistful memories.

According to Mary's account many years later, the poem was hers. She wrote her friend Mrs. Gideon Welles about the whole affair. General James Shields had been a member of the "little coterie in Springfield," and "was always creating a sensation & mirth by his drolleries. On one occasion [continued Mary], he amused me exceedingly, so much so, that I committed his *follies*, to rhyme, and very silly verses they were, only, they were said to abound in sarcasm, causing them to be very offensive to the Genl. A gentleman friend, carried them off, and persevered in not returning . . . them, when one day, I saw them, strangely enough in the daily papers. Genl Shields, called upon the Editor, and demanded the author. The Editor, requested *a day* to reflect upon it—The latter called upon Mr. Lincoln, to whom he knew I was engaged & explained to him, that he was certain that I was the Author. Mr. L. then replied, say to Shields, that 'I am responsible.' Mr. L. thought no more of it, when about two weeks afterwards, while he was 130 miles away from S. attending, court, Shields, followed him up & demanded satisfaction."

Shields's challenge was followed by ceremonious arrangements for the duel, made more elaborate by the excessive zeal of Lincoln's seconds. As the challenged party Lincoln had choice of weapons, and he shrewdly specified broadswords and spacing that made it impossible for Shields, a shorter man, to kill him. As he said to a friend later: "To tell you the truth, Linder, I did not want to kill Shields, and felt sure I could disarm him, having had about a month to learn the broadsword exercise; and furthermore, I didn't want the d——d fellow to kill me, which I rather think he would have done if we had selected pistols." In the elaborate correspondence about the matter which has been preserved, Lincoln's disgust with the dueling custom is made evident.

Of the deep anxiety, necessarily concealed from the Edwardses, which must have been in Mary's mind during this time we have no record. She had much for which to blame herself; she had carried the ridicule further than Lincoln had, and apparently without his authorization. Years later, writing to another friend, she referred to Lincoln's devotion and championship of her in the affair and revealed a sense of guilt. "I doubtless trespassed, many times & oft, upon his great tenderness & amiability of character," she wrote. They were words that could well be applied to the whole of their married life. Lincoln had no part in the verses, or in the letter written by Mary Todd and Julia Jayne; by his own statement he wrote only the Rebecca letter published on September 2 and "had no participation, in any form, in any other article" alluding to Shields. It was as typical of Mary to rush into things without consideration of the effect on others and then to be sorry for her impulsiveness as it was typical of Lincoln to protect her from her rash acts. Balanced consideration was his, but it was a quality which Mary was never to achieve.

Let her letter to Mrs. Welles again take up the story: "The party, with their seconds, repaired to 'Bloody Island,' opposite St. Louis [Alton] armed with swords, but doubtless, to the delight of each one, were reconciled. The occasion, was so silly, that my husband, was always so ashamed of it . . . we mutually agreed—never to speak of it . . ."

It might have been called Lincoln's most embarrassing moment. A matter lightly entered into had gotten out of hand and gone to ridiculous lengths. As Mary said in another letter: "This affair, always annoyed my husband's peaceful nerves . . ." She then told of an incident which occurred at a social occasion at the White House. An army officer was so ill-advised as to bring up the subject: "This Genl in the course of conversation, said, playfully, to my husband 'Mr. President, is it true, as I have heard that you, once went out, to fight a duel & all for the sake of the lady by your side.' Mr. Lincoln, with a flushed face, replied, 'I do not deny it, but if you desire my friendship, you will never mention it again.'"

Early in October Lincoln wrote to Speed: "You have heard of my duel with Shields, and I have now to inform you that the dueling business still rages in this city." Feeling ran so high that there were a couple of corollary duels proposed which were ceremoniously averted like the first one. But it was not dueling which Lincoln wanted to write of; it was "that subject which you know to be of such infinite solicitude to me." He asked Speed urgently, "'Are you now in *feeling* as well as *judgement,* glad you are married as you are?' From any body but me, this would be an impudent question not to be tolerated; but I know you will pardon it in me. Please answer it quickly as I feel impatient to know."

Lincoln had something on his mind more important than the duel. We infer from Mary's letter to Mrs. Welles that by the time of the duel incident the secret meetings between herself and Lincoln had resulted in their becoming engaged again. It apparently was as her fiancé that Lincoln had assumed responsibility for what Mary had done and the experience had drawn them even more closely together. Years later Mary in her loneliness was to warm herself by the memory of that championship, concluding her account to Mrs. Welles: "We were engaged & greatly attached to each other . . ." This was followed by the passage already quoted in which she mentioned how Lincoln repeatedly told her before and after marriage that she was the only one he had ever cared for.

A marriage was being planned at these secret meetings. Lincoln was soon to have a wedding ring engraved with words that seem to indicate the couple's ideal of their attachment for each other. "Love is eternal" was inscribed in the wedding ring worn by Mary Lincoln. These two young people were entering upon an obligation which both had carefully considered, an obligation they deemed lasting and sacred.

They were getting married for the same reason that has been in good standing through the years—because they loved each other and could not be happy apart. Herndon, adding to his imagined story of the defaulting bridegroom, suggested the theories that Mary was marrying for "revenge" and that Lincoln was doing so "to save his honor," even though "he knew he did not love her." It is hard to think of anything more ridiculous: that Mary would condemn herself to a life of misery for spite, and that Lincoln would be preserving his "honor" by doing a dishonorable thing, marrying a woman he did not love. As Herndon's biographer, David Donald, has remarked in another connection: "If Herndon were not taken so seriously, both by himself and by later Lincoln biographers, one could dismiss his analysis with a smile."

But these absurd theories have carried much farther than the simple truth of two young people getting married for the normal reasons. It is well to notice also how the words of the Herndon biography color the whole picture of the married life to follow. Lincoln "stood face to face with the great conflict between honor and domestic peace. He chose the former, and with it years of self-torture, sacrificial pangs, and the loss forever of a happy home." Such passages deserve the analogy that Lincoln himself used in another connection: they are like the "black fluid" thrown out by cuttlefish which makes the water so dark that the fish (and the fact) cannot be seen. The wedding of Abraham Lincoln and Mary Todd, the triumph of romantic love over family opposition and snobbery, was a dramatic event, but Herndon's treatment has produced such an obscuring and distorting that in telling the story one is forced seemingly to defend it. Yet defense should be unnecessary. All that is needed is to present the event in its true light and in its appealing human interest. The story speaks for itself when genuinely told. With Herndon's contribution removed there is the clear picture of two people who were marrying for love in spite of opposition and economic difficulties. Emilie Todd Helm, Mary's half sister, stated the obvious when she wrote: "Unless Mary Todd and Mr. Lincoln mutually desired it, there would have been no reason for the marriage."

At the stolen meetings the engaged couple had to work out details. Of course they could not have a festive wedding, much as Mary would have liked it, for there was no place to hold it. It was agreed that they would go quietly to Dr. Charles Dresser, the Episcopal minister, and have the ceremony at his home. (Had this plan been carried

out, they would have been married in the same house they
later bought and lived in for seventeen years.) All must be
kept secret from Mary's relatives until they were ready. A
member of the family said later (after Lincoln had become famous): "Some little misunderstanding had occurred which had prevented Mr. Lincoln from visiting
at Mr. Ninian Edwards' house . . ." (Again one notices the
understatement, the slurring over, of the family disapproval of the marriage.) The same account shows how
successfully the girl had kept her secret: "Mary had been
reticent and had not given the least intimation of her
purpose."

Things began to happen on the morning of November
4, 1842. Lincoln dropped around to the minister's home
on Eighth Street while the family were still at breakfast
and said to Dr. Dresser: "I want to get hitched tonight."
Some time early that morning the young lawyer met Ninian Edwards on that street, and announced to him that he
and Mary were going to be married at the parsonage that
evening.

Meanwhile Mary had broken the news in the Edwards
mansion. A storm of protest followed. Mrs. Edwards, according to her sister, Frances Todd Wallace, "with an outburst, gave Mary a good scolding," saying to her vehemently, "Do not forget that you are a Todd." The girl
stood her ground. The Edwardses were confronted with
the fact that Lincoln and Mary had made up their minds
to be married that evening and The Family were powerless
to prevent it.

Finally realizing this, Mrs. Edwards advanced the view
that since Ninian was Mary's guardian, the marriage must
be performed at the Edwards mansion with assembled
guests. Considerable discussion took place before this arrangement was agreed upon. There was so much bitterness in the background, Lincoln could hardly have wanted
to be married in the aristocratic home from which he had
been shut out so long, whose master and mistress had
snubbed him as a prospective brother-in-law. One suspects that the decision was Mary's, she so loved parties,
and that Lincoln gave in for her sake.

When this question was decided Mrs. Edwards, model
housekeeper and hostess that she was, faced the prospect
of arranging a wedding feast on short notice. Refreshments must be prepared in the home. As Ninian's sister-

in-law told the story, Springfield had only one bakery (Dickey's), and its choicest offerings were gingerbread and beer. Someone (perhaps in the hot words of that morning) "had spoke of Mr. Lincoln as a 'plebian.' . . . So when about noon of the wedding day Mrs. Edwards' feelings were sufficiently calmed to talk to her sister of the affair she said, 'Mary you have not given me much time to prepare for our guests this evening.' Then she added, 'I guess I will have to send to old Dickey's for some of his gingerbread and beer.' " Flinging back the word in hot defiance, Mary gave the spirited reply: "Well, that will be good enough for plebians, I suppose."

On the whole it was as well that the bride was able to leave the tense atmosphere of the Edwards home for a brief while that day. From her cousin, Elizabeth Todd, has come down the story of another incident on November 4. Elizabeth, unaware of the important event about to take place, wondered what was up when she saw a hurrying little figure running down the street toward her home. Breathless, Mary entered and exclaimed, "Oh Elizabeth, I'm going to be married tonight to Mr. Lincoln and I want you to stand up with me!" Feminine conversation ensued. "I've nothing to wear," said Elizabeth. "You must get something," said Mary. A solution was worked out and Elizabeth's preparations for the wedding consisted in washing and ironing her best white dress.

Another reminiscence presents the groom dressing for the ceremony. Salome Butler, daughter of the William Butlers with whom Lincoln had been boarding, remembered how she and her brothers as children loved Mr. Lincoln: ". . . he played with us and would toss me over his shoulder when we would run to meet him." On the evening of the wedding little Salome and her brothers followed Mrs. Butler when she walked down the hall to Mr. Lincoln's room to see if he was properly dressed for the marriage. Any motherly woman would know he needed help in that matter. In Salome's words: "As my mother tied Mr. Lincoln's necktie on him, little Speed called out: 'Where are you going, Mr. Lincoln? Mr. Lincoln [such is the reminiscence] jokingly replied: 'To the devil!' " It was probably a nervous young man's light answer to shut off the teasing questions of a child (or was it the expression of his feeling about going to the Edwards home for the wedding?)

but it has been added to the chorus of disparagement of Mary Lincoln.

According to Katherine Helm, Mary's close relatives and a few of the most intimate friends were notified; not more than thirty people were present. The Helm book mentions three bridesmaids, "Miss Jayne, Miss Rodney, and Miss Elizabeth Todd." James H. Matheny has been accepted as best man and Lina Lamb is mentioned as bridesmaid in another account; at the same time we uncover a statement that "no one stood up with" Lincoln—"Just he and Mary stood up alone."

One of Mary's relatives described the wedding as the story had come down in the family circle. The ceremony was held in front of the fireplace. The wedding supper was placed on a long table whose handsome linen cover had an appropriate turtledove design. Because of the hurried preparations the wedding cake was still warm. According to this account the nervous little bride spilled coffee on the bodice of her dress after the ceremony.

As to what that bodice was made of, one has a wide choice of materials. The bride wore, according to Katherine Helm, "one of her lovely embroidered white muslin dresses." Mrs. Frances Wallace, Mary's sister, is quoted in one interview as not being sure the dress was white, and thinking it was "delaine, or something of that kind," and in another interview as saying "Sister Mary was handsome in her beautiful bridal dress of white satin . . ." The only safe statement we can make is that she wore a nice dress of some pleasant material! We know that Mary was a most attractive girl with a pretty figure and vivid face and that she had a way of dressing herself becomingly. If that little bride of 1842, contemporary with the present generation's great-grandmothers, could be brought out of the past for inspection, she would be found quaint perhaps, but lovely and appealing as brides are in all generations.

The tall figure which stood beside her was undoubtedly grave, as serious-minded men are when they take their marriage vows. In addition there was the strained situation that existed after the bitter clashings that had occurred during the day. The sensitive man doubtless saw some tight-lipped disapproval on the faces of his bride's relatives. He could hardly have been at ease. It would have been easier to have gone to the minister's, as he and Mary had planned to do.

Nearly twenty-four years after the event, Herndon questioned James H. Matheny about the wedding and jotted down his answers. Matheny said "Lincoln looked and acted as if he were going to the slaughter" at the marriage. This passage was written into *Herndon's Life of Lincoln*, where just a few pages before we have the statements: "The sober truth is that Lincoln was inordinately ambitious . . . how natural that he should seek by marriage in an influential family to establish strong connections and at the same time foster his political fortunes!" This is followed by another of those insidious comments that serve to color the reader's mind: "This may seem an audacious thing to insinuate, but on no other basis can we reconcile the strange course of his courtship and the tempestuous chapters in his married life." Mary's sister Mrs. Wallace (who had no psychoanalyzing theories) said simply that Lincoln at the wedding "was cheerful as he ever had been, for all we could see. He acted just as he always had in company." To make contradictions complete, Matheny also stated, according to Herndon's jottings, that the marriage "was concocted and planned by the Edwards family."

It was this same James H. Matheny who told of a humorous incident which broke the solemnity of the marriage ceremony. This record is in his own handwriting, which is much better than getting it through Herndon's jottings. Matheny's letter reads: "The Wedding incident referred to was one of the funiest things to have witnessed imaginable. No description on paper can possibly do it justice. . . . Old Judge Brown was a rough 'old-timer' and always said just what he thought without regard to place or surroundings. There was of course a perfect hush in the room as the ceremony progressed. Old Parson Dresser in clerical robes—Brown standing just behind Lincoln— The Parson handed Lincoln the ring, and as he put it on the brides finger, went through the church formula, 'With this ring I thee endow with all my goods and chattels, lands and tenements.' Brown who had never witnessed such a proceeding, was struck with its utter absurdity and spoke out so everybody could hear, in an expression, used by him on all occasions by the way of emphasis, 'Lord Jesus Christ, God Almighty, Lincoln, the Statute fixes all that.'

This was too much for the Old Parson—he broke down under it—an almost irresistable desire to laugh out, checked his proceeding for a minute or so—but finally recovered and pronounced them Husband & Wife."

What do the various contradictory accounts of the wedding add up to? Human imagination is lively and memory plays tricks, telescopes events, switches labels and under suggestion often recalls things that never happened. What we know of a certainty is that on the evening of November 4, 1842, in the presence of the "Dearly beloved" gathered together, Abraham Lincoln and Mary Todd stood side by side before the minister, joined hands, and promised to take each other "for better for worse, for richer for poorer, in sickness and in health, to love and to cherish" till death did them part. It is said that rain beat against the windows as they were pronounced man and wife. "Tears for the bride the rain falls on," runs the old saying: it was to prove tragically so in the case of Mary Lincoln.

There followed feasting and merriment to the point where presumably the newlyweds passed from the illumination and rich furnishings of the Edwards home to a carriage which bore them through the dark and mud to a plain boarding house. Did the rain beat against the windowpanes of the room where Lincoln took his bride that night? Rain was destined to fall on another night then far in the future, a night also momentous with change for Mary Lincoln.

Seven days later the young husband wrote a friend: "Nothing new here, except my marrying, which to me, is matter of profound wonder." The phrase seems a bridegroom's perfect expression of a fundamental human experience.

chapter 7

"FOUR DOLLARS A WEEK"

In 1843 the Lincolns were living at the Globe Tavern. The two-story wooden structure made a plain setting for the young couple; its conveniences might be politely termed "early American." Mary was used to these conditions, but she undoubtedly missed the beautiful furnishings and the associations of the Edwards home. There were many new things to which she must become accustomed. There was the strangeness and dignity of being called Mrs. Lincoln. There was the frequent ringing of the bell on the roof of the tavern, its loud clanging followed by hurrying footsteps. When stagecoaches or even private conveyances would stop in front of the tavern, the clerk would ring this bell as a signal for the stablemen to come running from the rear to take charge of the horses. It was interesting to find out who had arrived. Mary always loved activity and excitement and had a gift for appreciating the color and joyousness of life. Now she had what has been fundamental in a woman's happiness from the beginning, the fulfillment of marriage to a man she loved, the tenderness he gave to his bride. "There never existed, a more loving & devoted husband," she wrote many years later, a simple statement, from the party most concerned, worth a thousand Herndonian theories.

She never called him Abraham; he was Mr. Lincoln to her except when he was "Father" after the children came. No proper wife of that era was so disrespectful as to call her husband by his first name.

The bridegroom, who had had the wedding ring engraved with the words "Love is eternal," had expressed his ideal of married life in other ways. To Speed he had written after the latter's marriage to Fanny, "You owe obligations to her, ten thousand times more sacred than any you can owe to others." He had what was new in his hitherto rather love-starved existence, someone who was interested in every little detail of what happened to him, a bright companion in the charm of her young womanhood who gave him ardent affection, and began in small maternal ways to look after his well-being. He continued through life to have the melancholy moods that were a part of his make-up but he was living on a more normal basis now.

As with Mr. and Mrs. Citizen in general, there were adjustments to make that first year. Many a wife has felt exasperation at masculine lack of perception; many a husband has been forced into a reluctant tolerance of feminine peculiarity. Lincoln's life up to that time had left him unaware of numerous details of living which Mary could not overlook. She did not have to teach him the foundation of courtesy which is consideration for others— in such fundamentals he was not lacking—but it was an age of rigorous etiquette, of forms and ceremonies, and Mary with her background of gentle breeding could help him learn social amenities which others as well as herself rated as extremely important.

As always one must get back into the mental attitudes of the time. From the eighteen-twenties on, literature on manners and good society "poured forth in a never-ending stream." People were etiquette-minded; there was an "unprecedented demand for dissertations on decorum in the generation before the Civil War . . ." To study one of these old books of conduct is to enter an amusing world of stilted modes and conventions, but such an "Emily Post" was taken in all seriousness in its day. Social *savoir-faire,* when so many considered it essential, was useful to a man who hoped to attain political prominence by votes.

There were the usual jolts before the marriage settled upon its foundation. Mary was nervous, quick tempered, and subject to migraine headaches, and Lincoln considered his own nerves defective. There were the adjustments of living closely together. From a fellow lawyer, Henry C. Whitney, who often slept with Lincoln when they were traveling on the judicial circuit, one learns that the latter had nightmares. Once before dawn Whitney was awakened by Lincoln sitting up in bed "talking the wildest and most incoherent nonsense all to himself." "A stranger to Lincoln would have supposed he had suddenly gone insane," added Whitney, who thought the matter an idiosyncrasy to laugh at. Neither he nor Judge David Davis, who was also in the room, considered it wise to speak to Lincoln in the "most sombre and gloomy spell" that fol-

lowed his awakening. Such an incident would not seem
laughable to a wife whose part it was to get the sleeper
awake and soothe him out of the night-terror mood. Mary's
natural cheerfulness was an excellent foil for Lincoln's
periods of depression.

All through the record run descriptions of his extraordinary moods of abstraction in which he was blind and deaf
to all around him, of his hours of melancholia in which he
was sunk in such a darkness of spirit that he could hardly
go on with the motions of living. He said himself that he
was not of a very hopeful temperament. John Todd Stuart
thought his "blues" were related to physical causes; he
had a sluggish liver and took the remedy then in use—
blue mass pills—but he gave them up during the Presidency, because as he said, they made him cross. When
masculine biliousness has to live with feminine sick headaches, there is bound to be at times a clash of nerves. It
was not always, of course, a clash. Rather it was the continuing adjustment that came as the loom of time began
to weave each shared experience into the fabric of a marriage.

One catches a glimpse of the new Mrs. Lincoln under
most entertaining circumstances the month following the
wedding. There was intense feeling against the Mormons
in Illinois, and in December 1842 their prophet Joseph
Smith was arrested by order of Governor Ford. A habeas
corpus proceeding having been instituted to have the famous prisoner released, a hearing was conducted in the
Federal courtroom in Springfield, with the townfolk assembled to see the show. The judge was Nathaniel Pope,
Smith's counsel was Justin Butterfield, and the picturesque scene was enhanced by the presence of the prophet's
twelve Apostles. Because of the crowding, several ladies,
Mary Lincoln among them, were seated on either side of
the judge. "Mr. Butterfield, dressed *à la Webster,* in blue
dress-coat and metal buttons, with buff vest, rose with
dignity, and amidst the most profound silence." Giving an
admiring glance to the pretty women surrounding the
judge and pausing a moment for oratorical effect, he delivered himself of the pun of a century:

"May it please the Court, I appear before you to-day
under circumstances most novel and peculiar. I am to address the 'Pope' (bowing to the Judge) surrounded by
angels, (bowing still lower to the ladies), in the presence

of the holy Apostles, in behalf of the Prophet of the Lord."

Another glimpse is in February 1843. Family tradition tells that Mary usually celebrated February 12 and recalls her pretty speech to her husband on his first birthday after their marriage; a speech that ended: "I am so glad you have a birthday. I feel so grateful to your mother." The warmhearted girl had tenderness as well as gratitude for that wilderness mother whom her husband "often described" to her, telling reverently of Nancy Lincoln's devotion to the Bible and her prayers for her son. In Mary's words she was "his noble mother." For both of the women who had watched over Abraham Lincoln's childhood his wife had tender feeling. We will find her later writing a letter of remarkable affection and consideration to his stepmother.

Living at the Globe Tavern was economical, which was necessary under the husband's slender financial resources. Lincoln continued to write letters to his friend Joshua Speed, and once mentioned the exact amount they paid: "We are not keeping house, but boarding at the Globe tavern, which is very well kept now by a widow lady of the name of Beck. Our room (the same Dr. Wallace occupied there) and boarding only costs four dollars a week." It is not clear whether he paid four dollars apiece or for both. In this connection it is helpful to find a comparable rate in Massachusetts; Sophia Peabody in the eighteen-thirties paid two dollars a week for room and board in Dedham. One might infer from this that four dollars covered the cost for both of them.

In January 1843 Lincoln wrote to Joshua: "Mary is very well and continues her old sentiments of friendship for you. How the marriage life goes with us I will tell you when I see you here, which I hope will be very soon." They had been married over two months and in their minds was either a question mark or a belief that Mary was pregnant. It was early to speak of it but perhaps by the time Joshua and Fanny came to visit (as the Lincolns hoped they would) things would be further along and one could talk about it. Joshua evidently had the inquiring mind about the matter, for on March 24, 1843, Lincoln wrote him, "About the prospects of your having a namesake at our house, can't say exactly yet." Lincoln by that time certainly knew there was to be a baby, but he would not commit himself as to whether it would be a boy or girl, and whether Mary would approve of the name Joshua.

It is always news in a small gossipy town when a newly married couple have prompt prospects of offspring. Lincoln's friend William Butler evidently wrote Speed what was being talked about with conviction by the month of May—that the Lincolns were going to have a baby—and Speed wrote Lincoln asking about "coming events." Lincoln answered with a twinkle: "I have so much confidence in the judgement of a Butler on such a subject that I incline to think there may be some reality in it. What *day* does Butler appoint?"

Mary did not need the authority of a Butler to tell her the news. There is no record as to whether she was fearful of the ordeal ahead of her in a day when the graveyards were filled with mothers who had died in childbirth, when there was great medical ignorance and seeming indifference on the subject. Mary's own mother had died at the birth of a child, as had Lincoln's only sister. There is evidence that Mary Lincoln did not let physical ills get her down. Years later the son that she was even then carrying was to say of her: "It is really astonishing what a brave front she manages to keep when we know she is suffering —most women would be in bed groaning, but not Mother! She just straightens herself up a little more and says, 'It is better to laugh than be sighing.'" Then her son added that if she were to reverse that sentiment, and give way to sighing, his father "would go all to pieces." We can infer her attitude toward childbirth only by her anxiety many years later about her daughter-in-law in "her time of trouble." Mrs. Lincoln's sympathetic words about her son's wife might almost be moved back twenty-six years to apply to herself that spring of 1843: "I am fearing a suffering time for her."

Then with the coming of April, a month dedicated to pilgrimages since the time of Chaucer, Lincoln went off on the judicial circuit. He was mostly in Springfield until April 5, 1843, but was apparently absent the rest of that month, coming back on May 5. Mary was left alone with her tightening waistline and much to think about. That was no time for a man to go off and leave his wife alone, with the Millerites predicting the end of the world on April 23! Even if one did not believe the prediction, all this talk of disposing of one's belongings and buying muslin for "Ascension Robes" made one feel jittery. Another young wife left a record of her terror on the subject. The branch railroad between Springfield and Jacksonville was trying out a new engine on the fateful day and when she heard "the screech of the whistle and roaring and rumbling of the engine," she was sure the prophecy had come true.

· Lincoln's absence on the circuit was to be one of the greatest hardships of the marriage. He was away nearly half the time, approximately three months in the spring and three in the fall. The practice of law in those days was largely itinerant; usually two terms of court a year were held in each county. Other young wives complained of their husbands' absence too, but Lincoln's was an extreme case; he traveled over the entire circuit, attending every court and staying until the end. The other lawyers, not going so far in those days of slow transportation, were able to get home more frequently. As will be seen, Mary came to resent these long absences.

It was a way of life Lincoln loved. He was not a ladies' man. Before his marriage he had been less at home in the more formal assemblies of the Edwards clique than in those nightly sessions of young men who gathered around the wood stove in the Speed store to have endless discussions of politics, people, and things in general. He had furnished a goodly part of their drollery and philosophical groupings. He liked to talk with men, to know what they were thinking, to find out what was happening over the state; and traveling on the judicial circuit was perfect for this. It was the best possible training for a man of political ambitions, as it enabled him to keep the common touch as well as to meet men of prominence. Court pleading also gave him practice in speaking and in testing his power to convince.

Henry C. Whitney, who traveled with Lincoln on the circuit from 1854 on, wrote an account of those journeyings over the prairies which he pictured "as desolate and almost as solitary as at Creation's dawn." Lawyers and judge traveled in "home-made" vehicles or on horseback, putting up at lonely farmhouses or village inns, sleeping two in a bed and eight in a room. Business was transacted "in unkempt court-rooms," offices were "ambulatory," being located now on the sunny side of a court house, then under the shade of a friendly tree, and anon, on the edge of a sidewalk."

Yet the little towns, when court met, waxed festive with parties and shows for the visiting lawyers. There was a gaiety like that of a county fair. Mrs. Judith A. Bradner of Bloomington in her old age remembered Lincoln as saying, when court broke up in Bloomington, "Well, our parties are through until fall." It was at her house that the tall lawyer (later in his married life) twice struck his head against the chandelier, and apologized the second time, saying: "Well, that was an awkard piece of business. You know we haven't got those things at our house."

There was color as well as discomfort in traveling on the circuit but there was less variety for the wives who stayed at home to tend the fires, to cook and nurse, and assume full responsibility without the help of a man around the house. It will be seen that Mary's nervousness made responsibility a burden to her. It was hard for her, for such long periods each year to give her husband up to his work. She was realizing the truth of what a poet who had died less than twenty years before her marriage had written: "Man's love is of man's life a thing apart; 'Tis woman's whole existence." In April 1843, Mary did not have her husband's companionship in attending the usual Springfield gatherings; there were none of the quiet evenings when they could plan for the future and talk of the coming child.

It would be difficult to find in history two people whose sympathy for children in general, and adoration of their own in particular, was more outstanding than that of the Lincolns. Mary's maternal instinct was of the very essence of her being. Intense affection was one of her strongest characteristics. Lincoln had a great soul's paternal attitude toward his wife, his children, and mankind in general. (There were to be times when Mary, viewing her abstracted husband, might have wished he would concentrate a little less on the troubles of humanity and a little more on the particular problems of a family.)

On July 26 Lincoln wrote Joshua Speed: "We shall look with impatience for your visit this fall. Your Fanny can not be more anxious to see my Molly than the latter is to see her, nor as much so as I am." He ended the letter significantly, "We are but two, as yet—" The child was born August 1, 1843, nine months less three days after the marriage. Ever after Mary remembered her husband's face at that time of her suffering. Years later, when her first grandchild came into the world, she wrote: ". . . it appears to me, *at times*, so short a time, since my darling husband, was bending over me, with such love and tenderness— when the young father of that babe—was born." And again years later, when her youngest son, Tad, nursed her through an illness, she recalled Lincoln's care of her when she was sick: "Taddie, is like some *old woman*, with regard to his care of me—and two or three days since— when I was *so very* sick—his dark loving eyes—watching over me, reminded me so much of his dearly beloved father's—so filled with *his* deep love."

One can picture the anxiety in the deep-set eyes at the birth of his first-born, and then their lighting with the joy of fatherhood. A basic human experience had come to the Lincolns to bind them together; two heads bent over the perennial miracle of a newborn baby, flesh of their flesh. From this time on the name "Molly" disappears from the record. Sometimes Lincoln called her playful pet names like "Puss," "child-wife," or "little woman," but mostly after this he called her "Mother."

Mary went through her labor at the Globe Tavern. It seems strange that she was not taken into the comfortable home of one of her sisters in Springfield for her confinement. The question arises as to whether there was still resentment because she had married against their advice and out of her class, a bit of the attitude that Mary, having made her bed, could now lie on it. Or the resentment, and resulting independence as to accepting favors, may have been Mary's; we have the statement of the son of Ninian W. Edwards that his Aunt Mary always held it against his mother that she had opposed the engagement. On the surface, after the marriage, invitations and visits were on the basis of family solidarity, but the Todds were always frank in stating each other's shortcomings. Mary herself excelled in outspoken criticism, combining with this trait, as so often happens, extreme sensitiveness at any criticism of herself.

Whatever may have been the circumstances of planning for this baby's arrival, we know that he was born at a second-rate hotel and that childbirth had no benefit or alleviation of competent medical attention, by modern standards, in 1843. At the birth of her last child, as will be seen, Mary received an injury which caused her trouble for years. Just how far-reaching was the effect of that injury cannot now be determined. Childbirth lesions were not repaired in the middle eighteen-hundreds; they were disposed of simply by not talking about them.

Among those living at the Globe Tavern at this time were Mr. and Mrs. Albert Taylor Bledsoe with their little girl Sophie. Years later the daughter gave her recollections of the humble circumstances attending the arrival of an impecunious lawyer's first-born. "Mrs. Lincoln had no nurse for herself or the baby," she wrote. "Whether this was due to poverty or more probably to the great difficulty of securing domestic help, I do not know." Mrs. Bledsoe went every day to Mrs. Lincoln's room, made her comfortable and the room tidy, and washed and dressed the baby. She continued this neighborly assistance for several weeks until the young mother was able to do these things for herself. Sophie remembered that she, a six-year-old, was allowed to take the baby out for an airing. One misses a record of Mary's sisters helping her at this trying time.

The child was named Robert Todd Lincoln for Mary's father. Joshua Speed did not get the namesake he and Lincoln had joked about. There was Mary's affection for a father who was good to her and her pride in the family name of Todd. And most people would agree that Robert was a more pleasing name than Joshua. Also Mr. Todd apparently did not look down on Lincoln as some other members of the family had done. According to family tradition he said, "I only hope that Mary will make as good a wife as she has a husband."

Katherine Helm records that Mary's father came from Lexington, Kentucky, to see his new grandson. "May God bless and protect my little namesake," he said with feeling. A pleasant, sensitive face looks out today from the portrait of Mr. Todd painted by Matthew H. Jouett; in it one can trace Mary's resemblance to her father. He was a kindly man with a genuine interest in his children's welfare, which took the concrete form of arranging, on that visit, to give Mary cash advances of one hundred and twenty dollars a year until Lincoln was firmly established in his law practice. (When Robert Todd's estate was finally settled it was found that during his lifetime he had advanced the sum of $1157.50 to the Lincolns.) One hundred twenty dollars meant a good deal at a time when girls doing housework (if one could get them) received one dollar and a half a week. It was fitting that Robert Todd should have his grandson named for him, but in fairness a later child was named for Lincoln's father. Contributions, however, on this side of the house went the other way; Lincoln had to give financial aid to his parents.

Those first years were very lean ones financially. "I reckon it will scarcely be in our power to visit Kentucky this year," wrote Lincoln to Speed in May 1843, mentioning their "poverty" as one of the reasons. Counting the pennies was new to Mary. A girl brought up as she had been in comfortable circumstances finds out, when she marries a poor man, that many things which she has always taken for granted cost money. It was not merely that there were not adequate funds for the things she needed; her husband had long owed money; there was what he called the "National debt" from his New Salem days. That hung over them. Mary was destined in her lifetime to shed many tears over debts.

Being poor, doing without pretty clothes and other things she loved, came hard to the young wife. Lincoln had doubtless warned her, as he had Mary Owens, that it would be the doom of the woman who married him to see "flourishing about in carriages" that she could not share, that she would have to be poor without the means of hiding her poverty. Mary was experiencing the realization of these predictions and finding out that her social standing, which was very dear to her, was not quite what it had been. And all the while there were those affluent sisters of hers (who had told her what would happen if she married a poor man), living near in fine homes and entertaining as expensively as they pleased. She was in no position to give parties in her early married life, and those who do not entertain gradually receive fewer invitations.

She had been trained to feel that social values were extremely important, and was quick to think herself slighted and out of the social whirl. Her awareness of the difference made by having ample funds became acute. She was the more concerned as it was soon evident to her that her husband was not primarily interested in money-making. Lincoln was not lacking in thrift, but other matters were more important to him. He was to say in the White House, "Money, I don't know anything about *'money.'* I never had enough of my own to fret me, and I have no opinion about it any way." Mary had an opinion all right and she did the fretting. She was also learning how many things a family needs and what they cost. A psychiatrist might trace a relation here to stories of her so-called "stinginess" and possibly to the later time when her conviction of her own poverty passed from normal thinking into irrationality.

It is fair to remember these factors when one picks up in reminiscence such incidents as the following. After the Lincolns had gone to housekeeping, two men and a boy one day, peddling the three pints of blackberries which they had spent the morning in gathering, offered them all to Mrs. Lincoln for fifteen cents. Examining the berries, Mrs. Lincoln said they were small and worth no more than ten cents. Lincoln, knowing what it meant to pick scarce berries for a whole morning, promptly paid the men more than they asked. Mary carried the habit of these petty economies into the years when they were no longer necessary.

Just what was the financial status of the family in those early years? In *The Personal Finances of Abraham Lincoln,* Harry Pratt estimates that between 1840 and 1850 Lincoln's annual income from the law was probably between $1500 and $2000. This was sufficient to provide a comfortable living a century ago, but those were years of heavy expenses. Doubtless to the vast relief of both the Lincolns the New Salem debt was paid off in that decade, an event on the home front well worthy of celebration. Who knows what economies Mary practiced in those first years to remove that burden?

Politicians, then as now, found that campaigning meant both extra expense and loss of income. Lincoln's political activities were a dominant feature of the life in Springfield and a matter of vital interest to both of them in their mutual ambition. He had to contribute to the support of his parents, always a burdensome thing to a couple who are starting their own family. Then in 1844 the Lincolns bought a house.

If the Globe Tavern had been a poor place for a honeymoon, it was even less suited to a couple with a baby. Springfield tradition has it that other guests complained of the baby's crying. No doubt he was voicing his own objections to their noise, and to the clanging of the bell. At all events, in the fall of 1843 the little family moved to a three-room frame cottage at 214 South Fourth Street. Little is known of their winter sojourn there, for the Lincolns were eyeing the story-and-a-half dwelling at the corner of

Eighth and Jackson Streets which belonged to Dr. Charles Dresser, the Episcopal minister who had married them. It was conveniently located not far from Lincoln's law office and was roomy enough for a family of three. In time both house and family were to be increased in size.

In January 1844 Lincoln drew up a contract for a deed with Dr. Dresser to buy his residence, but it was May 2 before the contract was completed and the Lincolns could move. For the house Lincoln paid $1200 plus a lot on Adams Street valued at $300. In the intervening four months Mary had become the owner of eighty acres of land three miles southwest of Springfield. It was a gift from her father. The financial stringency was beginning to ease up.

Mary's mind was concerned with household furnishings. A rising lawyer who was going to amount to something politically (she was sure of that) needed an adequate house. The "little brown cottage" could not compare to the stately brick mansions in which she had lived as a girl, nor to the Edwards splendor, but it was part of her buoyancy to take pride in her possessions and to view them in glowing colors. That story-and-a-half dwelling meant much to her; the Lincolns were establishing a home.

chapter 8

"WOMEN AND OXEN"

"Illinois is heaven for men and horses, but hell for women and oxen," ran a popular saying in the middle eighteen-hundreds. The house at the corner of Eighth and Jackson Streets, however desirable it seemed to Mary's home-longing eyes, had facilities as primitive as those of a none-too-desirable summer cottage of today. Housekeeping was painfully laborious. Planks laid down as sidewalks in the town gave scant protection from the "tracking in" of the all-pervading black and sticky mud, nor could one count on those boards being in place, as they were frequently uprooted by the hogs that had the freedom of the city.

Springfield was dirty and smelly. Outside toilets were a matter of course and there was a corollary to this: the oil lamps (which must be filled, have their wicks trimmed and chimneys cleaned) were not the only vessels requiring daily attention. The candles that were used were homemade. Gas for illumination was not available in Springfield until the fifties. Its coming caused wild rejoicing among the housewives. Mrs. John Todd Stuart, the wife of Mary's cousin, wrote her daughter on May 7, 1855, about the men digging in the yard to lay gas pipes and remarked exultingly, "Wont we be light and no lamps to fill either." There is a modern flavor in her comment a few days later: "We were expecting the gas men, to put the pipe in the house today, but they did not come." It was in that same month that the Stuarts took a "railroad excursion" on the wonderful new means of transportation, and fairly whizzed to Cairo at the breath-taking speed of twenty-eight miles an hour. They thought they were living in a most progressive age with all these new conveniences in the eighteen-fifties.

The house the Lincolns bought, of course, had no fly screens. At meals a fastidious housekeeper could try to keep the flies away by waving back and forth a stick to which was fastened paper cut in strips. If she wished to be very stylish, she used fancy paper. Windows, having no weights, were propped up on sticks, an arrangement which was a source of terror to mothers who had to tie up smashed fingers.

Heating of the new home in winter was by wood fires. This meant chopping the wood, which Lincoln himself did when at home, carrying it in, and constant watching and replenishing. Fires must be banked at night to keep coals over until morning.

There were apparently as many people who lived near the Lincolns in Springfield as there were beds in which George Washington slept. From these old-timers' recollections one gets glimpses of the Lincolns as they appeared to neighbors next door or down the street. One such account tells of a tall man in shirt sleeves and slippers with a shovel in his hand crossing the street early one summer morning to borrow live coals for the kitchen fire. It was that Mr. Lincoln who had moved to the Dresser house, and he was evidently a bit careless about banking his fire, for he had to come borrowing a number of times. Once the neighboring lady had no coals herself and offered matches. Mr. Lincoln in some surprise said he never would have thought of that. Matches cost money and could be dispensed with by an economy-minded family.

Stove and fireplace heating meant icy halls and parlors; it required also the wearing of heavy underwear and many clothes in winter. By the eighteen-fifties the Lincolns had charge accounts at Springfield stores, and faded business records of purchases show what they were buying. One can read a chilly domestic interior in such an unequivocal item as: "2 pair Heavy Drawers @ $1.25 per Son." Open fires also meant dirt which must be cleaned up with water carried from the pump in the back yard, and soap that was probably homemade, though by the later fifties "cakes of soap" appear on the charge accounts. Once they bought "1 box Palm Soap 62 @ .07," totaling $4.34, undoubtedly the large economy size. With the scarcity or nonexistence of commercial laundries, soap, and lots of it, was a necessity.

Laborious as cooking was, it had to be done on an extended scale that the present generation with its infinite resources of canned and frozen foods finds it hard to visualize. Large estates had their icehouses filled by cutting ice in winter, but even as late as 1860 refrigeration in the average household was almost completely absent. It has been seen that Springfield, when the Lincolns were married, had only one bakery, whose total offering was gingerbread and beer. Mary had to bake bread for her family and such a thing as buying cakes and pies was hardly thought of. In addition to these difficulties, Lincoln had the experience, common to new husbands, of discovering that his wife did not know much about cooking. She was a skillful seamstress and delighted in sewing, but in the matter of food she had grown up accustomed to the services of loved household slaves and the cooking of old Chaney, who never got over a feeling of indignation that in Illinois "Miss Mary didn't have no beaten biscuits at home," and that her servants (of whom Chaney had a very poor opinion) "didn't even know how to make good co'n bread." How much that Southern cooking meant to Mary is expressed in one of her letters. While in France, she was to write wistfully: ". . . *waffles, batter cakes,* egg corn bread—are *all* unknown here—as to biscuits, light rolls &c &c they have never dreamed of—*not* to speak of *buckwheat* cakes." There was nothing in her Kentucky background of ease and plenty that had given her training for housekeeping under Illinois conditions; at the same time her rearing had taught her high standards of homemaking which she lacked the means to achieve. She found her housekeeping hard to manage.

A small boy who lived near and ran errands for Lincoln in those days before telephones, remembered later that Mrs. Lincoln "was a high strung, nervous woman who frequently allowed her housecleaning or other activities to interfere with having her husband's lunch on time." The Herndon life of Lincoln, quoting Joshua Speed, says of Lincoln, "In all his habits of eating, sleeping, reading, conversation, and study he was . . . regularly irregular; that is, he had no stated time for eating, no fixed time for going to bed, none for getting up." How could she have a meal on time when she never knew when he would come home? She would not serve the meal until he came (that was her standard of respect for him) and this, when the children got hungry, created a problem, not to say a crisis.

Emilie Todd Helm recalled being at the Lincoln home for supper and the long hungry waiting for the man of the house to appear. The chickens burned and the rest of the supper got cold, and finally, at the end of two hours, "in sauntered brother Lincoln as innocent as a lamb of any infraction of domestic routine." The incident was taken lightheartedly by all. When Mary mentioned that she was afraid that the chickens were burned to a crisp, Lincoln (remembering Mammy Sally's theory about the jay bird) smiled quizzically and pointing his finger at his wife said, "Nem mine! Mr. Jay's gwine tell ole man Satan that Mary sets her hungry husband down to burned up vittals just caze he's two minutes late." He received a prompt and unanimous correction of "two minutes" to "two hours," but replied with irresistible good humor, "Nem mine, just bring on the cinders and see how quickly they will disappear."

Lovable as Lincoln was, he had traits that were very exasperating to one who had to keep house for him. Living in log cabins during the formative years, he was, through no fault of his own, ignorant of many details of refined living. He was notoriously unsystematic at the office, scattering papers about in such disorder that frequently documents were lost. Mary had enough to do at home without continually picking up after him. The office was dingy with dirt piled high in the corners, a condition that did not disturb either of those two untidy souls, Lincoln and Herndon, but Mary had a different standard.

She had been brought up to consider social conventions (including sweeping in corners) important. It rankled that her family had advised against her marrying this "mighty rough man," and this doubtless made her more determined that he should take on social polish. It annoyed her that he came to the dining table in his shirt sleeves. It was all right for him to lie on the floor reading, with the back of a turned-down chair for a pillow, but when the quaint little doorbell on the wall of the dining room tinkled, it was proper to let the maid (when they had one) answer it. Through a cousin of Lincoln's who lived at their home for about a year and a half comes the story of his going to the front door in his shirt sleeves to admit two lady callers (probably very stylish ones), ushering them into the parlor and telling them in his quaintly amiable way that he would "trot the women folks out." Mrs. Lincoln, with her usual failing for speaking her mind, scolded him sharply, which made a morsel of conversation that the visitors did not fail to circulate. When it reached the ears of Mary's relatives (who had apparently learned that Lincoln had something to offer), one of them said to her, "Mary, if I had a husband with a mind such as yours has, I wouldn't care what he did." This was consummate tact; praise of her Mr. Lincoln made Mary beam and she answered at once, "It is very foolish—it is a small thing to complain of."

An absent-minded husband whose thoughts turn inward while the fire goes out and the baby squalls, requires constant looking after, like a child. It has been said that Mary Lincoln's "soul inhabited the obvious;" it was a good thing for the welfare of the household that somebody's soul did. Records of Lincoln's appearance in early life mention his carelessness in dress; it fell to Mary to see that he did not go around with one pants leg rolled up and the other down as he had in New Salem days. She had to make sure that he took his warm shawl with him on cold days, and his umbrella on wet ones. She knew the proper dress for a rising lawyer and a gentleman and she intended that her husband should make a good appearance. Gamaliel Bradford has stated her social problem: "... it must always be remembered that she had the strange, incalculable, most undomestic and unparlorable figure of Lincoln to carry with her, which would have been a terrible handicap to any woman." There is no evidence that Mary, as proud as she was of Mr. Lincoln, looked at the matter quite like that, but she did give attention to his clothes and he profited by it. An old neighbor sized up the situation very neatly: "She looked her husband over carefully whenever he left the house to make sure that, in his thoughtlessness about his dress, he had not neglected some detail."

Mary Owens, when Lincoln was courting her in New Salem days, had concluded that as a husband he would not always know how to help with the babies. In her own words: "On one occasion did I say to Mr. L—— that I did not believe he would make a kind husband, because he did not tender his services to Mrs Green in helping of her carry her babe." Miss Owens continued with her accusation of thoughtlessness. "There was a company of us going to Uncle Billy Greens, Mr. L—— was riding with me, and we had a very bad branch to cross, the other gentlemen were very officious in seeing that their partners got over safely; we were behind, he riding in [front] never

looking back to see how I got along . . ." Piqued at his lack
of courtesy, the spirited young woman rode up beside him
and said tartly, ". . . you are a nice fellow; I suppose you
did not care whether my neck was broken or not." Lincoln
laughed and got himself out of a tight corner with a compliment that smacks of the frontier; he told the lady that
he knew she was "plenty smart" to take care of herself.

Miss Owens's comment on Lincoln's ineptness as to
helping with a baby recalls a well-known incident. On
Sundays while Mrs. Lincoln went to church, the neighbors
would see Lincoln pulling a little wagon with a baby or
babies in it, up and down the street in front of his house.
In one hand he would hold an open book, and, deeply absorbed, read from it as he walked. Once the baby fell out
and lay squalling upon the ground while the father went
on with complete unawareness of anything wrong. This
was the scene which greeted Mary as she returned from
her devotions at church, and many women will pardon her
for shrieking at him. She did not know at that time that
he would become a great statesman but it was borne in
upon her forcibly that he was not a reliable baby sitter.

It is illuminating to examine the manner in which
Herndon presented this incident to his collaborator Weik.
He begins his letter with a statement of his theory: "Mr.
& Mrs. Lincoln never lived a harmonious life"; then adds
that "when she wanted to go to church or to some gathering she would go at all events and leave Lincoln to take
care of the babies." Herndon was an infidel and proud of
it; he had no sympathy with her going to church in the
first place and in the second he thought she was imposing
upon her husband. "Mrs. Lincoln couldn't keep a hired
girl because she was tyranical to her," he wrote, "and Lincoln per force was compelled to look after the children."
Herndon's punch line is concerned with what followed the
wife's return from church: ". . . you know, a hell of scolding. Poor Abe, I can see him now running and crouching."
(Incidentally, he never presumed to call his partner "Abe"
to his face.) And Herndon, humorless and not familiar
with the Lincoln family circle, never knew that afterward
the spilling of the baby was a family joke, a topic of teasing and laughter.

Herndon thought that baby-tending was woman's work
and any husband who did it was henpecked, a point of
view that appears also in the recollections of a very frank

neighbor. She told Mr. Lincoln, apropos of his wheeling the baby, she thought that was "a pretty business" for him to be engaged in.

Herndon's biography makes the statement: "Mrs. Lincoln, on account of her peculiar nature, could not long retain a servant in her employ." This ignores the fact that other women were having the same difficulty. That young wife, Mrs. Benjamin S. Edwards, who rode into Springfield at the beginning of this story, left a record of her experience in this line: "It was almost impossible to get servants. I had brought a woman from St. Louis but found her so intemperate that in less than a year I was obliged to discharge her and my troubles in housekeeping began. I knew nothing of cooking and shed many a tear over my first attempts."

That Mary Lincoln had a difficult temperament is quite true but it is worth while to examine the testimony of servants who lived with her, some of them several years at a time, in spite of Herndon's assertion. We have the recollections of a colored woman who worked for the Lincolns when Robert, as she said, was about five. She waited on the table, washed dishes, laundered and scrubbed while Mrs. Lincoln (whom she described as "a very nice lady") did the cooking and sewing. This included sewing for the poor when the church society met at her house, for Mary was faithfully religious and did not neglect her church attendance or duties. The limited means of the Lincolns made a deep impression on this kind Negro servant; she recalled that Mrs. Lincoln's dresses were of inexpensive material, no silks or satins, and that Robert's small pants were adorned with patches. After this servant left, Mrs. Lincoln did all the work herself.

Mary always fares well in the testimony of colored people. She was kind to them; they understood her. So did a little Portuguese girl who served her and many years later managed to say more in a few words of broken English than many could express in the same number of pages. Mrs. Lincoln, she said, "taka no sassy talk, but if you good to her, she good to you. You gotta good friend." Of the husband and father, the Portuguese woman was equally discerning: "He so kind. He choppa the wood for fire, and little Robert choppa the little wood. When he passa me, he patta my shoulder. . . . Mr. Lincoln no verra style. He just common, like some one that is poor."

All the servants were devoted to the lovable master of the house but it is rather amusing to find a former maid saying frankly that Mrs. Lincoln was "a smarter woman than he was a man." That is the way it appeared on the domestic front. This same maid remembered that the Lincolns were "very domestic in their tastes," and that Mrs. Lincoln was a "good woman," who often helped her with her work to the end that the girl might have more time to play with the children. The cream of this recollection is the account of Lincoln wholeheartedly playing blindman's buff with his little sons.

From an aged woman who once worked for the Lincolns came an understanding account of Mrs. Lincoln's quickly flaring temper. She said these outbursts lasted only a few minutes and then Mrs. Lincoln was "all sorrow" and anxious to make amends. Mary's own numerous apologies in her letters and accounts from all sides bear this out. Her lack of emotional control was a burden to her as well as to others. "She had an ungovernable temper, but after the outburst she was invariably regretful and penitent," said Harriet Hanks, who lived in the Lincoln home for many months, and Mrs. Keckley, the colored dressmaker in Washington, said the same thing. Fundamentally affectionate, all Mary needed was a little time for cooling off, a fact well understood by her husband.

The Herndon life of Lincoln tells how Lincoln once secretly paid a servant an extra dollar a week in order to have her stay on with them, which she did for "several years." It was a pleasant conspiracy on the part of a husband who knew his wife's penny-pinching complex and also her need for help in the heavy household duties. Lincoln, who had infinite tact, understood how to get around the "little woman." There is a newspaper story, given here for what it is worth, telling that a group from Springfield's volunteer fire department once called on Lincoln and asked him for a subscription for a needed new hose. With a twinkle Lincoln outlined his policy to them: he would talk it over with his wife when he went home and suggest that they contribute fifty dollars. She would immediately say that he was always too liberal; that twenty-five dollars was quite enough. Lincoln concluded with a chuckle that they could call next day for the twenty-five.

The house on Eighth Street is now a national shrine.

The visitor there today sees in the family sitting room three chairs that create a picture of that former domesticity which is like a Currier and Ives print of married life in the Victorian era. There is the large rocker for the father with its lines suggesting a long pair of stretched-out legs, a child's chair symbolic of the dominant interest in that household, and the mother's low rocker in which she sat when sewing. Clothes could not be bought ready-made as now.

Refined gentlemen wore elaborate shirt fronts at the time, and Mary, sentimental wife that she was, "could not endure the thought of her husband wearing shirts made by any hands except her own." A neighbor's little girl who loved Mrs. Lincoln, as children invariably did, remembered her "stitching hour after hour on finely tucked shirt bosoms" for Mr. Lincoln. Unless her eyes were unusually good, she probably suffered in time from eyestrain. She also had the tasks of making clothes for her children, patching little pants, and contriving becoming attire for herself. Lincoln, like other husbands, was proud of his good-looking wife and liked to see her dressed up, and she delighted to make herself pretty for him. He learned in time to notice anything new that she wore and to give her the sought-for word or glance of admiring approval.

A study of old charge accounts of certain Springfield stores shows that she bought endless pieces of "Calico," "Fr. Merino," "Cross Barred Swiss," "Opera Flannel," "Wool Delaine," "Bobbinett," and yards of other materials with the spools of thread, buttons, whalebones, laces and ribbons required to make them up. Like the rest of womankind, she delighted in buying remnants, and frequently changed her mind and returned items which did not appear as alluring when she got them home as they did in the store.

Fashioning a costume was no simple task. It was a time of elaborateness in dress, although Illinois ladies, even with the help of *Godey's Lady's Book,* found it a bit difficult to keep up with styles in the East. "Heaven save the ladies, how they dress!" exclaimed Charles Dickens on his visit to New York in 1842. "We have seen more colours in these ten minutes, than we should have seen elsewhere, in as many days. What various parasols! what rainbow silks and satins! what pinking of thin stockings, and pinching of thin shoes, and fluttering of ribbons and silk tassels, and display of rich cloaks with gaudy hoods and linings!" Heaven save the ladies indeed, not to mention their bill-paying husbands.

The lagging behind in fashions due to slow communication sometimes led to amusing results. Some cotton net nightcaps were received by a store in Decatur, Illinois, in 1849. The clerk had not the faintest idea what they were intended for, but with commendable enterprise he sold them as the latest thing in ballroom headdress. No one knew the difference and the nightcaps, adorned with ribbons, appeared on the most style-minded heads at an elaborate ball.

It is not until the end of the fifties that Mary's simple materials were replaced, in the charge accounts, with such impressive items as "16 yds. Plaid silk @ 1.00 per Lady," and "16 yards Grenadine @ 2.00 per Lady." It took a great deal of silk for a hoop skirt. Mary's half sister Emilie recorded the story of a "white silk with blue brocaded flowers scattered over it" which Mary made into a dress for herself. When her husband came home from the office he found her arrayed in this new creation ready to go to a supper party at the Edwards home. Being reminded to change his own clothes, he said to her with an admiring smile: "Fine feathers enough on you to make fine birds of both of us." Then noticing the material more closely he added, "Those posies on your dress are the color of your eyes." Whereupon the delighted wife, with a smile that brought out her dimples, remarked to her sister: "You see, Emilie, I am training my husband to see color. I do not think he knew pink from blue when I married him."

Sewing for herself and her babies was one item alone calculated to keep Mary busy in the new home without the endless round of cooking, washing, cleaning, and baby tending. All these things must be achieved along with further childbearing. Three times the little brassy cry of a newborn infant was to be heard in the Eighth Street home as three more sons—Eddie, Willie, and Tad—were added to the household.

Mary was well centered in woman's sphere, which, as all good people of the time knew, was where any wife belonged. The mental circumference for females was as restricted as the physical one. *Godey's Lady's Book* (as revealing of thought patterns as of those for dress) left no doubt on this subject; home was woman's dominion and any circumstance which drew her from that sacred sphere was to be deplored. As the author of *The Fabulous Forties* has pointed out, the ideals of that decade were all directed toward making wives "unspeakably dull."

That, however, is one of the few accusations which has not been hurled at Mary Lincoln. Her impetuosity was often lacking in wisdom, but she was always lively and interested in all that was happening. "She was fond of home," wrote her half sister; "was a cheerful woman, a delightful conversationist, and well-informed on all the subjects of the day." Mrs. Keckley spoke of her "cheery voice," and another source mentioned that voice as "soft" and "sweet." Mary went into the new-bought house to make it into a home with her usual energetic enthusiasm. She had small dainty hands and was a bit vain about them—their quick pretty gestures were a part of her personality—but those hands did not hold back from any household task. When she finally went to Washington as wife of the President-elect, her hands were hardened with toil. A gentleman who shook hands with Mrs. Lincoln on March 1, 1861, recorded: "We are pleased with her. She had no gloves on & put out her hand. It is not soft."

The little family settled into domestic routine like young married people of all generations. The Lincoln home knew drudgery, monotony, illnesses, clashes of nerves and viewpoints, scoldings, "blues," fears, disappointments, small disasters—all the elements that go into the daily exasperation of the average household. It was also a home for a man who had been homeless, who had known loneliness, a home like others down the street where the husband returned after the day's work to tell his wife all that had happened to him that day, knowing she would be more interested than anyone else and more partisan. She on her side would tell him small important news: how their little son had had an adventure with a stray kitten, or how the baby had tried to say a new word and it had come out such a dear, funny combination of sounds that they both smiled with fond parental eyes.

It is difficult to recover the inner life of a marriage. Demonstration of affection is a private matter, not for witnesses. By chance we have had a glimpse of Lincoln, during the courtship, folding Mary in his arms, kissing her and holding her on his lap. One knows well there were times when mutual affection led to such caresses. There were the binding intimacies of the night. These were two people of unusual tenderness and affection. Mary's was a demonstrative nature. Lincoln had known small demonstration of affection up to the time of his marriage; the grimness of backwoods existence had crowded it out; he was in a position to appreciate its sweetness.

There was love in the house on Eighth Street, there was fun and playfulness, there was the joy of children.

chapter 9

"THE HAPPIEST STAGES OF LIFE"

The Fourth of July, 1845, was an exciting day for the Lincolns. Patriotic celebration began at three A.M. with reveille in the cupola of the Statehouse followed by thirteen guns. Lincoln was the orator of the day at the meeting held in that same prideful Statehouse at two in the afternoon. Mary's spirit would always rise to meet an event featuring her husband. It is a safe guess that in the audience was a bright-faced young matron, not yet twenty-seven, perhaps with a squirming little boy who was not quite two, and that the speaker was keenly aware of their important presence.

Later at home the wife could tell Lincoln how his speech impressed his listeners. There was much talk of politics in that home, for Lincoln was laying his plans to run for Congress. As Herndon said, "His ambition was a little engine that knew no rest." Mary had her own little engine of ambition that ran side by side with his.

When Springfield welcomed in the year 1846 the Lincolns had another important event, in addition to the Congressional election, to look forward to. Mary again was letting out her dresses and shunning the public gaze with Victorian modesty. A second son, Edward Baker Lincoln, was born March 10, in the home on Eighth Street. He was named for Edward D. Baker, who belonged to Lincoln's intimate circle of close friends, a handsome and personable man and a fellow Whig. Baker was a good companion at Lincoln's favorite sport, playing fives, a simple game now called handball. With partners choosing sides there was lively competition as well as fine physical exercise and Lincoln loved it.

So Joshua Speed lost out again as to getting a namesake; in fact, Lincoln was so busy with politics that it was October before he got round to writing his friend the news. "We have another boy, born the 10th. of March last. He is very much such a child as Bob was at his age—

rather of a longer order." There follows a very neat description of the three-year-old first-born: "Bob is 'short and low,' and I expect, always will be. He talks very plainly—almost as plainly as any body. He is quite smart enough. I some times fear he is one of the little rare-ripe sort, that are smarter at about five than ever after. He has a great deal of that sort of mischief that is the offspring of much animals spirits." (Herndon expressed the same idea in a more down-to-earth fashion by using the word "brat.") Lincoln added details of a small domestic crisis. "Since I began this letter a messenger came to tell me Bob was lost; but by the time I reached the house, his mother had found him, and had him whiped, and, by now, very likely he is run away again." The concluding words to Speed indicate that the Lincolns shared incoming personal correspondence: "Mary has read your letter, and wishes to be remembered to Mrs. S. and you, in which I most sincerely join her."

Mary Lincoln's irrepressible motherliness was in time to extend its intense affection and sympathy to her daughter-in-law. Among her most appealing letters are those she wrote the wife of her son Robert. One must go to these letters to get her attitude toward her own wifehood and motherhood.

Writing many years later to Robert's wife (who had apparently been upset by one of those inevitable ladies who consider it a virtue to offer free advice and pessimism to young wives), Mrs. Lincoln said: "Referring to that speech . . . that housekeeping and babies were an uncomfortable state of existence for a young married lady I think her experience was different from most mothers who consider that in the outset in life—a nice home—loving husband and precious child are the happiest stages of life." The letter in its sympathy, generosity, and affection is a model for mothers-in-law.

The Lincolns were genuinely sentimental about babies. When her half sister Emilie had *"expectations"* in 1857, Mary wrote her, eager for news, "I expect dear Em, ere this, they are fully realized & that now, you are a *happy, laughing loving Mama.*" Was this a picture of Mary herself when she first held her new baby in her arms? One does not get in Herndon's caricature of Mrs. Lincoln the face of a joyous young woman lighted with mother love which Lincoln so often looked upon.

The fulfillment of parenthood was fundamental in this marriage. Love and enjoyment of their children is a glowing theme in the letters which passed between the Lincolns. Mary's letters constantly praise her "darling sons." As to talents, she wrote, they "were perfect in that respect & so worshipping to us both!" In retrospect this woman of passionate maternity launched into a glorification of her children: "Sons the most *idolising*, the noblest, purest, most talented—that were ever given to parents—Their presence grand & beautiful—"

Other people, of course, could point out to the Lincolns how foolish they were about their offspring. Mary's sister, Frances Wallace, remembered Lincoln carrying his well-grown son Tad "half way to the office," and when she remonstrated, "Why, Mr. Lincoln put down that great big boy. He's big enough to walk," the answer was, "Oh, don't you think his little feet get too tired?"

It was Mary's joy to dress her children nicely, to teach them little verses and love of literature, to train them in the manners and courtesy of good society. Here is the scornful way Herndon described this devoted effort: "It was the habit—custom of Mrs. Lincoln when any big man or woman visited her house to dress up and trot out Bob—Willie or Tad and get them to monkey around—talk—dance—speek—quote poetry &c &c. Then she would become enthusiastic & eloquent over the children much to the annoyance of the visitor . . ." No passage could illustrate better the contrasting standards of Herndon and Mrs. Lincoln. Social refinements were not necessary in his rough-hewn environment; they were merely "monkeying around."

Emilie Todd Helm recalled Mary's reading the novels and poems of Sir Walter Scott to Robert with dramatic results. One day, hearing noise of conflict, she and Mary ran to the window to witness a battle royal between that sturdy youngster and a playmate. Fence palings served admirably as lances and Robert was loudly proclaiming, "This rock shall fly from its firm base as soon as I." Struggling with laughter but entering properly into the spirit of the thing, Mary curbed their zeal with "Gramercy, brave knights. Pray be more merciful than you are brawney."

The Lincolns both had that quality which enabled them to see a situation as it appeared to a child's mind. An example of this is in the letter Mary wrote Mark W. Delahay, a politician from Kansas. This gentleman had brought two flags from the convention of 1860 to Springfield and one of the Lincoln boys thought the smallest flag had been given to him. Mr. Delahay departed with both flags and Mary wrote him explaining the matter and saying: "I will ask you to send it to us, the first opportunity you may have, especially as he claims it, and I feel it is as necessary to keep one's word with a child, as with a grown person."

Mary went to great pains to give a child's party. The small guests received socially correct invitations beautifully penned by the mother. One which has been preserved reads: "Willie Lincoln will be pleased to see you, Wednesday Afternoon at 3 O'clock." She mentioned one of these birthday parties for Willie in a letter: "Some 50 or 60 boys & girls attended the gala," she wrote. No task was too great if it pleased the children.

Lincoln had mentioned in his letter to Speed that Bobby had been whipped for running away, but such spankings were not the rule. The Lincoln boys were notoriously spoiled, a fact Lincoln himself implied in a letter to Dr. A. G. Henry in 1860 in which he spoke of Robert promising very well "considering we never controlled him much." One obscure reminiscence tells of Mrs. Lincoln switching Tad when she thought (mistakenly) that he had stolen a dime. This story was the old-age recollection of a lady who said that she as a little girl lived near the Lincolns; it is much trimmed up with details of the scene:

Mary's switching of the boy in spite of his protests of innocence, with Lincoln coming in, locating the missing dime and reproachfully saying to his wife, "Mary! Mary!" The little girl was supposed to see and hear all this by looking from her kitchen window into the kitchen window of the Lincoln home, an amazing, not to say impossible, feat. The Lincoln home faced west, and the kitchen had no window to the north (the pantry being on that side), and anyone who looked into the kitchen from the south would have had to do so through a door from across Jackson Street, a distance that rendered such accurate seeing and hearing well-nigh impossible. There is no evidence that Mary Lincoln ever lost her temper with her children, or treated a child with anything but tenderness and consideration. She later wrote that they never required whipping: "A gentle, loving word, was all sufficient with them—and if I have erred, it has been, in being too indulgent." Perhaps in her mind the word "whipping" implied greater severity than was involved in the spanking which Robert received for running away.

In another lady's memories we have the picture of Lincoln carrying her as a little girl, accompanied by his small rambunctious sons and a group of neighbor children, watching a circus parade on the streets of Springfield. When the boys were slow to obey, the father would make a show of breaking off a switch from a bush, but somehow it was never used.

In an age when it was thought that children should be repressed and disciplined, seen and not heard, Lincoln's view was strikingly modern. Here is the way his wife described it: "Mr. Lincoln was the kindest man and most loving husband and father in the world. He gave us all unbounded liberty. Said to me always, when I asked for anything, 'You know what you want, go and get it.' He never asked me if it were necessary. He was very—exceedingly indulgent to his children. Chided or praised them for what they did—their acts, etc. He always said: 'It is my pleasure that my children are free, happy and unrestrained by parental tyranny. Love is the chain whereby to bind a child to its parents.'" Just how far Lincoln's method of encouragement by praise, now in high favor, was in contrast to the prevailing view is shown by the experience of a teacher of that day who was criticized for commending her pupils, on the ground that praise bred vanity.

Lincoln's gentle way with his children seems not to have been inherited from his father. That backwoods parent, perhaps believing that to spare the rod was to spoil the child, whipped his son Abraham severely. Whether there is a connection here with Lincoln's attitude is a matter of conjecture, but in that record one catches a glimpse of how deeply this punishment hurt the feelings of a sensitive boy.

All the evidence shows that the Lincolns had the modern theory that children should not be frustrated, a theory resulting then as now in frequent frustration of adults. On Sunday mornings while their mother was at church, Lincoln would bring his little sons to the law office, and how Herndon did suffer. As he told it, the unrestrained boys would pull the books from the shelves, scatter legal papers, smash pen points, spill ink over everything and otherwise tear things up from top to bottom. The office was untidy enough at best, but after such a visitation it undoubtedly looked as if it had been visited by a small tornado. The squirming Herndon wrote with much feeling that he "wanted to wring the necks of these brats and pitch them out of the windows." Herndon was an affectionate father to his large family of children, but if they disobeyed him they were punished, and if one was disrespectful to his paternal authority the razor strop was put to use. That wrecking crew of the Lincoln boys at the office went hard with him, and he harped on the theme in his letters. "I have felt many & many a time that I wanted to wring their little necks and yet out of respect for Lincoln I kept my mouth shut. Lincoln did not notice what his children was doing or had done." The junior partner did not dare remonstrate, for fear of consequences: "He [Lincoln] worshipped his children and *what* they worshipped[;] he loved what they loved and hated what they hated . . ."

From an old neighbor comes the account of Lincoln lying in the hall of his home, his shoulders on a turned-down chair, his feet up on the newel post, dangling a baby over him. It is a lovable close-up view of him in the happiness of fatherhood.

Some of the best pictorial flashes, perhaps, come from Herndon. He was at his vivid best when describing Lincoln, for he was telling what he had himself looked upon. Posterity owes him gratitude for photographic passages like this: "Mr. Lincoln sometimes walked our streets cheerily, . . . perhaps joyously and then it was, on meeting a friend, he cried—How'dy, clasping one of his friends in both of his wide long big bony hands, giving his friend a good hearty soul welcome. On a winters morning he might be seen stalking and stilting it toward the market house, basket on his arm, his old grey shawl wrapped around his neck, his little Willie or Tad running along at his heels, asking a thousand little quick questions which his father heard not . . ."

We have from a letter of Mary's a description of her husband's boyishness and mirth in his own home, "free from care, surrounded by those he loved so well & by *whom*, he was so idolized." She sought for words to express that dear whimsicality of his and the adjectives that came to her were "cheery," "funny," and "in high spirits." There was laughter in the Lincoln home.

In 1846 that home also knew the thrill of success. Lincoln was elected to Congress in November, an event toward which he had been shaping his plans for some years. He was emerging from state politics into national, and Mary's ambition for him was soaring. Her words expressing their elation have been preserved by a man whom Lincoln first met in the latter half of 1847, a young Virginian destined to become a close and valued friend. Ward Hill Lamon was quite a figure in his "fashionable toggery," "swallow-tail coat, white neckcloth, and ruffled shirt" when he was introduced to Lincoln, and the latter, eyeing all this splendor with a twinkle, made a remark to the effect that he did not think Lamon would succeed at splitting rails. The young man, a newcomer to Illinois, protested that he had done much hard manual labor in his time, and Lincoln, much amused, replied: "Oh, yes; you Virginians shed barrels of perspiration while standing off at a distance and superintending the work your slaves do for you. . . . Here it is every fellow for himself, or he doesn't get there."

Later Lamon was in Springfield and Lincoln invited him to a party at his house. When the young man was introduced to Mrs. Lincoln he remarked that her husband was a great favorite in the eastern part of the state where he had been stopping. "Yes," she answered, "he is a great favorite everywhere. He is to be President of the United States some day; if I had not thought so I never would have married him, for you can see he is not pretty. But look at him! Doesn't he look as if he would make a magnificent President?"

Taken from its context this might give the impression of a coldly calculating decision to marry Lincoln as the main chance. It was instead a wife's gay and bridling expression of pride in her husband, who was going to be in the United States House of Representatives.

When questioned as to their impression of Mrs. Lincoln, a majority of people will mention first her high temper. The next remark is apt to be that she "was very ambitious." Mary's lighthearted predictions that she would be the wife of a President have received heavy treatment. An old neighbor thought that a fortuneteller had once made some such prediction, which was all youthful optimism needed to make it dwell on the idea. Then Mary had grown up in an atmosphere of political awareness where much attention was given to Presidential possibilities in general and those of Henry Clay in particular. These factors throw light on her earlier remarks on the subject. Her faith in her husband explains the later ones. It has been said many times that Mary's ambition spurred Lincoln on, which is true. One of the most satisfying rewards of success to any man is his wife's delight in it.

But Lincoln's "little engine" of ambition was running full tilt before he ever met Mary. His ambitious plans stimulated her in turn; his political future was a matter in which they felt as one. The young Mary Todd, probably at the very time she was first considering marrying Lincoln, had put herself on record as expecting her lot to be a quiet one, adding that she would be happy indeed if it were only cast near those she *"so dearly"* loved. It is true that she delighted in prominence, excitement, and glory; it was part of her intense joy of life.

In the fall of 1847 Mary's spirits were riding high. The Lincolns were renting their house and starting on a journey east. How the quick-motioned little housewife must have hustled around with packing and preparations, and one suspects her deliberate and absent-minded husband was not too much help. What mountainous baggage was necessary in a day when dresses required about sixteen yards of silk, lined at that, and where would one tuck away the extra set of hoops for hoop skirts? The archaeologist of the future, if he used figures of yardage alone, might deduce that women were giants in the earth in those days, for the stouthearted ladies by 1855 were supposed to wear dresses of thirty square yards of silk, with twelve to fifteen yards of whalebone and sixty-three square yards of cotton underwear. Fortunately most women then, as now, made some sort of compromise with the extremes of fashion, but there is no doubt that Mary's packing was a far more formidable thing than the present-day custom of laying a few things in a suitcase.

One can almost follow the family's itinerary day by day. Their house was rented to Cornelius Ludlum beginning November 1, 1847, the rent being ninety dollars for one year, with "the North-up-stairs room" reserved to store the Lincoln furniture. The first lap of the journey, probably by stagecoach, was to St. Louis, whose *Daily Era* reported on October 28 that "A. Lincoln and family" and Joshua Speed were guests at Scott's Hotel. So they had arranged to meet Joshua, show him their remarkable children and talk over old times with this loved friend.

Mary was always at her joyous best on a journey, and such a journey as this was, when she was taking her husband (about to enter the United States Congress, if you please) home to Lexington to show him to the relatives. Her thoughts had often turned to the old home; she was homesick for "the sweet old garden," she wrote, and longed to stroll again along the path between the flowers that led to the well-remembered summer house. How she had missed the leisured and stately beauty of Lexington in the raw newness of Springfield!

The journey from St. Louis to Lexington required about a week. One had to take a packet steamboat down the Mississippi to Cairo, where its muddy waters were joined by the clear flow of the Ohio River. Looking down from the boat at that point the Lincolns could see, as one does today, the line of juncture, where great tawny swirls of the Mississippi create a vast pattern of plumes in the limpid waters of the Ohio. Then the steamboat had to push against the current up the Ohio and probably up the Kentucky River to Frankfort, where it was possible to take the train on the Lexington and Ohio Railroad to Lexington.

Imagination likes to play upon the Lincoln family traveling on a river boat: the tall rawboned father, whose face was certainly not "pretty" as his wife had said but upon whose rugged features character was etching lines that were to make it "magnificent," the plump, pleasant-faced wife, so amusingly short beside her lengthy husband (and a bit sensitive about that too), the lively youngsters requiring constant attention to keep them, or at least the older one, from climbing over the deck rail and, if one may judge by what follows, causing considerable annoyance to the other passengers. There was the excitement of lining up at the rail to see the boatmen tie up at the landings where all the population of the river town would come down to meet the boat. There was the endless loading and unloading, and the always changing drama of river life.

The train, consisting of a tiny steam locomotive and a single coach, that bore them to Lexington was a thing of up-to-date progressiveness to them. After a jolting journey, it rattled noisily into the station, whose plain-lined building still stands at Mill and Water Streets. Mary had come home.

Emilie Todd Helm gave an account of that homecoming as it appeared to her little-girl eyes. The whole Todd family stood near the front door of the stately brick mansion on Main Street to welcome them, the colored servants in the rear to make a "miration" over the babies. Mary came in first with little Eddie in her arms. To Emilie this half sister, eighteen years older than she, was very "lovely" with her vivid coloring of blue eyes, flushed cheeks and brown curls, all glowing with the excitement of the moment. Mr. Lincoln followed her into the hall, carrying Bobbie, and stooped to put the four-year-old on the floor. As he rose, little Emilie was frightened; his tall form unfolded to a height that made her think of the giant in "Jack and the Beanstalk." His long full black coat and fur cap with ear straps added to the strange and awesome effect. She almost expected him to say "Fee, fi, fo, fum!" Then Lincoln reached out and lifted Emilie in his arms, saying "So this is little sister," and her fears vanished. She was a beautiful little girl and his heart went out to her. Down the long years, through happy normal living, and through the bitterness and tragedy of the Civil War with its dividing of loyalties, Emilie was to remain "little sister" to him and to Mary.

Mrs. Todd's nephew, Joseph Humphreys, had traveled on the same train with the Lincolns, whom he had never met. It is a short distance from the railway station to the Todd home and, having no baggage, he quickly walked there. "Aunt Betsy," he burst out, "I was never so glad to get off a train in my life. There were two lively youngsters on board who kept the whole train in a turmoil, and their long-legged father, instead of spanking the brats, looked pleased as Punch and aided and abetted the older one in mischief." At that moment he noticed through the window the long-legged man and the lively youngsters alighting from the Todd carriage in front of the house. "Good Lord," he exclaimed, "there they are now." He made a prompt exit and was not among those who called to pay their respects to the visiting relatives.

Emilie remembered the visitings and the family fun and teasing. Sam Todd, Mary's half brother, with great glee taught little Robert to call him Uncle Sam, and poked fun at Mary because she was so short, expressing the hope that the Lincoln boys would inherit their father's long legs. "And their mother's lovely disposition," said Mary with a little grimace, for she knew her own shortcomings.

Lincoln, as could be expected, explored the Todd library. According to family tradition he read a book of poetry and committed Bryant's "Thanatopsis" to memory. Emilie recalled that her noisy romps with Bob never seemed to disturb him when he was absorbed in reading.

There can be little doubt that he observed with deep thought the slave pens that almost surrounded Grandmother Parker's home, a block or so distant from the Todds. Long consequences came from Lincoln's marriage to a girl whose family was in Kentucky: understanding of the Southern viewpoint and direct observation of slavery. The auction block and whipping post on the public square were there for him to consider in all their implications. Perhaps he attended an auction, or perhaps a gang of manacled slaves was driven by the Todd door. He was also able to see firsthand the relation between the master's family and the privileged household slaves.

This rich visit lasted about three weeks and then Congressman Lincoln and family started the tedious journey to Washington. Probably they traveled by stage to Winchester, Virginia, where they could get the Winchester and Potomac Railroad to Harpers Ferry, then the Baltimore and Ohio to Relay Station, Maryland, from which a branch line ran to Washington. This took about a week of exhausting travel, especially with children aged four and one-and-a-half years. The Lincolns arrived late at night on December 2, taking temporary lodgings at Brown's Hotel. Later they moved to rooms at Mrs. Ann G. Sprigg's boardinghouse on the site where the Library of Congress now stands. Congress convened on December 6, and Congressman Lincoln was soon up to his ears in politics.

Among the Lincolns' new experiences around the time of going to Washington was that of having their pictures taken, probably for the first time. Mary very likely was the one who thought that Congressman Lincoln and his wife deserved to be photographed by the new daguerreotype process. She carefully arrayed herself in her loveliest striped dress with a lace scarf around her shoulders fastened at her throat with a large cameo pin. One suspects it was her wifely inspection that caused Lincoln's hair to be brushed to an unaccustomed flatness. Both look a little strained and stiff at the new experience; posing is apt to be a trying business. Mary, judging by later pictures, never learned to take it in her stride as Lincoln did. She tended to freeze into a blank and stolid look that belied her vivacity. The long exposures required by photographs of the Civil War period often resulted in a sort of *rigor-mortis* expression.

Many years later Robert Lincoln wrote his aunt Emilie Todd Helm, sending her a print of this early picture of his mother and telling her how these two daguerreotypes of his father and mother hung as a pair in the Lincoln home in Springfield almost throughout his memory of that home. Though there are made-up pictures of them together, Mr. and Mrs. Lincoln never had their pictures taken on the same negative (probably because of the amusing contrast in height). But these companion likenesses were treasured. Mary's daguerreotype was not entirely satisfactory, however; her dainty hands looked too large in it. This little woman had her harmless vanity; it was part of her femininity. She was apt not to like her pictures, ". . . my hands are always *made* in *them,* very large and I look too stern."

Too little is known of the months the Lincolns spent in the boarding-house on Capitol Hill. Going to Washington was a great adventure to them, and perhaps a stimulation to their ambition. Both had a fresh, unspoiled interest in new scenes and new people. There were doubtless many thrills at visiting historic spots associated with the great men of the nation whom they admired. Lincoln had a deep sense of history and Mary's letters show she was singularly responsive to sight-seeing in storied places.

They were pleasantly located facing the Capitol. "The iron railing around the Capitol Park comes within fifty feet of our door," wrote Theodore Weld when he stopped at Mrs. Sprigg's five years before. "Our dining room overlooks the whole Capitol Park which is one mile around and filled with shade trees and shrubbery." He found his room delightful in all respects, including "a good fire place, and plenty of dry wood to burn in it." One can picture the pleasant-faced young matron of the daguerreotype taking the two little boys across into the park for an airing, a plump little figure dressed in what the well-dressed woman of '47 or '48 was supposed to wear, at least as this was understood in Illinois. Perhaps the more sophisticated ladies of Washington could have recognized that the dress originated in the "remote" West.

One catches a gimpse of Mary from a gentleman who was also boarding at Mrs. Sprigg's, but he reported that she "was so retiring that she was rarely seen except at the meals." Little Eddie was at an age when he required constant care, and Mary as a proper Victorian matron did not put herself forward. The same gentleman mentioned that Robert "was a bright boy" but "seemed to have his own way."

It is pleasant to think of the couple in the evenings before the fireplace in their room, talking softly (so as not to waken the children) of their new experiences and broadening horizon. What important people they were meeting! Why, most of the boarders were members of Congress! Both Mary and Lincoln reveled in talk of politics and there were undoubtedly lively discussions around that long table. And what quantities of food were placed on it: Graham bread, corn bread, great pitchers of milk, wrote Mr. Weld. "Mush we have always once and generally twice a day; apples always once a day; at dinner potatoes, turnips, parsnips, spinnage with eggs, almonds, raisins, figs and bread; the puddings, pies, cakes, etc." Mrs. Sprigg, a Virginian, had eight servants, all colored, "3 men, one boy and four women. All are free but 3 which she hires and these are buying themselves."

Living, however, in a boardinghouse with two little children proved complicated. With Bobbie and Eddie as spoiled as they were, the other boarders at times probably, like Herndon, wanted to wring the necks of those brats and throw them out of the windows. One may be sure that any criticism of her children would not be well received by Mary. The Lincolns both belonged to that happily fatuous group of parents who think their children can do no wrong.

There was no trouble with the landlady, however. In the first year of the Presidency one finds Lincoln giving her a wholehearted recommendation, and Mary, to strengthen it (for she loved to help people too), added hers, saying, "We boarded some months, with Mrs. Sprigg, & found her a most estimable lady & would esteem it a personal favor, if her request, could be granted."

By April 1848, Mrs. Lincoln with the children was back in Lexington visiting her old home again. Probably she had a chance to make the trip with some friends or some protector; she could hardly have made it alone. On April 16, Congressman Lincoln in Washington sat down to write his wife a letter.

We now come to supreme historical evidence as to the Lincoln marriage; four long letters between them at this time have been preserved, three of the husband's and one of Mary's. Reminiscence is subject to fallibility. Herndon's testimony as to the marriage is the spinning out of a theory in an eccentric mind; but in these unself-conscious letters, written with no thought of others ever reading them, it is as if the Lincolns themselves came back to bear witness to the relationship between them. To read these letters is like listening to husband and wife talking to each other at the end of the day in those moments of relaxation when they could review small events of mutual interest and take the time to express affection. To eavesdrop like this upon any couple would be to find out directly what they meant to each other.

What does Lincoln write his "Dear Mary" on April 16, 1848? He very properly tells her first how he misses her. When she was there, he thought she interfered some with his attending to business, but now that life is all business, no variety, it has grown "exceedingly tasteless" to him. "I hate to sit down and direct documents," he writes, "and I hate to stay in this old room by myself." He had told her "in last Sunday's letter" about a little speech he was going to make, but the week had gone by without his getting a chance to do so. (Only a man's wife would find that fact interesting.)

He had received two letters from her since he last wrote, and she had told him how the baby thought of him. He repeats the baby word—"Dear Eddy thinks father is *'gone tapila'* [Capitol?]." He had been shopping for the "little plaid stockings" she wanted but could not find "a single pair of the description you give, and only one plaid pair of any sort that I thought would fit 'Eddy's dear little feet—' I have a notion to make another trial tomorrow morning." She was always interested in his dress, so of course she would want to know about his shopping for himself: "Very soon after you went away, I got what I

think a very pretty set of shirt-bosom studs—modest little
ones, jet set in gold, only costing 50 cents a piece, or 1.50
for the whole."

He would sometimes tease her about her shortcomings:
"All the house—or rather, all with whom you were on
decided good terms—send their love to you— The others
say nothing."

There is gentle husbandly advice as to tactful behavior:
"I wish you to enjoy yourself in every possible way; but
is there no danger of wounding the feelings of your good
father, by being so openly intimate with the Wickliffe family?" (There was a long history of hate and litigation
between Mr. Todd and Robert Wickliffe.) He modestly
suggests, "Suppose you do not prefix the 'Hon' to the
address on your letters to me any more. I like the letters
very much but I would rather they should not have that
upon them." (One doubts whether they saw eye to eye on
this; who can measure Mary's satisfaction in prefixing that
"Hon" to her husband's name?)

He knew full well that too much work and tension contributed to her torturing headaches. At present she is relieved from housekeeping; he hopefully inquires: "Are
you entirely free from headache? That is good—good considering it is the first spring you have been free from
it since we were acquainted." Then follows a whimsical bit
of flattery, playing up to her coquetry: "I am afraid you
will get so well, and fat, and young, as to be wanting to
marry again."

This exemplary family man evidently worried about his
wife and children. "Tell Louisa I want her to watch you
a little for me—" he writes and adds as a sort of checking
up, "Get weighed and write me how much you weigh." His
anxiety had apparently come into his dreams—"I did not
get rid of the impression of that foolish dream about dear
Bobby till I got your letter written the same day— What
did he and Eddy think of the little letters father sent
them? Don't let the blessed fellows forget father." He
signs the letter "Most affectionately, A. Lincoln."

Her long newsy letter to "My Dear Husband" was written in Lexington one Saturday night after "our babies"
had been put to sleep. Outside her window lay the "sweet
old garden" where fragrant lilies were in their May blooming. She told him everything a family man would want to
know: who were coming and going and what the news

from home—Springfield—was. Frances Wallace was not going to send the box she wanted because, wrote Mary, throwing in a pleasant and complimentary parenthesis, "she thinks with you (as good persons generally agree) that it would cost more than it would come to, and might be lost on the road." Apparently the box contained childrens' clothes, as Mary continued, ". . . it takes so many changes to do children, particularly in summer, that I thought it might save me a few stitches."

Of course the main topic of Mary's letter is those wonderful children. "Our little Eddy, has recovered from his little spell of sickness—Dear boy, I must tell you a little story about him. Boby in his wanderings to day, came across in a yard, a little kitten, *your hobby*." Bobby brought the kitten to the Todd house and as "soon as Eddy, spied it his *tenderness*, broke forth, he made them bring it *water*, fed it with bread himself, with his *own dear hands*, he was a delighted little creature over it . . ." The story does not have a happy ending; Mrs. Todd disliked cats and had the stray animal thrown out, "Ed—screaming & protesting loudly against the proceeding . . ." Mary apparently held her tongue and there was no clash with her stepmother, who "has just sent me up a glass of ice cream, for which this warm evening, I am duly grateful."

There follows a bit of teasing: Mary threatens to go traveling with some friends who are planning a trip to Philadelphia. "You know I am so fond of *sight-seeing*, & I did not get to New York or Boston, or travel the lake route — But perhaps, dear husband . . . cannot do without his wife next winter, and must needs take her with him again—" She expects he would "cry aloud" against her going on such a trip. Then comes the expression of her longing for him: "How much, I wish instead of writing, we were together this evening, I feel very sad away from you."

One more bit of teasing coquetry. Her old beau Mr. Webb was going to be in Shelbyville, Kentucky, before long. "I must go down about that time & carry on quite a flirtation, you know *we*, always had a *penchant* that way."

He had asked her not to let the children forget him. Back went this reassurance: "Do not fear the children, have forgotten you . . . Even E— eyes brighten at the mention of your name— My love to all— Truly yours M L——"

His letter of June 12, 1848, contains a gentle, paternal reference to Mary's difficult temperament. It is the voice of one speaking to a willful, beloved child. He had just received her letter saying she wished to come East again. "Will you be a *good girl* in all things, if I consent?" he writes. "Then come along, and that as *soon* as possible. Having got the idea in my head, I shall be impatient till I see you——" He advises her as to money for the trip, apologizes for the shortness of the letter, as he was writing it in the House of Representatives, and concludes: "Come on just as soon as you can—I want to see you, and our dear, *dear* boys very much. Every body here wants to see our dear Bobby."

Lincoln wrote again to his "Dear Wife" on July 2, giving careful instructions as to the money draft for her journey, and asking about her arrangement for the forwarding of letters. One gathers from this letter that even at this time Mary was somewhat unreliable in money matters; she had left two small debts in Washington that he did not know of until he received the bills from the stores. There is a gentle implied reproof in what he said: "I hesitated to pay them, because my recollection is that you told me when you went away, there was nothing left unpaid. Mention in your next letter whether they are right." He also reminded her: "Write me whether you got the draft, if you shall not have already done so, when this reaches you." Lincoln already knew his wife's weakness in spending money, a failing that was to lead to fearful results in the White House. Her lack of knowledge of business details (which no wife at the time was expected to understand) is suggested in the passage: "I have had no letter from home . . . except short business letters, which have no interest for you."

He was sending her a copy of a recent speech he had made. He well knew her interest in his political activities. This letter is delightfully gossipy. There is a twinkle in the lines: "Mrs. Richardson is still here; and what is more, has a baby—so Richardson says, and he ought to know."

More light conversation with a dry humorous twist, and then this fatherly husband, who knew Mary's tendency to overdo and pay up for it in headaches or nerves, wrote: "By the way, you do not intend to do without a girl, because the one you had has left you? Get another as soon as you can to take charge of the dear codgers. Father expected to see you all sooner; but let it pass; stay as long as you please, and come when you please. Kiss and love the dear rascals."

A flock of witnesses close to the Lincolns have left testimony as to the happiness of their marriage. "They were in harmony on the larger affairs in their lives," and "Abraham Lincoln loved her," said Henry B. Rankin out of years of pleasant friendship. "Lincoln thoroughly loved his wife. I had many reasons to know this in my intimacy with him," wrote H. C. Whitney. Who knew the truth of the matter better than Mary's sisters? With careful consideration Emilie said, ". . . they understood each other thoroughly, and Mr. Lincoln looked beyond the impulsive words and manner, and knew that his wife was devoted to him and to his interests." Frances Todd Wallace, living in Springfield and intimate with the Lincolns, repeated that "He was devoted to his home, and Mrs. Lincoln . . . almost worshiped him . . . And they certainly did live happily together—as much so as any man and woman I have ever known."

Substantial as this testimony is, no evidence can be found to equal the voices of Mary and Lincoln themselves unconsciously saying in these pages that they are a loving and adjusted couple.

The letters give an epitome of the married life in Springfield. Every element is contained in them: mutual interest in his work and hers, feminine coquetry met with humoring flattery, tender longing for each other. The wife's two worst failings are suggested, her irresponsibility as to money and her difficulty in getting along with people, and the husband's mention of these weaknesses shows his light, paternal way of dealing with them. There is a mutual rare devotion to and enjoyment of their children. This is evidence of a happy marriage that will hold in any court of law, or historical investigation, where theories based on hearsay and gossip will be stricken from the record.

chapter 10

"TEARS ON THE JURY"

In writing of the Lincoln marriage today, it is necessary to deal fully with three personalities that form a unique kind of triangle: Mary herself and her husband on one side and Herndon at the opposite point busily spinning theories about them and the relationship between them. We have reached the chronological point of Herndon's entry into this story.

William H. Herndon had become Lincoln's junior law partner late in 1844. Lincoln, after serving as a junior partner first with John Todd Stuart and then with Stephen T. Logan, had reached a standing where he could be the senior partner himself and let a younger man be the one who, to use Herndon's own words, " 'toated books' & 'hunted up authorities,' " and did the other legal chores. Lincoln was fond of Billy, who had for a time been a clerk in Speed's store, and had slept in the big room over the store along with Charles R. Hurst (another clerk), Joshua Speed, and himself. He knew Billy, who was just twenty-six, had the inquiring mind, an eager intellectual curiosity with which Lincoln could well sympathize; he also knew he could count on the younger man's honesty and devotion. He was to learn later he could not trust Herndon's judgment or discretion. Billy had no inconvenient political ambitions (as Lincoln's two other law partners had had) and he would serve to keep Lincoln in touch with the rank and file of the Whig party who, like Herndon himself, were outside the aristocratic circle. Lincoln was understood, somewhat to his disadvantage, to be associated with that aristocratic group after his marriage. The younger man had learned much of law as a student in the Logan-Lincoln office; he was competent. He came in time to consider himself a better lawyer than Lincoln.

Herndon was to develop a way with juries, studying the art of bringing them to the viewpoint he wished them to have, and playing on their emotions. "When you get tears on the jury, you win your case," he once confided to his nephew. He would sway them to his purpose with every lawyer's trick of slanted evidence presented in vivid, salty, down-to-earth language. It was the method which he was later to use in presenting the case against Mary Lincoln to the public as jury.

We have Lincoln's own description of Herndon in a letter he wrote his junior partner in 1848. Herndon had written to Lincoln (then in Washington) complaining of "the stubbornness and bad judgment of the old fossils in the party, who were constantly holding the young men back." Lincoln, who considered himself one of the old men (though he was only nine years older than Herndon), replied: "I would save you from a fatal error. You have been a laborious, studious young man. You are far better informed on almost all subjects than I have ever been. You cannot fail in any laudable object, unless you allow your mind to be improperly directed." As so often, one finds in Lincoln's words the essence of a complicated situation reduced to a simple phrase that contains the ultimate truth. Herndon did "allow" his mind "to be improperly directed": he was, as the senior partner told him, "too rampant and spontaneous," he went off on the tangent of amateur psychoanalysis and transcendental intuition, and wove thereby his theory of the Lincoln marriage. He made a "fatal error" from which Lincoln would have saved him, and that error, by a strange twist of fate, was also fatal to the reputation of Lincoln's wife.

Lincoln's words may also suggest one personal reason why he brought Herndon into his office: his paternal helpfulness recognized that here was a young man of bright mind who was in need of proper guidance. Mary Lincoln many years later wrote of her "husband's kindness" to Herndon, saying, "Out of pity he took him into his office, when he was almost a hopeless inebriate," which may be an overforceful statement of what was basically true.

Herndon's biographer, David Donald, brings the new junior partner to life as follows: "He was a child of the frontier, a man's man. He had the earthy flavor of the prairies; he knew the talk of racing and cock-fights and horses and women; he liked ribald anecdotes and practical jokes. His was a horselaugh, not a titter."

It was not a combination of qualities calculated to appeal to a woman of refined tastes. Mary did not like young

Herndon or approve of him; he was unpredictable, loquacious about his unorthodox views (a matter of offense to one devoted to her church), was not acceptable socially in the Edwards circle, and drank too much. Many men used too much liquor at that time, but its commonness did not lessen Mary's disapproval and fear of it; she had a brother whose life was made a tragedy by drink.

She and Herndon disliked each other as a matter of incompatibility, in their first meeting at a dance shortly after she came to Springfield. Thinking to compliment her, the awkward young man told her "she seemed to glide through the waltz with the ease of a serpent." Quick to have her feelings hurt, as usual, Mary answered: "Mr. Herndon, comparison to a serpent is rather severe irony, especially to a newcomer." The incident itself (in which one feels rather sympathetic toward the gauche young man) had no special significance; a boy and girl had met but did not like each other, that was all. But down the years far ahead of them were to be various episodes and situations that grew out of that mutual antagonism and differing standard of values. When Lincoln took Billy Herndon as a partner, Mary probably expressed herself as usual in emphatic terms, ticking off his shortcomings in telling phrases, and then turned her mind to other things. She knew she could not change her husband's decisions, once he had made up his mind. After all, she considered, as she later wrote, that Herndon was in the office only in the capacity of "a drudge." Herndon himself said in one of his appealing moments of candor and affection for Lincoln that "[H]e was the great big man of our firm and I was the little one. The little one looked *naturally* up to the big one . . ."

It is likely that Mary resented one arrangement of the partnership very much: Lincoln divided fees equally between his junior partner and himself. This was a most generous action, as far as Herndon's interests were concerned; it was not so considerate toward the financial needs of Lincoln's own family. Mary with her great pride in her husband's talents and abilities had reason to feel that Lincoln should receive a larger portion of the office income, a point of view in which many in Springfield doubtless agreed. Lincoln's legal services with his experience and reputation were naturally, to her mind, more valuable than those of this fledgling lawyer who was just getting his license. Besides she knew how much she needed every penny for the family. Being married to an altruist on a limited income, is a trying business for a wife.

There were to be times when Mary had a chance to say "I told you so" and probably did. There was the morning when Lincoln had to arise very early and go into action to save his partner from jail. Herndon and two of his friends "had spent the night in a drunken spree, had broken in almost the entire front of a grocery or saloon and otherwise committed acts of such vandalism that before daylight the sheriff was forced to apprehend them." Lincoln was placed in considerable embarrassment to raise one hundred dollars before breakfast, but he managed to do it. One suspects that Mary made some remarks on that occasion, referring, as she did in a letter many years later, to her husband's "crazy drinking law partner."

There was a degree of incompatibility in the partnership. Herndon had a "complete lack of a sense of humor," and was apt to be bored with Lincoln's stories. Lincoln on his side grew weary, according to Mr. Donald, of the younger man's "meaningless metaphysics and gaseous generalities."

In the Lincoln home Herndon figured not at all. Mrs. Lincoln wrote in her widowhood: "Mr. Herndon had always been an utter stranger to me, he was not considered an habitué, at our house. The office was more, in his line." In the days of the partnership in Springfield relations between the two were distant but polite, an easy matter since they saw so little of each other. Mrs. Lincoln "rarely visited the office," said a young man who studied law with Lincoln and Herndon. Beneath the surface the antagonism was probably building up. According to a remote reminiscence, Mrs. Lincoln feared that Herndon was not attending properly to affairs at the office when Lincoln was away, and tried indirectly to check up on this. For a man who took himself as seriously as Herndon did, to have a mere female thus overseeing him would have been intolerable. And he would naturally resent the fact that he was never invited to a meal at his senior partner's house. Years later he described that home from which he was excluded and one can feel a certain sympathy for the man who did not belong to the so-called "best society," who was on the outside looking in. The people who went to the Lincoln dinners were prominent, wrote Herndon, "politicians

mostly," "Judges," "Legislators," "the belles of the city—
young ladies of wit—refinement—&c. Mrs. Lincoln got
up the parties herself & *selected* the aristocracy you may
'bet.' The suppers were very fine indeed." His slighted feelings are apparent in the following outburst: "The house
was cold—exclusive and aristocratic, with no soul—fire—
cheer or fun in it. . . . No wine—beer—or liquor was ever
used at such parties." The last item made his disapproval
complete.

Mary in the eighteen-forties was more concerned with
domestic problems than with parties. She was a nervous,
overanxious mother. Bobbie's tendency to run away, mentioned in his father's letter to Speed, terrified her. From
her husband's letters in 1848 it has been seen that he was
anxious that she should not overdo. Pregnancy, childbirth, household drudgery, and sick headaches were beginning to tell on this abnormally intense little woman.
She was easily frightened into a panic. An old neighbor,
Elizabeth A. Capps, recalled many years later how Mary,
finding her child missing, would become hysterical, and,
rushing out onto the terrace in front of the house, would
scream: "Bobbie's lost! Bobbie's lost!" The same neighbor
remembered how the little boy once got into the "lime
box" (a necessary accessory of the outdoor toilet), putting some of the lime in his mouth. The frantic mother,
losing her head, screamed in the terror that blotted out
her reason: "Bobbie will die! Bobbie will die!" It was the
father of Elizabeth Capps who rushed over and washed
out the child's mouth.

Mrs. Capps further recalled that an old bearded umbrella mender at the door frightened Mrs. Lincoln into
crying out "murder," so that a neighbor came and led
the man away. Mary came from a family characterized
by overintensity, a family in which Dr. Evans concluded
there was more than one abnormal personality. Her emotional instability was showing up. There is evident in Mrs.
Capps's account a scorn of this neighbor's inability to meet
her own emergencies. A person who loses self-control and
goes "out of her mind," creating a scene, may be either
pitied or censured. An age in which nervous and mental
disorders were not accorded much understanding or sympathy usually employed censure. There is the added factor
that some of these recollections were given after the pub-

lication of Herndon's life of Lincoln which so cruelly be-
rated Mrs. Lincoln. People tend to climb on the band
wagon of abuse.

Thunderstorms filled Mary with the same agonizing terror. It is well known that Lincoln at the first signs of a
storm would leave his office and go home to comfort her.
One old-timer remembered that Mary, knowing he would
come, would meet him at their gate just a step from their
front door, when his protecting arm would be slipped into
hers, and so arm in arm they would go into the house together.

But what about the weeks and months when Lincoln
was away on the circuit and there were no protecting arm
and calm balanced nature to steady her? When he was
gone, her responsibility with the children was doubled.
Another circuit-widow, Mrs. Benjamin S. Edwards, complained bitterly of her trials when her husband had gone
off to "hold court" and she was left alone to be father and
mother to her little brood.

Mary had a terrifying experience one night when Lincoln was absent. It was her misfortune to have at the
time a girl of bad character staying with her. In the night
this nervous woman became aware that men were coming
into her house. She screamed in an agony of fear to her
neighbor James Gourley to come and protect her. He left a
record of her hysterical pleading with him to sleep at her
house. Such fear is real suffering. Mary, for all her impetuosity and courage in certain respects, had a timidity
and childlike dependence upon the strength and calmness
of others. These qualities her husband supplied in full
measure when he was with her, humoring and comforting
her with a paternal touch. She said herself, with that facing up to her own weaknesses which she often achieved,
that he spoiled her with his indulgence. It is quite true
that in his love for his wife and children, Lincoln spoiled
them all; it is also true that after his death this factor
made life much harder for Mary.

All through the record one finds evidences of Lincoln's
trying to protect her. He did the best he could to prevent
those nights of trembling fear. He would engage a boy
to sleep at the house when he was absent, paying (as one
boy grown old remembered) the sum of five cents a night.
But as Mrs. Lincoln sobbed to James Gourley the

night she awakened him with her cries, she did not want boys because they went to sleep too soon and would not and could not watch. A twelve-year-old could not dispel her fear.

The husband knew, as no one else did, what Mary had to contend with. He had seen her in prostrating, nauseating headaches (like those now called migraine) when her head could not be raised from the pillow and a jarring step on the floor was torture. Lincoln was the only one who knew whether those hysterical outbursts of fear or anger had a time relation to her headaches or to periodic and other ills. Again we turn to him for a simple expression of the essential truth. He did not say his wife was in a tantrum (as others did); he would say merely, "Mrs. Lincoln is not well today," or that Mary was having one of her "nervous spells."

If people today know only one fact about Mrs. Lincoln, it is that she had an uncontrollable temper. Many people have quick tempers, but with her it was coupled with an emotional immaturity or weakness. Dr. Evans found her an abnormal personality. Episodes of such irresponsible outbreaks made choice morsels for clothesline gossip, items to be mouthed over, improved upon, and passed on with variations and additions, as is the way with gossip everywhere. As Carl Sandburg has understandingly commented, "That her husband had married her . . . in debt, that he charged low fees as a lawyer and was careless about money, and that she managed the household so well that her husband trusted her . . . didn't get into the gossip. That she was often sorry, full of regret, after a bad burst of temper, didn't get into the gossip."

These were the stories of Mary's irresponsible moments which were collected by Herndon years after the Lincolns left Springfield as the basis of his character sketch of Lincoln's wife. It would be a dreary fate for anyone to have his portrait for posterity based on his moments of anger or fear. There are enough of these stories from various sources to make it clear that Mrs. Lincoln was so afflicted, yet one would be hard put to it to collect even one for each year of the Lincoln married life in Springfield. A few such stories with these embellishments and variations have gone a long way. One does not know how often the explosions occurred or whether they were more frequent in the later part of the Springfield years, after Mary's child-birth injury in 1853, or as she approached the ills of the menopause. The stories remain, but the contributing factors have been lost or overlooked.

Mary did not develop this emotional instability until after she was married. There is no record of it in the buoyant girl. Let one notice how Herndon explains this change in her. Though he supported "women's right" as the term was understood in his day, he was not the type of man to give much reflection to the physical hardships of womenkind. His own first wife died from tuberculosis and the constant burden of childbearing, and, though there is no doubt of his love for her, in a few short months he was courting a pretty girl to start the same game over again in a man's world.

Herndon, of course, explained Mary's developing nervousness by remote psychoanalysis. After a description of Mary Todd in which it is admitted that she was "handsome and vivacious," "affable and even charming in her manners," and was "one of the belles" of the town, comes this sentence: "She was a very shrewd observer, and discreetly and without apparent effort kept back all the unattractive elements in her unfortunate organization." She is here accused of deliberate deceit in concealing faults which she did not know she had, as if any lighthearted young girl knows what the strains of life will do to her. On another page Mary's developing instability is related to a mere fabrication of Herndon's mind: the insinuation that she married Lincoln to get even with him after the (imaginary) wedding default. "Whether Mrs. Lincoln really was moved by the spirit of revenge or not she acted along the lines of human conduct," runs the biography. "If, in time, she became soured at the world it was not without provocation, and if in later years she unchained the bitterness of a disappointed and outraged nature, it followed as logically as an effect does the cause."

On another page Lincoln's theoretical "conjugal infelicity" is colored by the following statement: "That a lady as proud and as ambitious to exercise the rights of supremacy in society as Mary Todd should repent of her marriage to the man I have just described surely need occasion no surprise in the mind of anyone." This subtly creates the impression that Mary repented her marriage, this woman whose loving heart looked back, by her own statement, to the time of her wifehood and motherhood as the happiest stage of her life.

It is well to study Lincoln's attitude toward his wife's moments of hysterical anger. He accepted them with humor and a calm philosophy. It made a lot of difference that he could count on her regret when the explosion was over. One old-timer quoted him as saying after a wifely storm of angry words: "It does her lots of good and it doesn't hurt me a bit." That "protective deafness" which J. P. McEvoy calls the "mark of every happily married man" was his to the nth degree. He could sit lost in thought while his boys were shouting and turning the room upside down all around him. It was his custom to let Mary's nervous fussing pass by without penetrating his consciousness.

The Todd family had a well-established reputation for temper and the quick retort which was a matter of amusement to Lincoln. It was an age when the snappy comeback was especially well thought of. We will find him later teasing Mary, to enjoy—as a large, slow-motioned man is apt to do—a saucy answer from a bright and spirited little woman. Repartee has been a game between the sexes in all ages. Lincoln liked to talk about the spirit of the Todds.

When "Little Sister" Emilie later gave a provoking gentleman just the hit-the-target answer which he deserved, Lincoln's eyes twinkled and he chuckled: "The child has a tongue like the rest of the Todds." Once on the judicial circuit he and John Todd Stuart, with other lawyers, had stopped at an inn. After supper the landlady remarked: "Stuart, how fine and peart you do look!, but Lincoln, whatever have you been a doing? you do look powerful weak." "Nothing out of the common, Ma'am," was Lincoln's reply, "but did you ever see Stuart's wife? or did you ever see mine? I just tell you whoever married into the 'Todd' family gets the worst of it." In the laugh that followed the brother lawyers began running over the large Todd family connection and found to their great glee that with the exception of the hearty and portly William Wallace, all who had married Todds were thin!

One gathers that if Lincoln had seen the letter written by a friend in 1862, which described him as "an old *poke easy* that used to walk our streets and was said to be *hen pecked,"* the accusation would merely have caused his eyes to twinkle. A wife who was easily upset could not have had a more suitable husband. Of course there were times when Mary's hysterical seizures were no laughing matter. It is a terrible thing for an adult woman to go into a frenzy in which she is not responsible for her words or actions. Her neighbors could at times hear her hysterical screams. Lincoln used the best method available; failing to laugh her out of it, he would pick up the children and depart until she came to herself.

Let us examine one of the stories about Mrs. Lincoln which Herndon collected after Lincoln's death. Riding his theory that the Lincoln marriage was unhappy, he eagerly sought stories pertaining to their home life, being the better satisfied if he could twist them to an unflattering conclusion. But he found a scarcity of "evidence." As he wrote his collaborator Weik: "Lincoln, you know, was not a social man, and hence those little *incidents* in his office and around his hearth which you want so much are hard to gather and to get, for they are few and far between." It is easy to see the difficulty of presenting incidents "around his hearth" for Herndon, who was not invited to frequent that hearthside.

The story we will analyze as an example is the one which has probably gone farthest in convincing the jury of the public that the Lincoln marriage was unhappy. The Herndon biography tells how a man called at the Lincoln home to find out why Mrs. Lincoln had discharged his niece from her employ. Mrs. Lincoln used such "violent gestures and emphatic language" that he beat a retreat and hunted up Lincoln to "exact from him proper satisfaction for his wife's action." Lincoln was entertaining some of his friends with his stories in a store when the man "called him to the door and made the demand." Lincoln is quoted as saying, "My friend, I regret to hear this, but let me ask you in all candor, can't you endure for a few moments what I have had as my daily portion for the last fifteen years?"

Now let us get a little nearer the source by examining this story as Herndon wrote it to Weik in 1887, long after the event which he says took place about 1850. (It will be seen later that Mary's little boy died early in that year and she shortly thereafter became pregnant.) Herndon tells Weik that the story was related to him by Judge

Matheny, who got it from "one of the parties to it." This makes it third-hand evidence, and one might well ask which party to it; was it the man himself who would give only his own anti-Mrs. Lincoln version? That would not make any difference in this case, as Herndon, in relating any story about Mrs. Lincoln, habitually puts her in the wrong, and makes those opposed to her lily-white. He starts his letter with the statement that "Mrs. Lincoln was a tigress" and the man's niece "was a fine girl, industrious, neat, saving, and rather handsome, who would satisfy any body on earth." Maybe this was true, but such a paragon among Springfield's domestic help would have been, by all accounts, a seven-day wonder!

Herndon's letter tells us that the severing of relations between Mrs. Lincoln and the girl took place as the result of Mrs. Lincoln's getting very angry at the girl, but he fails to state what the girl had done to incur her anger. Instead, he assures us again that Sarah, the maid, was "a fine woman and rather intelligent, pleasant, and social." When the man, who had the somewhat alarming name of Tiger, came to the Lincoln home, so the story goes, he found Mrs. Lincoln in the yard with her broom. We are assured by Herndon (who was not there) that Mr. Tiger spoke to her "in a kind and gentlemanly way . . ." Another point of view has been suggested: "Maybe he went looking for trouble and found it." Mr. Tiger, according to Herndon, was a "powerful man physically"; it is possible that Mrs. Lincoln being approached and called to account by so formidable a figure was frightened, as she had been by the umbrella mender, and went into one of her panics. On the other hand, it has already been seen that she "taka no sassy talk." At all events she is reported to have defended herself with vigorous words punctuated by blows of her broom, until he retreated. The Herndon biography correctly informs us that she "was a plucky little woman."

Herndon's letter continues: Mr. Tiger sought out Lincoln "in order to make him correct the thing or to whip him—to apologize or to stand a thumping—licking—a severe whipping"; a very definite case of a belligerent individual "looking for trouble." Lincoln was telling a funny story when Tiger called him "out of the store," not "to the door" as Weik wrote it into Herndon's life of Lincoln. Tiger called him away from his friends so that the conversation could be private. It is possible that no one heard what passed between them, which leaves the question unanswered as to whether Lincoln's words were correctly quoted and transmitted. A direct quotation which comes third-hand can never be taken literally. As the public got the quotation in the book, it was really fourth-hand, for Weik toned down the rawness of the words Herndon had put in Lincoln's mouth: *"Friend* Tiger, can't you endure this one wrong done you by a mad woman without much complaint for old friendship's sake while I have had to bear it without complaint and without a murmur for lo these last fifteen years?"

Such a statement attributed to Lincoln is completely out of character; it was not his custom to speak slightingly of his wife. His authenticated statements about her show sometimes a gentle teasing, but always consideration and affection. Herndon's arithmetic also seems a bit "intuitive." If the incident occurred about the year 1850 as he says, and Lincoln had suffered "fifteen years," he would have had to marry Mary Todd in 1835, which was four years before he met her!

One does not know what Lincoln really said or how he handled the situation. We know he had a genius in managing human relationships, often with a light humorous touch that disarmed antagonism by bestowing in its place a sense of camaraderie. It is not known who repeated Lincoln's words to Matheny or whether the words were merely made up by that dramatic instinct in small-town gossipers which causes them to fill in details to make a good story. Lincoln's alleged words, said to have been spoken "mournfully"—". . . can't you endure for a few moments what I have had as my daily portion for the last fifteen years?"—are doubtful and unreliable to a degree. Yet the jury of posterity has been repeating them and figuratively shedding tears over them ever since the publication of Herndon's life of Lincoln in 1889. They have even been put into sermons on patience and in one such case (showing how stories continue to grow) the number of years Lincoln was supposed to have suffered was increased to thirty, in spite of the fact that the whole married life of the Lincolns was less than twenty-three years.

It is typical of the contradictions in Herndon's pages that immediately following the account of the Tiger incident in which Lincoln is supposed to have laid bare fifteen years of domestic unhappiness to a man on the street, one reads: "Mr. Lincoln never had a confidant, and therefore never unbosomed himself to others. He never spoke of his trials to me or, so far as I knew, to any of his friends." Then follows this enlightenment: "If, on arriving at the office, I found him in, I knew instantly that a breeze had sprung up over the domestic sea, and that the waters were troubled." The only way Herndon could have "known" that was by what he considered his infallible intuition. The paragraph continues: "He would not look up on my entering, and only answered my 'Good morning' with a grunt."

If Lincoln on such mornings was not his usual self, there could have been a dozen explanations. He might have been in one of his depressed moods, or bilious, or the baby might have kept him awake the night before. His feet may have hurt, as they sometimes did in the White House. Or Lincoln's curtness could possibly have been caused by smelling liquor on his partner's breath, for he disliked Herndon's drinking. Perhaps the husband had left Mary at home ill with one of her headaches. We have her own testimony that her illness upset him, a warm human statement from the person directly concerned. Once, after mentioning Tad's devotion, Mrs. Lincoln wrote: "In his loving & tender treatment of me at all times, & very especially when I am indisposed—he reminds me so strongly of his beloved father—for *he* was never himself—when I was not perfectly well."

Whatever the reason that Lincoln was not in happy mood, Herndon "knew" his wife was to blame for it. His inference here, and his use of the Tiger story, are perfect examples of his "evidence" about Mrs. Lincoln.

One more illustration will be used. It is in a letter which Herndon wrote late in his life. His hate of Mrs. Lincoln by that time had grown into a mental complex. Writing to Isaac N. Arnold, also a biographer of Lincoln, Herndon said Mrs. Lincoln "would curtain lecture L all night, till he got up out of bed in despair and went whistling through the streets & alleys till day &c. &c." In the same letter it is stated: "Lincoln was a good sleeper scarcely ever getting out of bed before 7–8 unless *Mrs.* Lincoln chunked beat him out with a stick of stove wood in order to make him go to the market for some beef for breakfast." Since the scenes thus pictured are strictly private ones and Lincoln never told anyone of his alleged domestic troubles, both statements are creations of Herndon's imagination which he gave to another Lincoln biographer as facts.

Herndon's evidence against Mrs. Lincoln is either theory generated in his mind, or town gossip passed from tongue to tongue through many years, both slanted in presentation to create the worst possible impression of Mrs. Lincoln before the jury of the public. Mary Lincoln has been "framed" for the purpose of proving his theory that the Lincoln marriage was unhappy.

chapter 11

IN-LAW PROBLEMS

Taking up the narrative from the point where Mary was visiting in Lexington in the early summer of 1848 and planning to return to Washington to rejoin Lincoln, we find the record somewhat vague as to her next movements. Lincoln made some speeches in New England in September that year, and Mrs. Lincoln wrote many years later that she and her children were with him there and that Eddie had an illness on their journey. Details of this are missing, but there is ample record of Lincoln's activities and speeches. Mary had the pleasure of reading much about her husband in the newspapers, and one doubts whether, if it caught her eye, she appreciated this comment in the *Boston Daily Atlas* on September 22: "Mr. Lincoln . . . is a capital specimen of a 'Sucker' Whig, six feet at least in his stockings, and every way worthy to represent that Spartan band of the only Whig district in poor benighted Illinois." She was to become very sensitive to the idea that they came from a crude part of the country and had no *savoir-faire*.

Absence of record as to Mary's presence in New England may indicate that she and the boys joined Lincoln at some point on the journey. At all events, they were with him at Buffalo, New York, when he took passage on the steamer *Globe* for Chicago. They evidently visited Niagara Falls together, and both Mary and her husband left record of being deeply impressed. A refreshing thing about the Lincolns is their responsiveness, their unspoiled enjoyment of travel. Many years later Mary, writing her grandnephew and rejoicing, with that sympathy in the pleasure of the young which she never lost, that he was to visit the White Mountains, Lake George, and Niagara Falls, said: "I have visited all these places & have always returned to Niagara with renewed interest."

Niagara Falls stirred long philosophical thoughts in Lincoln which he recorded in notes, apparently with a lecture in mind. The vastness of the amount of water and its irresistible force as it poured over the falls was overwhelming to him. Then he reflected upon the miracle of nature by which an equal amount of water was being constantly and quietly lifted up by the sun to be rained down upon the earth again. He looked back over the long sweep of history. "When Columbus first sought this continent—when Christ suffered on the cross—when Moses led Israel through the Red Sea—nay, even, when Adam first came from the hand of his Maker—then, as now, Niagara was roaring here."

Apropos of Niagara, David Donald, Herndon's biographer, relates a story showing how Lincoln sometimes humorously punctured the ebullience of his junior partner. When Herndon after a visit to the Falls expatiated grandiloquently on the Beautiful, the Grand, the Sublime, and asked the senior partner how he felt on seeing the great spectacle, Lincoln said dryly, "The thing that struck me . . . was, where in the world did all that water come from?" As Mr. Donald remarks, "What made it so funny was that Herndon did not know it was a joke. Thirty years later he chronicled that remark as proof that Lincoln did not appreciate nature."

On October 6, Lincoln was in Chicago making a two-hour speech at a Whig rally which was described in the *Daily Journal* as "one of the very best we have heard or read, since the opening of the campaign." On October 10 "Hon. Abraham Lincoln," looking "remarkably well," arrived with his family in Springfield. Since their house was rented, this may be the occasion when, according to an old-timer's recollection, they stayed temporarily at the Globe Tavern. The Tavern had its memories for them. One wonders whether they had again that room in which they lived the first year of their marriage.

A lady who was boarding there at the time later recalled Congressman Lincoln "going up and down the hotel dining room shaking hands with everyone," and how kind he was "about bringing up wood to the ladies' bedrooms." She also mentioned that Lincoln left his family at the Globe Hotel when he returned to Washington. It was as late as May 9, 1849, that Lincoln acknowledged, on the back of C. Ludlum's rent note, the receipt of full payment for the rental of his house. It was a sensible arrangement which relieved Mary of household drudgery and the terror of staying in a house alone at night. The deeper one gets into the story of their married life, the more apparent it is how Lincoln sought to protect his wife from strain and overwork. He left for the East the latter part of November 1848, and did not return until March 31, 1849. During this short session he was not at Mrs. Sprigg's but stayed elsewhere. We catch a glimpse of him attending President Taylor's inauguration ball with a group of friends and characteristically losing his hat, so that he walked back to his lodgings bareheaded at four o'clock in the morning.

In 1849 the Lincolns had a chance to move West. Lincoln in September wrote to John Addison: "I can not but be grateful to you and all other friends who have interested themselves in having the governorship of Oregon offered to me; but on as much reflection as I have had time to give the subject, I cannot consent to accept it." According to Herndon, it was Mrs. Lincoln who "put her foot squarely down on it with a firm and emphatic No." That is probably just what happened and the country can well be grateful to her, for she saved him thereby for the Presidency. The political wisdom of remaining in Illinois was a factor which she undoubtedly recognized and it is easy to understand why the prospect of leaving her home, her relatives and friends, and going into a remote, undeveloped part of the country to raise her children did not appeal to her.

Mary had nothing in common with untutored people in a primitive community and this brings up a problem that was always in the background of the Lincoln marriage, the question of in-laws. Lincoln's trouble was that his in-laws were too aristocratic; Mary's that hers were too poor and uneducated. Several letters of engaging illiteracy from Coles County, Illinois, show what a drag Lincoln's backwoods relations were to him and his wife, especially one who was really no blood kin. When Lincoln's beloved stepmother, Sarah Bush Johnston, married his father she brought with her to the Lincoln cabin her children by her former marriage, thereby bestowing upon Lincoln a stepbrother and two stepsisters.

In December 1848 Lincoln received a letter from his father (in the handwriting of his stepbrother, John D. Johnston), informing "Dear Son" that "I and the Old woman is in the best of health." In the good old-fashioned manner, Thomas Lincoln canvassed the physical condition of everyone concerned, including all the relatives, and then got down to business: "I was gratly in hopes that you would have Came a past hur on your way to Washington as I wished to see you, but as you failed to Come a past, I am Compeled to make a request by Letter to you for the Lone of, Twenty Dollars, which Sum I am Compeled to rayes, or my Land will be sold." There follow the details of a pitiful story; he thought the debt was paid but had "Lost the recpt if we ever had won," and was reluctantly making this request. "I am in hopes I will be able to make you requempence for all of your favours, I sopous it would be of Sattisfaction to you now [to know] how I have Disposed of them Notes you gave me."

On the same page Lincoln's stepbrother John D. Johnston wrote his own appeal for money, giving the details of his hard-luck story with a fluency that was unhampered by his illiteracy. He owed "80 Dollars in Small dribes" and was "Dund & Doged to Death." "Abe, I would drother Live on bread & wotter than to have men allways Duning me . . . & if you can send me 80 Dollars I am willing to pay you any Intrust you will ask & to make you Safe Father will make you a Deed for all of his Land when you come in the spring . . ." He managed to throw in a suggestion that Lincoln might just as well make it a hundred dollars with the land as security and he, Johnston, could then "goe to work, with Som hart, and not be a fraid of the Officer Taken the bread and meet out of my Childrens mouthes . . ."

On Christmas Eve Lincoln answered his father's request: "I very cheerfully send you the twenty dollars, which sum you say is necessary to save your land from sale." He cautioned his father to make sure he had not already paid the judgment, and ended the letter, "Give my love to Mother, and to all the connections. Affectionately your son."

To his stepbrother Lincoln wrote on the same page a kind but firm statement of facts: "Your request for eighty dollars I do not think it best to comply with now. At the various times when I have helped you a little, you have said to me, 'We can get along very well now' but in a very short time I find you in the same difficulty again. Now this can only happen by some defect in your *conduct*. What that defect is, I think I know. You are not *lazy*, and still you *are* an *idler*. I doubt whether since I saw you,

you have done a good whole day's work, in any one day."

Lincoln suggests that his stepbrother get out of his habit of idleness and go to work for someone who will give him money for it. To encourage this, he offers: "... for every dollar you will, between this and the first of next May, get for your own labor ... I will then give you one other dollar." He sizes up Johnston's offer of a deed for exactly what it is worth: "You say if I furnish you the money you will deed me the land, and, if you dont pay the money back, you will deliver possession. Nonsense! If you cant live now *with* the land, how will you then live without it? You have always been [kind] to me, and I do not now mean to be unkind to you."

These pleas for help and the futility of improving the situation made a harassing problem to the Lincolns. They had to give money to the poor relations when they needed it themselves. Lincoln's letters refer frequently to their "poverty." Only Mary knew in how many places of the household finances that twenty dollars or that eighty dollars could be used. It doubtless irked her for her husband to have to have this drain. She knew that it was by his own hard unaided struggle that he had pulled himself out of that environment. Now that he was making something of himself, it did not seem fair that he had to help shiftless relatives who would not help themselves. We will find good evidence that Mary had a kind attitude toward Lincoln's father and stepmother, that she, like Lincoln himself, desired that they should not be in want; but she may well have felt that his stepbrother, who was no blood kin at all, had no claim on him.

When the Lincoln Papers were opened in 1947 another letter from John D. Johnston to Lincoln came to light. This was written in May 1849, and is a masterpiece of trying to work on Lincoln's feelings in order to get him to come to see them. Lincoln's father, according to this letter, was "yet a Live & that is all & he Craves to see you all the time & he wants you to come if you ar able to git hure, for you are his only Child that is of his own flush & blood." The letter ended: "... he wants me to tell your wife that he loves hure & wants hur to prepare to meet him at ower Savours feet."

One phrase in this letter had special significance years later. After Lincoln's death Herndon, starting as so often with a flimsy piece of gossip, worked on the theory that

Lincoln was not the son of Thomas Lincoln, but was illegitimate. When his insinuations about this began to get about, Mary's grief and humiliation were overwhelming. Like many of Herndon's theories, the suggestion that Lincoln was illegitimate has been proved completely false. Herndon himself wavered back and forth between belief and denial of the illegitimacy, but his insinuations got abroad. One does not know whether Mary read this Johnston letter when her husband received it in 1849, but the time came in the eighteen-seventies when she would have been glad to look upon the misspelled phrase "of his own flush & blood" which was even then, had she but known it, lying among her husband's papers that were being fortunately preserved.

The story of Lincoln's trials with his Coles County relatives and his patient efforts to help them would make a book in itself. Others of the clan, as we will see, were writing him illiterate, begging letters, airing their own special troubles. John D. Johnston was a typical example of the "big talker, little doer"; his fortunes went from bad to worse. His pitiful, crippled son, Tom Johnston, presented a sad and embarrassing problem to Lincoln when he visited Urbana in 1856. Tom was in the Urbana jail on the charge of stealing a watch. Lincoln, accompanied by his friend H. C. Whitney (who tells the story), secretly visited the boy, who at once "set up a hypocritical wailing, and thrust out toward us a very dirty Bible . . ." Lincoln had remarked to Whitney in deep sadness, "He is already under a charge of stealing a gun at Charleston, I shall do what I can for him in these two cases, but that's the last. After that, if he wants to be a thief, I shan't help him any more." Lincolnian skill and tact procured Tom's release in both cases, but Whitney remarked that he had never seen Lincoln look more sad.

Tom Johnston continued to be what he called "unluckey in this life." The Barrett Collection contains two letters written by him in a jail at "Springfield Ills" in 1868. He had been mixed up in a fight where a man was nearly killed, though, of course, it was his "freinds" who "don the work," and he was trying to get his relatives to bail him out. One of his lawyers was "Mr. Herindon."

It was from this same Tom Johnston that Herndon in 1865 received the following story (which Mr. Weik has put into good grammar): "Mr. Lincoln took a fancy to my younger brother also named Abraham; wanted him to come to Springfield, live at Lincoln's home, and go to school so as to get a fair start in the world; but when Mrs. Lincoln was consulted she objected so bitterly her husband was obliged to write to my brother and tell him the plan could not be carried out because of domestic opposition." The statement further adds that Lincoln offered to pay for the boy's books and the schooling he received at home.

With the testimony of a Tom Johnston coming through a William H. Herndon, one is glad to be able to check the story by the most reliable of all witnesses, Lincoln himself. In 1851 he wrote the boy's father: "As to Abram, I do not want him, *on my own account;* but I understand he wants to live with me so that he can go to school, and get a fair start in the world, which I very much wish him to have. When I reach home, if I can make it convenient to take, I will take him, provided there is no mistake between us as to the object and terms of my taking him." This rules out the idea that it was Lincoln's wish to have the boy live with him, because of taking a fancy to him.

There are those who will see Mary's point of view in objecting to the arrangement. How could she take a twelve-year-old boy into her home to teach her sons (whom she was at such pains to train in manners and speech) to say "hure," "you air" and "them notes." Not to mention bringing into the family circle a whole bill of goods of backwoods standards when Robert was at the impressionable age of eight. Abram was no blood kin of her husband, and by that time Mary had bitter reason to know the unreliability and shiftlessness of the boy's father, John D. Johnston. In that same month Lincoln was struggling with this slippery individual to keep him from selling the land upon which he lived (in which Lincoln's stepmother had an interest) in order to get cash to move on. Lincoln's words are plain and urgent: "Now I feel it my duty to have no hand in such a piece of foolery. I feel that it is so even on your own account, and particularly on Mother's account. . . . I write it in order, if possible, to get you to *face* the truth, which truth is, you are destitute because you have *idled* away all your time. Your thousand pretenses for not getting along better, are all nonsense—they deceive nobody but yourself. *Go to work* is the only cure for your case."

Lincoln had also in Coles County a blood cousin, Dennis Hanks, whose picturesque personality is as tangy as a whiff of campfire smoke. He was doubly connected, as he married Lincoln's stepsister Elizabeth Johnston. Dennis's daughter Amanda left a reminiscence as to Lincoln's visits to the relatives. She said he called his stepmother "Mammy," and always gave money to her and to his father when he came. (No wonder he was urged to visit often.) Amanda remembered that the Springfield lawyer arrived once with his trousers having a conspicuously patched posterior, and Dennis, with that whimsical and picturesque twist characteristic of the Hankses, called them "Abe's spectacle pants." Lincoln's coat being short for his tall figure, the patches below, where most needed, could well have suggested twin lenses. Amanda furnished a good scrap of description of Lincoln when in animated conversation, "his expressive face beaming forth its joy, now seeming almost to laugh outright in its grimaces of fun, and now as solemn and sorrowful as a tomb."

Another daughter of Dennis Hanks, Harriet, came to Springfield to live with the Lincolns in order that she might go to school. According to Herndon, this happened about the year 1853, but according to Weik, Harriet wrote that Bob was the only child the Lincolns had while she was with them, and he was old enough to "correct." By Weik's account Harriet stayed about a year and a half. Since Eddie was born in March 1846, Harriet's stay must have been approximately mid-1844 to the end of 1845 and she left when Mary was expecting another baby. Harriet's marriage in 1847 rules out Herndon's date.

We know the "object," as Lincoln called it, of Harriet's coming but not "the terms" of the arrangement, but it seems proper that she should have helped with household duties in return for her room and board and education. Conflict of interests was inherent in the situation; unmarried girls are normally intent upon their own interests, and Harriet's limited background would have made her view things very differently from Mrs. Lincoln. The main point is that this backwoods origin did not deter Mrs. Lincoln who had both a kind heart and a sense of duty, from permitting the girl to come in the first place, and to stay a year or so. Harriet undoubtedly had her difficulties with her cousin's wife. Mary had not experienced the limited environment from which the girl came, was nervous, and there was a lot of housework that had to be done. There are two sides to this question and Mary's has not been considered, while Harriet's has been slantingly stated by Herndon. In a letter to Weik many years later, after calling Mrs. Lincoln "haughty," "aristocratic," and "cold as a chunk of ice," Herndon said that she tried to "make a servant—a slave of Harriet." Of course he added that Harriet was a "lady," and "a better woman than Mrs. Lincoln." He was not so complimentary, however, to Harriet's father, saying to Weik: "I am glad to know that your *eyes are open* about Dennis Hanks: he is a grand Exaggerator, if not a great liar." It should have meant much to Harriet that she lived in the home of the Lincolns. That she had the benefit of going to school is evident in a well-written letter she wrote to Herndon in 1866. It is in striking contrast to the misspelled scrawls of her father and the other Coles County relatives. She used this education to tell Herndon that "Mrs. Lincoln was very economical So much so that *by some she* might have been pronounced Stingy." On the same page she added that Mrs. Lincoln "loved to put on *Style*."

That economy and thrift may be accounted virtues seems to have been an idea frequently overlooked by some of the Coles County relatives. Mrs. Lincoln received no credit for working hard and stretching a limited income. Instead the interpretation has been that she economized in order to make a fine show in dress and entertainment. To take Harriet's account is to look through the eyes of a young backwoods girl who could not be expected to know the cost of bringing up a family by rules of genteel living, who would not realize that Lincoln's increasing prominence called for his wife's help to meet fittingly their social obligations. Whether an entertainment is "gracious hospitality" or "puttin' on style" depends upon the standards of the person describing it. Mrs. Lincoln had the best social ideals of the gentlewoman of her day.

In January 1851, when Lincoln's father was in his last illness, Lincoln wrote his stepbrother: "You already know I desire that neither father or Mother shall be in want of any comfort either in health or sickness while they live; and I feel sure you have not failed to use my name, if necessary, to procure a doctor, or any thing else for father in his present sickness."

Lincoln's love for his stepmother is well known. That he as a burdened President continued to look after her, as best he could at a distance, is shown by a letter which was found in the Lincoln Papers in 1947. This letter is from Harriet's father, Dennis Hanks, and the date is April 5, 1864. "Dere Abe," it reads, "I Received your Little Check for 50.00 I shoed it to mother [Lincoln's stepmother, Dennis's mother-in-law] She Cried Like a Child Abe She is Mity Childish heep of truble to us." This makes quite an appeal in spite of the amusing hint thrown out in the expression "Little Check," but the appeal turns into a question mark later when one uncovers a letter from another Coles County relative, John Hall, who wrote his "Dear Uncle" (Lincoln) in October of the same year: "I write to inform you that Grand Mother has not and does not receive one cent of the money you send her—Dennis & Chapman [Dennis's son-in-law] keep all the money you send her. I & my mother are now taking care of her and have for the last four years . . . he and Dennis had threatened to put her on the county."

There is one soft gleam in this pitiful record of poverty, old age, privations, and human failings. It appears in a letter which Augustus H. Chapman (who married Harriet) wrote Lincoln in 1858. Mentioning "Grand Mother," Chapman said: "I often take my Republican papers & read extracts from them that eulogise you & you can hardly form an idea how proud it makes her. She often says Abram was always her best child & that he always treated her like a son. I told her I was a going to write you to day & she says tell you she sends a heap of love to you . . ."

The Coles County relatives contributed to the sadness in Lincoln's eyes and the lines of patience around his mouth. They were also a continual humiliating problem to Mary, another exasperation which focused her mind upon that subject upon which she eventually became irrational—money. It was irritating to her to have her loved husband so imposed upon. "Father," she once said to him, "you should have been born a saint."

Herndon wrote Weik that if Lincoln's father and step-mother had ever come to Springfield, he doubted whether Mrs. Lincoln would have admitted them to the house. This was something in Herndon's mind; it will be well to examine what evidence there is on the subject. Mary named her youngest son for her husband's father. That father sent his love to her with the wish that he might meet her in heaven, as he apparently had not met her on earth. Later we find Lincoln's stepmother sending her "best & tenderest love" to Mary. This would seem to indicate that they had no reason to think of her in any but affectionate terms, but there is much more positive evidence of her attitude.

In 1867 we find Mary sending Lincoln's stepmother a box of clothing or the material therefor, and ten dollars. This was the year when Mary's son Robert wrote that his mother believed she was "in actual want and nothing I can do or say will convince her to the contrary." Dozens of letters written by her that year show she was in a constant panic over her limited finances, and her debts. She later referred to "*many dinnerless days*" around that time. Yet her sense of obligation to do something for the stepmother Lincoln had loved, to carry out his wishes, made her send money at a period when she was feverishly counting every penny.

She wrote Sarah Lincoln about the package on December 19, 1867. Distraught with grief over the loss of her husband, she poured out her feelings to one who was also grieving. "In memory of the dearly loved one, who always remembered you with so much affection, will you not do me the favor of accepting these few trifles?" she said. "In my great agony of mind, I cannot trust myself to write about, what so entirely fills my thoughts, my darling husband; knowing how well you loved him also, is a grateful satisfaction to me." Characteristically she longed to do something for the woman who had meant much to Lincoln. "Believe me, dear Madam, if I can ever be of any service to you, in *any respect*, I am entirely at your service."

Out of her understanding of a widow's feeling she continued: "My husband a few weeks before his death mentioned to me, that he intended *that* summer, paying proper respect to *his* father's grave, by a head & foot stone, with his name age & & and I propose very soon carrying out his intentions." She would not have her "loved one" thought lacking, so she added, "It was not from want of affection for his father, as you are well aware that it was not done, but *his* time was so greatly occupied always." She reminded Sarah "that our youngest boy, is named for your husband, Thomas Lincoln, this child, the idol of his father." The letter ended: "I am a deeply afflicted woman & hope you will pray for me . . . Affectionately yours, Mary Lincoln." Realizing she had laid open her heart, a feeling of reticence caused her to add a postscript: "This letter please consider entirely private—I shall be greatly pleased to hear from you."

She mentioned in this letter her wish to know when the package arrived. Evidently the matter was on her mind for the next day she wrote Sarah Lincoln a specific request for an acknowledgment. It is a businesslike note, as it was evidently intended to be, enclosing the express receipt; it was signed "Mrs. Lincoln." Many people, acquainted with this document, which has been published, and not knowing of the warmly affectionate letter which preceded it, have taken it to indicate a cold and haughty attitude on Mary's part toward Lincoln's stepmother. Even this note included an additional thoughtful gift; enclosed was also "ten dollars which please accept for the making of the dress &c &c." In view of John Hall's letter to Lincoln saying that things intended for the stepmother sometimes went into other hands, Mary's anxiety to know "whether the box, money &c &c has been received" is understandable.

Mary differed from the backwoods connections of her husband as much as the flowing script and literary finish of her letters differ from their illiterate scrawls. She saw little of them, but, against an idea in Herndon's mind, there is concrete evidence that she tried to fulfill her duty to her husband's less fortunate kinfolk. She had a conscience and fundamental standards of obligations to family and blood relations. The evidence indicates that her attitude was about the same as Lincoln's, to whom the welfare of father and stepmother was of deep concern. Indeed there is no record that Mary ever said anything as blunt as what Lincoln wrote his stepbrother when his father was ill: "Say to him that if we could meet now, it is doubtful whether it would not be more painful than pleasant . . ." Mary's tender letter to the one that Lincoln called "Mammy" has no hint whatever of difference between them; it is all affectionate consideration.

In the next chapter and later in the story will be found episodes in which Lincoln, in his turn, had serious in-law trouble with his wife's relatives.

chapter 12

"LITTLE EDDIE"

Around the middle of the century dark events were gathering for the Lincolns. There is an old saying that deaths
come in threes; this was to prove the case for them. Mary's
father, for whom she had named her first-born, died July
16, 1849, apparently of the dreaded plague cholera which
was then epidemic in Lexington. When one of the turbu-
lent Todd sons (George) objected to the probate of the
will, Lincoln was selected to represent the interests of the
four heirs in Springfield: Mrs. Ninian W. Edwards, Mrs.
William Wallace, Mrs. Clark M. Smith, and Mary Lincoln.
The fact that Robert S. Todd also left a lawsuit in progress
was an added reason for Lincoln's going to Lexington.

In October the Lincoln family of four started the complicated journey. There was gaiety on the boat going down
the Mississippi. A fellow passenger who had played several
pranks was punished by a mock arrest and trial. Lincoln
was the perfect choice to serve as judge. His playfulness
and sense of drama would have made him enter into the
role with a pseudo gravity which would accent every humorous twist of the situation. Then when they were cruis-
ing up the Ohio, there developed the supreme thrill of
steamboat days, a race with another boat. Lincoln's boat
at this critical time ran short of fuel, but fortunately managed to hitch on to a flatboat of wood. That wood must
be gotten aboard quickly; Lincoln jumped down, shouted
"Come on boys," and pitched wood with great enthusiasm. One can imagine Mary and the little boys on deck
cheering, but alas, the noble effort was wasted; with jeers
and laughter the other boat passed them to victory.

At Lexington there was the freshening of family ties,
with sound legal advice about litigation, visitings and gos-
sipings. Again Lincoln had opportunity to look on that
sight which was a "continual torment" to him, slavery. It
was early in November before they started the eight-day
journey back to Springfield, where mail and various matters had piled up for attention.

In January 1850 Grandmother Parker died, Mary's mother's mother, whose stately brick dwelling stood next door to the house where Mary had been born, their yards adjoining. Her presence had played a large part in Mary's early years. Grandmother Parker, like stepgrandmother Humphreys, arranged for the freeing of her slaves in her will, and even provided an annuity for one of them. Here one detects another emancipation influence in Mary's early life.

It was the second breaking of a fundamental tie within seven months. Death to Mary from that time on was not the vague, far-off thing viewed by youth; its visitation had taken an air of family reality, its menace a present focus. There was greater anxiety when the children became sick. It was an age when life expectancy was far below that of the present, when infant mortality was shockingly high, when germs, infections, and epidemics raged unchecked. Knowledge of medicine and sanitation, as it was then, seems unbelievably primitive to us now.

Mary did her best to guard the health of her husband and children. In the old charge accounts of the Lincolns with the drugstore Corneau & Diller, there are numerous entries such as "Castor Oil," "Calomel," "Box Ox Marrow," and "3 sticks Cough Candy," the last probably more popular with the little boys than the other items. One ounce "Syrup Ipecac," followed by the purchase of another ounce a week later, suggests harrowing scenes in the household. One "Bottle Vermifuge" shows that Mary was taking no chances on her children's having worms, though from their point of view the malady was probably preferable to the nasty-tasting medicine. The Lincoln boys were dosed in the good, old-fashioned way.

It was a helpless way when little Eddie was struck down with illness in December 1849. The news about Grandmother Parker reached the Lincolns when they were torn with anxiety for their youngset child. It added to their depression. Did Mary know the old superstition about three deaths in a row? There was no question of hospitals and nurses then; the father and mother themselves watched day and night over their ailing child, wishing, as parents always do, that they could take his suffering upon themselves, fluctuating between hope and despair. Mary was a tender and devoted nurse, but her nervousness and inability to control her emotions were against her. For-

tunately this was a time of year when Lincoln was normally in Springfield. The long illness dragged on for
fifty-two exhausting days; then on the morning of February 1, 1850, the innocent eyes that had brightened at the
mere mention of his father's name, closed in endless sleep.

Neighbors, doubtless, as was the custom, sat up all
night beside the still little body. There was a harsh intimacy with the dead at the time. Even as late as 1881 a
young girl in Cairo, Illinois, recorded in her diary how she
sat up with a dead child, changing wrung-out cloths on the
face and hands.

There was heard in the house the sound of Mary's weeping; she was never to learn how to hold back tears. She
had not known that life could be so cruel. The reminiscence of a neighbor tells how she lay prostrated, stunned,
turning away from food, completely unable to meet this
disaster. Her haggard husband, himself sunk in the deep
melancholia which death always produced in him, bent
over her, pleading, "Eat, Mary, for we must live." In the
end it was doubtless the wife's response to her husband's
need of her, and his response to her need for him, and the
need of Bobbie for both, that enabled them to pull them-
sleves together and take up normal life again.

In the Illinois *Journal* for February 7, 1850, appeared
"By Request" a four-stanza poem called "Little Eddie." It
is unsigned. Did either of those poetry-loving parents have
a part in writing it, finding an outlet thus for their love
and grief? Its poetic style is that of the middle eighteen-
hundreds, but the heartache in it is universal through the
ages to all who have lost a beloved child.

> *The silken waves of his glossy hair*
> *Lie still over his marble brow . . .*

> . . . . . .

> *Angel boy—fare thee well, farewell*
> *Sweet Eddie, we bid thee adieu!*

> . . . . . .

> *Bright is the home to him now given,*
> *For "of such is the kingdom of Heaven."*

Who wrote the verses is a matter of conjecture, but
one can safely guess whose tears fell on the printed page.

* * *

What is the best way for a couple to recover from the sorrow of losing a child? The answer might well be: take a trip for a change of scene, and look forward to having another baby. This is what the Lincolns did. Mr. Townsend, the authority on Mr. and Mrs. Lincoln in Lexington, Kentucky, tells how the little family of three came to that town in its early springtime, and saw "the Blue Grass country in its fairest aspects." The settlement of Grandmother Parker's estate gave an added reason for the journey. The Todd family in Lexington, like Mary herself, needed Lincoln's calm, balanced judgment. Settling any legal matters which involved the contentious and hotheaded sons of Robert S. Todd was apt to run into a lawsuit. This litigiousness was later to put Lincoln in a very harassing position.

Just as Mary had in-law problems, so did her husband. Mary's brother Levi was responsible for what Mr. Townsend calls "doubtless the most vexatious experience in all the years of his [Lincoln's] law practise." Prompted by Levi Todd, the surviving partners of Robert S. Todd's old firm, Oldham & Hemingway, brought suit against Lincoln in May 1853, alleging that he had collected certain debts in Illinois for that firm and appropriated the money for his own use. This astounding news reached Ninian W. Edwards at Springfield when Lincoln was out on the circuit. If Ninian told Mary, one can imagine her indignation and her agonizing anxiety to talk to her husband, find out what was involved, and know how he would meet this accusation. At the time the suit was brought, an attachment was also levied on about seven hundred dollars belonging to Lincoln and Mary.

Two weeks passed before Lincoln learned of the suit. From Danville, Illinois, he wrote his emphatic denial of the allegations, and enclosed it in a letter to his Lexington lawyer, George B. Kinkead. The suit was an attack on his integrity. Such an attack would injure him politically, a fact probably not overlooked by Levi Todd, for this seems to have been a "spite suit." Mr. Townsend points out that several weeks prior to the suit against Lincoln, he and Ninian W. Edwards had sued Levi (who was a problem individual in the full sense of the word), though the record as to the nature of the action against Levi is missing.

Lincoln was thoroughly aroused when the news reached him at Danville. He wrote his Lexington lawyer: "I find it difficult to suppress my indignation towards those who have got up this claim against me— . . . if they will name any living accessible man, as one of whom I have received their money, I will *by that man* disprove the charge." His answer to the accusation, properly sworn to and enclosed in this letter, is a model of clear legal statement. He explained that the only money he had ever collected for Robert S. Todd was fifty dollars on an old account which his father-in-law had turned over to him, telling him to keep what he could get out of it. It was another token of the wish of Mary's father to help the Lincolns financially. "With the exception of the fifty dollars aforesaid," ran Lincoln's answer, "received by Respondent under the circumstances aforesaid, Respondent denies that he ever received anything whatever, to which said firm, or said petitioners could have a pretense of a claim."

Lincoln had to attend court in Danville before going home, so Mary had additional days to worry over the matter without his reasurring presence.

The firm of Oldham & Hemingway did not try the case assigned for trial at the June term of court. Mr. Townsend says that a motion to dismiss for want of prosecution would have been sustained by the court, but Lincoln did not wish to get out by way of a technicality in a case where his personal integrity had been questioned. The plaintiffs were compelled to file the names of the persons whose accounts the defendant was charged with having collected, then Lincoln obtained from those persons depositions completely refuting every allegation made against him. The plaintiffs, realizing they were beaten, themselves filed a motion to dismiss the case, which was done on February 10, 1854, and one is happy to add that they had to pay the costs. But who can estimate the cost of long-drawn-out anxiety, outraged indignation, and fear of the wrong outcome with adverse effect on Lincoln's career, which was paid by Mary and her husband?

According to Mr. Townsend, Lincoln on the visit after Eddie's death found in the Todd library a thick volume called *The Christian's Defense*. He was especially interested when his eyes caught the name of the author, Dr. James Smith, as he was the understanding pastor of the

First Presbyterian Church at Springfield who had conducted the funeral services of little Eddie.

Mary had grown up, as might be expected of one with Scotch ancestors, a Presbyterian, but when she joined her sister's household in Springfield, she naturally attended the Episcopal Church, to which Mrs. Edwards belonged. This she continued to do after her marriage. But Dr. Smith spoke at Eddie's burial, and it was a message that apparently brought some measure of comfort to the parents. With Lincoln liking Dr. Smith and becoming interested in his views, Mary, when she returned from Lexington, began to attend the First Presbyterian Church.

One has no written word from her to prove that she felt distressed because her husband was not a church member. Her letters show that her religious faith was basic with her; one infers that she wanted Lincoln to share in all the fundamentals of her life. It is possible that one of her great objections to Herndon as Lincoln's law partner was that he was an unbeliever and talked so much about it. The impression has come down among some of her relatives that it was because she hoped Lincoln would join Dr. Smith's church with her that she began to attend it after Eddie's death. In 1852 we find her becoming a member of Dr. Smith's congregation. Lincoln did not join with her in formal membership, but he paid rent on the pew and attended church with her. They occupied that narrow pew for about ten years and Mary, when she went to Washington, was homesick for it and its comforting associations.

Dr. Smith's book, which examined the objections urged by infidels against the Bible and answered these objections point by point, had interested Lincoln deeply. In his growing years he had had such questionings himself, as young men who try to reason things out sometimes do. He had sought Dr. Smith out on his return from Lexington to talk over his questionings and deep depression, and a lasting friendship resulted. Henceforth Dr. Smith stood in the close relation of the pastor who, to use his own words, "buried their dead and baptised their living . . . and . . . is admitted to their full confidence." He was the welcome neighbor who dropped in at least twice a month, to "spend a pleasant evening in the midst of that family circle." Out of this intimacy he later described the Lincolns: he spoke of Mary's "intelligence, her fine conversational powers and capability at making herself very agreeable in any circle";

he noted that the husband gave his wife "a heart overflowing with love and affection." Dr. Smith must be remembered; he is to come into the story later at a time when Mary sorely needed him.

He and Lincoln would have long conversations when the latter came to see him or when they drove together over the prairies. Religion, as Lincoln had known it in the backwoods, was often a matter of feeling only, a revival or funeral, an orgy of emotionalism. Dr. Smith, who could write a book on the Christian's defense, could put religion on an intellectual basis without loss of faith. He could understand religious questioning that in primitive communities would have been merely denounced as infidelism. And he came into Lincoln's life at a time when his spirit was sensitized by a deep personal sorrow. It is not strange to find that Lincoln's views underwent a change after Eddie's death.

Lincoln's spiritual attitude, like his statesmanship, went through a process of growth and ripening. It is a coincidence that in the very spring of 1850, when he was pondering questions of mortality and faith, there was published in England a poem which gave expression to this common experience among young and thoughtful people. The poet Tennyson was also grieving with profound melancholy over the death of one he had deeply loved when he wrote:

> *He fought his doubts and gather'd strength,*
> *He would not make his judgment blind,*
> *He faced the spectres of the mind*
> *And laid them: thus he came at length*
>
> *To find a stronger faith his own . . .*

Eleven years later Mary could not talk of the dead child without bitter tears. Eddie's brief record is compassed by a chance reference or two: the love in his eyes for his father, his baby words "gone tapila," his tenderness over a homeless kitten. Yet his death was marked by a milestone in that father's spiritual gropings, and a scar that never quite healed in his mother's heart. At the poignant moment when Lincoln said good-by to Springfield as he left to assume the highest office in the land, he remembered that little grave.

chapter 13

"GOOD NEIGHBORS"

Lincoln returned to Springfield from Lexington ahead of Mary; he could not afford financially to be away too long from his business of making a living. Mary lingered in Lexington for a more extended visit but it was not long before they were settled again in the home that was lonely for the sound of a little boy's voice. Yet they had each other, seven-year-old Robert, and the birth of another baby in prospect for December. In February it had been nearly four years since Eddie was born, but about two months after his death Mary again became pregnant.

William Wallace Lincoln arrived December 21, 1850. Holidays and anniversaries always meant much to Mary and it was well that when December 25 came there was a new baby in her arms to ease her aching sense of loss when she remembered Eddie's presence at the last Christmas.

The newborn was named for Dr. William Wallace, Mary's brother-in-law, husband of her sister Frances. As a physician, eyeing Lincoln's thinness and knowing how widespread tuberculosis was in that day, he had warned Mary to watch over her husband's health. This she could and did do when he was at home, but it was a source of added worry to her when he was exposed to the rigors of life on the circuit.

Little Willie proved to be a beautifully endowed child who inherited his father's qualities and personality. It was not strange that he was to become his mother's favorite. Coming as he did after the loss of Eddie, having this calm, lovable, thoughtful nature, he was soon an object of complete adoration to both his parents.

As to Mary's slow recovery from this confinement there is a sidelight in a letter Lincoln wrote January 12, 1851, twenty-two days later. It was in answer to one from John D. Johnston, Lincoln's stepbrother, urging him to come to Coles County as Lincoln's father was ill. Lincoln replied:

"My business is such that I could hardly leave home now, if it was not, as it is, that my own wife is sick-abed." Lincoln, as has been seen, directed that everything possible be done for his father and promised to pay for it, but he did not leave Mary, still weak and nervous from her ordeal. We have already seen her own testimony as to his watching over her with loving care when she was ill.

On April 4, 1853, the fourth and last child was born. Mary and Lincoln, with their unlimited parental love, both left clues that lead one to guess they had hoped this baby would be a girl. "I regret the necessity of saying I have no daughters," wrote Lincoln in 1860, and Mrs. Lincoln said tenderly to sixteen-year-old Julia Taft in the White House, more than once, "I wish I had a little girl like you, Julia." How she would have delighted in making dainty dresses and curling the hair of a little daughter. Mary's world was fundamentally a feminine one.

Her love of little girls appears in the recollections of another Julia, the daughter of a dear neighbor, Mrs. John C. Sprigg, whom Tad with his appealing lisp called "Mith Spwigg." Julia Isabelle Sprigg when a small lass packed her tiny white ruffled muslin nightgown for the adventure of spending a night away from home with Mrs. Lincoln, whose husband was out of town. Julia was delighted because she had a good time when she was with Mrs. Lincoln; ". . . she was the kind of a woman that children liked, and children would be attracted to her." Mrs. Lincoln almost smothered her small guest with maternal affection and, in her eagerness to take good care of her, also smothered her with too many blankets. Perhaps for that one night Mary Lincoln made believe that she had a daughter.

Whether they wanted a girl or not, what arrived was a son. "Dear little Taddie was named, for my husband's father, Thomas Lincoln . . . was nicknamed Taddie by his loving Father," wrote Mary many years later. In contrast to an idea in Herndon's mind that Mrs. Lincoln would not have admitted her father-in-law to her home, is the established fact that she honored him by naming her son for him. The infant's head was larger than usual, so that his father, viewing the top-heavy baby figure, playfully called him a little tadpole and from this tiny incident, as so often, arose a nickname that lasted a lifetime.

That large head may account for the injury his little

mother received at his birth. Such injuries were not repaired or even talked of then; it was with great reluctance that Mrs. Lincoln mentioned it years later in a letter to an intimate friend. Sitting up for the first time in three weeks, she wrote: "I have been seriously sick. (My disease is of a womanly nature, which you will understand has been) greatly accelerated by the last three years of mental suffering. Since the birth of my youngest son, for about twelve years I have been more or less a sufferer." With true Victorian reticence, she crossed out the words in parentheses, doing such a thorough job that one can read them only with great difficulty. There are a few other veiled references to troubles "of a womanly nature" in her letters, but for the most part little is known of the effect of this injury on Mary's health or its relation to her extreme nervousness. Her husband knew of it, of course. If one could only have what was in Lincoln's mind when he would say at her hysterical scenes, "Mrs. Lincoln is not well," it might contribute to a more balanced understanding of her.

About the time Tad arrived, a son was also born to the Charles Dallman family, who lived a stone's throw from the Lincolns. Mrs. Dallman was very ill and unable to nurse her baby. Formulas were a thing of the future and babies in such cases usually died. Mary, secure in the joy of her own renewed motherhood, heard of her neighbor's trouble, and offered her help. Many years later when Mrs. Dallman was a dainty little old lady, she told the story of "how the tall, gaunt figure of Abraham Lincoln came across the street from the Lincoln Home, knocked at her door, entered with gentle step so as not to disturb the sick mother, and then gathered up the little mite of a new-born child into his big brawny hands, formed like a basket for that purpose and carried the infant across the street."

The tenderhearted woman whom Herndon called "cold as a chunk of ice" nursed her neighbor's baby at her breast along with her own child. The aged Mrs. Dallman "with tear-dimmed eyes" continued the story: "Soon he would return in that same eloquent silence with a tender expression of profound sympathy . . . as he deposited the little child in a cradle." The spotlight here is on Lincoln but after all it was Mary who furnished the essential nourishment.

The Dallman baby died in early childhood. The Lincolns knew only too well the agony of having the loved little body laid to rest in the earth, and the return to the empty home. They did what they could. Mary prepared food, making it as appetizing as possible with her best silver, placed it on a large tray, and Lincoln carried it to the sad parents.

It was a part of being a good neighbor in a day when neighborliness was vital. People were more dependent upon each other in those comparatively primitive days, and this interdependence led to a sharing of each other's troubles.

We have already met that excellent neighbor James Gourley, who lived so close that, as has been seen, Mrs. Lincoln could call him when she became frightened in the night. Herndon interviewed Mr. Gourley after Lincoln's death and jotted down in choppy fashion many things one is interested in knowing. Gourley tells how Lincoln "used to come to our house with slippers on—one suspender & old pair of pants—come for milk—our room was low & he said—Jim—you have to lift your loft a little higher. I can't stand in it well. He used to say to my wife that little people had some advantages: it did not take quite so much wood & wool to make their house and clothes."

Gourley observed how "Lincoln would take his children and would walk out on the Rail way out in the country— would talk to them—explain things carefully—particularly. He was kind—tender and affectionate to his children—very—very." Gourley also reported what he saw as he looked over into his neighbor's back yard: Lincoln "once for a year or so had a garden & worked in it: he kept his own horse—fed & curried it—fed and milked his own cow: he sawed his own wood generally when at home. He loved his horse well."

All through the record are scattered references to Lincoln's love of animals. Gourley mentions that the Lincolns kept cats, and we remember that Mary called cats her husband's "hobby." It was one of his relaxations to get down on the floor, to talk to and gently play with the current pet.

To Herndon's insinuating questions about the wife, Gourley replied: "I don't think that Mrs. Lincoln was as bad a woman as she is represented: she was a good friend of mine ... a good woman." He said husband and wife "got along" all right, except when Mrs. Lincoln had one of her hysterical seizures. Then Lincoln, if he could not laugh her out of it, took the children and left until she returned to her normal frame of mind.

From neighbor Gourley one learns Mary's resentment of Lincoln's prolonged absence on the judicial circuit. "She always said that if her husband had staid at home as he ought to that she could love him better." As usual Mary expressed herself in overemphatic language, but it is true that Lincoln spent more time on the circuit than the lawyer husbands of her friends.

In his old age Herndon wrote to Jesse Weik: "Lincoln would never come home while the court was grinding out justice on the circuit, to see his wife or family, while all the other lawyers, every Saturday night after court hours, would start for home to see wife & babes. Lincoln would see us start home and know that we were bound to see good wife and the children. Lincoln, poor soul, would grow terribly sad at the sight—as much as to say—'I have no wife and no home.'" This is a blatant case of working for tears on the jury. The "other lawyers" did not travel the whole circuit as Lincoln did; they could turn back toward home while Lincoln had to go on to more distant points from which it was impossible to get home in a short time. In the eighteen-forties travel was by horseback and buggy, and when the railroads began to play their part in the fifties, it was at first a lagging part. Paul Angle, studying a railroad map in 1854 and train schedules when the average speed was twenty miles an hour and connections poor, shows how frequently it was impossible for Lincoln to get home at the week end. When railroads had been extended until there were good connections between Springfield and all the county seats Lincoln visited, "Long absences from home," says Mr. Angle, "were things of the past."

Lincoln continued to make the rounds even in the later period of growth and development, when his own county was transferred to another circuit and when a Springfield lawyer would have enough business near home. The visiting of these county seats, with the opportunity to mingle with people and widen his acquaintance, meant much to him. We do not know at what period Mary made her complaint to Mr. Gourley or whether she qualified it. Her grievance could well have been that he rode the circuit more than other husbands did; his justification, that these contacts contributed to his political career. She needed his help with the children, especially when her headaches came, his calmness under emergencies when she lost her head, and above all she was lonely without him. This significant sentence slipped into a letter she wrote a dear friend: "I hope you may never feel as lonely as I sometimes do, surrounded by much that renders life desirable."

She also worried about him. She knew, out of her long care of him, he was as irresponsible as a child about dress. As late as 1859, Henry Villard met Lincoln on the prairie in an open buggy without top, clad in a short overcoat and without covering for his legs, all this on a bleak November day with a cutting wind out of the northwest. The young journalist offered a buffalo robe which was gratefully accepted, and the record continues: "He undertook, of course, to return it to me, but I never saw it again." Matters concerning clothes did not register with this absent-minded man.

The nervous woman had this worry as well as the responsibility of being both father and mother to the children. There was much to be said for her side of it and she doubtless said it.

The sum of James Gourley's testimony is that "Mrs & Mr Lincoln were good neighbors." That is the report from all sides. Reverend N. W. Miner, who moved to a house across the street in 1855, found Lincoln "delightful," and Mrs. Lincoln "a devoted wife, a loving mother, a kind neighbor and a sincere and devoted friend." When the preacher's house overflowed with visitors, as a preacher's house is apt to do, the Lincolns would help out by letting some of the visitors "put up" with them. Lincoln would at times lend the Reverend Mr. Miner his horse and carriage for church work.

Across Eighth Street lived the Solomon Wheelocks, whose teen-age daughter Ardelia was a favorite with the Lincolns. "Delie," as Lincoln called her, used to run in to help Mrs. Lincoln dress for parties. Getting arrayed in hoop skirt splendor apparently required assistance. Years later the Wheelock daughter told about the somewhat hectic evening the Lincolns attended a reception at the home of Jesse Dubois. Delie was helping Mrs. Lincoln dress when in came Tad and Willie from a candy pull, smeared with molasses candy from head to foot. They at once set up a lively howl because they wanted to go to the reception too. Mrs. Lincoln was firm that they should stay at home (with Robert as baby-sitter), but Mr. Lincoln could not stand the kicking and screaming; he told Mother if she would let the boys go, he would take care of them. Mrs. Lincoln pointed out that the reception was no place for the children, but the lawyer-husband countered that argument by saying he would take them in the back way and leave them in the kitchen. He won his case. Delie and Robert Lincoln quickly cleaned up the little boys and dressed them in such haste that Tad's little pants were put on backwards. At this Tad set up another howl, protesting, not unreasonably, that he "couldn't walk good." Of course the matter ended by the children attending the reception itself, where the dressed-up guests no doubt gave them, as Herndon once wrote in a similar case, "a wide birth." Willie and Tad were *"them* little devils" to Herndon and there were citizens of Springfield who were probably willing to concede something to this point of view, especially with regard to Tad. It may have been by a sort of premonition that the City Fathers, two years before Tad was born, drew up a special "Ordinance in relation to Boys," imposing penalties for such activities as exploding fire crackers, meddling with public pumps, and so on. But the imagination of the City Fathers in regard to pranks moved in slow motion compared with Tad's.

Delie Wheelock remembered being at the Lincolns' once when the family ate lunch in the kitchen and she was invited to join them. She described Lincoln as putting on a large apron and helping his wife with whatever needed to be done around the house.

Neighborliness sometimes took the form of looking after each other's children. One of the sons of Mr. Dubois remembered how he and other boys would play at the Lincoln home and the motherly sympathetic way Mrs. Lincoln would watch over them and give them cookies. When the Lincolns were out of town on one occasion Tad stayed at the Wheelocks'. It was the part of a good neighbor too that Lincoln, when he returned to town after a trip, would drop in to see Delie's grandfather, who was an invalid, and give him all the political chitchat of the day.

Mary Lincoln, when she went to Washington in 1861, wrote letters back to Springfield that testify to her love for her neighbors and her homesickness in retrospect for the sweetness of small-town life with its simplicity

and security. "You were always a good friend & dearly
have I loved you ... Will we ever meet, & talk together as
we have done," she wrote Mrs. Sprigg, the mother of little
Julia of the ruffled nightgown. Two months after reaching
Washington, Mary's thoughts turned to her trusted neighbor, Mrs. Samuel Melvin, whose boys had played with
hers so much that Lincoln, passing the Melvin house on
his way home from the office, was apt to stop and inquire,
"Are my boys here?" The Melvins had a back yard very desirable to boyish eyes and a kindly nurse who would watch
over the children. Mrs. Lincoln felt her boys were safe at
Mrs. Melvin's. The relationship between the mothers was
so close that when Mrs. Melvin was expecting a baby early
in 1861, it was understood that if the arrival were a girl,
she would be named for Mrs. Lincoln. The Lincolns were
giving a party the night before the baby was born; the next
morning Mrs. Lincoln sent over her centerpiece, "a large
pyramid of macaroons," by way of congratulation.

This is the background of the warm, affectionate, newsy
letter which the busy wife of the new President in 1861
wrote to her former neighbor whose "dear little sons" had
played with hers. "I take the liberty of enclosing some
photographs of the boys, also a little bonnet cap for my
sweet little namesake." There is further evidence in this
letter of wistful looking back: "I had intended requesting
Mr Melvin, to have given me a promise, that on our return to S—— we could be able to secure *our particular
pew,* to which I was very much attached, and which we occupied some ten years, may I hope that he will be able to
do so."

Mary Lincoln was a sincerely religious woman. She
loved that narrow little pew where she sat with her husband, surrounded by friends with whom, after the services
were over, she could exchange pleasant greetings and
items of personal views. It was a far cry from attending
church in Washington, stared at by crowds curious to see
the strange new President from the West.

One reminiscence pictures a neighborly scene in the
church at Springfield. Mr. Benjamin F. Fox had a pew just
across the aisle from the Lincolns. One Sunday in 1856 the
Lincolns observed that the Fox pew was resplendent with
new carpet and cushions, a mystery which was explained
when shortly therafter Mr. Fox brought his new bride to
church. When introductions took place, Mr. Lincoln re-

marked pleasantly to the newcomer that he wondered why Mr. Fox had been fixing up his pew so nicely, and now he knew. Mrs. Lincoln promptly suggested that Mr. Lincoln might do a little fixing up himself. Sure enough, it was not long before the Lincoln pew had a new carpet and cushions too. It doubtless needed them, but, on the other hand, Mary believed firmly in "keeping up with the Joneses."

Lincoln had a different point of view about this general question of keeping up with, or outshining one's neighbors. Once, when out on the circuit, he viewed a handsome residence, much superior to the houses around it, which was nearing completion. A friend commented on the impressiveness of the new home, and Lincoln replied, "Yes, it is a fine house, but I was thinking it isn't the best thing for a man in a town like Bloomington to build a house so much better than his neighbors."

A very dear friend of Mary's was Mrs. John Henry Shearer, who lived across the street from the Lincolns in the late fifties. She and Mrs. Shearer were both lively and quick-tempered and had occasional small fallings out, but those who understood Mary knew that her little flares were not deep-rooted; the two always made up and it was a lasting friendship, so affectionate that the son born to Dr. and Mrs. Shearer in October 1861 was named for Willie Lincoln by Mary's request. Mrs. Lincoln was in Washington when this baby was expected. In the complicated life of the White House, but with her truly fine quality of caring passionately about what happened to her friends, she took time to write Mrs. Shearer a long loving letter. She was impatient to hear that the ordeal was happily over: "Do write me, & tell me how you are coming in. You have so much more leisure, than I have, why do you not write? I want to hear, all about yourself— When *any thing* happens, make the Dr. write." She could not wait to hear about that baby.

As in most small towns, people in Springfield, Mary included, liked to gossip. One of her letters to Mrs. Shearer shows up Mrs. Lincoln's trait of using a sharp tongue against those who had offended her. In this letter she makes some femininely pointed remarks about *"that woman,"* who, fortunately perhaps, is not named. Mary would use stinging words one day and the next day, in forgiving mood, words of high praise for the very person she had derided. The bitter words would then be erased from her mind; what she did not realize was that the one who had been their target remembered. "Pass my imperfectations lightly by" is a recurring remark in her letters, but the instruction was not always followed. This trait of hers, one common to many individuals, was part of Mary's bundle of defects that, like the traditional peck of dirt, must be allowed to all fallible humans. Her neighbors all had their own special bundles of imperfections too. But words of appreciation and praise came as readily to Mary's lips as words of scorn.

An appealing letter with neighborly affection of a different sort was uncovered when the Lincoln Papers were opened in 1947, a letter William Florville, Lincoln's colored barber, sent to Washington late in 1863. "Billy the Barber" was unawed at the prospect of writing the President of the United States; he was writing only to a kindly friend whose sympathy for "the poor, and down troden of the Nation" he could count on. "I and my people feel grateful to you for it," he wrote. Of course Mr. Lincoln and the boys would want to know how things were at home. "Tell Taddy that his (and Willys) Dog is a live and Kicking doing well he stays mostly at John E Rolls with his Boys who are about the size now that Tad & Willy were when they left for Washington." Recalling doubtless the destructiveness of those two young irrepressibles, he reported on the house on Eighth Street and its tenants: "Your Residence here is kept in good order. Mr Tilton has no children to ruin things."

The neighbor boys (those young financiers who guarded the Lincoln home for five cents a night) left recollections that are like glimpses into the windows of that home. One of them, Howard M. Powel by name, attended school with Robert and reported that when the latter reached the stage where he began to study Latin, his father studied with him, going around the house declining Latin nouns as he did the chores of a paterfamilias. Howard also drove Mrs. Lincoln around for five cents an hour when the Lincolns in the fifties reached the point of "flourishing about in carriages."

Another small guardian and coachman in that decade, Joseph P. Kent, remembered how Willie resembled his father. "Will was the true picture of Mr Lincoln, in everyway, even carrying his head slightly inclined toward his left shoulder. (This Mr Lincoln always did while I knew him.)" Young Kent once asked Lincoln if he could borrow the carriage for his own use and Mr. Lincoln, smiling broadly, replied: "No Joseph there are two things I will not loan, my wife & my carriage." It was Joseph who, with several other small conspirators, hid behind a fence one dark night for the purpose of knocking off those irresistible targets, the tall hats of passing dignified gentlemen. Lincoln himself became a prize victim. Joseph summed up his impression of the family into which he entered so intimately: "Mr. Lincoln's home life was all happiness & content so far as I could ever know. He seemed to idolize his wife and boys and they, one and all sincerely loved him."

Albert Edwards, Mrs. Lincoln's nephew, who when a boy spent many Saturdays and Sundays at the Lincoln home, gave the same testimony. "I never saw a more loving couple," he said. During the days he spent with the Lincolns, he "never heard a harsh word or anything out of the way." Albert presented Lincoln as a "home man," going on Sunday downtown to get his mail, then returning to settle into the comfort of a quiet day of rest at home.

Lincoln seems to have assumed some of the duties of a Scoutmaster. He lived in a neighborhood well provided with boys, each family furnishing at least a couple of them, and the children all flocked to this lovable man who took so much interest in them. They understood, as one of them said, that when he "walked along with his hands behind him, gazing upward and noticing nobody," he was merely lost in thought and they had only to hail him to see the kind face light up with friendliness. He would sometimes gather up the boys of the neighborhood, put them in his "calash," a roomy kind of carriage, and take them out to the Sangamon for a day of fishing and picnicking. Years later one remembered that after lunch was eaten, "he told us stories and entertained us with his funny comments." It is pleasant to picture the tall kindly figure on the river's bank surrounded by the young boys of a century ago. There is also the theme for a painting in the account of Lincoln watching a circus parade on the streets of Springfield with a little girl in his arms, and his own boys, plus some of the neighbors', holding to his coattails.

With her husband away approximately half of the time, Mary often had occasion to turn to her neighbor James

Gourley for help. A woman's activities were restricted in those days and she felt the need of a man's assistance in carrying out certain business arrangements. Mr. Gourley told Herndon how he helped Mrs. Lincoln select a new carriage, "a fine one," and, when Lincoln returned, he "complained." This was a straw showing which way the wind was blowing. Mary loved handsome things and now that the early pinching days were over she could not restrain her impulses to buy them. But income was still irregular in the fifties and campaigning very expensive. After the Lincoln-Douglas debates, Lincoln wrote a friend in November 1858: "I am the poorest hand living to get others to pay. I have been on expenses so long without earning any thing that I am absolutely without money for even household purposes."

In the Lincoln marriage, as in many others, difference of viewpoint as to expenditures was a disturbing factor. Clothes, furnishings, and outward appearances did not matter to the husband, and they were extremely important to the wife. Her understanding of social obligations was an asset, but her gathering intensity about spending was a menace. In 1848 she had left Washington with some small unpaid debts. Now she was making expenditures of which her husband did not approve. These are items that show her increasing unreliability in money matters, a trait that was to grow, get out of bounds, and lead to distressing results.

Mr. Gourley's account continues, "While he [Lincoln] was gone—say in 1857—Mrs Lincoln & myself formed a conspiracy to take off the roof and raise the house." He was wrong about the date—he was speaking years later—and he can be checked against contemporary evidence; on April 3, 1856, Mrs. John Todd Stuart wrote her daughter that "Mr Lincoln has commenced raising his back building two stories high. I think they will have room enough before they are done, particularly as Mary seldom ever uses what she has." Mrs. Stuart used the name of the master of the house only by courtesy; it was Mrs. Lincoln who was doing it and it was apparently a surprise to Mr. Lincoln when he returned to find his house suddenly grown taller. With his usual humor, he inquired: "Stranger do you know where Lincoln lives he used to live here." But Mr. Gourley added significantly, "He scolded his wife for running him in debt." The cost of the improvement was $1300, and further changes in the house were made the following year which came to $200. It is possible Mrs. Lincoln paid for these improvements herself, as she had sold two years before the eighty-acre tract which her father had given her. But a difference of opinion between husband and wife is recorded; later it will be found that Mary concealed her financial transactions from her husband.

Mrs. Stuart's little dig, "Mary seldom ever uses what she has," possibly refers to the latter's economy in heating during the winters. Like many people before and since, she shut off certain rooms, and restricted living quarters to smaller dimensions to save fuel. One of her friends called upon Mrs. Lincoln on a winter's day and reported later that her hostess "had the fire lighted in the parlor and for a few moments it made a brave crackling, then died down, for it was nothing but chips and kindling, and they sat in the icy chill." Such an experience was apt to lead to later remarks about Mrs. Lincoln's "stinginess."

Old charge accounts show the buying of much wallpaper in 1856. In 1857, items like "36 yds. Buff Linen @ .25 per Lady," and "36 yds. cotton Damask" plainly indicate that Mary was making curtains, quite a task when sewing was done by hand. All in all the Lincoln home must have been thoroughly done over and made very attractive. Any woman knows the next step is to give a large party and let everybody see the fine improvements. Mr. Orville H. Browning recorded in his diary for February 5, 1857: "At night attended large & pleasant party at Lincoln's."

Mary supplied more of the particulars. On February 16 she wrote her sister with a certain air of feminine satisfaction: "I may perhaps surprise you when I mention that I am recovering from the slight fatigue of a very large & I really believe a very handsome & agreeable entertainment, at least our friends flatter us by saying so. About 500 hundred were invited, yet owing to an *unlucky* rain, 300 only favored us by their presence ... You will think, we have enlarged *our borders*, since you were here." The borders were undoubtedly enlarged but even so the house must have creaked at the seams, and it may have been just as well that a bridal party at Jacksonville "robbed us of some of our friends."

In a number of sources there is ample record of the Lincoln parties and small dinners, with "always on the part of both Mr. and Mrs. Lincoln, a cordial, hearty, western welcome, which put every guest perfectly at ease." Mary was in her best-loved element at these gatherings, busy, animated, and gay. As their friend Isaac N. Arnold said: ". . . it was the genial manner and ever kind welcome of the hostess, and the wit and humor, anecdote and un-rivalled conversation of the host, which formed the chief attraction, and made a dinner at Lincoln's . . . an event to be remembered." The Lincolns had fun when they enter-tained.

Mary wrote of a special and alluring kind of seasonal party. "For the last two weeks, we have had a continual round of *strawberry* parties," she said, and added, ". . . last week, we gave a strawberry company of about seventy . . ." This may have been mostly relatives, for we read else-where of "a little family gathering at Dr. Wallaces" which was "extended" to include fifty or sixty people. John Todd Stuart obligingly furnished further details as to these delectable occasions; he "was invited to come to cousin Anns [Ann Todd Smith] today *after church* to eat strawberries & ice cream. We had a fine dinner and plenty of cream & berries. Lincoln & Cousin Mary, Mother & my-self and Dr. Wallace were there."

These were the frivolous fifties and the letters of that decade bristle with parties. Springfield had come a long way from the raw little town of 1840. The "coterie" of gay young people then was replaced for the Lincolns in the fif-ties by a group of married friends and relatives. One can enter right into this Springfield society by aid of the de-lightful old-fashioned letters which Mary's cousins, the John Todd Stuarts, wrote their daughter Bettie when she was away at school. We meet some very likable people, men and women with warm personalities and high ideals, well educated and well bred. The letters are gossipy in a friendly way; they tell of the arrival of "little strangers," of the fun in large families, of visitors in town come to spend the winter, of bonnets and buggies, of calls where one "sat" for two or three hours, of protracted meetings in churches and baptizings, of public-spirited plans for a li-brary and the completion of a theater, ". . . just think of it a regular theatre where they play Othello, Hamlet etc!!" This object of pride was seventy-two by eighty feet and "brilliantly lighted with gas." There is no doubt that Mary and Mr. Lincoln were vitally interested in this; they both

delighted in plays and never missed a dramatic performance if they could help it. It was a shared congeniality that
gave them deep pleasure, another of the ways in which
they had fun together. Perhaps sometimes in that delicious
moment of anticipation when the lights were lowered for
the curtain, Mary slipped her hand into her husband's, as
she was to do one fateful night at Ford's Theater in Washington.

Springfield was beginning to put on grand airs. Mr.
Stuart told of one reception at the governor's for which
more than a thousand invitations were issued. It was
somewhat humiliating to have the cherished new gas illumination break down that evening, but candles were
hastily brought to the rescue. The next evening all the
children were invited to the governor's for a party of their
own, and they "danced or at least hopped around. John
[Stuart, Jr.] danced all evening *in his way*. Next day he
and Bob Lincoln were hunting up the dancing master."
Bob was growing up in more ways than in studying Latin.

Mr. Stuart with a twinkle described a typical entertainment which he and wife attended. "We press through the
crowd. We push and they push. We tread on their toes and
they tread on ours." He described how sweat rolled down
judicial foreheads that would rather argue a case in the
Supreme Court than struggle thus. "All the world is here.
All the sewing societies broke loose." "Cousins Mary Lincoln, Lizzie Edwards and Mrs. B. S. Edwards" were among
those who consumed "oyster sallad &c, then ice cream and
cake." (The digestive sequel was not revealed.)

"Cousin John" also described to his daughter a scene at
"Cousin Lizzie's" which seems like a flash back to the time
some sixteen years before when Mary as a girl was living
there. He and "Mother," as he called his wife, went to tea
at the Edwards mansion. "We heard . . . a great deal of
talk about love and beaux etc etc. And it seemed to me
that the girls heads were pretty full of such matters . . ."
This delightful father continued: "Don't it seem ridiculous! Now Bet. I hope you won't get any fool notions in your
head and for fear that you should I would advise if you
should see a nice young man any where even in church
just turn away your eyes, and if you cannot do any better
just *shut them* tight."

Such were the people among whom the Lincolns moved,
and such were their festivities. We can picture Mary and

her husband as we do our great-grandparents, an old-fashioned couple, dressed in heavy antiquated clothes, used to going in double harness, quietly understanding each other and the business of life, having with their neighbors in a century-past setting their hours of friendly sociability and laughter.

The fifties were good years for the Lincolns, a rich part of the happiest stage in life for them. These small-town gatherings were happy events and most of the friends and relatives they met at them were good and lovable people. They understood how "to neighbor," to use that verb in its finest meaning of mutual interest, helpfulness, and affection. Lincoln was to give immortal expression to the tugging at his heart when the time came to tell these old friends good-by.

chapter 14

"FIZZLE-GIGS AND FIRE-WORKS"

For several years after Lincoln's term in Congress, there was little to bolster Mary's gay assertion that she would be the wife of a President. Lincoln's greatest desire in 1849 was to be appointed commissioner of the general land office, a position that would have done little for his larger political ambitions. But how he wanted it! He wrote innumerable letters in his efforts to get the appointment, just how many was not known until the Lincoln Papers were opened in 1947. In one case when he was hurried in his letter-writing appeals because he was soon to leave for Washington, Mary, like a helpful wife, made a copy of the required letter to be sent to an additional friend and signed his name. They were disappointed, however; another man got the appointment.

For the next several years Lincoln quietly devoted himself to the practice of law. But by 1854 the political scene was changing. The country was being divided by the question of slavery with the focus on slavery in the territories. Lincoln, with his inborn love of politics and his deep feeling on the problems of the nation, could not possibly have refrained from getting into the game.

Early in 1855 a new senator was to be chosen by the Illinois legislature and, getting back into the swing of politics, Lincoln ardently hoped he might be elected to that office. "I have really got it into my head to try to be United States senator," he wrote his friend Joseph Gillespie on December 1, 1854. That fall he had been making speeches and conducting a vigorous campaign in what he afterwards described as an "agony" of political maneuvering. His letters show he was soliciting all the aid he could get while finding it necessary to define his position at a time when it was very difficult to do so.

His rival was Lyman Trumbull, a member of the young "coterie," now the husband of the same Julia Jayne who had conspired with Mary in writing one of the "Rebecca" letters. Wishful thinking, exasperations at the ups and downs (and sometimes double-dealing) encountered in campaigning, hopes and fears at fever heat were in the Lincoln home.

There was the presence of a loved visitor in that house when the year 1854 closed. Emilie Todd had come to town in December to visit her four married sisters who lived in Springfield. "Little Sister," who had been a beautiful child, had grown into a lovely girl of eighteen. Her six months' visit was marked by an epidemic of parties. Keenly intelligent and levelheaded, as well as spirited and handsome, Emilie observed shrewdly what she saw then, as later in the White House. Her account is one of the best sources for the home life of the Lincolns. She saw them continually for six months in Springfield but saw no trace of unhappiness between them.

Instead she noted the look of pride in Lincoln's eyes as they rested on his comely little wife, sprightly in motion and speech; and how that wife took pains to dress prettily and sparkle to bring that look to her husband's eyes. She noticed how Mary would watch for him when it was time for him to come home, and how she would sometimes meet him at the gate to slip her hand into his, and how, swinging their joined hands, they would come in the front door together. Emilie remembered the contrast between the dainty white hand of the wife and the big bony brown hand whose rugged contours are preserved today in the Volk cast. She heard Mary telling Mr. Lincoln the substance of the books she had read, and noticed how he discussed live topics and talked over his plans with her. The husband himself gave a glimpse of her love of reading when, in a letter acknowledging the receipt of certain books, he wrote: ". . . my wife got hold of the volume I took home, read it half through last night, and is greatly interested in it." For her literary interest Mary was probably called by some people what she herself called Emilie, "a regular blue."

The young visitor during those six months found her half sister always "gay and light-hearted, hopeful and happy." She knew as all the relatives did that Mary was nervous, had the Todd temper, and was quick to flare up. But, said Emilie, "Her little temper was soon over, and her husband loved her none the less, perhaps all the more, for this human frailty which needed his love and patience to pet and coax the sunny smile to replace the sarcasm and tears—and, oh, how she did love this man!"

The disrupting effect of having one in the household circle who, in sudden abstraction, would become blind and deaf to his surroundings, was not lost on the visiting girl. Playing checkers with Bob one evening in the family circle, Emilie noticed how Mr. Lincoln had gone into a brown study and was not hearing a word that was being said. Mary with a touch of pique remarked, "Your silence is remarkably soothing, Mr. Lincoln, but we are not quite ready for sleep just yet." Still he did not hear until she took his hand to get his attention. Then he came out of his abstraction good-naturedly and told such a funny story that it broke up the game of checkers.

Mary asked Emilie if Mammy Sally still believed that jay birds went to hell every Friday night with tales of wrongdoing. Then, pointing her finger at her husband and mimicking Mammy's voice and manner to perfection, she threatened him to his great delight: "Nem mine, Mr. Jay's gitten so plum full of tales of you-alls devil*ment*, I'm feared he'll bust befo' Friday night an' time-come fur him to trabble to the bad place." One can imagine the twinkling in Lincoln's eyes. Mary continued: ". . . po' Mr. Jay is so weighten down with the heavy burden of you-all's sins which he's been totin' roun' all week that he can scacely fly up to old man Satan's years which is just like a mule's, long, and hairy an' made plenty big on puppus so he won't have the yearache when Mr. Jay gets shet of his load." Lincoln broke into a hearty laugh.

Emilie also recorded the perennial anxiety of a young mother at a party wondering if everything was all right with the children at home. Her intense motherliness extended to her husband to see that he was warmly clad, to scold him for coming home in the rain without an umbrella, to help him look his best in broadcloth and tall hat, and to be proud of him when he was dressed up.

This maternal instinct included Emilie herself, eighteen years younger than her half sister. Attending church one morning Mary noted that Emilie's bonnet was not as fine as that of a beautiful girl, Lydia Matteson, the governor's daughter. Mary did not like other people to have prettier clothes than hers. It was not merely for herself that she wished lovely dress; she delighted to plan beautiful clothes for others, especially young girls.

Coming home that Sunday morning she said to the loved "Little Sister," "Emilie, you are just as pretty as Lydia, but I do not like your bonnet." Loving conspirators put a plan into execution that week, and when next Sunday rolled round, Emilie went to church wearing a white velvet bonnet from which waved enchanting white plumes, a gift from her sister and brother Lincoln.

Emilie, of course, was keenly aware of Lincoln's campaign for the senatorship, and was present, as were Mrs. Ninian W. Edwards and Mary, at the Statehouse on February 8, 1855, when the legislature assembled to elect the senator. Their tenseness may well be imagined, especially as the first ballot had Lincoln in the lead with forty-five votes where fifty-one were necessary for election. Lincoln gave the story in a letter he wrote next day: "The agony is over at last . . . I began with 44 votes [the records show he got one more vote than he gave himself credit for], Shields 41, and Trumbull 5—yet Trumbull was elected." Later voting had changed the picture. Lincoln held on until he saw his case was hopeless, then threw his support to Trumbull.

Emilie, in the gallery with the family group whose hopes had run so high on the first ballot, recorded: "I remember how indignant we were that our man was not the chosen one. We feared it would be a terrible blow to Mary, but if she was disappointed she kept it strictly to herself."

It is interesting to notice how Albert J. Beveridge (who accepted Herndon's estimate of Mrs. Lincoln) wrote about this event. As to Lincoln holding on so long in the voting, Beveridge said, "If eagerness had not dulled his judgment, the fact that Mrs. Lincoln was in the gallery is a possible explanation of the hazard he now took; for she was determined that her husband should win, and when, within the hour, she saw the triumph of Trumbull, her anger was so fierce, unreasoning, and permanent, that she refused then and forever afterward to speak to the wife of the victor, Julia Jayne, the intimate of her young womanhood and until now, her closest friend."

Beveridge here suggested a personal motive in Lincoln's mind as possibly influencing his conduct. By a coincidence Lincoln made a statement shortly afterwards which deals with this matter. Writing a friend and commenting on his own course of action in swinging his support to Trumbull,

he said, "I could not, however, let the whole political result go to smash, on a point merely personal to myself."

Lincoln's strong effort for the nomination is explained
by his ambition, while his shift to Trumbull was due to a
complex situation, with Shields, Matteson, Trumbull, and
others besides himself contending for the prize. These factors, which Beveridge himself treats at length, sufficiently
account for Lincoln's conduct without the labored explanation as to the feminine angle.

Beveridge gives no source as authority for his statement
that Mary never spoke to Julia again. Dr. Evans questioned
descendants of Senator Trumbull, who told him that the
night of the senatorial election the Lincolns attended a
reception given by the Edwardses and met the Trumbulls
in a friendly way without any unpleasantness. There are
further details from Trumbull's biographer, Horace White.
Someone at the reception remarked to Lincoln that he
must be disappointed, whereupon Lincoln smiled, went up
to his opponent, put out his hand and said, "Not *too* disappointed to congratulate my friend Trumbull."

That a coolness between the two women developed is
true. Fortunately that well-balanced witness, Dr. A. G.
Henry, left a record that throws light on the interplay of
the many factors contributing to that coolness. Dr. Henry
saw the Lincolns in the White House in 1863 and wrote
back to his wife in Springfield: "Mary & Julia have both
made me their confidant telling me their grievances, and
both think the other *all* to blame. I am trying to make
peace between them. It is as I told you, Mr. Trumbull was
jealous of Col. Baker's influence with Mr Lincoln, and this
was the cause of open family rupture." More light on the
situation appears in a confidential statement made by Lincoln's friend, David Davis: "Mr. Lincoln has no doubt that
Judge Trumbull is not his friend." Trumbull's coolness toward Lincoln is shown in a source which only recently
came to light. William Jayne, Julia's brother, wrote after
Lincoln became President: "Mr. Lincoln has not treated
Mr Trumbull as he should & Mr T said . . . that he should
not step inside of the White House again during Mr Lincoln's four years, unless he changed his course." Apparently the President would not make a certain appointment
according to Trumbull's wishes.

The attitudes of Lincoln and Trumbull toward each
other were the result of a number of factors, in which poli-

tics, public affairs, and patronage were far more important than the feelings of the wives. Differences between the husbands were naturally reflected in the emotions of the two ladies involved. Beveridge's assumption that the estrangement was due to Mrs. Lincoln's "unreasoning" anger over Trumbull's defeat of Lincoln in 1855 is another example of the unfavorable interpretation she has constantly received.

Politics continued to absorb Lincoln. Parties were shifting. The Whig party which Lincoln and Mary had both loved with their young enthusiasm was crumbling. The new Republican party, opposing the extension of slavery in the territories, was being formed. It did not go so far as to advocate using national authority to abolish slavery in the Southern states. Looking wistfully backward, Lincoln finally joined the Republican party.

His poignant regret at being "unwhigged" ran through his letter to Joshua Speed in August 1855. Joshua had written him suggesting that they now differed politically. Lincoln was hurt at this division with so loved a friend. He was also distressed that he could no longer be a Whig but must witness the disappearance of a party that included Southern friends. He did not relish the changed political scene in which he saw no alternative but to join a sectional party to which Southerners such as Speed could not belong.

The country was being torn apart by the question of slavery. Lincoln pleadingly stated his position to Joshua: "You know I dislike slavery; and you fully admit the abstract wrong of it. . . . I also acknowledge *your* rights and *my* obligations, under the constitution, in regard to your slaves. I confess I hate to see the poor creatures hunted down, and caught, and carried back to their stripes, and unrewarded toils; but I bite my lip and keep quiet." Scenes of slavery were a "continual torment" to him and made him "miserable." "You ought rather to appreciate how much the great body of the Northern people do crucify their feelings, in order to maintain their loyalty to the constitution and the Union. I do oppose the extension of slavery . . . If for this you and I must differ, differ we must."

He closed the letter with a friendly, wistful note: "Mary will probably pass a day or two in Louisville in October.

My kindest regards to Mrs. Speed. On the leading subject of this letter, I have more of her sympathy than I have of yours. And yet let me say I am your friend forever."

On that "leading subject," slavery, Lincoln also had the sympathy of his wife. Herndon said that Mrs. Lincoln "was decidedly pro-slavery in her views." He based this far-reaching pronouncement upon a casual remark which she was said to have made to friends (which he got by hearsay), "If ever my husband dies, his spirit will never find me living outside the limits of a slave State." Weik, Herndon's collaborator, later interviewed the man, John S. Bradford, who told this story. Incidentally Weik found out that Bradford had a grudge against Lincoln. According to Bradford's account, he and his family invited Mrs. Lincoln to take a drive with them. When she joined them, she was "very nervous and more or less wrought up." The Bradfords suspected that she had just had some trouble with the current maid, for she made some such remark as reported by Herndon.

Herndon's conclusion was utterly false. There were doubtless times when Mary, weary of household drudgery with little help, longed for the comfort and service of the loved house servants in Kentucky. Whatever may be said of her lightly tossed out remark, which may not have been correctly reported, her actual attitude was far from "pro-slavery." She had grown up influenced by those who believed in gradual emancipation. She left an unbroken record of sympathy for what she called "all the oppressed colored race." We are to find her during the Presidency working in their behalf, believing in emancipation, and in the end being called by that extreme term, "abolitionist." The evidence shows throughout that she shared her husband's attitude.

Lincoln's political activities continued to bring him into the public eye. When John C. Frémont was nominated as candidate for President by the new Republican party in June 1856, Lincoln's name was among those voted upon for Vice President. When the news came to him during a session of the circuit court at Urbana, he remarked simply: "I reckon that ain't me; there's another great man in Massachusetts named Lincoln, and I reckon it's him."

He made many speeches during the campaign for Frémont that summer and one of the newspapers remarked of him that "he attacks no man's character or motives, but fights with arguments." He was becoming more and more prominent in the Republican party.

It was natural, therefore, that when a new newspaper, the Springfield *Republican*, made its appearance in February 1857, a copy was left at Lincoln's house. Lincoln by his own statement "thought the establishment of the paper unfortunate," but it was not politic to oppose it, and he expected to take and pay for one copy. When the paper arrived, Mary, concerned as usual with economy, said to him, "Now are you going to take another worthless little paper?" Lincoln was not feeling well about that time and, like many a husband, he preferred to avoid an argument with a sharp-tongued little woman, so, as he put it, "I said to her *evasively*, 'I have not directed the paper to be left.'" That was all Mary needed; she sent a message to the carrier not to leave the paper again, with the result that a resentful paragraph appeared in the *Republican*, creating a misunderstanding which Lincoln had to clear up. It is an early example of how her impulsiveness was to make political difficulty for her husband. Yet she could honestly have thought that he meant for her to discontinue the paper.

Emilie left Springfield in the late spring of 1855. It had been a happy visit. She would always remember the long drives out into the country in the springtime to gather wild flowers. She remembered too that Bob, when not quite twelve, had been taught by his mother to help the ladies out of the carriage in the manner befitting a young gentleman. The six-months visit had created a close bond between the Lincolns and herself, one destined to be cruelly lacerated by the Civil War.

Three letters which Mary wrote "Little Sister" in 1856 and 1857 have been preserved and from them can be traced the course of life for the Lincolns. In the one of November 23, 1856, she apologized for her "past silence, forgetfulness you know it could not be." She loved to write letters but she had gotten out of the habit of it; one must not expect too much from "a staid matron, & moreover the mother of three noisy boys." Yet nothing delighted her more than to receive letters; would Emilie please write.

Emilie was by this time the wife of Ben Hardin Helm, whom the Lincolns, as always with interesting young people, took to their hearts. He visited the Lincoln home in

Springfield after the marriage and a genuine congeniality developed between him and Lincoln. Both had been born in Kentucky, only a few miles from each other; both were intensely interested in law and in politics. They differed as to the latter, but were the sort who could discuss serious questions together.

In her November letter Mary mentioned Mr. Helm's "great taste for politics" and this naturally brought up the subject of the recent Presidential election. Mary went to great pains to explain her husband's position in the contest. Above all she wanted it understood that he was not an "Abolitionist." "In principle he is far from it—" she wrote. "All he desires is that slavery shall not be extended, let it remain where it is." Mary was here defending her husband from a term that was deeply hated; an abolitionist was considered by many a dangerous subversive, a radical who believed in immediate emancipation without due consideration of the violent disruptions that would follow. Lincoln and Mary at that time believed in gradual emancipation with compensation to slaveowners.

It develops interestingly that the Lincolns had not agreed about the election. It was long before the days of woman suffrage, but one wonders whether, if she had had a vote, Mary would have voted differently from her husband. Lincoln had campaigned for Frémont, but, said Mary, "My weak woman's heart was too Southern in feeling to sympathize with any but Fillmore. I have always been a great admirer of his, he made so good a President & is so just a man & feels the *necessity* of keeping foreigners within bounds." Mary here fell short of her husband's broad sympathy and tolerance for the foreign-born. As usual she thought of public policy in personal terms; Irish servants were unsatisfactory to her, therefore she wanted all foreigners kept "within bounds."

Between the lines one can read that Mary too was upset at being "unwhigged." That was the party she had loved and believed in, and she took a solid satisfaction in the fact that in Illinois the Democrats had been "defeated in their Governor, so there is a crumb of comfort for each & all." She added with characteristic optimism, "What day is so dark that there is no ray of sunshine to penetrate the gloom?"

Another letter to Emilie nearly three months later is devoted to the personal items that would interest a much younger sister—parties, weddings, and family news. Mary used the affectionate nicknames that appear in any large family, referring to two of her half sisters as Kitty and Dedee. She hoped they would both come out for a visit next winter; she wrote affectionately that "we will endeavor to make it as pleasant as possible for them." She longed to hear again Emilie's young laugh and begged for more letters. The winter had passed rapidly away, "spring if we can call the month of *March* such, is nearly here." There had been much sickness among children and scarlet fever had swept several away.

By September of 1857 Mary had new and exciting items to write about. She thought that Emilie's baby had been born, though the news had not yet come. Any mention of babies enlisted Mary's full attention; she pictured Emilie's joy in her new motherhood but was impatient for details. "Do write me, all the news—I feel anxious to hear from you."

Mary had had a wonderful summer. Lincoln had to make a trip East in connection with his legal services for the Illinois Central Railroad and took his travel-loving little wife along. "We visited Niagara, Canada, New York & other points of interest," wrote Mary proudly to Emilie, "when I saw the large steamers at the New York landing, ready for their European voyage, I felt in my heart, inclined to sigh that poverty was my portion, how I long to go to Europe." Then out of her assured happy wifehood she made a teasing remark to her husband, "I often laugh & tell Mr L—— that I am determined my next husband *shall be rich.*"

Springfield was growing at a prodigious rate. "Almost *palaces* of homes, have been reared since you were here," continued Mary's letter, "hundreds of houses have been going up this season and some of them, very elegant." One catches a glimpse of her many tasks. She remarked of a niece who as yet had no children that "she has nothing but her dear Husband & silk quilts to occupy her time. How differently the daily routine of some of our lives are." Mary had to be mother and father both to those noisy boys so much of the time. "Mr L —— is not at home, this makes the fourth week, he has been in Chicago."

The New Year 1858 began with a day which was as expansive as that year was to prove to the Lincolns. Hoopskirted ladies and top-hatted gentlemen were making calls in the fine winter weather. At the governor's mansion several hundred guests were entertained. It was to be a year of highlights for Mary and her husband. Over fifteen years were now woven into the fabric of their marriage. The threads were close together and strong but the color and pattern were like those of most small-town American families. Now began the weaving of more vivid threads, the first edges of a design whose striking pattern would be revealed in crowded years soon to follow.

In April that popular speaker Abraham Lincoln gave a lecture to a full house in Bloomington on "Discoveries and Inventions," a lecture he would be called upon to repeat elsewhere. In May people were talking about his clever defense of a man charged with murder, Duff Armstrong, son of an old friend of New Salem days. Introducing an almanac to prove there could not have been sufficient light from the moon to see the deed as described, Lincoln discredited the testimony of the state's star witness. On June 16, the state Republican convention selected Lincoln as their candidate for the United States Senate. He made a speech that evening using a sentence destined to become famous: "A house divided against itself cannot stand."

In this connection one gets a bit of evidence of the underlying disapproval of Lincoln among Mary's relatives, undoubtedly a never-ending irritant to her feelings and a challenge to her loyalty to her husband, that loyalty which never wavered. One of the relatives later said, according to Herndon's jottings: "The Todd—Stuart—Edwards family— with preacher & priest—dogs servants, &c. got mad at Mr L because he made the house-divided-against-itself speech. . . . Lincoln was a radical—fanatically so . . ." (This description was, of course, an utterly wrong appraisal of Lincoln.) Mary was probably on the defensive much of the time. It has been seen how careful she was to explain to Emilie that her husband was not an abolitionist.

Lincoln's Democratic opponent as senatorial candidate was Mary's old beau, Stephen A. Douglas. His circle too had widened until he had become a national figure. He was a powerful speaker and new heights of excitement loomed ahead for Mary when her husband challenged him to a series of joint debates. There were carnival days ahead for the seven Illinois towns where the debates were to be held between August 21 and October 15. In the less complicated life of the time with its absence of modern diversion, political contest furnished fun, entertainment and, in this case, a grand dramatic show. Lincoln would be met at wharf or railroad station by a great crowd who would escort him to his destination marching to the music of a brass band and the ringing of courthouse bells. He learned what an uncomfortable thing it was for a long ungainly man like himself to be borne aloft on the shoulders of his friends; he learned also what a thrill it was to receive the deep-throated cheers of a thousand or more voices. At Freeport he rode to the scene of the debate in a Conestoga wagon drawn by six white horses. There were barbecues and ice-cream festivals. Country people, often in ox-drawn wagons, flocked into the towns for the excitement. In the evenings there was the stirring drama of torchlight parades, a long line of dark moving figures holding aloft flickering tongues of flame against the blackness of the night. The sheen of their oilskin coats reflected in the torchlight; behind them trailed smoke and the smell of kerosene. It was a huge American spectacle, thrilling and exhilarating.

Douglas may have been Mary's old beau, but she was strictly partisan in these debates. One is grateful to Herndon for recording what she said in the law office one day when the conversation turned on Douglas. "Mr. Lincoln may not be as handsome a figure," were her words, "but the people are perhaps not aware that his heart is as large as his arms are long." Herndon remarked what was as noticeable as a flying banner: ". . . she was inordinately proud of her tall and ungainly husband. . . If to other persons he seemed homely, to her he was the embodiment of noble manhood . . ."

Mrs. Lincoln's niece tells how Mary with her head lifted and eyes shining with pride said: "Mr. Douglas is a very little, *little* giant by the side of my tall Kentuckian, and intellectually my husband towers above Douglas just as he does physically." It was difficult for her to attend the debates—travel was so time-consuming and there was the question of someone to stay with the children—but she followed Lincoln's progress with passionate interest.

There is a glimpse of the manner in which this faith of Mary's was always bolstering him up, and fighting his self-doubts. On one occasion during the senatorial canvass Lincoln and a young journalist found themselves waiting for a late train at a flag railroad station not far from Springfield. A thunderstorm compelled them to take refuge in an empty freight car, and squatting down on the floor Lincoln began to chat confidentially to his companion: ". . . my friends got me into *this* business. I did not consider myself qualified for the United States Senate, and it took me a long time to persuade myself that I was. . . . Mary insists, however, that I am going to be Senator and President of the United States, too." Then followed his famous ringing laugh, his arms clasped around his knees while he rocked back and forth with mirth. "Just think," he chuckled, "of such a sucker as me as President!"

Lincoln got home only two Sundays during the debate period, as he was making many additional speeches at the same time. He had so much to tell Mary, and she could be a good listener, full of eager or sympathetic questions. Every united couple knows the satisfaction of the homecoming when the husband has rich and gratifying experiences to relate to the one most interested in them.

Perhaps he told her how clearly he saw Donati's comet which was in the sky that September. At Jonesboro he and Horace White had sat looking at it for more than an hour. Remembering her love for young girls, he may have mentioned to Mary how the two daughters of his landlord at Haggard House in Winchester came beseeching with their autograph books, and how he made up little verses for them. In Rosa Haggard's book was written in that precise yet individual handwriting over the signature, "A. Lincoln:"

> *Teach your beau to heed the lay—*
> *That sunshine soon is lost in shade—*
> *That* now's *as good as any day—*
> *To take thee, Rosa, ere she fade.*

The wife was able to have a taste of the excitement when Lincoln reached home on September 25. The Republican Club came to serenade him and he had to step outside his front door to speak to the enthusiastic crowd. One can imagine two bright-eyed little boys and a proud wife watching from a window with an older son in the background. Mary heard that evening the deafening cheers from those people who, like herself, looked up to Lincoln with faith and hope.

But an even greater thrill was to come. For the last debate at Alton on October 15, a large group of people were going from Springfield on a special train at excursion rates of half fare. The "Springfield Cadets," Robert Lincoln among them, and "Merritt's Cadet Band" accompanied them to make the trip festive with youth and music. Mary, who so loved excitement, was doubtless in her glory. Besides, Mrs. Douglas had been traveling around with her husband on his speaking tours, and had made him so many adherents by her beauty and charm that it would do no harm to let people see that Mr. Lincoln too had a good-looking wife with taste in dress, a soft voice, and pretty, refined manners. One can be sure that Mary gave full thought to her costume and hair arrangement that day. She must look her best for her husband's sake.

But it seems her spirits fell for a period at Alton. Perhaps she foresaw what did happen, that Lincoln would be defeated in the senatorial contest. Gustave Koerner, who was optimistic as to Lincoln's chances, met him at the hotel before the debate and Lincoln said, "Let us go up and see Mary." They joined Mrs. Lincoln and her husband requested Koerner: "Now, tell Mary what you think of our chances! She is rather dispirited." Perhaps Mary's depression was a reflection of Lincoln's for he was himself despondent that day.

It was once said that Lincoln looked seven feet tall when he spoke. To Mary's partial eyes he probably looked ten, especially with that sawed-off Mr. Douglas beside him on the platform. One listener carried away an impression which he handed down to his family, a picture of Lincoln "unlimbering himself to speak, like a tall ungainly bird, under whose wingspread arms his sleek, duck-built adversary could have walked." The short figure had a deep voice that spoke in a steady stream; the tall debater's high-pitched tones "sometimes stopped for repairs before finishing a sentence . . ."

Mary heard her husband that afternoon say things which have come down in history. He repeated what he had first said in June: " 'A house divided against itself cannot stand.' I believe this Government cannot endure permanently, half Slave and half Free." She heard him lament the evil of slavery, while at the same time explaining his position so as to overcome the impression that he was stirring up strife and antagonism.

It was one of the hottest of the debates and there may have been times when Mary's blue eyes flashed fire. But she is found in pleasant and hospitable mood after the debate was over. She and her husband dined at the hotel with an animated group including Lyman Trumbull, Horace White, and two brothers, John and Robert Hitt. Mrs. Lincoln courteously invited Horace White and Robert Hitt to go with Mr. Lincoln and herself to Springfield to rest for a day or two. Hitt in declining said "that he would never call at her house until she lived in the White House." Mary laughed at the suggestion and replied "there was not much prospect of such a residence very soon."

The senatorial contest ended with a bang in a giant Republican rally at Springfield on October 30. The great crowds were worked up to such a pitch of excitement that many did not hear the restrained but magnificent speech which Lincoln made to them. The people had to have action and demonstration. There were torchlight processions that night and doubtless the points of fire were reflected in the eyes of a proud wife and three excited sons.

Election day, November 2, as if prophetic of the gloom to come, was dark, with incessant rain and ever-deepening mud. The weather even cut down the usual number of street fights, but at that, by nightfall the city prison was nearly full. The tumult and the shouting died; Lincoln was defeated.

It went hard with him for a time. Two days after the election he wrote, "The emotions of defeat, at the close of a struggle in which I felt more than a merely selfish interest . . . are fresh upon me . . ." Few have considered the disappointment of the loyal wife who had proclaimed her confidence in her husband's great intellect and heart. Mary wanted things with such intensity that it was usually hard for her to be reconciled. By temperament she was a hard worker and a hard fighter. As she once said to Emilie, "one feels better even after losing, if one has had a brave, whole-hearted fight . . ."

Before long Lincoln achieved something of the same attitude. By November 20 he was looking forward to the future again. In spite of all the weary travel, the strain of two- and three-hour speeches in the open, the rain and hot sun, the mud and dust, and jolting, it had been a good campaign. The "fizzle-gigs and fire-works," as he called the trappings of the campaign, had been good fun. His feeling is summed up in a letter he wrote a disappointed friend: "I believe . . . [you] are 'feeling like h—ll yet,'" he said. "Quit that. You will soon feel better. Another 'blow-up' is coming; and we shall have fun again."

Lincoln lost the contest in the sense that Douglas was elected. But the country, through all the fanfare and through following the clear, logical speeches of a prairie lawyer who had pondered deeply the seething problems of the day, had become aware that there was an Abraham Lincoln in Illinois. There were even optimistic souls who were beginning to think of this man as a possible Presidential possibility. There is a certain symbolism in the fact that there was a comet in the sky in 1858.

chapter 15

WIDENING CIRCLE

When a stone is thrown into the water it starts a procession of ever-widening circles. Lincoln's life expanded in somewhat the same way. First there was the tiny circumference of a backwoods cabin. When young Lincoln reached New Salem the ripple had broadened to village size. His Springfield life was an ever-widening process, from junior law partner in a prairie town to prominent lawyer and state politician. Then the widening gained momentum and rapidly increased until it embraced the whole nation and reached in the Presidency international dimensions which even now can hardly be measured.

The year 1859 had life's usual ups and downs. Early in February the Lincolns gave one of their large parties, doubtless similar to the one of crushing proportions which had occurred in the same month in 1857. The dates have significance; the legislature met in the odd years and was in session in February; in other words, the Lincolns were doing their political entertaining. If Mary received a lift of pride from this party as she had from the one two years previous, her elation soon vanished to be replaced with anxiety.

Lincoln was in Chicago on a Monday late in February when a worried mother wrote their friend, O. M. Hatch: "If you are going up to Chicago to day, & should meet Mr L—— there, will you say to him, that our *dear little Taddie*, is quite sick. The Dr. thinks it may prove a *slight* attack of *lung* fever. I am feeling troubled & it would be a comfort to have him, *at home*." The underscoring of the word "slight" perhaps was to comfort both parents, but the appeal for Lincoln to come, while not at all hysterical, was urgent. The mother continued: "He passed a bad night. I do not like his symptoms, and will be glad, if he hurries home."

Lincoln was still in Chicago on Wednesday. Thursday found him at home again to share the nursing and anxiety. Threatened pneumonia was a bad business for Tad, whose lungs thereafter proved weak.

The illness passed, as did the spring months. When Lincoln had to take an unexpected trip to Chicago early in June, he took Willie along for the excitement and pleasure that a little boy going-on-nine would get from the thrilling adventure. That Willie inherited from both parents the gift of writing good letters is shown by his communication sent back to a playmate in Springfield. The town was "a very beautiful place" and "Me and father went to two theatres the other night." The companionableness of the two, and perhaps the words of the father stand out in Willie's description of the "nice little room to ourselves" and his explanation of the "two little pitcher[s] on a washstand. The smallest one for me the largest one for father." The two towels were likewise appropriately sized, as were the "two little beds" and the "two little wash basins." They went to an "exhibition" and the weather was "very very fine"; it was a happy expedition. "Mother" had a short expedition to Chicago about this time also, as she wrote Mrs. Shearer. Whether it was the same trip and she stayed with friends or had a room to herself, one cannot tell, as the date of her going is indefinite.

On July 14 the Lincolns with a group of friends started off on a long journey over the lines of the Illinois Central Railroad, the business of the men being the assessment of the road's property. For Mary it was a glorious excursion, as she wrote Mrs. Shearer: ". . . we . . . travelled *eleven hundred* miles, with a party of eighteen. . . . *Words* cannot express what a merry time, we had, the gayest pleasure party, I have ever seen." The indulgent husband, seeing her delight, had promised her a fine trip for the next summer: "Mr Lincoln says I may go up to the White Mountains, Niagara & take New York & Philadelphia, in our route."

The travel-loving wife had a number of trips in 1859. Tad, the youngest, was now six years old and she had a reliable maid, so she was free to go. "Mary, the same girl, I had last winter, is still with me," she wrote Mrs. Shearer, "a very faithful servant, has become as submissive as possible."

Bob went away to school (Phillips Exeter) that year and his mother voiced the perennial sense of emptiness which parents have when the first child leaves the home circle—

". . . it almost appears, as if light & mirth, had departed with him." A letter to Mrs. Shearer early in October told how "Mr L & myself visited Columbus & some beautiful portions of Ohio, & made a charming visit to Cincinnati," and added, "I miss Bob, so much, that I do not feel settled down, as much as I used to & find myself going on trips quite frequently." The Ohio trip had been in September for the purpose of Lincoln's making some political speeches. Mrs. Lincoln and one of the boys went along and got in some family visiting, spending a Sunday with a cousin of Mary's, Mrs. William M. Dickson, in Cincinnati. Mary's relatives seemed placed in strategic positions for visiting purposes; later in the year she spent a week in St. Louis, where she had as many as "four *own* cousins."

Lincoln's political activities continued to take him out of the state. In Kansas, on December 7, he responded again to a young girl's appeal for an autograph, beginning with the gently teasing lines: "Dear Mary With pleasure I write my name in your Album—Ere long some younger man will be more happy to confer *his* name upon *you.*"

But in spite of the lengthening diameter of the circle he was still the pessimistic member of the family. ". . . I must, in candor, say I do not think myself fit for the Presidency," he had written in April 1859. Mary the optimist knew better. He found, as public men often do, that acclaim does not pay grocery bills. "It is bad to be poor," he wrote in September of that year. "I shall go to the wall for bread and meat, if I neglect my business this year as well as last." So wrote in 1859 the Illinois lawyer who in the following year was to be elected President of the United States.

The circle widened with breath-taking rapidity in 1860. With Lincoln's increasing prominence the indiscretions of his junior law partner began to cause him some embarrassment. Early in that year Herndon spread reports which Lincoln described as "untrue and unjust" to Lincoln's friend Norman B. Judd. Moreover Lincoln pointed out to Herndon that he, Lincoln, "would be held responsible" for what had been said. Herndon, in Lincoln's words, "rather denied the charge, and I did not press him about the past; but got his solemn pledge to say nothing of the sort in the future." So much for that incident, but after 1860 Lincoln kept Herndon out of his affairs as much as possible. "For small things Billy could still be useful," writes Herndon's biographer. "But when it came to major matters of state, Billy was counted out."

A far-reaching event was scheduled for February 27, 1860. On that date Lincoln delivered in New York at the Cooper Union his notable address which made the East acutely aware of this Republican from Illinois. His plan for his trip included going to Exeter to see Robert and he was somewhat dismayed at the invitations to speak which crowded in upon him. Always mindful to keep Mary in close touch with what he was doing and feeling, he wrote her on March 4, "I have been unable to escape this toil. If I had foreseen it, I think I would not have come East at all." He had made his carefully prepared speech in New York; now the difficulty was "to make nine others, before reading audiences who had already seen all my ideas in print."

He spoke at Phillips Exeter, where his son was a student. It is said that when the tall awkward figure with rumpled hair and baggy knees rose to speak, his fellow students felt sorry for Bob, but their pity vanished when the orator began to speak. According to the recollection of one of the listeners, Lincoln would occasionally put a question to the audience and pause for an answer which was not forthcoming. Finally he remarked good-humoredly: "You people here don't jaw back at a fellow as they do out West."

After the Cooper Union speech Lincoln, who had achieved national recognition by his debates with Douglas, was not only "prominently mentioned" for the Presidency; he was one of a small number of leading contenders. In April he confessed in a letter to Lyman Trumbull, "The taste *is* in my mouth a little . . ." The gathering momentum of his prominence moved forward swiftly in its culmination in the wild drama of the Chicago Convention on May 18 when he was nominated on the third ballot as the Republican candidate for President.

The news reached Springfield about noon and at once the firing of a hundred guns commenced. Did Mary, tensely waiting, hear those guns and guess their tremendous significance or did her husband reach her first? For he said to his friends who were wildly rejoicing over the news: "There's a little woman down at our house would like to hear this. I'll go down and tell her." One must imagine that telling; the wife's triumphant pride and joy, the husband's answering emotion to her illumined face and loving touch. They did not have long to themselves; friends came trooping in to congratulate them all afternoon. A great crowd, to whom Lincoln had to make a short speech, descended upon the home in the evening. The simple dwelling on Eighth Street was to face many such crowds in the coming months, to resound to band music, speeches and cheers, to mirror the glare and shadows of torchlight processions. Mary, who was "the very creature of excitement," was destined to have it as her daily diet.

A committee of solemn and distinguished gentlemen arrived in town the next evening to notify the candidate of his nomination. Mary prepared sandwiches and cakes and—true to her Kentucky rearing—drinks for their visit in the evening. She took the precaution of asking two of Lincoln's friends, who called ahead of the committee, as to the appropriateness of her preparations and they raised objection to her liquid hospitality. Some of the expected delegation were "strictly temperance people." Mary argued the case "in her very lively manner," but Lincoln, hearing the discussion, came in and soothingly said, "Perhaps, Mary, these gentlemen are right. After all is over, we may see about it, and some may stay and have a good time." So all the committee received in the end was ice water. As they had just come from a dinner where they had had everything to drink except water and it was a hot evening, the choice proved a popular one. As Lincoln explained afterward, "Having kept house sixteen years, and having never held the 'cup' to the lips of my friends there, my judgment was that I should not, in my new position, change my habits in this respect."

As the committee reached the Lincoln home, two small boys seated on the steps (so as not to miss anything), greeted them. "Are you Mr. Lincoln's son?" Mr. William M. Evarts asked the older child. When Willie replied "Yes, sir," Evarts and the others ceremoniously shook hands with him. Tad, feeling the honors were not being fairly divided, promptly spoke up, "I'm a Lincoln, too!" Whereupon the gentlemen laughed, shook Tad's hand with equal impressiveness, and rang the doorbell.

Inside a dignified ceremony followed. George Ashmun made the formal speech of notification, Lincoln answered appropriately and briefly, then the group relaxed into informal talk. The delegates were presented to Mrs. Lincoln, drank their ice water gratefully, and departed. They returned to the hotel through streets bright with rockets and bonfires, along houses illuminated from top to bottom. "Bands of music played in the street," said Gustave Koerner. "Even the Democrats, who all liked Lincoln personally, joined in the jubilee."

Springfield continued to celebrate. The exciting weeks that followed were punctuated at frequent intervals with giant rallies; the Republican cannon was fired as often as if a war were on. An unknown photographer deserves gratitude for a picture of the Lincoln home during one of these great celebrations with Lincoln standing at the door surrounded by friends. The picture captured everything: the procession going by, the waving hats, the unkempt small-town surroundings of the home, the figures of the household in the upper window (Mary perhaps among them), everything except the deafening noise.

Newspapermen came to Springfield for interviews. They stared at the house on Eighth Street, the woodshed and other buildings in the back, taking notes to put into articles. Artists clamoring for sittings flocked to town. There were requests for details of Lincoln's early life, and for autographs. Letters of all kinds poured in. Some of these were so appealing that Lincoln kept them, with the result that they were found when the Lincoln Papers were opened in 1947. Three of them are worth noting here for their human flavor.

In the first letter a former resident of Springfield makes his feeling apparent in its salutation. It begins: "Mr Lincoln *Dear Father I might say*," and is signed "Your Boy." The writer was so rejoiced over the nomination that he "shed Tears like a child," he wrote. "The thought struck me what must Mrs Lincoln & Bob feel when they heard it. I almost imagined I could hear old Buck snicking in the stable." This correspondent wanted Lincoln to know he was doing his bit; he was agent for "Christy's minstrels" and "our funny Men are giving you good hits from the stag[e] . . . which of course before an audience of 1000 People in a strange plac[e]—Evy Every night does no harm." Another letter in the same spirit has a twinkle in the postscript directed perhaps toward Robert: "Please make my respects to Mrs. Lincoln and Little Chin-chopper."

September brought an epistle with a unique enclosure, a "Lincoln nail." "Sir," ran this communication, "this is a genuine article observe the 'L' on the head of the nail show it to your little wife, I think it will please her curiosity. I have a little wife myself."

There were few private and personal matters that were left untouched in the incoming mail. Eleven-year-old Grace Bedell wrote Lincoln suggesting he grow a beard. It was an age of whiskers—they were the style—and one may be sure Lincoln would not have adopted the suggestion if Mary had not approved. There is hardly a biography of Lincoln that omits this young girl, and she usually has a favorable press, but Lord Charnwood had a different view. He wrote: "To this dreadful young person . . . was due the ill-designed hairy ornamentation which during his Presidency hid the really beautiful modelling of his jaw and chin."

Having read some of Lincoln's mail, we may as well go to visit his home with an observing newspaperman who dropped in the latter part of June. The home was easy to find, he said, "A modest-looking two story brown frame house, with the name 'A Lincoln' on the door plate, told me that my pilgrimage was ended." The visitor was ushered in by a servant and apparently made some notes while waiting for Lincoln to come downstairs: "The house was neatly without being extravagantly furnished. An air of quiet refinement pervaded the place. You would have known instantly that she who presided over that modest household was a true type of the American lady."

The reporter continued to observe details. "There were flowers upon the table; there were pictures upon the walls. The adornments were few, but chastely appropriate; everything was in its place, and ministered to the general effect. The hand of the domestic artist was everywhere visible. The thought that involuntarily blossomed into speech was—'What a pleasant home Abe Lincoln has.'"

"Presently I heard footsteps on the stairs," continued the journalist, "and a tall, arrowy, angular gentleman, with a profusion of wiry hair, 'lying around loose' about his head, and a pair of eyes that seemed to say 'make yourself at home,' and a forehead remarkably broad and capacious, and arms that were somewhat too long and lank for a statue of Apollo, made his appearance. The lips were full of character, the nose strongly aquiline, the cheek bones high and prominent, and the whole face indicative at once of goodness and resoluteness. In repose it had something of rigidity, but when in play, it was one of the most eloquent I have ever seen. None of his pictures do him the slightest justice. His presence is commanding —his manner winning to a marked degree. After you have been five minutes in his company you cease to think that he is either homely or awkward. You recognize in him a high-toned, unassuming, chivalrous-minded gentleman, fully posted in all of the essential amenities of social life, and sustained by the infallible monitor of commonsense." (Mary had recognized these innate qualities twenty years before but she could have claimed some of the credit for the fact that he had become in the intervening years "fully posted in all of the essential amenities of social life.")

The two men had a pleasant talk together. In the words of the visitor: "I asked him if he was not very much bored with calls and correspondence. He replied that he liked to see his friends, and as to the letters, he took good care not to answer them. . . . His greatest grievance were [was] with the artists; he tried in vain to recognize himself in some of the 'Abraham Lincolns' of the pictorials."

The newspaperman was completely captured: "I found him to be one of the most companionable men I have ever met. Frank, hearty and unassuming, one feels irresistibly drawn toward him."

The caller saw the master of the house, not the mistress, and he possibly ran the risk of catching scarlet fever. Mary's elation had vanished in a mother's anxiety: Willie was ill. On July 4 Lincoln wrote to that always loved friend, Dr. Henry, then residing in Oregon: "Our boy, in his tenth year (the baby when you left), has just had a hard and tedious spell of scarlet fever, and he is not yet beyond all danger." Lincoln's words doubly identify the boy as Willie, who was ten in December 1860. Tad was not yet born when Dr. Henry left Springfield in 1852. Then the father added casually what seems very ominous in the light of present medical knowledge: "I have a head-ache and a sore *throat* upon me now, inducing me to suspect that I have an inferior type of the same thing."

One gets various glimpses in connection with the aspiring artists who were Lincoln's greatest grievance. They painted him in the room at the State House where he daily received visitors, and apparently it was Lincoln's wish that Mrs. Lincoln pass judgment on the portraits. Perhaps he wanted to ask her privately if he really looked like that. When Alban J. Conant finished his painting, to use his own words: "Lincoln came over and looking at the portrait, said: 'You're not going till this evening? I would like for Mrs. Lincoln to see that. If you will let it remain here, I will bring her at three o'clock."

They arrived promptly at three accompanied by their youngest irrepressible son. "Tad was everywhere at once, being repeatedly recaptured by his mother, and waiting but for a favorable diversion to be off again." The artist noticed "with what interested pride Lincoln's eyes followed him [Tad] about the room." When the canvas was uncovered Mary exclaimed with enthusiasm, "That is excellent, that is the way he looks when he has his friends about him." Then she added with a touch of apprehension, "I hope he will look like that after the first of November."

A visiting politician, Thomas Webster, strolled into the room when the artist, George P. A. Healy, was finishing up his first portrait of Lincoln in November 1860. He saw Mrs. Lincoln come to see the result, which pleased her greatly. While she viewed the portrait Mr. Webster studied her and gave a verbal sketch in a letter the following day: "Mrs. L has a soft sweet voice; quiet dignified self possessed undemonstrative manners, is graceful easy and unembarrassed." She was the one that captured him; he thought she had "all the refinements of the family..." He even liked her dress and was delighted with the two "chubby" sons who came with her; they were "really healthy smart boys." Lincoln did not fare so well in the letter. He was "slouchy ungraceful ... round shouldered, leans forward (very much in his walk) is lean and ugly every way."

One can view the Lincoln family that summer through the eyes of a young man, a friend of Robert at Phillips Exeter, Frank Fuller, who came to Springfield and called on Lincoln at the State House. Herndon once wrote: "Lincoln dare not even ask a friend to go to dinner with him, unless he first got *Mrs* Lincoln's *warm*—eager consent..." Nevertheless, Lincoln invited Frank to dinner and the two walked together down the street to the "pleasant home, where," as the young man said, he was "warmly received by Mrs. Lincoln." He had with him an interesting poster which he spread out on the floor "to the delight" of his hostess and the two little boys, who at once "climbed all over me . . ."

Young Fuller had with him a slender volume of poems by one Albert Laighton "and glad was I to find in Mrs. Lincoln a lover of poetry." Mary's full attention was instantly enlisted, as always at the mention of poems; she wanted to know all about the book and its writer and asked Frank to read some verses aloud. The young man presented the book to her with the result that it was taken to Washington, where he read again from it to Mrs. Lincoln when he visited the White House.

As they walked into the dining room Lincoln asked young Fuller if he said grace before meals. The latter answered it was his custom to recite a couple of lines from the book they had been reading. When they were seated at the table, Lincoln bowed his head while the guest repeated Laighton's words asking the blessing of the Supreme Power

> *That made our frames, sustains our lives,*
> *And through all earthly change survives.*

The young man found that Lincoln knew a great deal of the Bible by heart, especially the Sermon on the Mount and the twenty-third Psalm. The guest summed up his visit gratefully: "I was taken to the hearts and home of the charming family."

The visitors, even those who were opposed to him, liked the Republican candidate, and also liked Mrs. Lincoln. The representative of the New York *Herald* was delighted with his visit to the Lincoln home where "The conversation was lively, and occasionally interspersed with some brilliant flashes of wit and good nature from the Kentucky lady, his wife."

In July Carl Schurz, picturesque German-American with a powerful gift of language, came to town to address a huge crowd at one of the rallies. He spoke first in German and then in English. When he finished, Lincoln (as Schurz wrote his wife) "came and *shook hands* (ouch!) and said: '*You are an awful fellow. I understand your power now.*'"

The letter to Mrs. Schurz described the family: "In the evening I was at Lincoln's for supper. His lady had decked herself out very prettily and already knows very well how to wave a fan. She chats quite nicely and will be able to adapt herself to the White House without difficulty." As to those youthful enthusiasts who were wont to add their boyish yells to the cheers for their father, he thought they were "regular fellows." "One of them," he added, "insisted upon going barefoot." When Schurz took his leave, Lincoln and Mary urged him to bring his wife next time "and to be sure to stop with them . . ."

After a day of visitations in the room at the Capitol, Lincoln would return home to have more visitors in the evening. Mary began to find out that the limelight involved some distasteful features, such as hearing one caller ask another, "Is that the old woman?" Good as was her sportsmanship in dealing with the public, one may doubt her appreciation of this inquiry. Willie and Tad were the only ones whose delight was without drawback. When cheering was heard outside the home, their shrill yells gave an enthusiastic response.

Rally by rally, events had moved on to November 6, Election Day. Lincoln spent most of that day in his room at the State House. About three in the afternoon he went to the courthouse to vote, where he cut off the Presidential electors from the ballot so as not to vote for himself, and voted for the state officers. Mary apparently spent most of the day at home in an agony of waiting. Not that she was pessimistic, however. Mercy Levering Conkling ("dearest Merce" of girlhood days, now Mrs. James C. Conkling) had written her son Clinton a few days before: "I rejoice that this excitement will soon be over. Bob Lincoln . . . has been styled *Prince of Rails!* I saw Mrs. Lincoln a day or two since, she . . . feels quite confident of her husband's election."

Lincoln spent the evening with a group of friends in the telegraph office getting the returns. Mary was not there; it was not customary for women to be a part of such a gathering. In front of the Capitol local orators were addressing a huge and excited crowd. From time to time returns were read out. Lincoln and his friends sat in the office tense with that interest which all who have listened to election returns know. Lyman Trumbull, one of the party, had remarked that "if we get New York that settles it." The hour grew late.

Suddenly the man receiving the telegrams got a dispatch that electrified him. He was so excited he could not read it clearly and Jesse Dubois, who had dozed a little, sat up shouting "How is that?" Lincoln had carried New York! There was a moment of wild confused rejoicing, then the men rushed single file down the narrow stairs, Dubois in the lead carrying the dispatch, to inform the great crowd waiting across the street. He was so breathless with hurry and excitement that all he could yell was "Spatch! spatch!"

Lincoln did not cross to join the meeting where "10 000 crazy people were shouting, throwing up their hats, slapping and kicking one another." He had something he must do first. He was walking down the street toward home. He had said to Trumbull, "I guess I'll go down and tell Mary about it."

chapter 16

TANGLED TALES AND GOOD-BY SPRINGFIELD

Mary at the end of her long day of waiting had her taste of the excitement downtown. Later that evening Lincoln took her to Watson's Confectionery where the Republican ladies had prepared a victory supper. They entered into "a rich and very exciting scene." People were almost beside themselves with jubilation. At Watson's an artist in the midst of the confusion was making a sketch for *Harper's*. Mary, who never quite grew up in some ways, could enter into all this with the wholeheartedness of a child. Mrs. Conkling told of Election night in a letter to her son: "Father was out till half past two. He describes the scene as perfectly *wild*. While the votes were being counted the republicans were ... *singing, yelling! shouting!!* The boys (*not children*) *dancing. Old* men, young, middle aged, clergymen and *all!*" Even those who went to bed could not sleep for the noise.

Mercy Levering Conkling was among the friends who crowded into the Lincoln home during the next few days to offer congratulations. Mrs. Lincoln, she reported to her son Clinton, was "in fine spirits! As you may imagine!" and she "desired me say to you that when they are settled at Washington she will be glad to have you visit them with Bob." Mary was not to forget her friends in her new prominence. Another feminine letter that went out from Springfield at this time adds its evidence on this subject. "I spent an evening at Mr Lincolns a few evenings since," wrote Ada Bailhache to her mother, "and had a very pleasant time. Mr. L. has not altered one bit he amused us nearly all the evening telling funny stories and cracking jokes. I could hardly realize that I was sitting in the august presence of a *real live* President. Mrs L is just as agreeable as ever, does not put on any airs at all but is as pleasant and talkative and entertaining as she can be."

One visitor who called, Mrs. Judith A. Bradner, left an old-age reminiscence which ultimately found its way into print. According to Mrs. Bradner's account, she and her sister visited the Lincolns the day after the election and found Mr. Lincoln in high spirits. He told them he had a fine joke on his wife. Pointing a teasing finger at her he said she had locked him out the night before. The embarrassed Mrs. Lincoln tried to hush him, saying to "never tell that again." But he went on gleefully with the story. Mrs. Lincoln had said, when he went downtown in the evening to hear the returns, that if he were not home by ten o'clock she would lock him out. And she did. But, concluded Mr. Lincoln, "when she heard the music coming to her house she turned the key in a hurry."

This tale is contradicted by another account of election night said to have come from Lincoln himself. Henry C. Bowen, editor of *The Independent,* recalled in reminiscence that Lincoln told him the details of going home on election evening. Bowen quoted Lincoln's own words: "I told my wife to go to bed, as probably I should not be back before midnight. . . . On my arrival I went to my bedroom and found my wife sound asleep. I gently touched her shoulder and said, 'Mary'; she made no answer. I spoke again, a little louder, saying, 'Mary, Mary! *we are elected!*'"

One utterly fictitious episode presented as happening on the night of the election has unfortunately reached a vast audience. In Robert E. Sherwood's play, *Abe Lincoln in Illinois,* Act III, Scene XI, Lincoln on that night deliberately dismisses his friends from the room in order to curse Mary, twice savagely damning her to her face. This act comes with a grating shock; it is unbelievably out of character. Lincoln could display temper, he could boot a scheming rascal out of his office, he could, if the occasion demanded it, use the word "damn," he did at times become impatient with Mary, but the whole body of reliable record runs counter to his using words to his wife which were as violent as a blow in the face.

In answering criticisms of this scene in his essay "The Substance of 'Abe Lincoln in Illinois'" given in the published play, Sherwood refers to a certain story which was handed down by Herndon. This tale appears twice in Herndon's manuscripts and was printed in Hertz's *Hidden Lincoln,* which Sherwood had apparently seen before he wrote the essay. This story can be examined as testimony.

In Herndon's writing, undated, under the heading, "Mrs Lincoln & Lincoln—'a fuss,'" is recorded his recollection, not of an occurrence, but of a story in which two men were alleged to have seen parts of the same incident and to have pieced it together. Such piecing is apt to lead to supplying any parts that are missing, especially as the man who told the story did so ten years after it was supposed to have happened—that is, if he had the right year in mind, which he was not sure about either. According to this account a man by the name of Barrett, passing the Lincoln home, saw a little woman chasing Lincoln in the yard "with a table knife or butcher knife in her hand . . ." Herndon states that Barrett was a man of truth, "if I have the right Barrett in my mind." Barrett thought "what he saw was sport or fun." Apparently he was under this impression until he talked with the other man, named Whitehurst, who allegedly saw the rest of the incident, and was the one who told the story to Herndon. Lincoln, according to Whitehurst via Herndon, seeing people approaching along the street, turned, seized his wife from behind and hustled her back into the house. He said, according to this account, "There d—n it, now stay in the house and don't disgrace us before the Eyes of the world."

It was twenty-nine years after the incident (if he had the year right), that Herndon described it in a letter to his collaborator Weik. He omitted mention of any table knife but stated positively that Barrett "saw a long tall man running and saw a little low squatty woman with a butcher Knife in her hand in hot pursuit." In this letter Herndon gave Lincoln's words as: "There now, stay in the house and don't be a d—— fool before the people." In neither version does Lincoln directly damn his wife. The tale is secondhand, pieced together, and told long after the event; it is hedged in by uncertainties and ifs: the year uncertain, the day "Sunday if I recollect the time," a man by the name of Barrett "if I have the right Barrett in my mind," and it all came through Herndon, who was convinced he knew truth by his own intuitive powers and did not hesitate to put forth the results of his mental ramblings as truth. This flimsy tale offers little basis for making Lincoln step out of character to damn his wife.

The real blame goes back to Herndon. As so often his long arm has reached down the years to distort the Lincoln marriage in a modern play. Mr. Sherwood, like many others, has relied too much on Herndon, but his play was written before the Herndon-Weik manuscripts became available to the public, to be studied in full and evaluated, and before a definitive study of Herndon himself had been produced. There is no wish here to criticize so distinguished and admirable a dramatist as Mr. Sherwood, nor would the incident have been mentioned were it not that the scene has fixed in countless minds an erroneous impression of the Lincoln marriage. A great number of people think that Lincoln cursed his wife on Election night and a biographer, who finds no basis for such a scene in reliable evidence, must nevertheless cope with that unforgettable piece of dramatic fiction.

From the time of the election both the Lincolns suffered from the circulation of stories and rumors and the criticism and envy which prominence and politics always bring. An old neighbor did not hesitate to suggest that other Springfield women were jealous of Mrs. Lincoln and there is no doubt that her explosiveness and habit of speaking her mind made her vulnerable, and a favorite topic of the town gossipers.

With all her triumphant elation, Mary, in the later months of 1860, had her dark moments. On November 9 Lincoln received news that he had been hanged in effigy at Pensacola, Florida. Shortly after the election a visitor, viewing the home of the President-elect, reported "a broken pane of glass each side of front door, & two or three broken blinds on the side . . ." Whether this condition was due to political vandalism, windstorm, or small boy with rock or ball is not known, but in any case it was irritating to the mistress of the house. Mary, who had been abnormally nervous when younger, was forty-two in December 1860; the ailing forties of a woman's life were upon her. It was more than ever difficult for her to endure tensions. Perhaps the apprehensive, depressed moods of the menopause, from which she was to suffer in the White House, had already begun.

A trip to Chicago with her husband and a group of friends the latter part of November probably did nothing to ease the strain. On the train, two manacled convicts, one a murderer, were seated between the families of Mr. Lincoln and Mr. Trumbull, the sheriff in charge of them being a Douglas Democrat. Donn Piatt, a newspaperman of Ohio, and his wife were of the party and if the journalist's emotions showed in his face, he probably cast disapproving looks at Mrs. Lincoln. He was unappreciative of the hospitality he had received at the Lincoln home, describing the supper as "an old-fashioned mess of indigestion, composed mainly of cake, pies and chickens . . ." He turned an equally dyspeptic attitude toward Mrs. Lincoln that evening, saying later: "This good lady injected remarks into the conversation with more force than logic, and was treated by her husband with about the same good-natured indifference with which he regarded the troublesome boys." He also found fault with the President-elect, speaking of his "hard, angular, coarse face," and doubting whether he "had at all a kind, forgiving nature." Piatt's critical faculty was operating in high gear.

With all the drawbacks Mary probably got a thrill from viewing the Wigwam, which had been the scene of the tumultuous nomination of her husband for the Presidency. At a public reception next day she learned what a strain it is on hand, feet, and nerves to stand in line and shake hands with an endless stream of people. She was good at this sort of thing and liked it, but it was fatiguing.

There was newspaper comment that Lincoln returned to Springfield looking "rather the worse for wear," and by December she had cause to worry about him. There were too many demands upon him. "Mr Lincoln, I understand, is at present indisposed, if not seriously unwell," ran a letter written in Springfield on December 8, ". . . I think, Mr Lincoln may well pray often 'Save me from my friends,' for, I certainly believe, they could not have acted more cruelly towards him, than to have him made President. It will kill him and set his wife beside herself, I verily believe."

Early in January 1861 Mary received from South Carolina what was probably intended as a ghastly Christmas present, a painting on canvas showing Lincoln "with a rope around his neck, his feet chained and his body adorned with tar and feathers," an object to give a nervous wife nightmares. There were dark moments of apprehension for Mary.

Her husband helped out, as usual, with a bit of fun now and then. He not only received much mail, but also various presents, and among the latter was "a very elegant hat." Lincoln playfully and ceremoniously tried it on before a mirror and, glancing from his reflection to Mary, who was watching the whole performance with great interest, he remarked with a twinkle: "Well, wife, there is one thing likely to come out of this scrape, any how. We are going to have some *new clothes!*"

He did not need to tell Mary she was going to get some new clothes; she could be depended upon to think of that herself. Incidentally the fact of Lincoln receiving presents may have given her the wrong idea and may have some relation to certain unhappy events to follow in the White House. That Lincoln received many gifts while he was President is shown extensively in the Lincoln Papers. To one with such a well-developed acquisitive sense as Mary, the idea that the new position carried perquisites with it was dangerous; as we are about to discover, her thinking on finances and goods was now getting out of focus.

She intended, properly enough, to fill her new situation becomingly. That involved appropriate dress. The President's wife must have the finest and most exquisite of apparel. Nothing was more to her taste than beautiful costumes and now there would be no more long hours of laborious stitching in order to have them. She went to New York early in January 1861 to do her shopping, and had her first glorious and foolish spree of buying. Salesmen flattered her, merchants extended credit to the wife of the President-elect. New York's best stores, filled with luxuries she had not known before, opened up a new world to her, a world of color, of rich fabrics and shining jewels. She had had to save and scrimp so long; now it seemed that she could spend as much as she pleased. Was not her husband to be President of the United States? To complete her overthrow, it was a time of fearful extravagance in dress.

Fashionable ladies studied the styles set forth in *Godey's Lady's Book* and appeared in more and more elaborate and costly costumes. American women were said to be spending two and three times as much as Englishwomen on their clothes. There was criticism of all this extravagance; the moralists of the time were indignant about it. Women bought bonnets costing two hundred dollars, lace scarves costing fifteen hundred. Into this glittering world of fashion, urged on by designing merchants, stepped an impulsive, well-intentioned Illinois wife and mother dazzled by her sudden rise to prominence. She lost her head and bought extravagantly. Most people know the power of a charge account to make actual payment seem a far-off, unreal thing that need not be bothered with at the moment, but with Mary it was more than this. Buying was an intoxication with her. In the end it became an utterly irrational thing, an obsession.

Dr. Evans, who made so invaluable a study of Mrs. Lincoln's impaired personality, calling on specialists in mental diseases to help him interpret her actions, says: "At this point is recorded her first evidence of poor judgment in money matters; the peculiar direction and bent of this error were later to become a quality of her insanity." He finds in her unreasonable purchases the first act indicating "that she might not be mentally 'right'—the first suspiciously false note." Modern psychology does not use the word "insane" in a case where a mind is abnormal within a certain limited area while the rest of it is untouched; it is too comprehensive and misleading a term. Mrs. Lincoln was to become increasingly irrational on the subject of money and property; she could not think straight on these subjects. There are other known cases where such a peculiarity has developed at the menopause. Like many people now receiving psychiatric treatment, she was "off" on one topic, but that is a condition far removed from a general mental breakdown.

In New York people were eager to meet the wife of the President-elect, and Mary, quick to respond to personal attention, was always ready for a social gathering. Hermann Kreismann, a German-born politician, wrote from Washington on January 16, 1861, to a newspaperman in Chicago: "Mrs Lincoln's journey is considered very much out of place, the idea of the Presidents wife kiting about the country and holding levees at which she indulges in a multitude of silly speeches is looked upon as very shocking." Perhaps it was especially so to the German idea that a woman's interests should not go beyond cooking, church, and children. Others would praise Mary's social responsiveness. Kreismann's letter continued: "Among other interesting speeches of Mrs. L—— reported here is that she says her husband had to give Mr Seward a place the pressure was so great. But he did it very reluctantly." The phrase "reported here" smacks of sheer gossip and Kreismann's wording indicates an unfriendly attitude. One does not know what Mrs. Lincoln said, if anything, but the remark about Seward as reported is off the beam; his appointment to the cabinet was a most logical one. Mary's indiscretion, however, in making remarks with political implications cannot be denied. Lincoln had a vivacious and loving wife, but not a discreet one. Mary's acknowledgment of any of her shortcomings can usually be found in her letters. One catches a glimpse of the husband's attempts to curb his wife's unconsidered and troublemaking statements when she wrote years later, apropos of indiscreet talking, "My husband always enjoined upon me to be quiet."

While "Mother" was in New York the burdened Lincoln in Springfield had found home very forlorn. Robert was to return with her. "Dutiful husband and father that he is," wrote the reporter for the New York *Herald*, "he had proceeded to the railroad depot for three successive nights in his anxiety to receive them, and that in spite of snow and cold." One's sympathy goes out to the tall lonely figure that waited three times in vain, peering through the dimness to see a quick, bright-faced little woman emerge from the car accompanied by a well-dressed young man. She would bring color and the joy of life with her as she told him of her adventures; he could borrow lightness of spirit from her as one does from a child. The reporter recorded that Lincoln was "delighted" when mother and son arrived on January 25, and that Mary was in "excellent spirits."

Affairs had become almost unbearably complicated. Troubled by political tangles and misquotings, besieged by visitors, newspapermen, portrait painters, and office seekers, all this at a time when the nation was breaking apart, Lincoln let it be known on January 27 that he would depart February 11 for Washington, and asked for "the utmost privacy" during the rest of his stay in Springfield. There was so much that must be attended to. They must arrange to rent the house, break up housekeeping, and move to the Chenery House for the last few days before their departure. He must work in a trip to Coles County to see his loved and aged stepmother once more. There he would make a pilgrimage to the grave of that backwoods father whose circumscribed life could hardly have visualized the possibility that his boy Abe would ever become President. He must prepare his inaugural address, a declaration of policy in a desperate national crisis.

Carl Sandburg's *Lincoln Collector* describes a scene in the Lincoln back yard one winter day early in 1861, a scene which makes historians feel like tearing their hair. A bonfire was merrily burning presided over by a busy little woman. Mrs. Lincoln, like benighted housecleaners before and since, was destroying old letters and papers. A neighbor asked for some of the pages as souvenirs, a request which was good-naturedly granted, and thus were preserved the priceless letters which Lincoln and his wife exchanged in 1848. We have proof then that Lincoln preserved at least one of his wife's letters. Perhaps others written by her went up in smoke that day.

Mary did not burn all the letters her husband had written to her. From early days she had saved certain special ones and treasured them. In her widowhood we will find her reading over "that large package of *his,* dear, loving letters to me," some of them yellow with age, and drawing comfort from their words of affection. But the urgency of getting the house ready for its new tenants led to the destruction of valuable evidence that day.

Mary's hands were full. She had a final social duty to perform before they left the home: their reception on February 6 must be the biggest, most brilliant affair they had yet given. And what a providential opportunity it was to let her Springfield friends see some of the splendor of her New York shopping!

Again Mercy Conkling obligingly furnishes the description: ". . . such a crowd, I seldom, or ever saw at a private house. It took about twenty minutes to get in the hall door. And then it required no little management to, make your way out." Bob, going-on-eighteen and with Eastern clothes and manners, "figured quite largely. While I was standing near Mr. L. he came up, and in his humorous style, gave his hand to his father, saying: 'Good evening *Mr. Lincoln!*' In reply his father gave him a gentle slap in the face."

As the time for departure drew near, the pull on the emotions of the Lincolns became stronger. Mary loved her friends with passionate intensity. Now she had to leave these old, tried, faithful neighbors who had suddenly grown more dear. She was also much upset as to the plans for the trip East; she and her husband were not in agreement as to whether she should leave on the same train with him or meet him in New York. Lincoln was opposed to her going with him on his circuitous journey; there were newspaper rumors of intended attacks on the President-elect on his way East. Mary's friends were pointing out these rumors to her as arguments to delay her going to Washington, but they produced the opposite effect from the one intended. The correspondent of the New York *Herald* wrote: ". . . the plucky wife of the President met all these well meant propositions with scorn, and made the spirited declaration before she started on her Eastern trip that she would see Mr. Lincoln on to Washington, danger or no danger." When a dispatch came from General Winfield Scott in Washington saying it would be safer for Lincoln "to be surrounded by his family," Mary made up her mind to go with her husband. Like any wife worth her salt, she intended to be at his side when danger threatened.

It will be seen that when the Lincolns reached the White House, there was a political smear campaign deliberately launched against Mrs. Lincoln in order to injure her husband. It is possible the following story was influenced by rumors already afloat inducing a readiness to believe or imagine the worst about the First Lady-elect. Henry Villard, already frequently quoted, was a German-American reporter who went to Springfield in November 1860 to cover the movements of the President-elect for the New York *Herald*. Villard was quick to criticize Lincoln for his robust stories, and he states in his *Memoirs* that he did not wish to know Mrs. Lincoln because he had heard unfavorable comments about her. On the same page where he thus states his prejudiced approach, he speaks of her "inordinate greed, coupled with an utter lack of sense of propriety," and makes the positive assertion that she "allowed herself to be persuaded, at an early date, to accept presents for the use of her influence with her husband in support of the aspirations of office-seekers."

Villard's statement seems to relate to a story of Hermann Kreismann, whose unfriendly letter about Mrs. Lincoln has already been quoted. As Villard's version of that story is told in *Lincoln on the Eve of '61*, Lincoln was delayed in arriving at the depot on the morning of February 11, and Kreismann was sent to see what was wrong.

Kreismann went to Lincoln's room and "opened the door in response to Lincoln's 'Come in.' Mrs. Lincoln was lying on the floor, evidently quite beside herself." The account continues: "... with his head bowed and a look of utmost misery, Lincoln said: 'Kreismann, she will not let me go until I promise her an office for one of her friends.'" Lincoln is said to have yielded, and have started for the station with his family. There is good reason to believe that Kreismann was not even in Springfield at this time.

There is an inconsistency in this account as to Lincoln's conduct. For him, kind husband and astute public-relations man that he was, to call out in answer to a casual knock on the door by an unknown person, "Come in," when his wife was in the condition described, is uncharacteristic in the extreme. Likewise one who guarded his utterance as President-elect with almost superhuman caution would never have made to a casual politician so damaging a statement as to say that his wife was forcing him to appoint a man he did not want to appoint.

Villard makes unfavorable statements about Mrs. Lincoln in his *Memoirs* that can be proved untrue. Later mentioning that in Washington she regularly visited the Union soldiers in camps, he wrote: "... the truth was, that she had no liking for them at all, being really, as a native of Kentucky, at heart a secessionist." The rumor that Mrs. Lincoln was disloyal was part of the whispering campaign during the war. It will be shown later how completely she was for the Union in thought and in action. She was never a secessionist; a native of Kentucky, yes, but for that matter, Kentucky did not secede. Villard's statement is ignorant in more respects than one.

The account of the Kreismann story as happening on the day of Lincoln's departure from Springfield is not acceptable. Mary was doubtless in a highly emotional state then, with rumors of danger to her husband and with her determination to be at his side on the journey. If she was begging for anything that morning, it was possibly his consent that she join him next day in Indianapolis, which is, of course what she did.

But the Kreismann story as it appears in the Herndon-Weik manuscripts is not placed on the day of Lincoln's departure. According to a letter of Horace White, written January 26, 1891 (thirty years after the event), Norman B. Judd and Hermann Kreismann went to Springfield after

Lincoln's election and made an appointment to see him. When Lincoln was late for the interview, Kreismann was sent to his home to find out what was wrong, and a servant ushered him into the room where Mrs. Lincoln was having hysterics. According to Kreismann's story, she was trying to persuade Lincoln to make a certain appointment in which case she was to receive a diamond brooch as a reward for using her influence. The story rests entirely upon the word of one man, into whose mind and motives one cannot look fully. We do know, however, from his letter already quoted, that Kreismann was unfriendly to Mrs. Lincoln and was accepting and repeating gossip about her. A good deal hinges on the point as to where he got that detail about the brooch; that part of the story smacks of certain fabricated rumors that circulated later in Washington and we do not know at what time Kreismann told his tale. By the time Horace White wrote Herndon in 1891, Kreismann had gone back to Germany to live. Realizing the dubiousness of the story, White cautioned Herndon not to use it on his (White's) narration, adding justly that it would be best not to use it at all.

Herndon, of course, seized eagerly on the tale, saying: ". . . I will venture all I have that the story is correct." His reply gives a glimpse of his methods: "I am still diligently gathering well authenticated facts of Lincoln. Many I reject because they are not in harmony with the fundamental elements of L's nature . . . Every day or so I think of some fact or facts & they suggest to me some other fact or facts which make in me a conscious state, as if the thing—conditions & time were just present."

It goes without saying that Herndon played up the story in writing to Weik. Out of his imagination he produced variations on the theme of Mrs. Lincoln's hysterics, together with other unflattering details, and remarked apropos of the making of the appointment, "Lincoln had no true notions of the propriety of things, as a general rule." This letter reveals another of Herndon's methods. It had been his custom, he wrote, when he "wished to say something smart," to take "a Toddy as *Exciter.*"

A second- and third-hand story told thirty years after the event under these conditions cannot be accepted as reliable evidence. This is not to deny these three facts: Mrs. Lincoln did occasionally have hysterical seizures; she was, according to her own statement, spoiled by her husband's indulgence; and at the time mentioned, her thinking on matters of money and goods was becoming abnormal. Without conceding the authenticity of that particular brooch, it can be stated that both Lincoln and his wife constantly received gifts from that time on; this frequently gave rise to rumors that Mrs. Lincoln accepted bribes for using her influence.

In January the furniture of the Eighth Street house was advertised for private sale: "Parlor and Chamber Sets, Carpets, Sofas, Chairs, Wardrobes, Bureaus, Bedsteads, Stoves ... etc." The household articles accumulated in the Springfield years, invested with the importance of long familiarity, had now become useless to them, mere leftovers in living. When the Lincolns moved to the Chenery House, there was no longer a place which they could call "home." The last arrangements were checked off one by one. With his own hands the unassuming President-elect roped his own trunks, took some of the hotel cards and wrote on the back of them: "A. Lincoln White House Washington, D.C."

The morning of February 11 was depressing with gray skies, rain, and black mud. But they were all there at the Great Western Railroad depot to see him off, the faithful old neighbors and friends of office (except Herndon), street, and home. In the dingy station's waiting room Lincoln stood while they filed by to shake his hand, these fellow townsmen whose familiar faces were charged with deep feeling. As he passed through the crowd to the train platform, hands reached out to touch him again for the last time. Over all there hung the threat of a civil war.

Lincoln had not intended to speak (at least he had notified newspapermen that there would be no speechmaking on his part till he had left Springfield), but as he stood on the platform, out of his deep emotion came the words of a last farewell to these loved people whose lives were interwoven with his own. It was not only these personal ties which were being pulled apart; a way of life which he had found good was over. No more passing along the simple streets to friendly greetings and interchange of small personal news, no more dropping in for neighborly chats. No more would friends, with the understanding that only years can bring, come to share their troubles.

To them he owed everything, he said. "Here I have lived a quarter of a century, and have passed from a young to an old man. Here my children have been born, and one is buried." Mary was in that crowd, comforting herself with the last-minute plan that she would leave that evening and join him on the morrow. One knows well that her tears came at the mention of Eddie's grave. Where they were going, there would be no one who had wept with them in that sorrow, no one who would remember. Mary's loving and dependent heart was torn even as her husband's.

She heard that loved voice continue: "I now leave, not knowing when, or whether ever I may return, with a task before me greater than that which rested upon Washington." Again there was the chilling suggestion of danger. The rest is like a prayer: "Trusting in Him who can go with me, and remain with you and be everywhere for good, let us confidently hope that all will yet be well." That was better; Mary's faith was a comfort to her. Lincoln's breast was heaving with emotion and there was "scarcely a dry eye in all the vast crowd." He concluded: "To His care commending you, as I hope in your prayers you will commend me, I bid you an affectionate farewell." The train began to move. The married life of the Lincolns was four-fifths over. The "happiest stage" had come to an end.

chapter 17

"PITS AND PINNACLES OF CHANGE"

"Mrs. Lincoln left here last evening to overtake him [Lincoln] at Indianapolis at the suggestion of Gen. Scott," wrote James C. Conkling to his son on February 12, 1861. Lincoln was fifty-two that day, so Mary rejoined him on his birthday, a fact one may be sure she did not overlook. Her hurried departure was a pleasing bit of enterprise, of pluck and planning, on her part. It lends a certain point to a remark that Lincoln made about that time. Telling a story relating to missing articles and spouses, he commented humorously, ". . . if it were nothing but a wife that was missing, mine would be sure to pop up serenely somewhere." The words suggest laughter and joking over Mary's catching up with him so promptly. With the two young irrepressibles, Tad and Willie, in tow, she arrived about eleven in the morning, just in time to board the Presidential train before it pulled out. Since Robert had left Springfield with his father, the entire family was moving east at the dizzy rate of over thirty miles an hour.

It was a triumphal tour. "Men with Union flags were stationed every half a mile. Every town and village passed was decorated." Thousands stood by the tracks, shouting and waving flags as the train "swept by."

At stations where it stopped briefly Lincoln had the public man's perennial problem—to appear and please the waiting crowd, yet not to make a speech involving too many commitments. After a while he worked out a technique to deal with this difficulty. He would sit quietly in his seat until the conductor notified him that the train was about to start. "Then he would appear on the back platform to bow, with no time left for speaking." This was not his wish, for he was always ready to talk to the people, but it became necessary in the rigors of the journey that lasted nearly two weeks. The continued demands upon his time and energy included, besides arduous travel, numerous speeches, crowds to greet in the streets on long stops, receptions, hundreds of handshakings, and (at state capitals) formal meetings of legislatures. It was not merely that everyone wished to meet the incoming President; the country was in a fearful crisis and was looking to Lincoln to save the Union.

Indianapolis greeted the approach of the train with thirty-four guns, one for each state then in the Union. At that city even Robert, by this time dubbed, the "Prince of Rails," was called on for a speech, much to his disgust. He responded only by a wave of the hand. His kindly father smiled engagingly at the crowd and made everything all right by remarking that "his boy, Bob, hadn't got in the way of making speeches." Robert could not adapt himself to public appearances as his father and mother did. They both made a good job of it, but he apparently lacked their natural outflowing interest in people. He had written his mother two months before, apropos of an occasion when he feared being called upon to make a speech: "Just phancy my phelinks mounted on the rostrum, holding 'a vast sea of human faces' &c. I stop overwhelmed." Robert had grown up in a playful family which knew the fun of nonsense words.

At Indianapolis two close Illinois friends hid their deep feeling under a bit of roughhouse. In Lincoln's hotel room Jesse Dubois and Ebenezer Peck "took hold of him in a melo-dramatic manner. They hugged him, and told him to behave himself like a good boy in the White House, and lastly even cut a lock of hair off his head, with which they rushed triumphantly out of the room."

It is not to be wondered at that by the time the party reached Columbus, Ohio, Lincoln was hoarse and had a cold. But he was in the best of humor and "chatted and laughed continually. Mrs. Lincoln was likewise in her most pleasant mood and conversed with the ladies and gentlemen around her in the most lively manner." To quote a more folksy record, "she was tickled to death with all she had seen since leaving home." For her it was a glorified version of that other trip of which she had said, "*Words* cannot express what a merry time, we had, the gayest pleasure party, I have ever seen." It was all that and, in addition, the husband of her faith and pride was now the most important man in the country.

Glimpses along the way show the couple in their relation to each other. At Ashtabula, Ohio, when the cheering crowd called for Mrs. Lincoln, her husband told them he "didn't believe he could induce her to come out. In fact he could say that he never succeeded very well in getting her to do anything she didn't want to do." The crowd laughed delightedly. The throng at a station in Pennsylvania was equally tickled when he brought Mrs. Lincoln out on the platform and said he had concluded to give them "the long and the short of it!" One suspects that Mary did not think that as funny as the crowd did.

She did not approve of the shockingly bad hat and worn overcoat he was wearing on the trip and she did something about it, with the result that shortly after the train left Utica, New York, a colored servant "passed through the car with a handsome broadcloth over-coat upon his arm and a new hat-box in his hand." As the New York *Times* approvingly remarked: "Since then Mr. Lincoln has looked fifty per cent. better, and if Mrs. Lincoln's advice is always as near right as it was in this instance, the country may congratulate itself upon the fact that its President elect is a man who does not reject, even in important matters, the advice and counsel of his wife."

The interior of the Presidential car was the latest thing in railroad elegance. Light-colored tapestry carpet contrasted nicely with richly dark furniture complete with the scrolls and tassels dear to the Victorian heart. The side walls of the car beneath the windows were covered with crimson plush, while between the windows hung heavy blue silk studded with thirty-four silver stars. Two national flags of rich silk were crossed at each end of the car. Patriotism ran high at that time of crisis; it was emphasized in the red, white and blue festoons that hung from the molding.

The exterior also was a thing of vivid color, with glistening varnish and orange panels splashed with flourishes of black or brown. That bright train, with flags and streamers waving from engine and cars, presented a thrilling sight to the thousands who watched it pass. Fine traveling this for a man going East who came West walking beside oxen drawing a clumsy wagon.

Even without all this color, there could not fail to be gaiety on a train that carried so much youth. Willie and Tad were having the time of their lives, and doubtless added their boyish yells, as they had in Springfield, to the acclaim of the crowds. One of them (presumably the prank-loving Tad) amused himself nearly all the way by asking outsiders, "Do you want to see Old Abe?" and then pointing out someone else.

But even Tad seems to have got an excess of excitement. At Poughkeepsie, Mrs. Lincoln, seen through the windows, was warmly welcomed by the crowds. She promptly raised the window and returned the salutations. "Where are the children? Show us the children?" shouted one of the spectators. Mrs. Lincoln called Robert to the window, where he was greeted with cheers. "Have you any more on board?" was the next shout. "Yes, here's another," called Mary, entering into the spirit of the occasion, and turning to get Tad. That refractory little representative of the house of Lincoln promptly threw himself on the floor, and made a door mat of himself that refused to be budged. Mary, doubtless with laughing face, had to get the idea across to the crowd that the "pet of the family" objected to being exhibited. Tad fell down here as to public relations, but his mother gave a fine performance. There was reason for the New York *Herald* to make the comment that "Mr. Lincoln and Mrs. Lincoln produced a decidedly favorable impression" upon those who saw them.

Robert Lincoln, whose seventeen years plus were glorified with a stovepipe hat, was unanimously reported as very gay and carefree on the journey. A little too carefree, as, with the thoughtlessness of his age, he mislaid the little black satchel with which his father had entrusted him. That bag contained Lincoln's inaugural address and its loss would have had fearful consequences. Lincoln was in great anxiety until the "gripsack," to use his own words, which held "my certificate of moral character, written by myself" was recovered.

There were three young and gifted men aboard whose names are familiar in the Lincoln story. Two were to serve as secretaries in the White House throughout the war, John G. Nicolay and John Hay. Bavarian-born Nicolay was an able, quietly efficient young man on whom Lincoln could and did rely. John Hay, Illinois-bred, was young, brilliant, charming, and destined to a distinguished career. Both young men were to clash with Mrs. Lincoln, and Hay, with youth's intolerance and lack of understanding, was to turn the stiletto of his unforgettable phrasing against her with far-reaching effect down the years.

Associated with the bright image of the third young man,

Elmer Ephraim Ellsworth, are glamour and grief. His magnetism drew all hearts to the handsome military figure that in less than four months was to lie crumpled in death at the Marshall house in Alexandria. Mr. and Mrs. Lincoln loved him with that outpouring parental affection so characteristic of them both. They made a pet of him, an easy thing to do, for he was "brimming, running over with health, high spirits, ambition, hope, and all the exuberant life of a rarely vigorous nature."

Two mature gentlemen whose striking figures fitted well into the picturesqueness of the Presidential car, were Judge David Davis and Ward Hill Lamon. Judge Davis, with whom Lincoln had traveled the judicial circuit, had a circumference of such mighty proportions it was said he had to be surveyed for a pair of trousers! Lamon, also of large figure, had been Lincoln's law partner at Danville, Illinois, and was to be marshal of the District of Columbia. He was ready, at the drop of a hat, to use his remrkable strength in defense of Lincoln. The two men, strikingly different, had long had a tried and affectionate friendship. Lamon had "brought a banjo along," and entertained the party with Negro songs. With his robust figure plus banjo and joviality he seems the subject for a Hals painting with the red plush and silver-starred blue of the car somewhere in the background.

Lincoln passed from ovation to ovation. At Buffalo the pressure of the crowd was so great that one member of his escort had his arm dislocated in his efforts to keep people back. But the visit to Buffalo had its highlights too. The Lincolns lunched with ex-President Millard Fillmore at his home, doubtless a real thrill to Mary, who had written of him five years before that he had been a good President and she admired him greatly.

At Westfield Lincoln had bestowed a kiss upon Grace Bedell, the little girl who had advised him to grow whiskers. When the train reached the lordly Hudson, skaters greeted the President-elect with waving and cheers. Again one visualizes a scene for a painting: that festive train with its orange splashes, the great frozen river, the skating figures with their grace and the color of flying banners.

On February 19 the exhausted Lincolns arrived in New York and were taken to the Astor House. A gentleman also staying at that hotel eyed the new President from the West curiously and wrote his nephew and niece: "He is

a clever man, & *not so bad* looking as they say, while he
is no great beauty. He is tall (6 f. 4 in.) has a commanding figure; bows pretty well; is not stiff; has a pleasant
face, is amiable & *determined.*" The writer had gone to
Mrs. Lincoln's reception on February 20 and reported:
"She is a plump, amiable, modest, pleasant, round faced,
agreeable woman; with no silly airs; & they say is a pious woman. We feel a deep interest in them both, & trust
they have gone to deliver our country from the thraldom
of imbecility, knavery & slavery."

Whether Mary would have appreciated it or not, that
word "plump" appears in many of the descriptions, though
not oftener than the adjectives "amiable" and "pleasant."
She "looks like a good Motherly kind of a woman," ran
another of these informative letters, and very definitely
Mrs. Lincoln would not have cared for that way of putting it. As her youth receded, this petted woman had a
feminine desire to appear young and girlish, which is
no great novelty in her sex. Nor was her method of lop-
ping off a few years when she gave her age entirely
unique. On one matter all the accounts agree. At receptions and other public functions, Mrs. Lincoln did "her
part of the honors with becoming grace."

The trip had its shocks. At one station, a cannon was
placed too near the train for its salute, so that its discharge broke a window, covering this nervous woman with
shattered glass. Then, when they reached Pennsylvania,
Mary's high-soaring spirits were destined to take a deep
plunge. Allan Pinkerton, a Chicago detective, having
strong reason to suspect an assassination plot in Baltimore, urged and arranged a plan by which Lincoln was
taken secretly through that city by night ahead of the
rest of the party. The details of that exciting detective
story are told in Norma Cuthbert's *Lincoln and the Baltimore Plot,* which gives both Pinkerton's own account and
his Record Book. Both sources relate that Lincoln insisted that Mrs. Lincoln alone be told of the secret plan
in advance, "as otherwise she would be very much excited at his absence." No matter how intense the emergency, this husband never failed to consider his wife.

A. K. McClure recorded with a nuance of disapproval
that Mrs. Lincoln "was much disturbed by the suggestion
to separate the President from her, and she narrowly escaped attracting attention to the movements which re-

quired the utmost secrecy." Who would expect this excitable little woman to act otherwise? She had hurried her plans for her trip in order to be at his side in possible danger; now he was to leave her and be taken secretly at night through a city thought to harbor those who sought his life. Here was threat to the one who was dearer to her than life itself. She had never learned to control her emotions. Fear threw her into an unreasoning panic; she probably did create a scene. She could not go with him herself, but she knew one person who could be counted on to defend Lincoln with his own life, Ward Hill Lamon, and she insisted that he be allowed to accompany her husband. At Columbus it had been Lamon who placed his mighty form in front of Lincoln and protected him from being crushed by the crowd.

It has been recorded that Lincoln did not sleep that night as he lay in the train berth which was too short for his length, but little thought has been given to the wife who had to lie through hours of darkness in an agony of fear. In the morning (Saturday, February 23) came the relieving telegram announcing the safe arrival of the President-elect in Washington. The detective story has one glint of unconscious humor. Upon arrival Pinkerton sent a code telegram: "Plums arrived here with Nuts this morning—all right," which being decoded meant that Pinkerton had reached Washington safely with Lincoln!

Mary and the children with the rest of the party passed through the hostile city of Baltimore according to the original schedule, an ordeal to try nerves far steadier than hers. A lurid account of threatened mob violence appeared in one of the New York papers, but according to Nicolay, while they witnessed great crowds in the streets of Baltimore, they encountered no trouble. The "travelling show" ended in an anticlimax of secrecy and a flood of ridicule. Mary arrived in Washington in the late afternoon of February 23 and the Lincolns were united at Willard's Hotel, where they were to stay until the inauguration.

The days were crowded with meeting people, but when Judge and Mrs. H. N. Taft called upon the Lincolns on the evening of March 3, they noted a significant fact— few Washington women were there. The newcomers were not welcome in the capital, which had buzzed for weeks with stories of the uncouthness of both Mr. and Mrs. Lincoln. Washington "society" was horrified that this rustic couple were to occupy the White House. An incident in New York had brought home this arrogant attitude to Mary. She and her cousin Elizabeth Todd Grimsley had overheard from an adjoining table in a dining room such questions about Lincoln as these: "Could he, with any honor, fill the Presidential Chair?" "Would his western gaucherie disgrace the Nation?" At length one gentleman struck the table and exclaimed with great emphasis, "Well! if nothing more is effected it will help civilize the Illinoisans." No woman of Mary's high spirit could hear such things without resentment. There was the background of her sensitiveness as to her marrying a man reared in the backwoods. She knew she was socially well qualified. For that matter, so was Lincoln. He was not naïve; there was method in his simplicity. He was the skilled craftsman in human relations "who in all essential things had few superiors in easy dignity of manner . . ."

Her indignation at such unjust accusations was to result in a determination to show her critics that she could dress better, refurnish the White House better, and entertain as well or better than the best of them. It became a factor in her subsequent extravagance. Such acclaim as Mary had been receiving was calculated to turn any human head which was not exceedingly well fortified with humility. By February 27 the New York *Herald* was noting that "Mrs. Lincoln begins to feel her importance, has a great deal of dignity, and accepts becomingly enough the deference which all pay her."

But the graph of the days ahead was to rise and dip in sharp points; there was never a time from the election of Lincoln on that the glory for Mary was not tarnished at frequent intervals by criticism, hostility, threat, anxiety, illness, or sorrow. The same was true for her husband. Along with cheers he was receiving a stream of almost unbelievable abuse. An illustration of this shocking contrast and the grimness of the situation is found in a letter which was waiting for him at Washington at the end of that triumphal journey. The letter was preserved perhaps as a supreme example of depravity and only recently came to light. It began, "If you don't Resign we are going to put a spider in your dumpling and play the Devil with you." Then followed about nine lines of unprintable abuse, ending ". . . you are nothing but a goddam Black nigger." The last sentence shows not only the fanatical hatred of Lincoln, but also the cruel attitude toward what Mary Lincoln sympathetically called "all the oppressed colored race."

Elizabeth Todd Grimsley, "Cousin Lizzie," who had been a bridesmaid at the Lincoln wedding, was one of a number of Mary's relatives who came to Washington to attend the inauguration. Old differences of opinion sank beneath the surface where family solidarity was concerned, and there was the added fact that the Todd women were attractive social assets and could be a real help to Mary. "The papers announce the presence of 100 Todds and all wanting office," wrote Cousin Lizzie in March to Cousin John T. Stuart, back in Springfield. This figure was considerably exaggerated, but, in addition to Mrs. Grimsley herself, Mrs. Ninian W. Edwards, with her two daughters, Julia Edwards Baker and Elizabeth Edwards, was at the White House and so was Margaret Todd Kellogg, Mary's half sister.

Crowded confused days moved swiftly to March 4. That morning Lincoln read his inauguration address to his family, then asked them to leave him alone for a while, which they did. From an adjoining room, Mary thought she heard her husband's voice raised in prayer. It was a day of days for prayer, March 4, 1861, with the country falling apart and facing the dark menace of war. Little Julia Taft, shortly to trip delightfully into this story, was awakened the night before by "a curious jarring rumble" as a battery passed to be posted on the corner of 12th Street and the Avenue. The air was tense with apprehension of violence. General Scott had received over three hundred letters of hostile and threatening character and he was safeguarding the incoming President with every possible precaution. Julia's mother, Mrs. Taft, did not want her husband to go to the Capitol, so sure was she that there would be trouble. The Taft family, therefore, watched from a window of Woodward's hardware store on Pennsylvania Avenue, noting as they took their seats a file of green-coated sharpshooters going up to the roof to guard the movement of the Presidential carriage as it passed. Troops lined the Avenue and street corners were under armed guard. As Julia Taft got her first view of Lincoln seated beside the outgoing President, James Buchanan, in the passing carriage, she heard a voice nearby say: "There goes that

Illinois ape, the cursed Abolitionist. But he will never come back alive."

Just what was Mary's reaction to this air of menace as she rode toward the Capitol, one can only guess. The weather, which had been cloudy at dawn, had fortunately cleared; there was sunshine for the inaugural parade. Street sweepers the night before had done what they could with Washington's inevitable mud or dust. Mary with her three sons and party of relatives sat in the diplomatic gallery of the Senate Chamber to watch the Vice President take the oath of office. Outside at the Capitol's east front a platform large enough to hold several hundred people had been erected. Behind it at the center of the Capitol rose, not the low inverted-bowl structure with which Mary had been familiar in 1847, but a new unfinished dome, its truncated top ending in a derrick which pierced the sky. That half-constructed dome was to become symbolic of the Union, threatening to break in two and never to be a completed whole.

Mrs. Lincoln and the family party sat on the platform back of those figures which held all eyes, President Buchanan, Chief Justice Taney, and Abraham Lincoln. Cousin Lizzie Grimsley remembered afterwards the "sea of upturned faces, representing every shade of feeling; hatred, discontent, anxiety and admiration," which crowded the East Plaza. Since she was sitting behind him, Mary probably could see only the back of her husband's head, with the dear familiar shagginess of the black hair. She could not see the sensitive face, but she heard the earnest, pleading voice that was saying to all the country and especially to the inflamed South: "We are not enemies, but friends. We must not be enemies. Though passion may have strained, it must not break our bonds of affection." Did Mary's thoughts turn at those words toward her blood kin in the South who, if war came, would fight against her husband? The compelling voice went on: "The mystic chords of memory, stretching from every battle-field and patriot grave to every living heart and hearthstone all over this broad land, will yet swell the chorus of the Union when again touched, as surely they will be, by the better angels of our nature." Mary's poetry-loving soul could rise to salute the perfection of those lines.

At the close of the ceremony President and Mrs. Lincoln were driven to 1600 Pennsylvania Avenue, where

"Old Edward," doorkeeper since the days of President Taylor, opened the doors of the White House to welcome them in. Lincoln had a strong sense of history and this quality was not lacking in Mary. Did a strange awe affect them as they crossed that historic threshold? It was reported that General Scott ("Old Fuss and Feathers") gave a sigh of relief; when the new President was safely inside he said: "Thank God, we now have a government."

Exalted events must give way to human need for food and rest. Elizabeth Grimsley relates briefly that about seventeen sat down to dinner in the White House that evening and then scattered to their rooms for a short rest before dressing for that brilliant event, the Inauguration Ball. Every detail of that elaborate dressing was important to Mary with her pride in clothes, especially as the ball was like a dress parade for the President and his family on exhibition.

It was a quarter to eleven when the Presidential procession, two by two, entered the ballroom, Mary—so strange is history—on the arm of Senator Douglas, who had once in young Springfield days been her beau, and had later become Lincoln's opponent in the famous debates. Those two could have had much to talk about concerning the ways of Providence as they took their part in the pageant. "The band struck up 'Hail Columbia,' and the party marched from one end of the hall to the other, amid inspiring strains of the national air, causing an era of tremendous good feeling."

Mary danced the quadrille of the evening with Douglas, and a striking couple they undoubtedly made. Lincoln left a little before twelve-thirty, but the ladies stayed on to dance a while longer before returning to the White House. So closed the momentous day. Perhaps the President and First Lady were able to rest, perhaps not. But there was to be little sound, untroubled sleep for them in the coming four years under the historic roof which sheltered them that night for the first time.

"EMPANELED TO CONVICT"

The inauguration was on a Monday. Tuesday morning at eight o'clock a mulatto woman with a fine, intelligent face and dignified carriage entered the White House. Mrs. Elizabeth Keckley, formerly a slave, was a skilled mantua-maker or modiste and had come by appointment to arrange for making some dresses for the new First Lady. She was a woman of strong and soothing personality, and Mrs. Lincoln, who had grown up relying on colored servants and was soon to find herself very lonely in the White House, came in time to depend upon her as maid and companion. Thus Mrs. Keckley became an important witness in the story of the Lincoln marriage; she left, as we have already seen, an intimate (though ghost-written) account of what occurred behind the scenes. Mrs. Keckley had seen Mrs. Lincoln briefly the morning before at Willard's and had noted her "cheery voice" and tendency to stoutness.

In spite of late hours the night before, Mary, with her usual energy, was up and at breakfast. Shortly thereafter Mrs. Keckley was taken upstairs, where Mrs. Lincoln greeted her warmly. Mary was surrounded that morning by a little group of female relatives. One often wonders how hoop-skirted ladies dressed in less formal moments. Hoops would have been a serious impediment to household duties. Mrs. Keckley supplies the answer: Mrs. Lincoln was dressed in a "cashmere wrapper, quilted down the front; and she wore a simple head-dress. The other ladies wore morning robes."

An old familiar trait of Mary's cropped up in the interview which followed; she wanted Mrs. Keckley's services in sewing only if her terms were "reasonable." "I cannot afford to be extravagant," she is quoted as saying. "We are just from the West, and are poor." Elizabeth Grimsley was encountering the same attitude. Writing back to Springfield, she mentioned that Mary told her, apropos of her coming to Washington, "to count the expense well and know how I was to get home." In other words Mary was indicating to Cousin Lizzie that borrowing from the Lincolns was not in order. It was partly Mary's penny-pinching complex, but there are other suggestions of a shortage of cash in the Lincoln family at this time. Ward Hill Lamon makes the statement that Lincoln had to borrow money "to defray expenses for the first months of his residence at the White House." Mary's mind was getting increasingly tangled on the question of being poor but up to this time there are in the record more statements of their poverty by Lincoln himself than by his wife.

Tuesday, March 5, was, as it would have been for any household, the busy day of settling into new quarters. The house must be inspected from top to bottom, a duty in which Willie and Tad proved most zealous. They interviewed every member of the staff with a thousand boyish questions, especially "Old Edward," the doorkeeper, who was probably quite equal to the occasion, for he has been described as "a short, thin, humorous Irishman, to be trusted equally with state secrets, or with the diplomatic management of the President's unpredictable young son Tad."

As Mary and the consignment of relatives made the tour, they became more and more disappointed and dismayed. The only elegance of the mansion was in the East, Blue, and Red rooms and their splendor was decidedly tarnished by daylight. Paint, furniture, and almost everything about the house needed renewal. The shabbiness of the family suite was found to be amazing. Mrs. Grimsley recorded with a touch of scorn that "A mahogany French bedstead, split from top to bottom, was the best piece of furniture in it . . ." The basement had "the air of an old and unsuccessful hotel." One can imagine the indignant comments of Mary and her kin at such makeshift furnishings. Since they had the Todd habit of expressing themselves emphatically, Mary's determination to improve conditions doubtless received no little stimulation during this tour. She was to go at this task with her usual good intentions, but with questionable judgment and an excess of zeal.

In the household arrangement as the Lincolns worked it out, the east half of the White House, roughly speaking, was devoted to business and public affairs; the west half, except for the state dining room, was for the family.

Downstairs on the left as one entered was the East Room, the great drawing room where the large receptions were held. At the back, facing south, were three smaller parlors, the Green, Blue, and Red rooms. "The last named of these is the favorite sitting room of Mrs. Lincoln," runs a description written two years after the Lincolns moved in, when some refurnishing had taken place, "where she receives private calls every evening in the week when in town, and where the President usually meets his friends socially after dinner." The interior sounds typically Victorian: "The furniture is very rich— of crimson satin and gold damask, with heavy gilded cornices to the windows and a profusion of ormolu work, vases, etc., some of which stuff is very ancient, being bought or presented during Monroe's and Madison's administrations. There is a grand piano in this room and a full length portrait of Washington . . ."

The family dining room was toward the front on the west side of the house; the state dining room was at the southwest corner. Attached to the house on the west was the conservatory, where one could escape from the stuffiness of Victorian interiors into the moist, green and fragrant world of growing plants and flowers. Upstairs the west half was given to family and guest chambers. Over the East Room were the President's office, the waiting room, and the office of the private secretaries, Nicolay and Hay.

Another young man with secretarial duties was soon to be added to the staff, William O. Stoddard, of pleasant and tactful personality. Between him and Mrs. Lincoln developed a warm liking and friendship. She saw far more of him than of Nicolay and Hay as he was the one delegated to open the flood of mail that came to the First Lady. There were likes and dislikes blowing about the White House like winds that cannot be seen but nevertheless are keenly felt. They are discernible only in their effects. Nicolay's daughter has written that Mrs. Lincoln liked "Stod" better than the other two secretaries. Nicolay and Hay were described by a reliable witness with direct knowledge as "snobby and unpopular." They had a difficult position in protecting Lincoln from the impatient crowd of people always wanting to see him, but it was suggested that "an inside guardian of affable address" would have created a better impression on the public.

Stoddard had a smooth-flowing pen as well as a sympathetic approach. Let him tell of the arrangement between himself and Mrs. Lincoln. Carrying a consignment of letters and a letter opener, he met her by appointment one morning in the Red Room. He found her "a pleasant-looking woman" and apparently "in fine health and spirits." He explained the business in hand with a playful touch such as Lincoln himself so often used: "This rascally paper-folder, Mrs. Lincoln. A lot of your letters—here they are—were lying on their faces on my table, and he got at them and opened every one of them. I caught him and choked him off before he had time to read them, but I'd like to know what I am to do about him?"

Mrs. Lincoln with a pleasant "Oh dear me! Is that all?" told him to read all of her letters before presenting them. She had evidently read a few by the time Stoddard came, and she continued: "I do not wish to open a letter, nor even a parcel, of any kind, until after you have examined it. Never!" The young man understood the vehemence of the last word when he came to inspect her letters. "The insane, the depraved and the fiendish have by no means restricted themselves to the President in their infamous penmanship. His vilest foes are willing to vent their infernal malice upon his unoffending wife . . .".

Mrs. Grimsley tells how, before the first day in the White House was half spent, the place was overrun with office seekers who filled waiting rooms, halls and corridors, and even invaded private apartments. This "throng continued and increased for weeks, intercepting the President on his way to his meals . . ." Lincoln, under the intolerable pressure of people wanting to see him as well as a thousand and one duties crowding upon him for attention, would have forgotten his meals altogether if his wife had not seen to it that he ate sufficient food. The first day gave some indication of the strain that living in the White House was to be, but only a faint hint, as war had not yet come. That proud dwelling which had loomed as the destination of Mary's hopes was not only shabby, it was like a madhouse in its turmoil and certainly no place for a woman of her nervous temperament.

The first of a regular series of Friday evening receptions or levees was held on March 8. This was the function for which Mrs. Keckley had been engaged to make

"a bright rose-colored moire-antique," undoubtedly a becoming choice for fair skin, blue eyes, and rich brown
hair. The ultraelaborate costumes required endless stitching by hand, and Mrs. Lincoln complicated matters, womanlike, by changing her mind as to some details of the
style. She also gave Mrs. Keckley orders for a waist
of blue watered silk for Mrs. Grimsley.

With these delays Mrs. Keckley was behind in her schedule and it was the evening of the levee itself when she
finally arrived at the White House with the dress. She
found Mrs. Lincoln in a state of upset nerves and full of
reproaches for the tardiness. Mrs. Keckley apologized,
and offered to help her dress, saying it would take only a
few minutes. It was not without reason that Lincoln sometimes called Mary his child-wife and it is also revealing
that she liked the name. To act like a child in order to be
petted while at the same time bolstering a masculine feeling of strength and superiority has been a method long
known to the feminine mind. There is distinctly a suggestion of the humored child in what Mrs. Lincoln is quoted
as saying: "No, I won't be dressed. I will stay in my room.
Mr. Lincoln can go down with the other ladies." Mrs.
Edwards and Mrs. Grimsley supplied the needed soothing persuasion and, once she saw herself dressed in the
flattering rose-color with pearl earrings, necklace, and
bracelets and with roses in her hair, Mary was—again
like a child—in joyful spirits once more.

Lincoln came into the room, threw himself on the sofa,
and commenced pulling on his white kid gloves. They
made his powerful hands very conspicuous—great white
lumps against the blackness of his attire. He was quoting
poetry all the while until his wife remarked that he
seemed to be in poetical mood. "Yes, mother," he answered pleasantly, "these are poetical times." Then, the
becoming effect of the rose-color not being lost on him,
he continued, "I declare, you look charming in that dress.
Mrs. Keckley has met with great success." He always enjoyed seeing Mary dressed for a party, just as she liked
to see him in the best attire. This artist in dealing with
people soon had the roomful of nervous women all feeling
good again. Of course he did not fail to compliment the
other ladies on their charming appearance too.

There was a last-minute hitch when Mary's handkerchief could not be found, that prankster Tad having ap-

propriated it as a practical joke. But in the end Mary took her husband's arm with smiling face and the two, perhaps with a pleasant sense of playing a role in a drama, went down the historic stairs together.

Mrs. Keckley, who had heard the gossip with which Washington tongues were wagging—that the new First Lady was ignorant, vulgar, and unused to polite society— felt surprised at her grace and composure. The hostess who greeted the crowd below was dignified, calm, and completely charming. Conditions were trying. The throngs were immense and much "crinoline suffered mercilessly." Ladies in hoop skirts filled up space very quickly; dented crinoline was as common as dented fenders are today.

There was little reason for the brightness in the face above the rose-colored moire. Many eyes that met Mary's were unfriendly and searching for faults. Few women have been placed in as difficult and lonely a position as Mrs. Lincoln. To be raised to high position is usually to be lonely, but there are many varieties of hostility and it seemed that she was the target of them all.

Washington entrenched society looked down on her as coming from "uncivilized" Illinois. It was the fashion to pass around stories of her alleged crudity and lack of education. Mrs. Grimsley, who knew herself, as all the Todd women did, to be well-born and well-bred, gave her opinion of those tilted noses in a letter back home: "I have seen *so many* disagreeable ones, who value themselves and other people only by their laces and diamonds." Then she added with quiet dignity: "But after all there are none so very elegant as to make me wish myself at home or in a corner."

In spite of her excellent cultural and social training Mary's horizon had been mostly limited to two small towns; hers had been the restricted rearing allotted to genteel females in the eighteen-twenties and thirties. She had lived in the personal and local in a time when poor communication cut sections of the country off from each other. There were real differences in social usages between East and West. Young Nicolay wrote his fiancée that the manner of dancing in Washington seemed strange to him, adding, "It may be fun to dance in this way, but according to a 'barbarian's' view, there is very little sense or reason in it." He was not yielding his Western point of view, nor was Mrs. Grimsley, who said meaningly, ". . .

we were all reared in the free air of the prairies, with a certain sense of independence . . ." A gentleman from Denmark, when a guest at dinner in the White House, summed up the situation very neatly: "My observation leads me to think there is too much snobbishness . . . in the East towards the West, which is returned with greatly exaggerated prejudice." Southerners, soon to vanish from the Washington social scene, despised Mrs. Lincoln, the wife of the Republican President, as a traitor to her own people. This despising, combining sectional and political antagonism, was soon to deepen into actual war hatred, especially as a number of Mary's own family would be fighting on the Confederate side.

Northerners, already antagonistic to her as a Westerner, were, with the actual outbreak of war, to hear wildly circulating rumors of her disloyalty and to be suspicious of her as a Southern spy in the Executive Mansion.

Mary herself said (after she had been in the White House for a year, made many blunders, and had begun to realize the tangled net in which she was trapped) that she had been the victim of *"evil counselors."* The friend to whom she said this wrote indignantly: "Women who knew the wire-pulling at Washington, whose toilet arts and social *pretensions,* society-lobbying and opportunity-seeking, taught them to lie in wait and rise in the social scale by intimacy at the White House, these basely laughed at the credulous woman who took counsel from them, and struck aside the ladder of her friendship by which alone they had been able to climb. Some said to her, 'They say you are a Western woman, and that brilliant life is unknown to you. Prove by your style and splendor that to be Western is not to be a boor.' Others said (and these were wives of certain army officers and office-holders, rebels in heart, but protected by disguise of loyal livery), 'We rejoice to have a Union Southern lady in the White House, one who will understand to be our friend.' And so they found a welcome to her home, where they evinced their chivalric spirit by ridiculing her 'attempts at Southern hospitality.' "

Mary, used to relying on neighbors at Springfield who, however much they might gossip, could be depended upon to be kind and helpful, was as defenseless as a trusting child among these scheming females.

There was also jealousy of her as the wife of the highest official. Beautiful, sophisticated, ambitious Kate Chase, whose father, Secretary of the Treasury Salmon P. Chase, was quite willing to be President, could not be expected to like this outspoken little woman from Illinois who was in the White House where Kate herself wanted to be. There was a peculiar feminine quality to that dislike and Kate Chase had no monopoly of it in Washington. It did not help matters that Mary herself liked a great deal of attention, and was jealous of other women talking with her husband.

One thing she had probably not foreseen was the way ladies in Washington would flock around the President. Lincoln was distinctly a man's man. In Springfield at social gatherings, instead of talking with the women, he liked to get off with the other men and tell stories. But in Washington there were handsome and sophisticated ladies who delighted to talk with and perhaps use a bit of Victorian coquetry on anyone as important as Mr. President. Mary herself was good at coquetry, but to her the sight of a pretty woman flattering her husband, or fawning upon him, would have been unbearable. Her intense love was possessive.

To Lincoln the situation had at times its amusing side. After all, jealousy in a wife is flattering. He had always a gentle way of speaking to women and doubtless at times used a bit of the playfulness which he employed with Mary and their boys, but as far as romantic interest was concerned his wife filled his life and other women did not exist. Perhaps Mary's jealousy had its source in a feeling of inadequacy. Emotionally unstable, she could not rely upon herself, knowing that she would at times flare up and say things for which she later realized she must apologize. In calm moments she could recognize and be sorry for her own shortcomings.

All this is the background of a scene presented by Mrs. Keckley in which we catch Lincoln in the act of teasing his wife. Just prior to going downstairs to one of the receptions he came into her room as she finished dressing for the occasion. Pulling on his gloves as he spoke he began "with a merry twinkle in his eyes" to ask which ladies he would be permitted to talk to that evening. As he mentioned this or that one, Mrs. Lincoln scored her off as "deceitful" or detestable or, worse still, "young and handsome," Lincoln all the while enjoying a tall man's amused indulgence of a spirited little woman. She told him in heated terms that she did not approve of his "flirtations with silly women, just as if you were a beardless boy, fresh from school."

"But, mother," he argued, "I insist that I must talk with somebody. I can't stand around like a simpleton, and say nothing." Then, his teasing over, he offered "mother" his arm and in perfect harmony they went down the stairs together.

It will be seen later that in the bitter politics of wartime, there was a deliberate launching of a whispering campaign against Mrs. Lincoln as a way of injuring her husband. Opponents were quick to recognize her vulnerability in human shortcomings. Fierce searchlights of hostile publicity and the red glare of war were turned upon this well-intentioned woman to throw into distorted relief every flaw in her nature. Mary in Washington was surrounded constantly by "a jury empaneled to convict on every count of every indictment which any slanderous tongue may bring against her ..." These are the words of that understanding secretary who knew her best, Mr. Stoddard, and he adds to them this well-considered judgment: "That she should make a success here, under such circumstances, under the focalized bitterness of all possible adverse criticisms, was simply out of the question; but she has done vastly better than her ill-natured critics are at all willing to admit."

Mary brought to her position as White House hostess fine qualifications: the birth and rearing of a gentlewoman, an excellent cultural education, a bright, quick, responsive mind, the charm of a vital and joyous personality, a conscientious desire to help her husband by fulfilling her duties, and the love of social life that stems from a genuine interest in people and events. That she was not acquainted with the superficial sophistications of Washington society was important only to that society itself, but the said society was extremely vocal about the matter. She had the fortitude required for standing in line to greet an endless chain of people and to be gracious and interested in each one. She could sit through a four-hour dinner of notables stiff with their own dignity, keeping the conversation lively, meeting unexpected contingencies with composure, taking care to neglect no guest.

Few women at the time could have met as well the awkward situation of entertaining the Chilean ambassador and his wife who could not speak a word of English. Mary reached back in her mind to the training at Madame Mentelle's and conversed with her guests in her long unused French. This incident seems to have a connection with an item which appeared in a newspaper that fall to the effect that Mrs. Lincoln was studying French. This lady was willing to work at her new job. That she reviewed to good purpose was evident in her later life when she was living in France and using the language constantly with perfect ease.

There is appealing evidence that Lincoln was proud both of his wife's appearance and her social grace and that his sensitive face gave that fact away whenever he looked at her. One close to them in friendship described his expression as "the *pleasing look* of *Abraham Lincoln*—for *her whom he so loved.*" Another woman chatting with the President in the great East Room on a social evening found his attention wandering from the conversation as his eyes followed Mrs. Lincoln. Caught in the act he laughed pleasantly and explained: "My wife is as handsome as when she was a girl, and I, a poor nobody then, fell in love with her; and what is more," he continued, "I have never fallen out." Still a third lady, noting that telltale light in his eyes when Mary entered dressed in white silk with roses in her hair, said to him tactfully: "How very young she is looking." The President smiled warmly and was evidently much pleased at the remark. Some felt she was overdressed at times—it was a grandiloquent age—but what Mary wore evidently looked good to him. One does wonder, however, what was the reaction of his sense of humor to a bonnet presented to Mrs. Lincoln by the ladies of New York, a bonnet whose strings were adorned with a likeness of himself surrounded by a wreath. The question of low-necked dresses was a controversial one. Mary probably considered Lincoln's attitude behind the times. There was another engaging scene just before a reception when he viewed her dressed in a satin gown with long train. "Whew!" he remarked teasingly, "our cat has a long tail to-night." Then, in the gentle paternal manner he used when offering her advice, he said: "Mother, it is my opinion, if some of that tail was nearer the head, it would be in better style."

It is amusing to find this same difference of masculine and feminine approach causing argument in another historic family of the time, that of General U. S. Grant. The occasion was a reception in 1865. Presenting a friend, Mrs. Grant said: "Now, General, here is Mrs. Tripler with a low-necked dress. I have a neck, too. But you don't let me wear such a dress." Mrs. Eunice Tripler, receiving a nudge, rose to the occasion with this impressive statement: "Every woman is bound to make the best appearance she can in observance of the proper customs of her time and station." The general could win battles, but two women with their minds made up were too much for him. At a later reception Mrs. Tripler noted with great satisfaction that Mrs. Grant wore a low-necked gown.

That Mary Lincoln "had a neck" white and beautifully molded is well attested. Naturally she wanted to wear the low-necked dresses so alluringly pictured in the fashion books of the time. But that too brought its flood of criticism. A roughhewn and dairy-minded senator from Oregon wrote to his wife from Washington early in 1862 telling of his attendance at "Mrs. Lincoln's party" in the East Room, which was "about the size of our big red barn ..." He looked upon the assembled ladies with a cold and disapproving eye; not one was "handsome" but they "were all distinguished for paint and big Hoops, with dresses a great deal too long at one end, and quite as much *too short at the other*." He and Lincoln evidently agreed on that point. The senator continued: "There were big fat dowagers in *low-necked* dresses who would have excited the envy and admiration of a *Dairyman*."

The gentleman from Oregon came to that reception to criticize and criticize he did. "The weak minded Mrs. Lincoln had *her bosom* on exhibition, and a flower pot on her head, while there was a train of silk, or satin draging on the floor behind her of Several yards in length, as I looked at her I could not help regretting that she had degenerated from the industrious and unpretending woman that she *was* in the days when she used to cook old Abes dinner, and milk the cows with her own hands." He continued with more of the same, the lacteal theme predominating. His language was typical of letters being written and of gossip being mouthed in Washington. It was the fashion to criticize the Lincolns and everyone was doing it.

It was as Stoddard said: that she could make a success under existing conditions was out of the question. A paragon of all the feminine virtues could not have done so, and Mrs. Lincoln's personality included its list of liabilities. In impulsiveness and imprudence, in emotional immaturity, in that tendency to view things personally which shuts out broader wisdom, in susceptibility to flattery, in nervousness aggravated by migraine headaches and the mental tensions of the menopause, in growing irrationality as to money, she had hidden weaknesses that were to pull her down in one of the most taxing situations a woman ever faced. These defects were not apparent like blindness or a crippled limb. She was like a foot soldier with secret lameness who must march long distances day after day through four years of war.

Lincoln at this time was probably finding Mary's moods unpredictable, as has happened to other husbands when their wives reached the forties. "It was not easy, at first," wrote Stoddard, "to understand why a lady who could be one day so kindly, so considerate, so generous, so thoughtful and so hopeful, could, upon another day, appear so unreasonable, so irritable, so despondent, so even niggardly, and so prone to see the dark, the wrong side of men and women and events."

Strange dark moods when all interest in living faded into an overwhelming feeling of insecurity came intermittently to Mary Lincoln. Stoddard had talked the matter over with a doctor when he wrote: "Probably all physicians and most middle-aged people will understand better than could a youthful secretary the causes of a sudden horror of poverty to come, for example, which, during a few hours of extreme depression, proposed to sell the very manure in the Executive stables . . ."

On the same page where he mentions that Mrs. Lincoln was at times unreasonable, Stoddard tells of one of her redeeming traits which has been largely overlooked. She had an authoritative manner of speaking, "but it is entirely easy, for all that, to meet her with the most positive and strenuous negatives. She is always ready to listen to argument and to yield to plainly put reasons for doing or for not doing, provided the arguments come from a recognized friend . . ." Mary, like most people, would take no advice or criticism from those she disliked; as Stoddard added: ". . . her personal antipathies are quick and

strong, and at times they find hasty and resentful forms
of expression."

Just how unaware Mrs. Lincoln was at first of this
barbed-wire entanglement of hostility is evident in a most
unusual description of her as she appeared at one of her
early receptions. It was written by a woman who is a most
fascinating study in her own right. Laura Catherine Redden Searing, who wrote under the pen name "Howard
Glyndon," was a poet and journalist who was sent to
Washington as correspondent for the St. Louis *Republican*
during the Civil War. An illness at eleven had rendered
her completely deaf and as a result she was unable to
speak except in a sepulchral tone; she therefore in conversation at this time depended much upon writing. Except that she was not blind, she reminds one of Helen
Keller in her indomitable spirit and literary gifts. Perhaps
as compensation for her misfortune, she was able to look
beneath the surface of trivialities and penetrate to essential meanings.

She gazed at Mrs. Lincoln with coolly analytical eyes
and wrote down what she saw. Many of the word portraits of the First Lady are in the colorless conventional
language which Victorian taste dictated. They are dry
leaves of description, where this one comes to life.

The newspaperwoman was in the Blue Room toward
the close of a reception when Mrs. Lincoln, mindful of a
hostess's duty to circulate and greet all the guests, approached her. She did not care for the elaborate lilac
dress which Mrs. Lincoln wore: "It was made very
decolleté as to the shoulders, bust, and arms; but she
had a certain dimpled chubbiness as to these which justified the style. That portion of her skin visible was of a becoming whiteness." It was typical of the critical atmosphere always surrounding Mrs. Lincoln that when the
journalist audibly admired that white skin, she was
"jeered at for not detecting cosmetics." But, the writer
continued, "At all events, the charm of her face was not
owing to cosmetics. It was a chubby, good-natured face.
It was the face of a woman who enjoyed life, a good
joke, good eating, fine clothes, and fine horses and carriages, and luxurious surroundings; but it was also the
face of a woman whose affectionate nature was predomi-
nant." Another shrewd judgment followed: "You might
safely take your oath that she would be fussy on occa-

sion; but the clouds would not last long with her, and she would soon be laughing as heartily as ever." Descriptions of Lincoln's famous laugh have been written in many places; it has been overlooked that his wife also had the gift of laughter. The lady journalist continued: "There is no doubt but that Mr. Lincoln found in her, despite her foibles and sometimes her puerileness, just what he needed, and that she was a most loyal wife and mother and a good woman."

Mrs. Searing (or Miss Redden as she was during the Civil War) sized up with the same clear-sightedness the situation in which Mrs. Lincoln was placed. Her "want of success socially" was due to the circumstances. "It is true that she did not appreciate these difficulties, and, by injudiciousness, she increased them . . ." "It was Mrs. Lincoln's fate from the first to be pilloried by all the viler elements of society, as the wife of the first Republican President; and it was her misfortune that she was not fitted by Nature to bear herself sublimely in the pillory. She refused to pose as a martyr, and insisted on enjoying herself in her own way all she could." The last statement was true only the first year in the White House. After February 20, 1862, Mary Lincoln was a chastened and grieving mother who was never again to feel complete wholehearted enjoyment.

This discerning woman, Laura Redden, saw as Stoddard had seen the hopelessness of Mary's dilemma: "It would have been quite impossible, under any circumstances, for her to have satisfied the opposing factions of the day." Equally understanding is the comment: "Her blunders annoyed her husband, but made her not less dear to him."

"Poor, outspoken, impulsive, frank-hearted, and uncalculating woman" was the summing up of the First Lady's qualities by Laura Redden. She added one significant statement that may be transferred down the years to express in part a present injustice: "I am ashamed," she wrote, "that to-day, nothing of Mary Lincoln's goodness of heart . . . is remembered or spoken of."

The wife of Abraham Lincoln in joyous humor on that train moving toward Washington in February 1861 had been like Icarus soaring toward the sun with wings attached by wax.

chapter 19

ATTENTION OF THE PRESIDENT'S WIFE

The new First Lady soon found herself swept along in a
stream of events. There is always the increment of the unexpected; the family was scarcely settled in the White
House when the boys were taken ill. Any mother who has
raised a family knows that when life is especially complicated and busy, the children are sure to catch something.
What Willie and Tad caught was the measles. They were
sick for two or three weeks, and Mary, as usual, was much
upset. Mrs. Grimsley explained the situation: "The
mother, always over-anxious and worried about the boys
and withal not a skillful nurse, was totally unfitted for
caring for them." The pampered youngsters did not take
to their attendant maid, so the one who did the nursing
was "Cousin Lizzie," with frequent visits from the burdened but devoted father. "I never regretted the days
thus spent," wrote Mrs. Grimsley, "for then I learned to
know the depth, tenderness, and purity of Mr. Lincoln's
nature, his gentleness and patience."

Elizabeth Grimsley stayed on at the White House for six
months after the inauguration—not that she wished to, as
she had left her children in Springfield, but, as she wrote
"Cousin John" Stuart, "Whenever I mention my return
home Mary instantly objects . . ." The relatives evidently
understood that Mary, nervous and impulsive, was fundamentally dependent upon the calmness and balance of
others. As her nervous condition and sense of insecurity
grew worse in the White House, it is pitiful to discover
how Lincoln, knowing her need, begged first one and then
another of her sisters to stay with her. The family all knew
what the Springfield neighbors had found out—that, in
spite of high spirit and courage in certain respects, Mrs.
Lincoln "was a very timid woman, usually in time of
trial."

She went into a panic in a carriage accident in June

1861. Mrs. Lincoln, Mrs. Grimsley, and the Lincoln boys, accompanied by General Hiram Walbridge, were driving over to Virginia to have a look at the camps, when the horses of the Presidential carriage stumbled and fell, throwing the driver off the box and breaking the pole. The newspapers played up Mrs. Lincoln's presence of mind, but Mrs. Grimsley's account to Cousin John dealt laconically with the plain facts: "I suppose you saw by the N.Y. papers the narrow escape we made on Friday evening. I am confident had it not been for General Walbridge who was with us, that Taddy would have been crushed by the wheel. You will certainly think Mary and I have changed characters as the papers represent her as acting with great coolness while I had to be assisted from the carriage. So much for reporters." There was no serious physical hurt to Mrs. Lincoln, as there was to be in a carriage accident two years later, but it was one of the many shocks that beat in upon the Presidential family.

April 1861 found the country in Civil War. Early on the morning of the 12th, the Confederates fired upon the Union-held Fort Sumter, and on April 15 Lincoln called for seventy-five thousand troops. That all-pervading gloom that only war can bring settled over the city as the government geared itself for fighting. Washington society was disintegrating. Southerners soon disappeared, taking with them, as Mrs. Grimsley regretfully recorded, the charm of Southern culture. She commented with some distaste upon certain new-rich elements which took their place. "The city is full of strangers . . . and many are here whose sole business it is to *'invigorate* the *war.'*" The public buildings were barricaded and guarded by sentinels. There was a tense period when, exposed, unprotected, fearing attack from the Confederates, the city held its breath in fear and prayed for the coming of the Union troops to guard it. The Northern soldiers were having trouble getting through Baltimore.

"Frontier Guards" were organized and camped in the East Room and corridors of the White House, so that Mary met soldiers on the way to breakfast in the morning and saw them the last thing at night when retiring to her bed-chamber. Washington was like a city under siege; the streets were empty except for hurrying patrols. As day after day of anxiety dragged on, even the President looking wistfully out of the window in the direction from which help was expected, joined the refrain: "Why don't they come! Why don't they come!"

The Sixth Massachusetts, which had been assaulted by a mob in Baltimore, reached Washington, and on April 24 Lincoln received and spoke to the wounded of that unit. There was nothing, however, in the sight of injured flesh and bone to bring reassurance; that was a day of deepest gloom. But when on the 25th the Seventh New York arrived and marched up Pennsylvania Avenue to the White House, with band playing and flags flying, it was a deliverance never to be forgotten. Here was strong disciplined glorious young manhood ready to defend.

Hollow-eyed from the strain, Mrs. Lincoln and Mrs. Grimsley with the excited little boys were watching when the President gave the soldiers his heartfelt welcome. The women were roundly cheered by their deliverers and it is not strange that their overwrought emotions gave way to tears.

"Thousands of soldiers are guarding us, and if there is safety in numbers, we have every reason, to feel secure," wrote Mary Lincoln in a homesick letter to Springfield two days later. Washington became an armed camp but the Executive Mansion remained a house of fear. One night every member of the family except the servants was taken ill and there were frenzied whispers of "poison." The trouble proved in the end to be a case of tainted Potomac shad but fear and suspicion were always present. Mrs. Grimsley tells vaguely of a guest in the house who listened at doors and gave out state secrets until discovered and dismissed.

There was a slimy stream of letters of abuse and threats of assassination of the President. Although Mrs. Lincoln was shielded from the knowledge of some of these letters, she knew enough of them to be increasingly worried. From this time on one finds an appealing theme woven into the evidence, more and more incidents which show how this middle-aged couple in the midst of terrifying forces drew close together, each trying constantly to help and shield the other.

Lincoln was determined to save the Union but he had tried to avoid war. He had said to the South, "We are not enemies, but friends," this man so scrupulous as to literal truth that he would not use the conventional greeting, "I am delighted to see you," unless that really was the case. The following year he was to tell an earnest lady presenting the views of the Quakers: "If I had had my way, this war would never have been commenced." Months after the war was joined, Mary expressed the poignant wish: "If we could accomplish our purpose without, resorting to arms & bloodshed how comfortable, it would be. But that is impossible."

Between the inauguration and the firing on Fort Sumter Lincoln had hoped for and worked for peace. He said of the trials of that interval; "They were so great that could I have anticipated them I could not believe it possible to survive them." John Hay was to say of Lincoln: "He bore the sorrows of the nation in his own heart." The four years' agony of that compassionate heart had begun. He said to one of his generals in those first few months of his Presidency: "If to be the head of Hell is as hard as what I have to undergo here, I could find it in my heart to pity Satan himself."

Mary knew of his worried sleepless nights. She did not need a wife's instinct to note the lines that were etching themselves around the patient eyes and mouth. Mrs. Grimsley told of Mrs. Lincoln's campaign to take care of her husband's health and lighten his spirit. She instituted a daily carriage ride, making quite a point that she wanted and needed him to accompany her, as she knew that would be the most compelling argument. What he would not do for his own good, he would do for hers. The drives were her method of getting him away from his work into the fresh air.

To get Lincoln to come to his meals had always been a problem; now it was worse than ever. Mary and "Cousin Lizzie" conspired together. If Lincoln could not be enticed to the table, one or the other would carry a tray to the room where he was working and try to maneuver herself in, to lighten the atmosphere with a feminine remark or two while he ate. Too often they were told to leave the tray outside and later they would find it untouched.

Wifely strategy also involved good friends to breakfast, especially jolly old friends who would laugh and jest. Courtesy required Lincoln to come and eat with his guests, although he usually had to be sent for. He would arrive looking sad and worried and sit down with a bare nod of recognition, saying, "Mother, I do not think I ought to have come." Like as not the stage had been set for his entrance with some pleasant anecdote in progress as he entered, which of course had to be finished. By the time the story was ended, Lincoln, beginning to relax, would say "This reminds me," and Mary would know her little scheme had succeeded.

One of Mary's most valuable wifely duties was helping Lincoln fight his moods of depression. He borrowed from her a quality he did not possess, a natural childlike buoyancy in living. He constantly turned to her for relaxation, seeking her room to sit or to stretch out on a couch and read or chat for a few moments. He would often reach for a certain Bible that was seemingly kept in place for the purpose, and like as not would slip off his shoes to rest his feet. "Cousin Lizzie" presented a pleasant picture when she wrote how, at such times, she and Mary would give him a cup of tea and how "He would read aloud to us, recite some poem, until recalled to the cares of state by the messenger." All present must have hated the sound of approaching footsteps.

When, as is normal in a congenial marriage, Lincoln would seek his wife's companionship, her bright interest in the small affairs of daily living undoubtedly gave him relief from his tremendous problems. Another source from which he drew strength stands out in Mrs. Keckley's account of an incident in the middle year of the war. The President entered his wife's room one day and threw himself on the sofa, "a complete picture of dejection." Mary, of course, was quick to notice this and asked where he had been. To this Lincoln gave a "brief, almost sullen answer" that he had been to the War Department. To his wife's inquiry as to news, he said despairingly, "Yes, plenty of news, but no good news. It is dark, dark everywhere."

He then reached for the Bible and began to read. At the end of fifteen minutes, the "dejected look was gone, and the countenance was lighted up with new resolution and hope." Mrs. Keckley, who had both piety and normal feminine curiosity, wished to see what part of the Bible had produced the change. She made some excuse to pass behind the sofa, and discovered the President had been reading Job.

Mary tried to conceal from Lincoln her own dark days and increasing ill health. As if either husband or wife, with the sixth sense that comes with long association, could ever fool the other. Mary, like so many in her day, was a victim of ague, a malarial affliction marked by a regular succession of chills and fever. One finds her writing in September 1861: "I have been quite sick with chills for some days, this is my day of rest so I am sitting up. I am beginning to feel very weak. If they cannot be broken in a few days, Mr. Lincoln wants me to go North and remain until cold weather. When so much is demanded of me I cannot afford to be delicate, if a different climate will restore my health." In that day a trip was considered a panacea. Mary continued: "If at the close of this week I am still sick, I expect I will go up to Boston . . . for two or three weeks and return here in November." She always hated to give in to her ailments and went on: "I trust, however, I may not be under the necessity, yet I am feeling very far from well. September & early in October are always considered unhealthy months here, my racked frame certainly bears evidence to the fact."

The passage throws considerable light on the frequency of her trips during the Presidency. The Civil War plus a combination of ailments was placing a severe strain on this nerve-shaken woman. It was essential for her to get away at frequent intervals from the tension of the Executive Mansion.

Her unaccustomed depression was written into this letter: "The weather is so beautiful, why is it, that we cannot feel well. The air feels very much like the early days when I used to have chills in Ill., those days have passed, and I have no cause to grieve over my lot. If the country was only peaceful, all would be well." That agonizing desire for the war to cease appeared in her homesick letter to Mrs. Melvin on April 27, 1861. Looking back to the sweet security of quiet neighborly days at Springfield, she expressed the helpless and urgent wish common to women in wartime: "We can only hope for peace!"

Painful family cleavage in the crisis was soon brought sharply into focus. In April 1861 Lincoln wrote Ben Hardin Helm, the husband of "Little Sister" Emilie, to come to Washington. There the President offered Helm a coveted position, that of paymaster in the United States army with the rank of Major. It was about as tempting an offer as an ambitious young man could receive and its acceptance would have opened a career of the very sort that Ben and Emilie most desired. Lincoln was using every inducement to get them on the side of the Union and near himself and Mary. The Lincolns wanted this passionately; they both loved the young couple with a deep parental affection. Mary needed Emilie's presence in Washington. Young Helm's difficult decision was somewhat like that of Robert E. Lee. On the one hand was all that he most desired in life—high position, affluence, opportunity; on the other was conviction of a loyalty that he felt he could not, in honor, deny. He declined the offer and entered the Confederate army. Few disappointments could have been more bitter for Lincoln and his wife.

Endless official duties, quite in contrast to the quiet existence which Mary's health required, crowded upon the Presidential couple. Some of them contained bright and thrilling moments when her spirit rose to meet pomp and circumstance. She probably enjoyed the military reviews when she was cheered along with the President. Mrs. Grimsley has told how she and Mary spent much time visiting the encampments and assisted in several occasions in christening them. The two were always recognized and welcomed with music and cheers, especially if the President was with them. One suspects that the First Lady was thrilled to visit "Camp Mary Lincoln," and Ma's camp was the favorite of the two affectionate little sons— the parents were Ma (Maw) and Pa (Paw) to Willie and Tad. On one occasion, when a hamper of choice wines was sent to Mrs. Lincoln, and she, as usual in such cases, sent it on to a hospital, there was protest from the little boys because it had not been reserved for their camp. In passing it may be noted that the Lincolns had no use for the wine themselves. Mrs. Lincoln said simply to young Stoddard, "I never use any, and Mr. Lincoln never touches any." It was not their custom to serve it at White House entertainments.

After military reviews where President and Mrs. Lincoln appeared, the soldiers would write their impressions in letters home. "The Pres. is not half so ugly as he is generally represented," wrote a cavalryman in the fall of '61 —"his nose is rather long but he is rather *long* himself so it is a Necessity to keep the proportion complete. . . . The Crowd Cheered him loudly as he left the Camp bowing and waving his hat. His Lady is charming enough to make up for all his deficiencies."

There is an American quality of independent judgment in these letters. One written in May from New York offered some advice to the Commander in Chief of the Army and Navy in unequivocal terms, though the good intention of the writer is as evident as his confidence in his own opinion. This letter came to light when the Lincoln Papers were opened in 1947: "They say when you are on horseback, and platoons of men marching by you, that you lean about and turn your head to talk with people behind you, when they claim that you should sit erect & talk to nobody and look straight at the saluting soldiery—" The Lincolns delighted to take their little sons with them on all possible occasions, whether convention approved or not. The letter continued: "And when you are passing lines of soldiers, reviewing them, afoot, they say you take your boys along, and straddle off as if you were cutting across lots, to get somewhere in the quickest time you can, and pay a good deal more attention to your own getting along, than to the soldiers whom you start out to review. These things dont sound well at all."

Having pointed out further deficiencies in the kindly manner of one who felt, after all, the President was worth saving, the writer launched into praises of the First Lady, who was making a real success of her public appearances: "Mrs Lincoln is growing popular all the while, because people say she is mistress of her situation. She aptly, fits herself to the times. . . . people think she is 'in town.' They like to talk about her and say she has a good deal of sense and womanly wit about her. She is coming into excellent reputation in this naturally prejudiced city against you and her both."

Soldiers, like college students, have excellent mass judgment; it is hard to fool them in regard to the personality on the platform. The men in uniform recognized that Mrs. Lincoln was a lady and that her motherly interest in them was genuine. They found her pleasant, responsive face good to look upon. The President and his wife were like comfortable neighbors back home. But Mary's upbringing made her careful to observe the proprieties. She liked attention but she did not wish to be "unwomanly" or "forward," two dread words in the Victorian code. One finds her respectfully declining a military salute from a regiment which chanced to be in front of the White House as she passed to her carriage one day.

War's bloodshed was brought home to the White House family on May 24, when a young man whom they all loved was killed. Elizabeth Grimsley wrote Cousin John on that very day: "This is a sad morning to us here on account of Col. Ellsworth's death of which you will hear before this reaches you. He was a great pet in the family and Mr. Lincoln feels it very much. He was shot immediately after having taken down the Secession flag in Alexandria . . ."

Elmer E. Ellsworth had been such an intimate of the White House that he had even caught the measles, much to his disgust, from Willie and Tad. The Lincolns loved him almost like a son. Together they went to the Navy Yard, where the body lay, and gazed on the still young face with deep emotion. Lincoln wept at the mention of his name. To a newspaperman who asked about the tragedy the President said, "Excuse me, but I cannot talk," and burst into tears.

The beautiful figure, almost the embodiment of youth's endearing qualities, was brought to the East Room of the White House that had so recently known his voice and living presence. A military funeral was held there for one whose promising military career had been cut off at the beginning. Upon the casket was a picture of Ellsworth "surrounded by a laurel wreath in wax placed there" by Mary Lincoln, who was completely unable to control her emotions during the services. Because of the motherly love she had given him, the bloodstained flag he held when he was shot was given to her, though it filled her with horror and she put it away. "Colonel Ellsworth's Funeral March," composed by Sousa the elder, was dedicated to Mrs. Lincoln.

This blow was the first of many war deaths that were to beat down the spirits of the couple. "This is only the beginning of terrible scenes I fear, through which we shall have to pass," wrote Elizabeth Grimsley to Cousin John, adding how she longed for the "quiet of home." She was extremely anxious to return to Springfield but "Mary has urged and urged and seemed to feel hurt at the idea of my leaving her, and now I am no nearer getting away than I was six weeks ago. You all write you are getting along so well without me, that Mary thinks me very selfish if I speak of going home." Elizabeth suggested that the situation be met by "Father or Mother" writing her "word to *come home* . . ."

One suspects that the relatives in Springfield thought it desirable that so well-balanced a person as Elizabeth stay with a member of the family so impulsive as Mary. "Brother John insisted upon my remaining with Mary until this time and longer if I could." But Elizabeth's letter showed her unhappiness in such a storm center as the White House and her sensitiveness and desire to be independent as to her expenses. She did not wish to deal with Mary on such a touchy subject as money. The family all knew Mary was peculiar about dollars and cents but the fair-minded Elizabeth was careful to report to them that "Mary has been uniformly kind & polite to me and evidently wishes me to enjoy my visit," and "on no occasion" has she "failed to do all she could to make it agreeable to me, and urge me to stay longer." As to Elizabeth's children, Mary wanted the younger boy brought to Washington to be with his mother; "She thought the trip, and all would be so nice for the little fellow."

Early in June the White House was again draped in mourning. Stephen A. Douglas, whose life had been interwoven with that of the Lincolns since early Springfield days, died suddenly in Chicago. "Dug" (so-called by some of the lighthearted coterie in those young days that now seemed removed a thousand years), who had debated with Lincoln, who had been Mary's beau, who had so recently danced with her at the Inauguration Ball, who had loyally stood by the President's side in defense of the Union, how could he, so full of life, be dead?

The deadly fear of those first days of war when Washington felt itself exposed to enemy troops, was revived with the battle of Bull Run on July 21, 1861. Mrs. Grimsley has recorded the high hopes at the White House when the regiments so long encamped about the city moved toward the Potomac, "amid cheering, enthusiasm, and hopefulness, for the general feeling was that this March was to be 'On to Richmond', to be crowned with brilliant victory; 'the backbone of the rebellion was to be broken,' and the war ended." As is tragically usual with the beginning of a war, it was expected to be a short one.

Early on the morning of July 21 the roar of artillery at Bull Run could be heard. "Pa says there's a battle in Virginia," said Willie in great excitement, "that's big cannons going off that sounds like slamming doors." Perhaps this was the time of which Mrs. Grimsley spoke later, perhaps not, but at all events she described a scene in which she and Mary went to the highest outlook of the White House to strain and listen to a distant battle. Elizabeth, tall and self-controlled, held the trembling little hands of Mary tight in her own to still the convulsive jerking that followed each distant, ominous report.

At first the news from the battle was good; the Union forces were reported as winning. Delight changed to consternation with a telegram saying that the battle was lost and it was a question of saving Washington and the remnant of the army. Elizabeth has described the feeling of panic which enveloped the city with the belief that Washington would be shelled and captured at once, a feeling made more poignant by the rumble of ambulances bringing the wounded to hospitals and the tramp of retreating soldiers through a dismal rain.

With Washington thus exposed, General Scott insisted that Mrs. Lincoln and the children and Mrs. Grimsley be sent north away from danger. "Mrs. Lincoln turned to her husband saying, 'Will you go with us?' and his speedy answer came 'Most assuredly I will not leave at this juncture'; and the response was just as prompt, 'Then I will not leave you at this juncture.'" Her reaction was exactly the same as when she had heard he was in danger on his trip to Washington; that settled it that she would be at his side. Mrs. Grimsley noted Lincoln's quiet pride in his wife's quick answer to General Scott's suggestion and the husband's satisfaction that she was staying with him. General Scott was not able at any time to make Mrs. Lincoln leave because of danger, and Mrs. Grimsley wrote back to Springfield how Lincoln wanted Mary with him.

October brought the death of another cherished friend. In May, Elizabeth Grimsley had written, "Col. E. D. Baker breakfasted with us." Being a Todd, Elizabeth had pronounced dislikes. "I cannot bear that man," she added, but to the Lincolns he was the beloved and tried companion of years for whom they had named their second son. It was like a visit home to have him to breakfast that morning; the face of an old friend was beginning to mean so much.

Lincoln saw him again in the autumn. A passing officer noted a scene on the White House lawn on a glorious October afternoon. Lincoln was seated on the ground with his back against the trunk of a tree; Colonel Baker lay at full length with his head supported by his clasped hands. Nearby Willie Lincoln was playing with the fallen leaves, tossing their scarlet and gold about in boyish glee. The two men were in serious low-voiced conversation. Perhaps they spoke of the battle which would take place on the morrow. Finally they rose, shook hands, Colonel Baker lifted Willie and kissed him, and then mounting his horse rode away to the west. Lincoln's eyes followed him until he disappeared. The next day Colonel Baker was killed at the battle of Ball's Bluff. When the news came to Lincoln he "left headquarters, utterly unheeding the orderly's salute, both hands pressed to his heart, his features convulsed with grief." So much that they had treasured in life seemed crumbling about the Lincolns.

Against this background of fear and heartache, it was still the duty of the First Lady to do the White House entertaining. She was criticized for having the usual receptions and dinners in time of war; criticism was equally inevitable if she failed to have them. These social obligations ranged from formidable state dinners for foreign ministers and visitors and the administration's own dignitaries to receptions or levees for the public. Under normal conditions no program could have been more to Mary's liking.

A little packet of invitations and answers saved through the years and only recently made accessible brings the important functions of White House hospitality very close. Undoubtedly it was Mary who saved these stately papers. Examining them, one reads on fine heavy stationery: "Lord Lyons will have the honour of waiting upon the President and Mrs. Lincoln on Tuesday June 4th at half past seven o'clock." This was placed in a handsome envelope, addressed to "Mrs. Lincoln, Executive Mansion," and sealed with the official seal of the British legation, a large seal on red wax. Equally impressive was the seal of the stately note in which the French Minister and Madame Mercier replied to "*l'aimable invitation*" of the President and Madame Lincoln. One notes with pride in this dossier that the American Secretary of State has the biggest and reddest seal of them all!

The first levee, at which Mrs. Lincoln wore the rose-colored moire-antique, was one of a series of Friday evening entertainments. Most people in public life know the terrific ordeal of shaking hands with hundreds of persons.

Lincoln endured it for two hours and a half on that occasion, remarking at the end of it that his hand was too lame to sign anything. Mrs. Lincoln started out bravely to follow his example, but had to give it up. Her hand, being very small, could not take the crushing which wore out even the big and powerful fist which had once split rails.

Apparently an arrangement was worked out which somewhat protected the hostess. Stoddard described a typical reception. The President stood in the foreground between his two secretaries, Nicolay and Hay, whose task it was to introduce to him the people who filed past. The human tide seemed endless; the whole performance was an endurance test.

Young Stoddard's post of duty was by Mrs. Lincoln, who stood a few paces to the right of her husband, and somewhat farther back in the room. This meant that the larger part of the procession, after greeting the President, passed her by with a smile or bow, or perhaps a rude stare. When someone of special interest greeted Lincoln, however, it was his custom to take that person over and present him to Mary. Francis Lieber, writing his wife on July 10, 1861, said that he had seen Lincoln at a levee and "He at once introduced me to Mrs. Lincoln and her companion against the rule." The last phrase shows the arrangement, but of course there were personal friends and many others who, as Stoddard says, swept "inward for a word with her." This last-named young secretary liked to be at her side; he found her "bright, cheerful, almost merry," and her instructions were "given in a very kindly and vivacious manner." He added: "As you look at her and talk with her, the fact that she has so many enemies strikes you as one of the moral curiosities of this venomous time, for she has never in any way harmed one of the men and women who are so recklessly assailing her." We will later find Benjamin B. French acting also as her aide at receptions, praising her in similar terms, and expressing a like indignation at the malicious rumors about her.

At intervals one can "look at" the White House hostess through various eyes. John Lothrop Motley wrote his wife that Mrs. Lincoln "is rather nice-looking, youngish, with very round white arms, well dressed, chatty enough and if she would not, like all the South and West, say 'Sir' to you every instant, as if you were a royal personage, she would be quite agreeable."

Lincoln is considered the great exponent of American democracy, and it is appropriate to find that the receptions during his Presidency were more democratic than those of preceding administrations. The levees were a mixture of elegance, fashion, and the crudity of frontier life. Cowhide boots and hickory shirts appeared along with the latest finery. Every class and condition from every section of the country came to the White House. Well might Lincoln call entertainments his "public opinion baths" that kept him in touch with the "plain people" who had elected him.

One who attended the receptions for "high and low" remembered "that the President was punctiliously polite to and considerate of those who appeared to be of humble estate . . ." His wife was at one with him in this; it was recorded of her that she "was equally gracious to all." Mrs. Lincoln, like her husband, was democratic. She was not snobbish in an age when snobbery was rampant. She could and did give the cold shoulder to people she disliked, but it was a matter of personal antagonism, not of class.

In addition to Friday evening levees, there were regular Saturday afternoon receptions. For these occasions Mrs. Lincoln would sometimes lend her support to her husband by inviting people whose friendship was valuable to the administration. On Saturday, March 30, William Howard Russell, the correspondent of *The Times* of London, recorded in his diary: "On returning to the hotel, I found a magnificent bouquet of flowers, with a card attached to them, with Mrs. Lincoln's compliments, and another card announcing that she had a 'reception' at three o'clock." He went to the White House where he found the gathering a scanty one, which caused him to comment that "The Washington ladies have not yet made up their minds that Mrs. Lincoln is the fashion."

This Englishman had been present at the first state dinner two days before. The sending of that bouquet indicates either that Mrs. Lincoln was being unusually diplomatic or else she liked him. The conservatory adjoining the White House on the west was a source of genuine pleasure to her. She delighted to give flowers to her friends, and—which seems a bit strange now—frequently gave bouquets to men. Mr. Russell, however, looked upon her (and upon most of what he saw in Washington) with a supercilious eye. Like Mr. Motley he objected to her habit of saying "Sir," though Mary had undoubtedly been taught

that it was good manners to do so. Mr. Russell also recognized the strain on Mrs. Lincoln in the dizzying transi-
tion from housewife in a country town to mistress of the
White House, where she was surrounded by "flatterers
and intriguers."

He described the First Lady's physical characteristics
in grudging terms but conceded she had a "well-propor-
tioned arm" and an energetic way with a fan. "Mrs. Lincoln struck me as being desirous of making herself agreeable," he confided to his diary, "and I own I was agreeably
disappointed, as the Secessionist ladies at Washington had
been amusing themselves by anecdotes which could
scarcely have been founded on fact." Coming from William Howard Russell, this amounts almost to a eulogy.

"We have music here in the President's grounds every
Wednesday and Saturday evening, when the grounds are
open to everybody," wrote young Nicolay that first year to
his sweetheart back in Illinois. There were gay scenes on
those evenings with the liveliness of the Marine Band, the
promenaders on the lawn, and perhaps the Presidential
family appearing on the south balcony. Mrs. Grimsley,
however, thought the view to the south rather spoiled by
the unfinished, truncated Washington monument, surrounded by piles of rubbish.

The regular receptions or levees must be distinguished
from the official receptions. The first of these was on April
8, 1861, and, according to Mrs. Grimsley, it involved a
clash between Mrs. Lincoln and Secretary of State Seward.
It might have been predicted that Mary would not like
Seward; he had wanted to be President instead of her husband. He was also making it very clear at the beginning of
Lincoln's Presidency, that he, Seward, considered himself
the power behind the throne. He sent to the President a
memorandum dated April 1 which practically amounted to
saying that he would do the thinking for Lincoln's administration. The discreet President, perhaps, did not tell this
to the indiscreet First Lady (he managed the matter quite
well by himself), but Mary's keen interest made her aware
of anything stirring in the world of politics, and she
knew Seward's attitude. When he even indicated that he
proposed to give the first official reception, there was an
irate First Lady in the White House. In those early Presidential days, she was constantly fearful that the sophisticated Eastern politicians would impose upon her honest

and confiding husband. In her loyalty and anxiety she frequently cautioned him: "Those men should realize, Mr. Lincoln, that you are the President," or "Don't forget that you are President," to which he would answer with a smile, "Never fear, Mary, there is no doubt who is President."

It is understandable, therefore, that when Seward moved to take over the first official reception, Mary's quick tongue (so it has been reported) informed him: "It is said that you are the power behind the throne—I'll show you that Mr L is President yet." Inasmuch as Lincoln himself was making that fact abundantly clear to Seward around that time, the family seems to have acted with considerable unanimity. But spirited conduct and even being right does not always add up to being diplomatic. Mary had the kind of tact that can deal with children, with understanding friends and friendly people, but she did not have diplomacy. Of course, she carried her point and the Lincolns gave the reception.

"And what a crush and jam it was!" wrote Mrs. Grimsley. Lincoln's hand was again lamed by handshaking, and the Presidential family gave a sigh of relief when they heard the Marine Band strike up "Yankee Doodle," the signal for retiring. The President offered Mrs. Grimsley his arm and they made the circuit of the East Room together, being much amused at the remarks they overheard, such as: "The President bears himself well, and does not seem the least embarrassed." "How much alike the President and Mrs. Grimsley are!" "Yes! brother and sister. They must belong to a very tall family."

It was a great trial to Mary that White House etiquette did not permit her on such occasions to march by her husband's side. She must promenade on the arm of some other distinguished gentleman. The jealous little woman endured this custom as long as she could but late in the Presidency decided to do something about it. Since custom gave first place to the President she reasoned: "I am his wife, and should lead with him. And yet he offers his arm to another lady in the room, making her first with him and placing me second." This was not to be borne any longer; after that she either marched with the President, or he marched alone or with another gentleman.

That reception of April 8 was the last in which North and South were to mingle for four torturing years. Within a week war became a reality. Mrs. Grimsley gives a close-up incident showing the tension of the time with its bitterness and its air of suspicion in which men and women looked askance at each other. Her relative, John C. Breckinridge of Kentucky, though a member of the United States Senate in the summer of 1861, joined the Confederate army later that year and became a general. Before leaving Washington he called several times at the White House and said to Mrs. Grimsley somewhat arrogantly in Mrs. Lincoln's presence: "Cousin Lizzie, I would not like you to be disappointed in your expected stay at the White House, so I will now invite you to remain here as a guest, when the Confederation takes possession." Mary quickly answered him: "We will be only too happy to entertain her until that time . . ." Whereupon ensued a seemingly merry war of words, but underneath, as Mrs. Grimsley says, was "storm and sting, as would naturally be the case, when two bright, quick, embittered brains and tongues wage a contest."

The amiability emphasized in so many descriptions of Mary Lincoln was apparent in her dealing with certain inflated egos. Mrs. Grimsley mentions the "inordinate vanity" of Nathaniel P. Willis and the "constant draft upon those with whom he was thrown, for pabulum upon which this vanity could feed . . ." Most people will recognize this type, which like the poor we have always with us. Fishing perhaps for praise, Willis said to Mrs. Lincoln one day: "You do not approve of me, you think me a very wicked man, say, truly, do you not?" The First Lady answered with tact and sincere appreciation of literary skill: ". . . how could that be with one who wrote such exquisite sacred poems, that have made ours, even through our school readers, where we and our children have learned to love them?" Poetry was always an open sesame to Mary. One gathers from Mrs. Grimsley's account that the gentleman would not have fared so well had she answered him.

At the dinner to the diplomatic corps early in June, Mary introduced something new. "Through the good taste of Mrs. Lincoln, the stiff, artificial flowers heretofore ornamenting the Presidential tables were wholly discarded and their places delightfully supplied by fragrant, natural flowers." She was justified if she looked with satisfaction at the beauty of the Blue Room, fragrant with blossoms, some even woven into the graceful festoons that hung from the chandeliers. The White House was her home at this time; her natural wish was to make it a beautiful and gracious place to live and entertain.

Early in August the French Prince Napoleon came to Washington. Before his arrival Seward called to announce his coming to President and Mrs. Lincoln, and to arrange for his entertainment. The Secretary of State offered to give the dinner the evening following the prince's arrival. Of course Mrs. Lincoln objected to this suggestion, and she went into action promptly to arrange for a formal dinner at the White House.

It was a brilliant affair occurring on Saturday, August 3, at seven in the evening. The Marine Band was just concluding its Saturday serenade to the people on the White House grounds when the prince arrived, so he was invited to step out for a moment on the south balcony, to view and be viewed by the crowd. He was in full dress, "his breast a flame of decoration," over which was crossed a broad crimson sash. For Mary, with her capacity for being thrilled, there was doubtless a high moment as she stood on that balcony with so resplendent a figure. Her sense of drama was equally gratified when later she entered the state dining room in procession on the arm of the prince. She had reason to think gratefully of Madame Mentelle that evening, for the conversation was largely in French. Twenty-seven guests sat down at the dinner which had been prepared in the White House. It was a glorious occasion but there was gossip about the paying of the bill. Six years later when Mary was an impaired and frantic widow, that gossip was to be revived and published in the newspapers to lacerate her wounds.

This gossip may have had relation to Mary's wish later to drop the costly state dinners from the social program, and give receptions instead. She had an argument with her husband about the matter, she urging economy in wartime, he cautiously pointing out that it was not a good thing to break an established custom. But when the wife said, "Public receptions are more democratic than stupid state dinners—are more in keeping with the spirit of the institutions of our country, as you would say if called upon to make a stump speech," Lincoln capitulated and she won her case.

On August 3 Elizabeth Grimsley had written Cousin

John: "Today Mary has a large dinner-party for the Prince Napoleon and suite. . . . Tell Cousin Mary [Stuart] she could scarcely realize there was to be a dinner-company of 30 in the house today. What a comfort to be able to entertain and feel no care over it."

Mrs. Grimsley was overlooking the very great care and diplomacy required in official entertaining. It was a delicate question as to who should be invited; those omitted were apt to become critical of the administration. To Nicolay fell the important task of seeing that invitations to official functions were issued to the proper people, that guests at a dinner were seated according to protocol, and that the entertainments were conducted with correct form. The etiquette book was always at hand, the rules were studied, and the dignity and feelings of officials and nations were carefully considered. Young Nicolay was very competent in the matter, and later in the Presidency, in 1864, his following of the rules caused a clash with Mrs. Lincoln, who was apt to make her own rules when it came to a question of her personal dislikes.

She disliked Secretary of the Treasury Chase as much as she did Secretary Seward and for much the same reason; Chase was willing to be President too. There was no love lost between Mrs. Lincoln and Chase's ambitious daughter Kate Chase Sprague. It should also be remembered that by 1864 Mrs. Lincoln had received shocks that had taken heavy toll of her.

When Nicolay in January of that year prepared to send out the invitations for a cabinet dinner he found that the names of Secretary Chase and of his daughter and her husband, William Sprague, had been stricken from the list. Of course this would never do, and Nicolay took the affair to the President, who in matters of consequence never allowed his wife's prejudices to influence him. He, of course, ordered the names restored at once to the list. Furious at Nicolay, Mrs. Lincoln made things quite unpleasant for him for a day or two. She seemed determined to get along without his help in arranging the dinner, and to see that he should not be present. There is no doubt this willful woman could get into a formidable state of mind, but in this incident one has a later glimpse: she got over it and expressed regret. All accounts agree that she would be sorry for her anger after she cooled off. On the afternoon of the dinner she sent for Nicolay, offered him her apologies, and asked for his help in planning the dinner. Her conscience had been hurting her; she told Nicolay that the affair had worried her so she had not slept for a night or two. Nicolay wrote John Hay, who was out of town: "I think she has felt happier since she cast out that devil of stubborness." Official entertaining for all its glitter had complications very difficult for one of such strong personal feelings.

Yet there was fine dignity in Mary Lincoln's social performance as First Lady. It was summed up more than two years after she entered the Presidential mansion by Ben: Perley Poore, experienced journalist and observer who knew well the ins and outs of Washington affairs: ". . . I am sure that since the time that Mrs. Madison presided at the White House, it has not been graced by a lady as well fitted by nature and by education to dispense its hospitalities as is Mrs. Lincoln. Her hospitality is only equaled by her charity, and her graceful deportment by her goodness of heart."

Mrs. Lincoln has been called "the most tragic woman character in American history, the most maligned and pilloried." But not even the unprecedented mudslinging from which she has suffered has been able to obscure her record as a lovely White House hostess. To her credit be it said that at parties she kept her self-control, even under most trying circumstances. As to the quality of her hospitality, it is well to notice that Mr. Poore ends up on the theme of her goodness of heart. Hers was not the manner of sophistication; it was the genuine friendliness of a motherly woman who liked people and welcomed them heartily.

chapter 20

FURTHER ACTIVITIES OF THE
FIRST LADY

In August 1861 Mrs. Lincoln and Mrs. Grimsley, accompanied by that close neighbor of Springfield days, Mrs. John Henry Shearer, went to Long Branch, New Jersey, together. Mrs. Lincoln "came here to rest and enjoy herself" reported the New York *Herald* on August 19. There was no rest to be had in the supercharged atmosphere of the White House, and Washington in summer was anything but a healthful place. The sewage system was primitive and odor as of "ten thousand dead cats" floated in the south windows of the White House from the swampy Potomac flats. There were no screens in the windows to keep out flies and mosquitoes and there was much illness. While Mrs. Lincoln was away John Hay had an attack of what he called "bilious fever" with "a gay old delirium." He added in a letter to Nicolay: "The air here is stifling. You had better stay as long as you like . . ."

Mary with her ague and headaches could not endure hot weather. She was not one to complain of physical discomforts, but she did mention in a letter that fall that even driving gave no relief from the heat because it was so dusty. "We will welcome cool weather, *dust,* I presume we will never be freed from, until *mud,* takes its place."

Mary's letter to Mrs. Shearer inviting her to be one of the party at Long Branch gave full details of the proposed trip. Three different hotels had offered suites of rooms, they would ride on railroad passes, "and the trip will cost nothing, which is a good deal to us all these times." She told Mrs. Shearer: "Bring your boys with you, it will be more pleasant all around. I am going to take my boys, with me, with a servant man, who will take charge, of your children also." There was never a time when the presence of children was not welcome to Mrs. Lincoln. The letter breathed affection and thoughtfulness: ". . . there is no one I am so anxious to see, as your dear self. If you are not well, my word for it, you can always keep yourself, as quiet as you wish." Mrs. Shearer was expecting a baby in October.

Mary's joyousness in the richness of her new life flashed out in her next paragraph: "We have the most beautiful flowers & grounds imaginable, and company & excitement enough, to turn a wiser head than my own. . . . There was so many lovely drives around W. and we have only *three* carriages, at our command." Three carriages caused pure joy when she had had to work and wait so long to have any carriage at all in Springfield.

A good example of the way in which comunications had increased and ideas about publicity for women had changed lies in the fact that the New York *Herald* had a special correspondent cover the movements of Mrs. Lincoln at Long Branch. There was as much fanfare and activity in her honor as the First Lady, who had a good sense of the value of public appearances, would permit.

Mrs. Shearer was quite ill upon their arrival. They had stopped for a day's shopping in New York and one suspects that going shopping with an energetic little woman like Mary was a strenuous business, especially for a prospective mother. And any travel of that time involved considerable jolting. When it came to a conflict between public activities and the need of a loved friend (especially one expecting a baby who was to be named after Willie Lincoln), Mary's choice can easily be predicted. Affection and personal loyalty came first with her; she kept her word and remained in seclusion until Mrs. Shearer recovered from her brief but alarming illness.

It is evident that Mrs. Lincoln was seeking on this trip the comfort of personal friendships, so difficult to attain in that lonely structure, the White House. She had been homesick for the old neighbors in Springfield, and for the warm intimate contacts that were so essential to her. It is a remarkable fact that, in spite of abnormal conditions and encircling hostility, Mary Lincoln formed in the White House rich and enduring friendships. Among these friends were Mrs. James H. Orne, a prominent lady of Philadelphia, whose husband was an active Republican and whose brother, Charles O'Neill, was a member of the House of Representatives, Mrs. Gideon Welles, wife of the Secretary of the Navy, and Mrs. Albert S. White, whose husband was a member of Congress until Lincoln appointed him to a federal judgeship. Mrs. White came from the

Randolph family of Virginia. Like Mary herself, she knew the traditions of a genteel Southern family. These three cherished friends were alike in being cultured, intelligent, high-minded, accustomed to the best standards, and confident of an assured position in society. That these fine women loved and respected Mary Lincoln is an indication of the genuineness, warmheartedness, and rich companionship that she gave to her friends.

Her interest, of course, embraced their familes. It was therefore a great pleasure for her to have a visit in Long Branch with the two daughters of Mrs. White, given in the New York *Herald* as "Mrs. Mack and Miss White." She probably asked them to sing for her, as amateur singing was a specialty with them, and Mary enjoyed music.

This taste of hers was mentioned in stately fashion in *Leslie's Illustrated Newspaper* on August 24 in connection with some of the plans for her stay in Long Branch. "As Mrs. Lincoln is a great admirer of music, never misses an opportunity to visit the opera, and has already delighted the *habitués* of the White House by a few *recherché* private concerts at Washington, it is designed to secure Carlotta Patti, the only rival of Adelina, for a grand concert in Mrs. Lincoln's honor, to be given some time next week." The article in *Leslie's* mentions other arrangements made for the First Lady's visit to the "Seagirt Shore": thirty-four little girls dressed in white were to "receive her at the depot, but only 27 could be found and got ready in time." The plan for the concert fared worse than this; it fell through entirely, but the mention of Carlotta Patti as planning to give a concert for Mrs. Lincoln raises an interesting conjecture in regard to a well-known story.

There has been a widely circulated anecdote to the effect that Adelina Patti, the famous prima donna, visited the Lincolns at the White House in the fall of 1862 and sang for them. Every detail of the pathetic incident has been told: how Mrs. Lincoln (then in mourning), wept at "The Last Rose of Summer" and how Lincoln, shading his sad face with his hands, asked for "Home, Sweet Home," which, being sung, filled his eyes with tears. The trouble with the story, as the researches of F. Lauriston Bullard have shown, is that it could not possibly have happened because Adelina Patti was in Europe all of 1862 and indeed from 1861 to 1881. She was still living when Mr. Bullard made his investigations and he wrote to her. In answer she had her secretary write him that the story "is quite untrue."

Carlotta Patti, elder sister of Adelina, while not as famous as the latter, was a well-known vocalist in her own right. Mr. Bullard found that she had been in Washington in 1862. So the conjecture arises as to whether the story, minus embroidered details, might be true except as to the first name of the singer. Could it have been Carlotta Patti (not Adelina) who visited the White House and sang to the Lincolns? This is offered merely as a speculation; details to prove this conjecture are at present lacking.

The sea breezes at Long Branch were apparently too much for Tad, as he was taken ill with a cold. By the time he recovered Mrs. Grimsley was getting very anxious to turn her face westward to Springfield and Mrs. Lincoln's ever-present wifely concern for her husband was making itself keenly felt. She told people "with much feeling" that he was lonely without her and explained rather appealingly that he needed her as a listener for his jokes and jests at table. No matter what the labors and fatigues of the day might be, she said, he was always lively, sociable and agreeable. There is a pleasing glimpse here of an animated little woman proudly adding touches to a portrait of her husband.

Mary accompanied Elizabeth Grimsley as far west as Niagara Falls. Once more the grandeur and sweep of the great spectacle uplifted her responsive spirit. From Niagara Mrs. Grimsley continued her journey to Springfield and Mrs. Lincoln returned to Washington. It had been hard to give "Cousin Lizzie" up. At their parting Lincoln had put his arm around her with a fervent "God bless you, my cousin."

The trip to Long Branch had been exciting and Mary had made an excellent impression. The New York *Herald* was loud in its praises of her public grace. "Others occupying the same high position have failed to excite a similar interest," said that newspaper. "Its explanation is to be found in the personal popularity of the distinguished lady who is the object of it." The articles expanded on her "discrimination and tact, joined to a great amiability of manner." Mrs. Lincoln's reputation for saying exactly what she thought without regard for the feelings of other people does not tie up with her undoubted social agreeableness; emphasis on her sharp tongue is out of perspective in the whole picture. On the other hand one does not expect entire consistency from any human. In her social resourcefulness there was reason for the *Herald*, in another article, to refer to her "infinite tact." This was a real achievement considering the vexations and awkward situations of her position.

When at Long Branch the ex-governor, William A. Newell, showed her in fatiguing detail one of the life-saving stations of which he was the originator, she gave him the impression that inspecting a life-saving station was exactly what she most desired. There is possibly a connection here with the fact that Lincoln appointed Newell superintendent of the life-saving service in New Jersey. Following this inspection there was "a sort of extempore reception" at which people crowded up to meet her. "With each she conversed most affably and agreeably, displaying the great tact which always distinguished her in the choice of her subjects and the manner in which she conducted the conversation." At the "Grand Ball" given in her honor the same evening it was reported that she equally charmed all who were present.

All this praise and attention, of course, pleased Mrs. Lincoln. She had said herself that the new grandeur and importance was enough "to turn a wiser head" than her own. But it was one thing for her to admit this and another for someone else to suggest it. That most sharp-tongued of her sisters in Springfield, Ann Todd Smith, made some sarcastic remarks likening Mary's position and attitude to "Queen Victoria's Court." It is indicative of the pettiness and jealousy that existed in the home town that the remark was relayed to her in Washington.

On September 29 Mary wrote Elizabeth Grimsley a confidential letter which takes one into the uninspiring circle of family bickering. Mary was resentful at the barbed reference to Queen Victoria's court and paid "Poor unfortunate Ann" back in kind, giving full treatment to the latter's "malice," envious feeling," and *"vindictiveness."* Mary's relatives usually presented a united front to those outside the clan, but within it they had a wonderful time talking about each other, a diversion in which Mary indulged herself in this letter. She had received, she wrote, from her sister, Elizabeth Todd Edwards, a letter "Very kind & aff. yet very *characteristic.* Said if rents and means permitted, she would like to make us a visit, I believe for a season." Mary continued: "I am weary of *intrigue*, when she [Mrs. Edwards] is by herself she can be very agreeable, especially when her mind is not dwelling on the merits of fair daughters and a talented son-in-law. Such personages always *speak for themselves*."

A new source of resentment had arisen between Mary and her kin. In Springfield years there had existed under the surface irritation because their views differed so radically from those of Lincoln. It had been a bitter dose for some of them that this man whom they had tried to keep out of the family had achieved the highest office in the land. But along with that achievement went power to confer benefits upon others. In the Lincoln Presidency the nation for the first time saw, centering at Washington, what might be called "big government." There were many offices to fill and millions of dollars to be spent. It was natural that Mary's relatives should hope that appointments and advantages would result from having a brother-in-law in the White House. This was only human, especially when times were becoming more difficult and war was upsetting the economy of the country. On the other hand, if Lincoln showed favor to his wife's kin, he was sure to be severely criticized. He acted with caution and moderation, making a few suitable and minor appointments where the applicant was qualified. In this same letter Mary mentioned such an appointment—as paymaster of volunteers —for the husband of her sister Frances Todd Wallace. "Dr. Wallace has received his portion in life from the Administration," wrote Mary, "yet Frances always remains quiet." The First Lady's feelings were hurt by this silence and seeming indifference of her sister. "I often regret E. P. E. [Mrs. Edwards's] little weaknesses," she said, "after all, since the election she is the only one of my sisters who has appeared to be pleased with our advancement." Inevitably there were disappointed expectations, injured feelings, jealousies and misunderstandings in the circle of relatives.

Continuing her letter to Mrs. Grimsley, Mary for a moment realized how petty the whole performance of backbiting was—that is, she realized it on the part of her sister Ann. "How foolish between us to be discussing such a person. Yet really it is amusing, in how many forms, human nature can appear before us." The letter thereupon launched into recent bits of news, and then Mary wrote from the genuinely kind and sympathetic heart that was hers along with the sharp tongue: "I know you will be sorry to hear, that our colored Mantua-maker, Elizabeth [Keckley], lost her only son and child in the battle of Lex., Mo. She is heart broken. She is a very remarkable woman herself." Mrs. Keckley appreciated "the kind womanly letter . . . full of golden words of comfort" which the First Lady wrote her when she heard of her sorrow. Many fine ladies of that class-conscious era would not have taken pains to write a beautifully expressed letter of condolence to a colored dressmaker.

Among the employments engaging the First Lady's attention were what might be termed extracurricular activities. She unwisely took a hand in political matters and it was done because she wanted to help her husband. She knew how often his goodness led to his being imposed upon. It had been his habit in Springfield to discuss matters of his career with her and he had profited both by the uplift of her buoyancy and the shrewdness of her judgments. "My husband placed great confidence in my knowledge of human nature," she once said proudly. "He had not much knowledge of men." Like many wives she had rather too much faith in her woman's intuition. Lincoln defined the situation when he said to her: "Mother, you are too suspicious. I give you credit for sagacity, but you are disposed to magnify trifles." She could not see things with his broad perspective.

Yet for years she had been his arbiter in food, clothes, and social etiquette, and it had become her habit to tell him what to do. It is a common human failing to reason that if one excels in one field, one is also an authority in others. Lincoln himself, with the years of companionship back of them, liked for her to take part in certain matters pertaining to his position. For example we find Mary sending a bouquet to General George B. McClellan on September 8, 1861, and on that same day the General wrote: "Mr. Lincoln came this morning to ask me to pardon a man that I had ordered to be shot, suggesting that I could give as a reason in the order that it was a request of the 'Lady President.'"

Mary revealed her attitude regarding her interest in politics in a letter to James Gordon Bennett, editor and proprietor of the New York *Herald,* an unpredictable newspaper that blew both hot and cold upon the Lincolns. For her to write to such a wily gentleman at all was playing with fire and she was dealing here with the important subject of the cabinet. "From *all parties*," she wrote, "the cry, for a 'change of Cabinet' comes." Bennett had written her a note about the matter, as had another gentleman. "Doubtless if my good, patient Husband, were here, instead of being with the Army of the Potomac," she went on, "both of these missives, would be placed, before him, accompanied by my *womanly* suggestions, proceeding from a heart so deeply interested, for our distracted country." As a proper Victorian female she was careful to add: "I have a great terror of *strong* minded Ladies, yet if a word fitly spoken and in due season, can be urged, in a time, like this, we should not withold it." Mrs. Keckley indicates that Mary gave the President so many "womanly suggestions" full of suspicion that he finally said to her, "if I listened to you, I should soon be without a Cabinet."

Yet politics is often a cutthroat game and Mrs. Lincoln was quite aware that other men wanted to be President. She told Lincoln she thought the Secretary of Treasury "was anything for Chase." Lincoln replied that he received letters daily from all parts of the country telling him not to trust Chase. Many such letters came to light when the Lincoln Papers were opened in 1947. Mary had a good idea of the political maneuvering that was going on around her husband's patient head and like any high-spirited, loyal wife she resented it fiercely. Her participation in politics, however injudicious, stemmed from her intense desire to watch out for and assist the mild and unself-seeking man she loved.

William H. Seward she disliked intensely. He had wanted to be President and, failing that, he wished as Secretary of State to be the most important man in the Lincoln administration. He and Mrs. Lincoln had clashed on the matter of official entertaining. An additional factor soon developed in Mary's thinking. That good friend, Dr. Anson G. Henry, found out in the spring of 1863 that Mrs. Lincoln believed Seward was responsible for some of the malicious rumors circulating about her. Dr. Henry thought these rumors "more likely emanated from the Treasury Department." He "knew this to be so," he said, on the West Coast (he was then in Washington Territory), "for I have traced many of them to the special friends of Sec. Chase . . ."

A conversation between the Lincolns concerning the Secretary of State, as reported by Mrs. Keckley, tells a great deal about the interesting give-and-take of this marriage. The wife made the statement that "Seward is worse than Chase." Lincoln replied: "Mother, you are mistaken; your prejudices are so violent that you do not stop to reason. Seward is an able man, and the country as well as myself can trust him."

There was a wife's protectiveness, a degree of wisdom, and considerable heat in Mary's answer: "Father, you are too honest for this world! You should have been born a saint. You will generally find it a safe rule to distrust a disappointed, ambitious politician. It makes me mad to see you sit still and let that hypocrite, Seward, twine you around his finger as if you were a skein of thread." It was a good lively argument over a difference of opinion, such as occurs in all marriages between two keen-minded and pronounced personalities.

Milton Hay in Springfield, who called Lincoln "an old *poke easy*" and *"hen pecked,"* should have heard the remark with which Lincoln closed the discussion: "It is useless to argue the question, mother. You cannot change my opinion." That Mary knew the truth of what he said is shown by her words at a later time: "He was a terribly firm man when he set his foot down. None of us—no man nor woman—could rule him after he had made up his mind." She added out of her long wifely experience: "I could tell when Mr. Lincoln had decided anything. He was cheerful at first, then he pressed or compressed his lips tightly, firmly, one against the other. When these things showed themselves to me, I fashioned myself accordingly, and so did all others around him have to do sooner or later, and they would find it out."

Mary's interest in politics, of course, got into the gossip. Such conduct on the part of a female, such a getting out of woman's sphere, was especially shocking to the public mind of the eighteen-sixties. A protest went up to Lincoln and his answer throws a great deal of light on this marriage. "Tell the gentlemen not to be alarmed, for I myself manage all important matters. In little things I have got along through life by letting my wife run her end of the machine pretty much in her own way."

Sometimes Mary exerted her influence for action which Lincoln wished to take anyway. Mrs. Grimsley tells delightfully of such an incident: "Mrs. Lincoln and I took the President by storm, one morning, with the demand for an appointment, which so surprised him that he could only hold up his hands and exclaim 'Et tu Brute.'" It was a merry interview, the President, with a twinkle, making the ladies argue their case, which they did with great enthusiasm. What they wanted, as Mrs. Grimsley explains, was "Nothing less than the consulship at Dundee for our Scotch Minister of Springfield, the Rev. Dr. James Smith, to whom we were all very much attached." This loved old friend wanted to spend his last days in his native Scotland. Lincoln teased Mary and Elizabeth a bit more before telling them to send the minister to the cabinet room to see about the appointment. But he exacted a promise from the two feminine conspirators that this should be the last time they would "corner" him.

No one of the laughing trio could know that the future held a time when widowed Mary Lincoln, living abroad, would make a journey to Scotland, although almost too ill to travel, "to see," as she said, "a very dear old friend of my husband's & my own, whose days I fear are numbered." Such was the steadfastness of her friendship.

Mrs. Lincoln followed the fortunes of the Union army with breathless, passionate interest, and we will find Lincoln constantly reporting military events to her. A nation at civil war is like a person in the grip of a dread disease. There are conflicts of opinion as to the treatment and cure, experimentation, blunders, fluctuations of improvement and reverses. Lincoln was patiently working with the human material he had, and took into consideration all the circumstances, but Mary was fierce in her blame of the military men who seemed to her so slow in winning the war. There were many staunch Unionists like herself who felt the same way. When a general was not winning battles she was inclined to say, like the Queen of Hearts, "Off with his head."

She had at an early date sent bouquets of flowers to General McClellan but there were no bouquets later in her remarks about him to her husband. The general was too slow and cautious for her, and, while Lincoln explained some of the circumstances, she brushed the explanations off and urged that he be removed. She disliked General Grant keenly. "He is a butcher," she would often say, "and is not fit to be at the head of an army." Lincoln mentioned

Grant's victories, which she admitted, but "He loses two men to the enemy's one," she protested. "He has no management, no regard for life." There was further opinion and advice. Then, with "a twinkle in the eyes, and a ring of irony in the voice," Lincoln said: "Well, Mother, supposing that we give you command of the army. No doubt you would do much better than any general that has been tried." Perhaps after all the point to note is that one could argue with Mrs. Lincoln on even terms.

Much of her entering into public matters came from her kindness and goodness of heart. Mary Lincoln, like her husband, enjoyed helping people. "There is difficulty enough to be encountered in preventing kindly Mrs. Lincoln from making matters worse, and breaking the official rule all to slivers in her good-humored desire to oblige a persistent stream of applicants who appeal to her personal friendship for them," wrote Stoddard, who read her mail and also, having access to Mrs. Lincoln, was sometimes forced into the role of go-between. He was referring here to requests for invitations to official functions.

In the letters appealing for aid (many of them very pitiful) which flowed in a great stream toward the White House, there were a number addressed to the First Lady. Frequently, in her busy life as the President's wife, she wrote letters that could have had no other motives than those which arise from pity and a sense of justice. Such a letter was the one written to Secretary of War Edwin M. Stanton urging that Frank Jones, "a young man of more than ordinary promise," be retained as a cadet at West Point. With the understanding of a mother of sons, she went to great pains to explain that he had been laboring under certain personal difficulties, not his fault and she pleaded that he be given another chance, a six-month trial. It is a tactful, graciously worded letter, typical of many she wrote.

There is eloquence in her plea to Governor Edwin D. Morgan of New York in behalf of one Mary Real, who was in Sing Sing convicted of manslaughter. "I think *her,* entitled to your clemency," wrote Mrs. Lincoln. "She must have acted under the influence of a mind, distrait, besides there is but little evidence, that she contemplated or committed the deed, she is punished for." There is poignancy in the phrase "a mind, distrait"; this letter was written in 1862, when Mary was crushed with grief. "Pray, let me know, if my signature, to a petition for mercy with other names of respectability, will induce you to remit her sentence? ... I shall feel grateful, if you think proper to signalize your retirement from office, by an act of grace, which I cannot but feel, is well deserved." We are reminded here of Lincoln's constant granting of pardon for condemned soldiers, because he took into consideration their human failings and limitations. The Lincolns were at one in being on the side of the person suffering from injustice or misfortune.

One finds a number of appeals addressed to Mrs. Lincoln in the Lincoln Papers. A good example of these begins: "Mrs. President Lincoln Highly respected Madam." The writer was "emboldened" to address her "first because those knowing you best say you possess a heart full of lofty patriotism and devotion toward our beloved Country, and of the kindest and tenderest sympathy for suffering humanity when and wherever want, sorrow and suffering may exist." Such letters tended to increase her idea that she should take part in public affairs.

Lincoln himself encouraged her in this point of view. In at least two cases he let her join him in making recommendations for personal friends, both putting signatures to the document involved. But that was a different thing from writing to editors and members of the cabinet. A letter she wrote the Secretary of the Interior, Caleb B. Smith, speaking in behalf of John Watt, head gardener at the White House, launches one directly into a tangled situation in which Mrs. Lincoln soon found herself involved.

John Watt had been head gardener for a number of years and had been accused of padding expense accounts and forging payrolls long before the Lincolns came to Washington. He has been referred to as "a cheat and a liar." But he evidently had a smooth personality and Mrs. Lincoln believed in him. He probably quickly learned, as did certain other evil advisers, that the First Lady could not think straight about money and had an obsession as to being poor. He was not the only villain who played upon her incompetence in financial matters for his own purposes.

It was said that Watt was the one who suggested to her that bills could be juggled so that expenses for one purpose could be charged to another. Perhaps he suggested that people who knew their way around in Washington did this frequently, or perhaps he made her believe that as First Lady she had certain prerogatives and it would be foolish not to take advantage of them. Such a man, long versed in rascality, could foresee that if he involved Mrs. Lincoln in dubious precedures he could either use blackmail against Lincoln or sell his knowledge to Lincoln's opponents later on. He ultimately tried to do both those things. Watt was also accused of being a secessionist; he certainly acted the part in doing all he could to sabotage the Lincoln administration.

There was nothing in Mrs. Lincoln's sheltered experience to warn her against a man like this. One can only guess at the line of talk he gave her, but he won the confidence of the credulous wife of the President and she considered him her friend, so much that in September 1861 she wrote Secretary of the Interior Smith a letter defending Watt in vigorous terms from a charge of dishonesty and stating that in all his accounts he had been "rigidly exact."

That fall there was a shakeup of the White House domestic staff. The Commissioner of Public Buildings wrote to the President on October 15: "... such a general outcry has been made against some of the employees at your house, that I did not know but it might be expedient to try to get rid of some of the clamor by the removal or resignation of some of them."

Further light is thrown on the situation by one of the most indispensable witnesses for the Lincoln story, Noah Brooks, who came to Washington in 1862 as correspondent for the Sacramento (California) *Daily Union*. He had known Lincoln in Illinois days, and was soon seeing him almost daily at the White House. Combining literary talents and high ideals with a delightful personality, he won the close and confidential friendship of both Mr. and Mrs. Lincoln. Perhaps the fact that he had lost both his young wife and baby son contributed to his sympathetic understanding of the Lincolns in their bereavement and was an added bond. The evidence of their faith in him lies in the fact that Lincoln selected him to be his private secretary at the beginning of his second administration when Nicolay and Hay were to leave.

Noah Brooks explained that when the Lincolns entered the White House there were "suckers who grew rich on the pickings and stealings from the kitchen, garden and conservatory and who had spies in every room in the house . . ." It is thanks to Brooks that one gets evidence on Mrs. Lincoln's motives in the shake-up. Writing later, Brooks said she "caused a terrible scattering of ancient abuses which once accumulated below stairs." He added that dismissed employees "circulated innumerable revengeful yarns concerning domestic weaknesses at the White House." These yarns of course joined the mighty barrage of abuse always being hurled at the Lincolns.

However much one doubts Mrs. Lincoln's discrimination in ridding the Executive Mansion of dishonest servants, her intentions as told by Brooks were good. The story of the domestic upheaval explains a situation that has been mostly known one-sidedly in striking phrases from the pen of that brilliant young secretary John Hay, who did not like Mrs. Lincoln. Apparently Hay brought with him from Springfield antagonism to her family connections as well. He remarked contemptuously in a letter to Nicolay in March 1862 that the "enemy," as he called Mrs. Lincoln, "is rapidly being reinforced from Springfield. A dozen Todds of the Edwards Breed in the house."

Friction between this young man and the First Lady was increased by the fact that he concealed certain vital matters from her. Mrs. Lincoln in the White House lived in a constant agonizing dread of danger to her husband. Hay recorded in his diary as early as April 1861: "I had to do some very dexterous lying to calm the awakened fears of Mrs. Lincoln in regard to the assassination suspicion." In this case Hay was justified in not alarming Mrs. Lincoln, but she would have been quick to sense that he was keeping something back and she was not the woman to appreciate being talked down to by a self-confident young man of twenty-three. It is a question whether he was as good at "dexterous lying" as he thought he was.

Young Hay was properly wary of Mrs. Lincoln's idea that in government expenditures money allotted to one purpose can sometimes go to another. Yet she may well have known the "subterfuge" by which John Hay himself happened to be doing secretarial work in the White House. Nicolay was chosen and appointed as private secretary and he himself explained at the time: "As the existing laws do not provide for an assistant for me, I have had John Hay appointed to a clerkship in the Department of the Interior and detailed for special service here at the

White House . . ." There was nothing wrong in this but the distinction between a justifiable subterfuge and a doubtful one may not have been clear in Mrs. Lincoln's mind, which was already confused in matters involving expenditures.

All this background is necessary to understand a passage which Hay wrote Nicolay in the fall of '61. It looks as if the misguided First Lady in selecting members of the domestic staff to be dismissed was being advised by the rascal Watt. Apparently Watt, using Mrs. Lincoln as a tool, even wished to get rid of Hay himself. The young secretary stood in the way because upon occasion he dispersed certain funds for household expenses. One can well sympathize with Hay's disgust at the way Mrs. Lincoln was taken in by the unscrupulous gardener. "Hell is to pay about Watt's affairs," wrote the young secretary. "I think the Tycoon [Lincoln] begins to suspect him. I wish he could be struck with lightning. He has got William and Carroll turned off, and has his eye peeled for a pop at me, because I won't let Madame have our stationery fund. They have gone to New York together." To allow Watt to go with her to New York was, to say the least, imprudent in Mrs. Lincoln, but the fact gives some indication of his influence over her at this time.

Watt seems to have had control in several ways. His wife served as stewardess from April 1861 until February 1862, when the gardener's rascality was brought into the open by the judiciary committee of the House. After that exposé (which will be treated later) his wife naturally lost her position as stewardess and the vacancy led to another struggle between Hay and the President's wife. By that time Mrs. Lincoln had suffered a deadly shock and was in a state of nervous collapse and her judgment was more defective than ever. In justice to Hay neither he nor people in general knew at that time that mental illness was involved.

"Madame has mounted me to pay her the steward's salary," wrote Hay to Nicolay on April 4, 1862. The next day he gave vent to his exasperation in a second letter to "Nico": "The devil is abroad, having great wrath. His daughter, the Hell-cat, sent Stockpole [Stackpole] in to blackguard me about the feed of her horses. She thinks there is cheating round the board and with that candor so charming in the young does not hesitate to say so. I de-

clined opening communications on the subject." One wonders whether Watt by his false representations had fooled
Mrs. Lincoln into suspicions of Hay himself. If so, the
young man's resentment and sarcasm are understandable.

The letter continued: "She is in 'a state of mind' about
the Steward's salary. There is no steward. Mrs. Watt has
gone off and there is no *locum tenens*. She thinks she will
blackguard your angelic representative into giving it to
her 'which I don't think she'll do it, Hallelujah!' "

Four days later young Hay, who was subject to bitter
depressed moods, again wrote Nicolay: "Things go on here
about as usual. There is no fun at all. The Hell-cat is getting more Hell-cattical day by day." And on the very day
Hay wrote these barbed words another letter was being
written in the White House describing Mrs. Lincoln's condition and asking a niece from Springfield to come on to
stay with her. She was so crushed and impaired by her recent bereavement that a companion to nurse, cheer, and
watch over her was "absolutely necessary." In the self-
centeredness of youth, John Hay had no understanding of
the devastation which grief was causing in an ill-balanced
personality. Yet these bitter phrases written in irritation by
an immature secretary in private communication to his
friend have been among the loudest notes in posterity's
chorus of denunciation of Mrs. Lincoln. It has been well
said that "it is a terrible fate to be disliked or distrusted
by a young man with a pen like John Hay's." Yet in justice to him it should be added that he probably never
dreamed that his off-the-cuff remarks would ever be published.

Mrs. Lincoln's association with Watt involved further
serious complications. Prone to act by the emotion of the
moment rather than by deliberation, and misled by unscrupulous advice, she was destined, with the best of intentions, to make some grave blunders, a fact she fully acknowledged in the end.

chapter 21

"FLUB DUBS" WITH COMPLICATIONS

Mrs. Lincoln was engaged that first year in another activity for which she received much censure. The "deplorably shabby condition as to furniture (which looked as if it had been brought in by the first President)," was so unarguable that Congress appropriated $20,000 to refurnish the White House. Even before she reached Washington the matter was on Mrs. Lincoln's mind. A gentleman who met her in New York on the President-elect's journey in February wrote: "She feels some anxiety as to the appropriation for refurnishing the White House, & putting new things in the place of the old." He continued in the stately fashion of the time, ". . . the dominion and the world of women is in the charmed & beautiful circle of Home. Mrs. Lincoln cannot but feel anxiety as to her future Home, for the next four years, & of having that home adorned . . . as becomes the residence of the President . . ."

Knowing, as one does now, Mrs. Lincoln's history of irrational thinking in money matters, and that shopping by that time had become a kind of intoxication to her, one can see the danger of placing $20,000 at her disposal. She was not used to spending large sums of money. There are even women, not listed as abnormal, to whom, under the stimulus of shopping, a total in expenditures fails to register. Mrs. Lincoln, loving beautiful things and conscious that she had discriminating taste, having a high standard of what was fitting for the Presidential mansion, and stung by the accusation that she was an uncivilized Illinoisan, made up her impetuous mind that she would make the White House over into a model of appropriate splendor. No task could have been more to her liking.

The world of furnishings, frills, and fabrics was her very own. Her love of minute detail, her nervous intensity, particularness, and desire to have only the finest and best, stand out in a letter she wrote that first year in regard to the making of a bonnet. It was to be "a purple *silk* velvet head dress of the *exact* shade of the flowers in this dress," and it must have "real silk velvet strings, behind— trimmed exquisitely with heartease before & behind of the same shade." She wanted it "very beautiful," the maker must exercise her very best taste, but it must be ready in three days and must not cost over five dollars. Then she repeated her urgent instructions: "I want it the exact shade of this purple & real—a little green & gilt would not hurt it—I want a lovely affair—the velvet gracefully twisted." The letter is an epistolary Godey's print.

Like flashes on a screen are the frequent newspaper items about her shopping trips to Philadelphia and New York that first year. The reporters sometimes showed excess of zeal. Mrs. Grimsley told of a pleasure trip to New York which she and Mrs. Lincoln made in May in which they "had not even driven by the stores." To their amazement after their return they read in the papers that they had been "on an extensive shopping trip" with the names of various stores visited, that "Mrs. Lincoln had bought, among other things, a three thousand dollar point lace shawl, and Mrs. Grimsley had also indulged, to the extent of one thousand, in a like purchase . . ." Mrs. Grimsley remarked dryly that was the nearest she ever came to having such a shawl.

The fact that other ladies accompanied Mrs. Lincoln on the shopping tours probably did not tend to reduce the expenditures. They could join her in admiring the alluring objects ceremoniously set forth for her inspection. There was the flattering deference and subtle salesmanship of the store managers. One may be quite sure top prices were charged the First Lady, who was spending government money. She was one of those women who should never have a charge account. Yet a Chicago paper recorded one likeable bit of down-to-earthness on her part. She was not ashamed to carry some of her bundles home herself. Some of New York's aristocrats probably looked down their noses at this, but it is a pleasing outcropping of Springfield informality.

Old receipted bills in the National Archives show the vast array of objects bought. There is every possible item of furniture for Victorian interiors: bedsteads, chairs, sofas, velvet hassocks, "Bell Pull Rosets & Cords," washstands, "Ewers & Basins," "Covered Chamber," "foot bath," and—to strike a modern note—"Pattent Spring

Mattresses." One almost wades through costly fabrics: damask, brocade, pink tarlatan, "French Brocatelles," "French Plushes," "French Satin DeLaine." There is even an item for "hanging 221 pieces of velvet paper." It took 508 yards of blue and white "Duck" for the tent placed on the White House lawn for the use of the Marine Band in their Wednesday and Saturday concerts. New rosewood furniture and regal purple and gold hangings were selected for a stately guest chamber. It is an epitome of what happened to Mrs. Lincoln that these splendid draperies, selected when her spirits were riding high in her new prominence, should hang in the room where her beloved child was to lie dying.

Any woman who delights in entertaining is drawn toward the glass and china departments. The Dorflinger glassware Mrs. Lincoln bought was the finest produced and a specimen of it now in a museum is a valuable item. Many people of today have seen, on exhibition in the White House, pieces of the set of Haviland in "Solferino and gold" which was one of her purchases. Solferino seems to refer to the reddish-purple color of the wide borders around the plates and other pieces. In the center was the American coat of arms. The splendor of that Solferino and gold so delighted Mary that, according to Mrs. Grimsley, she ordered a similar set made for herself with her initials, "M. L.," in place of the arms of the United States. Mrs. Grimsley is careful to point out that this was paid for privately. Lincoln's account in the banking house of Riggs and Company shows that on November 4, 1861, he was charged with $1106.73, presumably the cost of the dinner service.

It was an ill-considered purchase at best; a characteristic extravagance by a woman who had so recently impressed upon Mrs. Keckley that she was poor, and an indiscretion in that it was bought along with purchases made with government money. Of course she was accused of having paid for it out of public funds and the "crockery business" continued to be used in abusive stories. In the heat of the election campaign of 1864 the New York *World,* opposed to Lincoln's re-election, published an editorial charging that the bill for the set had been padded, so that the difference between the price and the amount of the bill could be used for private purchases for the Lincolns. The store involved, Haughwout & Company, indignantly denied the accusation, but the sad thing about political smear campaigns is that they do smear.

Receipted bills for labor show that housecleaning and redecorating were part of this energetic doing over of the Executive Mansion. There was an item of a new stepladder for $12.50 and $196.75 paid "To washing windows, paints & floor of lower part of house." Some intrepid workman cleaned, repaired and varnished the countenance of Andrew Jackson in his portrait for $25.50. There were women who would have felt sorry for themselves in having so large a task as doing over the White House. Mary did it with her characteristic interest and enthusiasm.

There was a special appropriation for books and she reveled in making the library up-to-date. Lovers of old books may wince a little to read in one of her letters, "There is a very poor set of Waverly—also Shakespeare in the house library, so I replaced each with a fine new edition." The bill for these two items plus a set of Cooper totals $62 and one speculates upon a note on this document: "The President pays of the above bill $47. leaving the Govt. to pay $15.00." Perhaps Lincoln wished to buy the books for himself, but one occasionally finds him paying out of his own pocket for unjustified or extravagant expenditures by his wife. The bills show that Mary continually bought books of poems: those of Hood, Goldsmith, Mrs. Browning, Spenser, Bryant, and Longfellow are listed among many others.

Many a wife would have bogged down in the multiplicity of things required for the White House but Mary had a nervous driving energy and she wrote truthfully: "No one has the interest of the place, more at heart than myself." It has been conceded that she showed fine taste. "The most exquisite carpet ever on the East Room was a velvet one, chosen by Mrs. Lincoln," wrote Mary Clemmer Ames, who certainly did not go out of her way to praise that unfortunate First Lady. "Its ground was of pale sea green, and in effect looked as if ocean, in gleaming and transparent waves, were tossing roses at your feet." If a guest's taste ran to stronger color, he could step into the Red Room, whose floor was covered with 117 yards of crimson Wilton at the cost of $292.50.

By November a newspaper was commenting on the "modern conveniences" the White House had acquired—furnaces, gas and Potomac water. The First Lady took a hostess's natural satisfaction in this up-to-dateness and transformation. She concluded her letter to Elizabeth Grimsley that fall by saying she was expecting a caller, Mrs. Donn Piatt, adding playfully, "I must mount my white Cashmere and receive her." She proudly told Elizabeth: "We now occupy the stately guest room. She [Mrs. Piatt] spoke last winter of the miserably furnished rooms. I think she will be astonished at the change." Her final sentence shows her handicap amidst all these activities: "I am not well enough to go down."

As so often happens in government expenditures, Mrs. Lincoln exceeded the appropriation. Her pride soon gave way to tears. To get the inside story of what followed, we turn to that astute and entertaining gentleman, Benjamin Brown French. He was appointed Commissioner of Public Buildings by Lincoln in September 1861, a position which brought him into close contact with the First Lady. He obligingly kept a journal and also wrote long newsy letters to members of his family; his papers are preserved today in the Library of Congress. The keen observations of this genial and sophisticated man (who wrote with a twinkle in his eye) furnish many plums in the pudding of historical research.

Having been in various government positions from the eighteen-thirties, French knew his way around in the intricacies of Washington society. We find him on December 24, 1861, writing his sister-in-law Pamela French about certain scenes at the White House. Pamela had evidently asked questions in regard to the stories being circulated about Mrs. Lincoln. French replied: "I certainly know of nothing 'unspeakably ridiculous at the White House,' & it seems as if I should know it were there any thing, for I am often there, & Mrs. L. & I are on the most cosey terms. We introduce *each other* to the callers every Saturday afternoon and on reception evenings."

The French Papers cover the Lincoln administration, and through French's recorded impressions can be traced Mrs. Lincoln's increasing deviation from the normal. It must be remembered that at this time people did not realize that mental illness was involved in her case. They felt with a certain puzzlement that something was wrong and called her peculiar or eccentric. French wrote: "Mrs. Lincoln is —Mrs. Lincoln, & no body else, & like no other human being I ever saw. She is not easy to get along with though

I succeed pretty well with her." Today we know she was
in need of medical treatment. Her contemporaries of the
White House period did not understand that; yet their
judgments, made harsh by this ignorance, are still quoted
against her.

French was encountering Mrs. Lincoln on the one topic
where she was irrational—money. His letter to Pamela
continued: "There is no denying the fact that she is a curiosity, but she is a lady and an accomplished one too . . . "
He then told Pamela of a recent experience. In December
1861 Mrs. Lincoln sent for him to come to the White
House "on urgent business." When he arrived she told him
in great distress and with many tears that she had exceeded the appropriation for refurnishing the White House
by $6700. She wanted Major French to see the President
"and tell him that it is common to overrun appropriations
—tell him how *much* it costs to refurnish, he does not
know much about it, he says he will pay it out of his own
pocket (tears) you know, Major, he cannot afford that, he
ought not to do it, Major you must get me out of this difficulty, it is the last, I will always be governed by you,
henceforth . . . now do go to Mr. Lincoln and try to persuade him to approve the bill, Do Major for my sake (tears
again) *but* do not let him know you have seen me." She
reminds one of a penitent wife who has foolishly bought a
too expensive hat and is faced with the bill and a husband
of a differing viewpoint.

French probably discounted her resolve to be governed
by his advice henceforth. On September 28, 1861, the Commissioner of Public Buildings had written her there were
no funds available for repairing the President's house.
In spite of this, Mrs. Lincoln went ahead with her un-
authorized spending. On October 11 she bought expensive
paper for the East, Blue, "Crimson," and Green Rooms,
the whole bill including labor totaling $3549.00. This bill
is significantly marked, *"as selected by Mrs. Lincoln &
not by Com. Pub. Bdgs."*

According to her wishes French left the tearful Mrs.
Lincoln and sought out the President to ask his approval
for a deficiency appropriation. Lincoln got "a leetle excited" and exclaimed: "It never can have my approval—I'll
pay it out of my own pocket first—it would stink in the
nostrils of the American people to have it said that the
President of the United States had approved a bill over-

running an appropriation of $20 000 for *flub dubs* for this damned old house, when the soldiers cannot have blankets."

Lincoln called for the bill sent by the store from which certain furnishing had been bought and examined it, commenting as he went along: ". . . elegant, grand carpet, $2,500 I would like to know where a carpet worth $2,500 can be put." By this time he had learned that his wife was the one at fault: ". . . well I suppose Mrs. Lincoln *must* bear the blame," said Lincoln, "let her bear it, I swear I won't!" Knowing only too well her irresponsibility in regard to money, the realization that this weakness of hers had become a matter of public policy threw him into distressed agitation. "It was all wrong to spend one cent at such a time," he continued, "and I never ought to have had a cent expended; the house was furnished well enough, better than any one we ever lived in, & if I had not been overwhelmed with other business I would not have had any of the appropriation expended, but what could I do? I could not attend to everything." The President's usual reserve was broken, he rose and walked the floor in his distress. As an indulgent husband he was vulnerable to anything that touched his wife, but on a matter of his convictions, he was uncompromising. French's account concludes that Lincoln "ended by swearing again that he *never* would approve that bill." "So ended that *interesting* morning *call* on the President & ess."

But there was nothing corrupt in a deficiency appropriation. Mrs. Lincoln spoke truly when she said it was a common thing to overrun appropriations. There was also point to her opinion that things bought for the White House should be paid for by public funds. In the end Congress passed two deficiency bills to balance the account.

Mrs. Lincoln's request to French not to tell Lincoln that he had talked with her shows clearly that she knew she could not influence her husband in a matter of this kind. Her failure to take him into her confidence was, of course, a mistake. But she knew he was already burdened to the breaking point with affairs requiring his attention and this was a matter "in the dominion and the world of women." She also knew that he would not see eye to eye with her in such expenditures. She spoke the truth when she said he did not know much about it. There was an honest difference of viewpoints. Material objects or beauty of sur-

roundings meant little or nothing to him. He did not notice or care how the mansion looked. She, feeling that the
social side of their position was her responsibility, cared
very much. She was aware that the hostile eyes which
came to official functions would view the run-down condition of the furnishings critically and make capital of it
to the effect that uncivilized Illinoisans did not know how
ladies and gentlemen lived. With good reason she trusted
her sense of the social fitness of things more than his. Her
intentions were of the best, and except for exceeding the
appropriation she had accomplished her task extremely
well, showing excellent taste and the sense of what was
appropriate that only a woman of cultured background
could have had.

In the French manuscripts one finds genuine appreciation of Mrs. Lincoln's good qualities as well as exposure
of her weaknesses. As her strain and feeling of insecurity
in the White House increased, she demanded more and
more material things. Perhaps acquiring things served as
a palliative. The urge to buy had become pathologic and
was to remain so the rest of her life. In the first year of
the Lincoln administration French in exasperation called
her " 'The Republican Queen' who plagues me half to
death with wants with which it is impossible to comply . . ." If he went to the President he encountered another difficulty with "honest old Abe who calls me
'French' and always tells me a story when I go to talk
with him." Three years later French wrote that Mrs.
Lincoln was "boring" him "daily to obtain an appropriation" for a new summer home for the President and herself, and by 1865 he confessed that her urgings combined
with the pressure of his various duties had him more
"*driv*" than ever before in his life. The commissioner was
having a hectic time like everyone else in wartime Washington, but like all who came in contact with Mrs. Lincoln he knew she was not the terrible woman pictured in
malicious gossip. He was indignant at the *"vile slander"*
heaped upon her for political purposes. He noted at the
White House receptions how she "bore herself well and
bravely, and looked queenly." He spoke of her little acts
of thoughtfulness for others, "excellent lady that she is."
He recognized that the bedrock of her character was a
fundamental goodness and kindness of heart.

By Christmas of 1861 the White House undoubtedly

presented a more beautiful and suitable interior. The color and richness of the new furnishings were a daily delight to Mary's feminine heart. But her fundamental values were always those of the devoted wife and mother. These splendid objects became merely what Lincoln called them, "flub dubs," in comparison to the joy of having all the family together at Christmas. Robert came home from Harvard so grown-up he seemed in some ways like a stranger. To people of such overwhelming parental instinct as Abraham and Mary Lincoln, having their children together was a wonderful thing. This was the essence of their Christmas.

January 1862 was the eleventh month of their stay in the White House. It would soon be a whole year. Early that month, who should turn up in Washington but Billy Herndon, to tell Lincoln, of all things, that he wanted help in his second courtship!

Herndon's first wife had died not long before and Billy was courting a pretty girl eighteen years his junior. The middle-aged widower with his drinking habits and a houseful of children was, as his biographer says, "no marital prize" and the young lady had an understandable reluctance. It happened that her brother-in-law wanted a federal job and Herndon figured that if he could use his friendship with Lincoln to obtain such an appointment it would advance his wooing. He laid the whole story before Lincoln, who found it "wonderfully funny" and took pleasure in arranging for the desired post for Herndon's future brother-in-law.

It is to be doubted that Mary found anything "funny" about Herndon's coming to the White House. Her opinion of him had not changed. His drinking and lack of refinement were as repulsive to her standards as ever. We do not know just what happened between them on that visit. After Herndon left he confided to a friend: "I was in Washington some days since and saw all. Mrs. Lincoln is a very curious—excentric—*wicked* woman. Poor Lincoln! He is domestically a desolate man—has been for years to my own knowledge."

Perhaps she had found out the fact that Herndon ran short of money and borrowed twenty-five dollars from the President while in Washington. With her complex about money and her distaste for Herndon that would have been hard to take. Perhaps she made her dislike evident

or perhaps Herndon picked up some of the malicious stories circulating about the First Lady. In addition to his
conviction that he "saw all," he could usually be counted
on to hear all when it came to gossip. It has been suggested that she snubbed him, but what happened is conjecture; one only knows that the visit was another item
in the long story of Herndon's antagonism toward Mrs.
Lincoln.

The Springfield gossips had a field day speculating
about Herndon's visit. They rolled up a snowball of rumor—that he had gone to ask Lincoln for an appointment for himself, probably as minister to Italy, that he
had been found drunk on the streets of Washington.
Herndon's biographer finds no evidence that he asked for
any appointment for himself on this visit but he appealed
later to Lincoln and was offered a small job of about a
month's duration, which he declined. In 1864 Herndon
tried a roundabout approach through a friend in Washington, writing him: ". . . if you see Lincoln tell him for me
that if he has any large, honorable, & fat office with a
big salary to give away and cannot get any person on
earth to take it that I'll take and run it . . ." The hint was
not taken. Springfield tradition had it that Mrs. Lincoln
influenced her husband not to give Herndon an appointment. One doubts whether any influence was necessary,
as Lincoln himself knew that Herndon's drinking habits
and indiscretion unfitted him for a responsible government position, but if Herndon thought Mrs. Lincoln was
to blame for his disappointment, it would have added to
his accumulating hatred of her.

Herndon came to Washington when Mary Lincoln was
at the height of her exhilaration, that peak from which
she was to be hurled to the depths by the tragedy of
February 1862. It was her continual fate to have what
she valued in life either spoiled or taken from her. The
glitter of silver, the sheen of rug or drapery remained
about her, but in a short time she was to write: "Our
home is very beautiful, the grounds around us are enchanting, the world still smiles & pays homage, yet the
charm is dispelled—everything appears a mockery, . . .
and we are left desolate."

chapter 22

WHITE HOUSE FAMILY

The foundation upon which Mary Lincoln's life rested was her family. Her refurbishing of the White House, her dipping into politics, her playing the star part socially as First Lady were all activities precious to her. She enjoyed the importance and drama of these things, but the well-being of husband and children was basic. In the White House as always her most important role was that of wife and mother and to this she gave her best attention.

The Lincoln sons have romped on and off stage in the Springfield phase but, as with the parents, the spotlight was not focused upon them until Presidential days. The eldest son Robert decidedly wished to dodge that spotlight. He could not adjust himself to publicity. His personality had hidden kinks. Possibly a psychiatrist would search his early life for causes of this maladjustment.

He had been somewhat cross-eyed as a young child. A fragment in the Herndon-Weik Papers sets forth the interesting information that he cured this defect by peeping through a keyhole. His schoolmates gave him the nickname of "Cockeye," which certainly was no psychological boost. Possibly also Robert fits into the theory that first babies sometimes get out of adjustment when the second child arrives to share parental attention.

Let the psychiatrist answer these questions, but historical evidence indicates that Robert was a bumptious, difficult individual and somewhat of a problem child to the Lincolns. His tendency at three years to run away from home was noted, as has been seen, in a letter of his father in 1846 with the comments that the child was very mischievous and that he, Lincoln, feared his son's smartness might be of the rare-ripe variety. Lincoln's remarks about Robert are characterized by a curious restraint which seems strange coming from one who gave out such an all-embracing parental affection to young people in general. The father was careful to be fair; Robert was "smart" and, as he approached seventeen, promised "very well, considering we never controlled him much."

If Lincoln's references to Robert usually lack warmth, Robert's account of his relation to his father is even harder to understand. To a request for details about Lincoln, the eldest son wrote that in his boyhood he had seen very little of his father, as the latter was away from home so constantly. The prolonged absence of the father is quite to the point, but almost any boy in the neighborhood would have answered that inquiry with a flood of affectionate reminiscence about the beloved and kindly man who was interested in all the children. Robert's answer was partly due to his curious, almost abnormal shrinking from giving out any personal information about his parents, but in the Lincoln home scene he seems aloof and sometimes in conflict with the rest of the family. His letter amounts to saying he did not know his father very well. Nor does his mother's presence seem to have registered to any extent on the young man's consciousness. In later years he did not remember that she attended the Alton debate and that, on the journey to Washington in '61, she and his two younger brothers reached Indianapolis on a later train than his father. These are both established facts. Of course Robert went away to school in 1859 and was at Harvard during most of the Presidency, figuring little in the Washington scene except at vacations. Even so, it is strange that he could say that he scarcely had ten minutes' quiet talk with his father in White House days, that father who could find time to tell stories and laugh with his young secretaries.

The theater was a favorite recreation of Mary and her husband. Lincoln's interest in plays and the appeal to him of poetry and drama, an interest which Mary fully shared, are well known. The following statements written by the eldest son seems more like that of a distant relative: "Personally I never attended a play with my father ... as I was very little in Washington while he was there. I have a general understanding that he frequently visited the theatre there as a matter of recreation, but I know nothing of the particulars."

It is a bit amusing to find that a certain word is chosen to describe Robert. Mrs. Conkling wrote her son just before the Lincolns left Springfield for Washington: "The young ladies say that Bob was greatly improved, and that he is much more gentlemanly ..." Mrs. Lincoln in a letter to a former neighbor in Springfield in the following year said: "He has grown & improved more than any one you ever saw." The consistent choice of the word "improved" implies there was room for improvement and perhaps involves also a certain we-must-hope-for-the-best attitude. Mary, like loving mothers through the ages, played down her son's shortcomings and expanded on his virtues until that tragic period late in her life when he, as she thought, betrayed her.

Occasionally one finds an incident of conflict between Robert and the rest of the family. The artist F. B. Carpenter was in Nicolay's room in the White House when Robert came in with a flushed face and said: "Well, I have just had a great row with the President of the United States!" Carpenter naturally wanted to know what the row was about and Robert explained. It seems Tad had gone that day to the War Department and Secretary Stanton, humoring the spoiled youngster, had commissioned him lieutenant. Tad, reminding one here of his mother, promptly assumed too much authority, ordered muskets, dismissed the regular White House guard, drilled the servants, gave them the guns, and put them on duty in place of the men he had discharged. Robert, on learning the situation, went to the President with the idea that Tad needed a bit of discipline. Lincoln looked upon the whole matter as a good joke and refused to do anything about it. After Tad was in bed, matters were quietly adjusted. Robert, like many older brothers, apparently did not approve of the way in which his parents were rearing the younger children. There were many in and around the White House who heartily agreed with Robert in this.

Herndon, disliking both Robert and his mother, said they were alike, and like many of Herndon's slanted ideas this one has been widely accepted. Robert may well have inherited certain traits from his mother's people but he did not have her personality. He was like her in being extremely sensitive. Both in old age were tortured with nervousness. But where Robert was close-mouthed and constrained, a man with deep hidden motives, his mother's feelings were an open book. He lacked her demonstrative, overflowing affection, her sparkle, her spontaneity, her giving of herself in love of people and life, her ability to have a good time. When Robert told his father that he wished to study law at Harvard, Lincoln replied: "If you do, you should learn more than I ever did, but you will never have so good a time." It seems a shrewd recognition that so unadjusted a personality could never let itself go in wholehearted enjoyment. There he was like neither father nor mother. One suspects that at times the Lincolns wondered from whom Robert got his traits. Within the limits of his eccentric personality he had ability, conscientiousness, kindness, and affection.

No, Robert was not like his mother, but she had her replica in Tad. He was, according to Cousin Lizzie Grimsley, "a gay, gladsome, merry, spontaneous fellow, bubbling over with innocent fun, whose laugh rang through the house, when not moved to tears. Quick in mind, and impulse, like his mother, with her naturally sunny temperament, he was the life, as also the worry of the household." Those were exactly the qualities of a young woman in Springfield with whom Abraham Lincoln had fallen in love over twenty years before.

To get best acquainted with Tad and Willie we turn to Julia Taft Bayne, one of the most captivating of the witnesses whose eyes we borrow to look at our central figures. Shortly after the Lincolns entered the White House there tripped into it a sixteen-year-old girl, Julia, daughter of Judge and Mrs. Horatio N. Taft, who were prominent in Washington society. Willie was going-on-eleven, and Tad nearly eight at this time and Julia had two younger brothers, "Bud" and "Holly," who were approximately the same ages. As soon as Mrs. Lincoln found this out she said to Mrs. Taft: "Send them around tomorrow, please, . . . Willie and Tad are so lonely and everything is so strange to them here in Washington." The mother tried constantly to keep life in the White House normal and happy for the children.

From that time on a quartet of irrepressible little boys romped through and threatened demolition of the Executive Mansion and the Taft home, visiting back and forth and eating meals indiscriminately at either place. Bud was Willie's crony and Holly was Tad's. On one occasion at least Mrs. Lincoln arranged for the Taft boys to live at the White House while she was out of town on a shopping trip.

It was Julia's dubious privilege to look after the four children. Being at the White House almost daily for nearly a year, she becomes an almost ideal witness. She saw things straight with honest, intelligent eyes and wrote them down conscientiously in her diary.

President Lincoln seemed to her "a good, uncle-like person, . . . smiling and kind," who with a teasing twinkle called her a "flibbertigibbet." When she asked him in open-eyed wonder if that were a French word, he explained it meant "a small, slim thing with curls and a white dress and a blue sash who flies instead of walking."

Julia's mother was a Victorian parent who thought young girls should not air their opinions in the presence of their olders. When Julia first met Mrs. Lincoln and the latter with genuine interest asked her questions and let her talk, it was a new experience. Mrs. Lincoln, who "was dressed in a fresh lilac organdy and looked very attractive," seated Julia beside her on the sofa, put her tactfully at ease and ended by winning her confidence and deep affection. She was soon telling the First Lady intimate thoughts which she would not have dared to confide to her own mother, and Mary Lincoln with equal naturalness was opening her heart to the sympathetic girl. In the account of this interview, for a moment a warmhearted woman comes alive and one feels that element hardest to capture from the record of the past— personal magnetism. It was the author's privilege to get this reflection of Mary Lincoln's lovableness more directly; I met Julia Taft Bayne in her old age and heard her talk of Mrs. Lincoln's sweetness and tenderness to her. There was a look of pain in Mrs. Bayne's fine eyes when she spoke of the cruel way in which public opinion has regarded Abraham Lincoln's wife.

She remembered the tact with which Mrs. Lincoln passed over a young girl's painful embarrassment. Julia wore her first long dress to a Presidential levee and a great hulking cavalryman with spurs walked on her train. With people showing their amusement all around her, the shy girl was in an agony of mortification but the Lincolns gave no evidence of noticing the accident; they received Julia graciously and as if nothing had happened. Later Mrs. Lincoln comforted her by saying, "You carried it off well for a schoolgirl."

Julia could confide to Mrs. Lincoln the shy secret of the boy friend who had joined the Confederates and asked her to fly with him "to the Southern clime." She would not have dreamed of telling this to her own mother. Mrs.

Lincoln understood: "Yes, dear, it is sad when our friends are in the rebel army." The girl dreaded to play the piano for anyone else but she did not mind playing for Mrs. Lincoln, who stood by in sympathetic companionship and turned the pages of her music for her.

The motto of the Lincolns was: "Let the children have a good time." Julia often heard Mrs. Lincoln say this with a smile as her two sons and the Taft boys rushed noisily or devastatingly through the room. She saw the principle being carried out when she entered a chamber to behold the President lying on the floor with four boys trying to hold him down. They could attend to his arms and legs but there was so much of the long powerful man, whose broad grin indicated his enjoyment, that reinforcements were desired and Tad yelled as soon as he saw her: "Julie, come quick and sit on his stomach." The proper Julia declined the invitation. But she did join the listeners when Lincoln gathered the four wriggling little figures on top of him in one big chair to tell them stories of hunters and settlers attacked by Indians. Somehow the long arm managed to reach out and sweep Julia into the group.

One night when Bud and Holly Taft stayed at the White House because it was raining too hard for them to go home, Mrs. Lincoln dressed the four boys in fresh blouses and let them attend a state dinner, sitting near the foot of the table. Mrs. Taft was horrified to hear of this next day. She evidently did not believe that "letting the children have a good time" was as important as that. The boys had their own reactions to the occasion; Tad and Willie thought "Pa" looked pretty plain with his black suit in contrast to those of the ambassadors "all tied up with gold cords," but they took comfort in the thought that "Ma was dressed up, you bet."

Julia as chaperone for the four boys was in as difficult a position as the teacher of a "progressive school." Tad was her greatest trial. When she took him to church he sat on the floor of the pew, negotiated the loan of a knife from a young officer, and promptly cut his finger, and Julia had to apply first aid with her best embroidered handkerchief as bandage. When she hissed at him she would never take him to church again, he put her in her place by saying out loud: "Just you keep your eyes on Willie, sitting there good as pie." The main reason

Tad went to church at all was to be with Willie, who liked to go. The Lincoln boys preferred to attend church with Julia rather than with their parents because the Taft family church was "Lots livelier." Its special attraction lay in the fact that, when the preacher prayed for the President of the United States, the "seceshes," as Tad called them, would get up and leave in a marked manner banging the pew doors behind them. This entertaining performance ceased abruptly when an order was issued for the arrest of anyone leaving before the service was over. Tad was frankly disappointed that no spirited "secesh" looking for trouble challenged this order.

One thing about the affair puzzled him and he asked his father about it a few days later. Lincoln was sitting book in hand near his wife, shoes off, legs crossed, one stockinged foot waving slowly back and forth. "Pa," demanded Tad, "why do the preachers always pray so long for you, Pa?" The father's smile faded. "I suppose it's because the preachers think I need it and," half to himself, "I guess I do."

The Lincoln boys also enrolled themselves in the Sunday school which the Taft boys attended. Mrs. Lincoln, mindful of church duties, was delighted to have them do this. To Julia fell on Saturday mornings the unwelcome assignment of teaching the four boys their Sunday school lesson. The scene reminds one of that in *Tom Sawyer* where Tom's cousin Mary had the same task of getting a bit of Biblical knowledge into a boy's mind that wished to occupy itself with any other topic but the one in hand. Tad interrupted a discussion of the moral law to ask, "Julia, what is a mud sill?" Tad gave his reason for the question, ". . . a boy in Lafayette Square said we were 'em and we am not." Tad, even if he did not know what the term meant, thought it sounded uncomplimentary and wanted to punch the boy on general principles but was restrained by Bud and Willie on the ground it would get into the papers.

To call the Lincoln boys mudsills implied that they belonged to a low stratum of society. Willie and Tad, like their parents, were encountering the snobbishness of the East and South. Tad found this as hard to take as his mother did that expression "uncivilized Illinoisans." Perhaps the mudsill remark that been prompted by the fact that the Lincoln boys did not look stylish. Mary dressed them practically and they, like their father, were indifferent to or unaware of appearances. They arrived one day at the Taft home in a driving rain under a dilapidated umbrella which they had borrowed from the cook.

Their style of dress was described as "homely" and "altogether different from that of the curled darlings of fashionable mothers." The pictures of Willie and Tad reveal no cherubic beauty, but boyish haircuts and honest bright faces that at least one observer thought showed marked resemblance to their father's. We have a delightful description of Tad as "rather a grotesque looking little fellow, in his gray trapdoor pants, made, in true country style, to button to a waist—and very baggy they were . . ." Willie's clothes were equally baggy "but there was a glow of intelligence and feeling on his face which made him peculiarly interesting and caused strangers to speak of him as a fine little fellow."

The antics of the two in the White House were legion. Both parents had the somewhat Western viewpoint that found pranks funny; both on occasion had been guilty of prankish jokes themselves, so the children came by it honestly. It was well that the White House was in stronger condition during the Lincoln administration than in the nineteen-forties, for its historic timbers had a lot to take from the romping, clattering little figures that raced through it from roof to basement, and turned it into a warlike playhouse.

Its roof served in various capacities. It was a circus ground (admission five cents for white or colored, the boys being as democratic as their parents), where Tad was blacked up and Willie wore a lilac gown of his mother's, very low as to neck and very long as to train. Both were liberally swabbed with the beautifier "Bloom of Youth." Tad was singing at the top of his voice "Old Abe Lincoln came out of the wilderness." He was wearing the Presidential spectacles at the beginning of the performance but an exasperated John Hay soon rushed up the stairs to reclaim them for their rightful owner. The President of the United States later attended the circus, paying five cents for the privilege and getting out of it a laugh worth at least a gold coin.

The roof had to double as a fort or the deck of a ship. With a small log to represent a cannon and a few old guns out of working order the boys were prepared to defend the White House against the enemy at all costs. "Let 'em come," said Tad, "Willie and I are ready for 'em." Further military resources consisted of a soldier company called "Mrs. Lincoln's Zouaves," made up of all the boys that could be mustered. With Willie as colonel, Bud major, Holly captain and Tad drum major, any foe had reason to beware. The President and First Lady reviewed this company with due ceremony and presented it with a flag.

The company's gun did not function but once Tad and Holly Taft got hold of one that did. They promptly fired it out of an upstairs window of the Taft home to the great consternation of a Negro mammy who was washing clothes next door. Tad was no more to be trusted with a loaded gun than his mother with a twenty-thousand-dollar appropriation. Julia in exasperation once told him he was not fit to have a revolver, but he protested that if he had one he would give her his "after-David" never to point it at anybody. His benightedly indulgent parents finally did give him a pistol that seems to have operated in some fashion. This got into the record through the father's anxious telegram to the mother when she was out of town with her youngest: "Think you better put 'Tad's' pistol away. I had an ugly dream about him."

Tad's boisterousness kept the household staff in a state that varied from exasperation to actual terror. When he discovered the White House bell system in the garret and, aided and abetted by Willie, achieved a wild ringing of the bells in all the offices at once, there was a frantic running to and fro of secretaries and messengers punctuated by muttered imprecations. When Tad ate up all the strawberries being forced for a state dinner, Major Watt, the gardener, made an emphatic remark about "The Madam's wildcat." One gathers, like Herndon, he "wanted to wring the necks of these brats and pitch them out of the windows."

Many pets were given to the two boys—dogs, ponies, goats—and this caused added complications. A goat hitched to a wagon or a chair and urged on by small boys is a formidable battering ram, and to make matters worse, Tad believed in giving his pets the freedom of the White House. Julia Taft tells of a wild chase after Nanko when he escaped from the stables and Nanny had the honor of being featured in a Presidential letter. Lincoln wrote sadly to his wife, who was on a trip with the youngest,

"Tell dear Tad, poor 'Nanny Goat,' is lost . . ." The father loved animals as intensely as the children, was in distress about it and continued: "The day you left Nanny was found resting herself, and chewing her little cud, on the middle of Tad's bed. But now she's gone! The gardener kept complaining that she destroyed the flowers, till it was concluded to bring her down to the White House. This was done, and the second day she had disappeared, and has not been heard of since. This is the last we know of poor 'Nanny.'" One has one's suspicions about that gardener. Lincoln had delighted to watch the antics of the little creatures upon the lawn; he believed that they were "the kindest and best goats in the world." Seeing one take an unusually active leap he playfully remarked: "He feeds on my bounty, and jumps with joy. Do you think we could call him a bounty-jumper?" The pets served, as did the children, to make the worried man forget his troubles.

It has not been realized that Lincoln had a dog in the White House. In an obscure little book one reads: "Even his little dog Jip was instrumental in relieving his master of some portion of the burden, for the little fellow was never absent from the Presidential lunch. He was always in Mr. Lincoln's lap to claim his portion first, and was caressed and petted by him through the whole meal."

Returning to the antics of Tad, we find him, in company with Holly Taft, bombarding a cabinet meeting with his toy cannon. The Commander in Chief of the Army and Navy had to stop cabinet proceedings to restore peace. The next prank seems to have been entirely Tad's own. He discovered the Confederate flag, the one young Ellsworth had torn down at the cost of his life, and took great delight in displaying it on the White House lawn at times when it would cause the most embarrassment. On one occasion Lincoln stood reviewing Union troops from the portico of the White House. Tad sneaked behind him waving the rebel flag until his father, becoming aware of some strange reaction in the spectators, turned and saw what was going on. He pinioned boy and flag in his arms and handed both over to an orderly who carried them inside.

One incident which shows the father's method with Tad's temper may well indicate the husband's way of dealing with the same quality in his wife. Some photographers who had come to the White House to take pictures of Lincoln requested a room in which to develop them. They were shown to a room which Tad had taken possession of for the purpose of making it into a little theater. Stage curtains and other properties had already been installed for him. When he discovered the invasion he flew into a passion, locked the door, with the photographers' chemicals inside, and refused to let them in; "they had no business in his room!" His father mildly told him to unlock the door but Tad went muttering to his mother's room without obeying. After waiting a reasonable time, the father went after him, returning in a short while with the key and unlocking the door himself. "Tad," he said somewhat apologetically, "is a peculiar child. He was violently excited when I went to him. I said, 'Tad, do you know you are making your father a great deal of trouble?' He burst into tears, instantly giving me up the key." An appeal to affection was the best method of bringing penitence and tears both to Mary and the son who was so like her.

In the fall of 1861 Mrs. Lincoln had desk and blackboard put in one end of the state dining room and engaged a tutor for the boys, inviting Bud and Holly Taft to join the little school, which they did. But the way of the tutor was much harder than the way of Tad the transgressor and tutors "came and went, like the changes of the moon." "If he [Tad] found one with obstinate ideas of the superiority of grammar to kite-flying as an intellectual employment," wrote John Hay, "he soon found means of getting rid of him." One kind and understanding young Scotsman, however, Alexander Williamson, formed an affectionate and lasting friendship with the Lincolns. Mrs. Lincoln was to turn to him for help in bitter months to come. Lincoln took Tad's abhorrence of study with great calmness. "Let him run," he would say, "there's time enough yet for him to learn his letters and get poky. Bob was just such a little rascal, and now he is a very decent boy."

Tad's acquisitive sense resembled his mother's. Julia noted that no matter how often the four boys started out with an equal number of marbles, all the said marbles would be found in Tad's possession by the end of the week. Both mother and son, being petted and indulged, expected a measure of leniency in financial transactions. Lincoln on one occasion offered Tad a dollar if he would cease to pester him for a certain period. Tad kept the bargain very poorly but he collected the dollar.

He was, again like his mother, full of schemes for raising money for reasons that seemed to him excellent. Once he stood at the foot of the stairs in the White House and collected toll of all who passed up; "Five cents for the benefit of the Sanitary Fund," he explained. The Sanitary Commission corresponded to the Red Cross of today. Tad turned merchant, set up a table in the corridor of the White House, stocked it with fruit and candy and sold his wares. This worked so well that he bought up the stock in trade of an old woman who sold gingerbread near the Treasury and moved his business to the portico of the Executive Mansion, where there were even more customers to be had from the endless crowd of office seekers. He made money but was too kindhearted and impulsively generous to keep it.

During the war the President would at times issue a proclamation for a national fast. When Tad found out the meaning of a "fast-day," he was filled with dismay. He promptly established a food depot under the seat of a coach in the carriage house, and stocked it from the White House kitchen. When the cache was discovered he was furious. The President laughed heartily over the incident and remarked gleefully: "If he grows to be a man, Tad will be what the women all dote on—a good provider." He had the gift, inherited from both parents, of choosing the apt word; combined with his lisp, this made his sayings very appealing. He called Elizabeth Keckley "Yib." The statue of General Jackson in Lafayette Park was a "tippy-toe" statue to him.

Tad was a problem but one cannot assemble the evidence about him without understanding and sharing the tenderness in his father's rugged hand as it stroked the restless little head. The boy loved intensely and like both parents had a compassionate heart. We see him tearing into the library in search of something and "having found it, he threw himself on his father like a small thunderbolt, gave him one wild, fierce hug, and, without a word, fled from the room before his father could put out a hand to detain him." So close was the feeling between them that the child, watching the father's face, would laugh uproariously whenever he saw a twinkle begin in the deep-set eyes.

Tad's tender heart prompted him to gather up street urchins of all descriptions and take them to the White House kitchen to be fed. The last Christmas in the White House he brought the whole gang in for Christmas dinner. He "would espouse the cause of some poor widow or tattered soldier, whom he found waiting in the ante-rooms, dragging them into the executive presence, ordering the ushers out of the way and demanding immediate action from headquarters. The President rarely denied a hearing, no matter how closely pressed in other directions."

Tad was an ardent Unionist and was constantly begging for flowers, fruit or books for "his good soldiers." One Christmas he told his father he wanted to send his Christmas books to the camps they had visited because the men looked "lonesome." His father held the tender little face against his own for a moment, then said, "Yes, my son, send a big box. Ask mother for plenty of warm things and . . . pack in . . . good eatables . . . and . . . mark the box 'From Tad Lincoln.' " He reminds one of both his father and mother in his compassion on that Easter Monday when he shared his Easter eggs with a little cripple at the White-House egg-rolling, having a chair brought out for him and watching over him with tact and sympathy.

We have an unforgettable description of a scene at a Union meeting where President and cabinet were in attendance. Lincoln brought Tad with him as he did on many unsuitable occasions. The boy, bored with the long speeches, moved from one member of the cabinet to another whispering to them (no doubt asking when that man was going to stop and let them go home). Finally he climbed on his father's lap to "nestle his head down on his bosom." The account continues: "As the long, bony hand spread out over the dark hair, and the thin face above rested the sharp chin upon it, it was a pleasant sight. The head of a great and powerful nation, . . . soothing with loving care the little restless creature so much dearer than all the power he wields . . ."

Lincoln wanted Tad's baby tooth saved for him and the not less sentimental mother promised to see that it was done. The overworked President could find time to write a card to the Secretary of War requesting him to let Tad have the flags he wanted, or a letter of thanks to someone who had sent Tad a gift of rabbits. The child would hang around the father, who was working at his desk late at night, until he fell asleep. The father would lift the sleeping boy and, stooping under doorways and dodging chandeliers, carry him off to bed, all the tenderness and joy of parenthood concentrated in the feel of that drowsy trusting head on his shoulder.

Along with his dark hair Tad's eyes were spoken of as dark. Willie with fair or light-brown hair, blue eyes and more open countenance, was handsomer. Between the two boys was contrast as great as that between the parents and for a good reason: where Tad was the duplicate of his mother, Willie was his father over again. By the same token their devotion to each other was outstanding. There were occasional clashes, of course, as between all small brothers. Once young Stoddard, noting the youngsters playing under their father's desk, which was covered with a battle map, heard a sudden yell. Tad was trying "to make a war-map of Willie" and there were "rapid movements in consequence on both sides." The President, as fathers are apt to do, disposed of the belligerents by sending them to the maternal parent. Willie would try to head off Tad's indiscretions and at times would reprove him. The boys delighted to question an old French soldier for the fun of seeing him pull off his cap whenever Napoleon's name was mentioned. "I made him pull off his old cap nine times," bragged Tad after a visit, and Willie promptly answered: "Yes, but you asked questions out of turn, Tad Lincoln, and that isn't fair."

But the older boy could not endure seeing the younger one unhappy. At breakfast one morning Tad was in tears and deeply hurt. He had taken some tracts to his beloved soldiers instead of the usual flowers or food and they had laughed heartily at the gift. His father tried unsuccessfully to console his "little man" while Willie looked on in deep distress. Finally the older boy fell into an absorbed silence, thinking deeply for some minutes; "then he clasped both hands together, shut his teeth firmly over the under lip, and looked up smilingly into his father's face, who exclaimed, 'There! you have it now, my boy, have you not?'" Evidently Willie had worked out in his mind some scheme to cheer Tad up. His father turning to a guest said: "I know every step of the process by which that boy arrived at his satisfactory solution of the question before him, as it is by just such slow methods I attain results."

Julia Taft called Willie "the most lovable boy I ever knew, bright, sensible, sweet-tempered and gentle-mannered." Cousin Lizzie Grimsley lists his virtues in glowing terms, ending up with the conclusion that he was "a counterpart of his father." It has been seen that he made little speeches and wrote quaint letters. He even essayed verses, surely a joy to his literary-minded parents. He wrote a poem on the passing of Colonel E. D. Baker, the handsome soldier who had kissed him tenderly on a bright October afternoon and then mounted his horse to ride toward the sunset and his death. It was not the subject for a child and the only notable thing about the poem is that it was written by a boy not yet eleven years old. Its stilted verses exalted patriotism and the glory of dying for the Union; one cannot tell how much was due to immaturity and how much to the prevailing poetic vogue.

Willie's thoughtful and studious nature was shown in his habit of collecting memoranda of important events, such as his father's inauguration, dates of battles and deaths of distinguished men. One day his father would show that little collection to his friend Orville H. Browning, who would write about it in the diary he was keeping. Willie makes one think of little Abraham Lincoln in the backwoods as his stepmother described him, eager for knowledge and books and the "best boy" she ever saw.

Mary Lincoln's whole heart was given to this son who was so like his father. She loved the unpredictable "Taddie" dearly; he was, as she wrote, her "little troublesome *sunshine*," but Willie was her comfort and her favorite child, the one she often said (with her ever-present feeling of insecurity) "would be the hope and stay of her old age." Her letters are starred with descriptions of him: "a very beautiful boy, with a most *spiritual* expression," a "peculiarly religious child, with great amiability & cheerfulness of character." She betrayed her dependence upon him when she said he did not seem like a child to her. In the special "nearness and dearness" between them Willie called himself "Mother's boy." But he was not less the very idol of his father's heart.

The noisy playing of little boys in the White House became subdued in February 1862. As Lincoln and young Stoddard returned to the White House one evening, "Old Edward" stopped the President at the door to say that "the Madame" wished to see him right away, adding,

"The doctor has been here, sir." Willie was sick. Lincoln quickly vanished up the stairway. Stoddard lingered to ask the doorkeeper if Willie was seriously ill. "I think he is, indeed," was the answer; "but she told me not to alarm the President."

Invitations had been issued for a large entertainment and Mrs. Lincoln thought they should be recalled. However, when the doctor was consulted, he said that there was every reason to think Willie was getting along satisfactorily and plans went forward for the elaborate event. But when the scheduled date arrived, Willie suddenly became worse.

That evening Mrs. Keckley arranged Mrs. Lincoln's hair and helped her put on a white satin dress trimmed with black lace, the one of which Lincoln remarked that it had a "long tail" and a neck too low for his taste. But talk of dress fashions was merely on the surface of their thoughts; what mattered to them that evening was the menace that hung over their child.

With worried faces the President and First Lady descended the stairs to go through the same old merry-go-round of official entertainment, greeting an endless blur of faces, hearing the brilliant music of the Marine Band, trying to say the proper and tactful word to each individual, while all the time their thoughts, sick with dread, were upstairs in the bedroom where Willie lay burning with fever. Several times during the evening Mrs. Lincoln left the glittering scene and went upstairs to hold the hot little hand a moment and watch with sinking heart the labored breathing. Then she returned to the hated social duty which up to this time she had counted a joy. One can picture the anxious eyes of the father catching hers with a mute question when she returned.

The days dragged on. The newspapers said Willie had bilious fever and in them one can trace the fluctuations of the illness: very ill, improved, out of danger, and then, by February 17, the ominous words, "hopelessly ill." Willie had asked for Bud Taft and the stanch little pal spent much time at the bedside. One night late the President found him there. Lincoln laid his arm across Bud's shoulder to stroke, as so often, the boyish head on the pillow, then said gently: "You ought to go to bed, Bud." Bud answered simply, "If I go he will call for me." Later the President found the faithful little companion fast asleep and carried him tenderly to bed.

After Willie's illness was recognized as dangerous Mrs. Lincoln did not leave his bedside. She became more and more worn out with the prolonged and agonizing watching. At some point Tad was taken ill too, apparently with the same disease, and the anxiety became a double one. On February 20 Willie had a momentary brightening, he held Bud's hand and seemed better. But as darkness began to close down, the long struggle ended and the little form became forever still.

The father, his features distorted with grief, pulled back the cover and looked on the dead face of his child. Choked with sobs, he tried to express acceptance of God's will but his words went into that pitiful cry of bereaved parents through the ages: "we loved him so."

The exhausted mother was wild in her agony. The sight of that still white face threw her into strange convulsions. There was not in her defective nervous equipment the strength, balance, and maturity necessary to meet this disaster. Between paroxysms of grief she lay stunned and prostrated. Tad was very ill but not even his need of her could make her muster a self-control which had never been hers. The tragedy had struck her when she was at a peak of exhilaration. She had been like a lighthearted, petted child playing a part in a drama with gorgeous costumes and dazzling settings. She would in time try to solace herself with these things again and would find them shoddy trappings.

Mary had rallied from Eddie's death, with the help of youth, the birth of two more children, and the normal surroundings of home. But now youth was behind her, health was impaired, and she was in the midst of war, suspicion, criticism, slander and hate. The future was dark and uncertain. She would never recover from this blow.

There was a violent storm in Washington the day of Willie's funeral. Trees were laid low, roofs were blown off, steeples toppled. Nature seemed to be in a convulsion of grief like the woman who lay ill in the White House. In time the roofs and steeples would be repaired, new trees would be planted, but for Mary Lincoln there would be no restoration. The wholeness and glamour of life for her were dead.

chapter 23

"FURNACE OF AFFLICTION"

Various appeals for help went out from the stricken family. Immediately after Willie's death a White House carriage was sent to bring Senator and Mrs. O. H. Browning, who came and stayed all night sharing, according to the old custom, the burden of sitting up beside the body. From Thursday, the day of Willie's death, until the funeral on the following Monday, these old friends of Illinois days were in almost constant attendance. It was Senator Browning who went to Georgetown to examine the vault into which the President's son was to be placed pending ultimate removal to Illinois. After the funeral services in the East Room, he rode with the President in a carriage drawn by two black horses. It was a long imposing procession; white horses drew the hearse, and the last carriage held the colored servants who had loved the little boy so well. The mother was far too ill to attend.

Lincoln desperately needed help in caring for his sick wife and son. When Dorothea Dix, superintendent of women nurses in Washington, called, the President asked her to recommend a good nurse. She suggested Mrs. Rebecca R. Pomroy, a woman of fine personality who had lost loved ones of her own and had found strength and consolation in her deep religious faith. Mrs. Pomroy did not wish to leave her wounded soldiers, but she was under military rule and was given ten minutes to get ready before being driven to the White House.

She found Lincoln where one would expect to find him, sitting by the bed of his sick wife. Here again comes to mind Mrs. Lincoln's description of her husband, anxiously watching over her with eyes "filled with *his* deep love." The President greeted Mrs. Pomroy warmly saying, "I am heartily glad to see you, and feel that you can comfort us and the poor sick boy." She was soon taken to Tad, who was in a pitiful condition between the fever of his illness and his spasms of crying over Willie, "who would never speak to him any more." Mrs. Pomroy was the right person; Tad and Mrs. Lincoln both received her care and gave her their affection.

She soon found a third patient. Lincoln himself had some kind of illness following Willie's death. Most of all he was sick in heart and he turned to this woman who had lost those dearest to her and still found peace. His mind was in an agonizing groping for help, for some source of strength to bear this unbearable loss. He questioned the nurse: "Did you always feel that you could say, 'Thy will be done'?" When she told him how faith in God came finally to comfort her, he walked the floor with tears streaming down his face. "This is the hardest trial of my life," he said. "Why is it? Oh, why is it?" Again and again he asked her to tell him how she obtained her faith and the secret of placing herself in God's hands in peaceful trust. Lincoln's deep-thinking mind was grappling with the age-old problem of death and immortality.

He was facing the tragedy as a mature person will. Mary, emotionally immature, could not face it or even reach out for help. The blow had struck her in a vital part, her affection. Her grief was as passionate as her love.

Robert was in Washington and he was the one who sent an urgent appeal to his aunt, Mrs. Edwards in Springfield, to come as soon as possible. Mary's oldest sister tried at all times to meet any emergency in the family circle; she left for Washington on the day of Willie's funeral. In her letters back home during March and April one has a new and intimate source showing human reactions back of the columned entrance of the Executive Mansion in the spring of 1862. Writing unguardedly to her daughter, Julia Edwards Baker, the sister gave a remarkable close-up of Mary's impaired and miserable condition.

The letters have reservations in their sympathy. It is the old story of the elder sister disapproving of certain qualities in the younger one, of her not understanding Mary's natural love of gaiety, dress and furnishings. Given the room with the regal purple and gold hangings (the room in which Willie died), she commented: "I would have preferred a smaller apartment, but she [Mary] insists that I deserve the honor—and any thing suits me from the *least* to the greatest, so I gladly submit." The older sister stated frankly that she felt "but little interest in society" and did not care especially for the pretty present which Mary gave her. However justified her criticism of Mary's "frivolity" was, it came from one who was not tempted by frivolous things.

Mary was confined to her bed for about ten days after her son's death. On March 2 Mrs. Edwards wrote: ". . . this morning . . . I persuaded her to put on the *black dress,* that so freshly and painfully reminded of the loss, that will long shadow her pleasures— Such is her nature, that I cannot realize, that she will *forego them* all, or even long, under existing circumstances."

Mrs. Edwards had not wanted to leave her family in Springfield but her fine conscience made her glad to give help where it was so badly needed. "It is enough to feel, however," she wrote her daughter, "that my presence here, has tended very much to soothe, the excessive grief, that natures, such as your Aunt's experience. And moreover to aid in nursing the little sick Tad, who is very prostrated with his illness, and subdued with the loss, he evidently suffers from, yet permits no allusion to." Nothing reveals Mrs. Lincoln's condition more completely than the words that follow the reference to Tad: "His mother has been but little with him, being utterly unable to control her feelings."

By March 12 Mrs. Edwards was writing her daughter that her visit had been "gloomy indeed." "Your Aunt Mary still confines herself to her room, feeling very sad and at times, gives way to violent grief." Mary was "so nervous, and dependent upon the companionship of someone," that the Lincolns wanted Mrs. Edwards to stay on indefinitely. It was "absolutely necessary" for a competent person to be with the sick and broken woman. There is pathos in Lincoln's constant effort to get some member of her family to stay with his wife and help him safeguard her from her own irresponsibility. He urgently pleaded with Mrs. Edwards to remain, saying: ". . . do stay . . . you have such a power & control, such an influence over Mary."

In order to get away herself Mrs. Edwards tried to arrange for her niece, Mary Wallace, to come to Washington in her place. There apparently she ran into some family resentment that Frances Todd Wallace cherished against Mrs. Lincoln, although the latter wanted Frances' daughter to come and offered to pay her expenses. Mrs.

Edwards was eager to leave the house of mourning and get back to her main interest in life, her children and grandchildren; "the sunny smiles of dear little Lewis," her grandson, were drawing her back to Springfield. One must note that little boy, Lewis Baker, because he comes prominently into the story later. There is mention in Mrs. Edwards's letter that he received the toy cars that had belonged to Willie: "Tad insisted upon sending them to Lewis, saying he could not play with them again." In the end Mrs. Edwards (perhaps by arrangement) received a sudden summons home, and the problem of a companion for Mrs. Lincoln was solved by the President's getting Mrs. Pomroy to return for some weeks. Her personality, serene in religious faith, brought healing to both the Lincolns. Husband and wife reached out to attain the comforting visitor's peace of mind. Mrs. Lincoln told her she "would live on bread and water" if she could find such inner happiness. The Lincolns were good to Mrs. Pomroy, taking her with them on their daily drives and showing their usual thoughtfulness and kindness. Mrs. Lincoln begged Mrs. Pomroy to remain all summer.

Ever after Willie's death Mary was apt to weep over any object associated with the lost son. It tore her to pieces to look upon his picture and she never again entered the purple-draped room where he died or the Green Room where he was embalmed. She knew if she did she could not control her emotions.

Yet the mother wanted Willie's memory cherished and even in her benumbed state she remembered his little playmates in Springfield. Mrs. Edwards wrote her daughter: "I enclose a notice of 'Willie' from Willis Home Journal." This was a beautifully worded appreciation of the boy written by N. P. Willis, editor of *The Home Journal*, and Mrs. Lincoln wanted it reprinted in the *Illinois State Journal* because she thought "Some of *his* little friends will enjoy seeing it . . ." But the clipping must be returned; it was the only one she had. The mother also sent a copy of the funeral sermon to a former neighbor in Springfield. They had seen Willie grow through a beautiful babyhood into a little boy and they would care, those old friends. A President's wife had no neighbors.

Mary always took great pleasure in giving presents. The trunk of the elder sister when it went back home contained various feminine gifts and also much shrubbery from Washington. Mrs. Edwards gave full details of this generosity but criticism predominated in her letters. "Your Aunt Mary's manner is very distressed, and subdued," she wrote her daughter. "It is a serious crush to her *unexampled frivolity,* such language, sounds harsh, but the *excessive indulgence,* has been revealed to me, fully justifies it."

This private censure was as nothing to the public excoriation that was going on. Mary herself realized and regretted her thoughtless gaiety and extravagance; she was undoubtedly subdued and for good reason. Beyond the walls of the White House hostile tongues were building fabulous structures of misinterpretation of everything she had done. That February entertainment which had taken place while Willie was ill had been a colossal blunder from start to finish. It was a private party running counter to established social tradition; some of the right people had not been invited and some of the wrong ones had; there were pointed declinations to so elaborate a festivity during the hardship and suffering of war. In Mrs. Lincoln's mind there had been possibly at first only the desire to refute the charge of crudity by showing how beautifully she and the President could entertain. But she had had her own doubts about giving the party and had asked advice. She had certainly wanted the invitations withdrawn when Willie became so ill but the doctor had assured her the boy would be all right.

She poured out her bitterness to a woman who came to weep with her over Willie's death, a mother to whose sick child Mary, with her unfailing sympathy for children, had sent books and flowers. Suddenly Mrs. Lincoln arrested herself in the midst of her tears and said with that touchiness which was one of her handicaps in public life: "Madam, why did you not call upon me before my ball? I sent you word I wished to know you." The visitor answered wonderingly: "Because my country was in grief, as you now are, and I shunned all scenes of gayety." "I thought so!" said Mary bitterly. "Those who urged me to that heartless step (alluding to the ball) now ridicule me for it, and not one of them has . . . come, to share my sorrow. *I have had evil counselors!*"

Newspapers on all sides were denouncing the invalid who wept in the White House. The February entertainment, shrieked the *Liberator,* had been worthy of "a woman whose sympathies are with slavery and with those who are waging war . . ." It had not been "worthy of man or woman with ears open to the wails of the bereaved throughout the country." Another journal raged over the "disgraceful frivolity, hilarity and gluttony," adding that "The White House may have its Delilah." Printed statements of this nature were legion. The cruelest blow of all was a widely read poem by Eleanor G. Donelly called "The Lady-President's Ball." Its lines were supposed to come from a pain-racked and dying soldier who could see through his window the glowing lights and the festive crowd at the President's mansion on the night of the ball. Three of its six stanzas will show its poignancy.

> *What matter that I, poor private,*
> *Lie here on my narrow bed,*
> *With the fever gripping my vitals,*
> *And dazing my hapless head!*
> *What matters that nurses are callous,*
> *And rations meagre and small,*
> *So long as the* beau monde *revel*
> *At the Lady-President's Ball!*
>
> *Who pities my poor old mother—*
> *Who comforts my sweet young wife—*
> *Alone in the distant city,*
> *With sorrow sapping their life!*
> *I have no money to send them,*
> *They cannot come at my call;*
> *No money? yet hundreds are wasting*
> *At my Lady-President's Ball!*
>
> *Hundreds, ay! hundreds of thousands*
> *In satins, jewels, and wine,*
> *French dishes for dainty stomachs*
> *(While the black broth sickens mine!)*
> *And jellies, and fruits, and cold ices*
> *And fountains that flash as they fall,*
> *O God! for a cup of cold water*
> *From the Lady-President's Ball!*

These verses were printed in a newspaper four days before Willie's death, at a time when his mother in despair was ceaselessly watching over him. Anything more calculated to inflame hatred for the First Lady could hardly be imagined, yet ironically enough no woman in Washing would have had more pity for that dying soldier than Mary Lincoln.

Inevitably there were accusations that the President's private party had been paid for by public funds. B. B. French, the one person best qualified to answer this question, evidently received letters from his family reflecting the gossip of the time. He wrote his brother a week after Willie's death, mentioning the "great party at the President's," and saying: "It was a magnificent affair, and the President will pay for it *out of his own purse.*" That settled, he turned to the stories about the First Lady's callousness. French knew her failings as few did but he also knew her tender and well-intentioned heart. "I think you Northern people are too hard on poor Mrs. Lincoln," he wrote. "She did all a mother ought or could during Willie's sickness—she never left his bed side at all after he became dangerous, & almost wore herself out with watching, and she mourns as no one but a mother can at her son's death."

With so much public abuse Mary had burning resentment and regret piled on her grief. She was by nature quick to flare up at criticism. It was not given to her, as to Lincoln, to take abuse philosophically or to put it out of mind. There was nothing philosophic in her nature. She could not bend her head to sorrow; she was rebellious; there was a sort of fighting against fate in the paroxysms of convulsive weeping that swept over her at intervals. Once when she was giving way to a wild outburst of grief, Lincoln gently led her to a window and pointed out a building that housed mental cases. In Springfield he had known that her hysterical seizures resulted from not being well: "nervous spells" he had called them. Now in his words we have evidence of his recognition that mental illness was threatened or involved. The tall patient husband with his arm in that of his frantic wife said: "Mother, do you see that large white building on the hill yonder? Try and control your grief, or it will drive you mad, and we will have to send you there."

With this couple struck down by mutual sorrow there was always the pathetic effort of each to help the other. Lincoln was himself plunged into almost unbearable melancholy. The first and second Thursdays following Willie's death he shut himself away from all society to grieve. As often in deep bereavement he would in his sleep see Willie alive and well again, then wake to the crushing reality it was all a dream.

Mrs. Lincoln in her turn was alarmed over the effect of his grieving on her husband's health. The artist F. B. Carpenter has told how she and Mrs. Edwards, learning that a minister they had formerly known was in Washington, sent for him to come and talk to the President. This minister found that Lincoln responded to assurances of immortality, to the thought that the precious spirit of Willie was still alive.

Out of the citadel of character Lincoln gradually shouldered his grief and carried on with his endless duties. He treasured keepsakes of Willie. Sometimes visitors would notice "over his mantel piece" "a framed picture of Illinois" and he would tell them with pathetic eyes that it had been painted by his little boy. Another minister offered what comfort he could. Rev. N. W. Miner, good friend of Springfield days, came to see the Lincolns. The President took him driving (perhaps so that they could talk together without interruption) and opened his heart to the old neighbor about his religious gropings. They spoke too of the dark state of the war. Lincoln said, "You know I am not of a very hopeful temperament. . . . But relying on God for help, and believing that our cause is right, I think we shall conquer in the end."

The death of Willie, even more than that of Eddie, seems to have had a profound effect upon Lincoln's mature religious belief. It was said that he referred later to the "*change*" in his feelings as a "true religious experience" which brought him a deeper faith.

Her letters show that Mrs. Lincoln's religion gave her an unwavering faith in immortality. She believed confidently that Willie lived on beyond the veil; with her the greatest agony was her mother's need to reach through the veil and find contact with the loved child who had gone out into the immensity alone. This made her susceptible to the wave of spiritualism that was sweeping the country, as always in the wake of war. Fathers, mothers, and wives in the anguish of loss were ready to listen to anyone who promised communication with the loved ones who had gone into the long silence.

Up to this time Mrs. Lincoln had been too interested

and busy with concrete details of living to dabble with the supernatural. Lincoln had been disturbed by dreams and premonitions and she had made light of them. Now it was suggested to her, distraught with grief, that there were mediums who could put her in touch with Willie's spirit. She wanted so much to believe this that it is understandable how she was induced to permit a charlatan who went by the alias of Colchester to hold a séance at the Soldiers' Home, where the Lincolns were staying in the summer of 1862. Of course the bereaved mother received "messages" from Willie, and that made Colchester a privileged visitor to Mrs. Lincoln. Lincoln's attitude toward spiritualism seems to have been one of healthy skepticism combined with curiosity as to how the tricks were done. As always, he wanted to protect his wife from impostors; so he asked a scientist, Dr. Joseph Henry, superintendent of the Smithsonian Institution, to hold a séance at Henry's office to find out, if possible, how Colchester got his effects. Dr. Henry discovered that the sounds which came from different parts of the room were caused by the medium himself. Colchester had an instrument strapped around his arm with which he could produce tappings by expanding or contracting his muscles even while his hands were held by others.

Noah Brooks, good friend of the Lincolns that he was, made a more spectacular investigation. In company with another skeptical friend, he attended one of Colchester's séances. There was the usual hocus-pocus of weird manifestations, in this case the thumping of a drum, the twanging of a banjo, and the ringing of bells. Brooks, who had carefully seated himself between two unbelievers, detached himself from the circle and "grasping in the direction of the drum-beat, grabbed a very solid and fleshy hand in which was held a bell that was being thumped on a drum-head." He shouted for his friend to strike a light. At that moment he received a blow on the forehead and the lighting of a match revealed Brooks with blood streaming down his face, firmly grasping the so-called medium Colchester. The séance broke up "in the most admired disorder."

A day or two later Mrs. Lincoln sent for Brooks and showed him in some agitation a note she had received from Colchester in which he demanded a pass to New York "and intimated that in case she refused he might

have some unpleasant things to say to her." It is another
incident showing how this impulsive lady tended to become the victim of unscrupulous men. Brooks arranged
with Mrs. Lincoln that Colchester should be summoned
to the White House next day, where he would meet him.
Mrs. Lincoln introduced the two men and then withdrew.
Brooks lifted the hair from the unhealed scar on his
forehead and said, "Do you recognize this?" Then he continued: "You know that I know you are a swindler and
a humbug. Get out of this house and out of this city at
once. If you are in Washington to-morrow afternoon at
this time, you will be in the old Capitol prison."

Brooks had supreme contempt for the impostors who
were preying on Mrs. Lincoln's grief. It may well be that
the sympathy and understanding of this man was a factor
in Lincoln's choosing him finally to replace Nicolay and
Hay, who could exchange letters belittling the President's
wife or calling her a "Hell-cat." Thanks to Noah Brooks,
Colchester was disposed of. He sneaked out of the house
and was heard of no more.

But there was a lady medium, Mrs. Nettie Colburn
Maynard, who held séances for Mrs. Lincoln and wrote a
book about the whole affair. This book gives an account
of various meetings with Mrs. Lincoln, of a séance in the
Red Room where Lincoln was present, and of numerous
spooky happenings. One evening, according to Mrs. Maynard, the First Lady was starting to leave the White House
when her husband asked where she was going. "To Georgetown; to a circle," was the answer. "Hold on a minute
and I will go with you," said the President. Then follows
a highly detailed account of the Georgetown séance, but
one is skeptical of accepting as historical evidence information from a lady subject to trances. Lincoln naturally
went with his wife to protect her; also he was curious.
Skepticism seems to have been constantly present, for Mrs.
Lincoln herself required Nettie to undergo a test case. A
military figure wrapped in a long cloak completely concealing his person was presented to her and the lady was
challenged to show her supernatural powers by identify-
ing him. According to Nettie Colburn Maynard's book, her
control, "Pinkie," a little Indian maid, at once identified
the unknown soldier as "Crooked Knife," meaning General
Sickles. (A sickle is a crooked knife.) The identification
was correct. Mrs. Lincoln's demand for the test indicates

her doubts about the cult, although Mrs. Maynard, of course, represents her as a believer in it.

By the summer of 1863, with many frauds exposed, spiritualism was having a setback. Mrs. Lincoln, ill in body and spirit, seems for a time to have found comfort in the thought that Willie visited her. But, even though she attended séances and wanted to believe she could reach Willie, one does not know that she ever fully accepted spiritualism, and in later life she emphatically repudiated it. "Time . . . has *at length* taught & convinced me, that the loved & idolized being, comes no more," she wrote Mrs. Welles. The charge of believing spiritualism pursued her in later life. "I am not EITHER a spiritualist," she wrote in 1869, "but I sincerely believe—our loved ones, who have only 'gone before' are permitted to watch over those who were dearer to them than life."

Death struck again in 1862. One of the First Lady's great handicaps was the fact that she had so many relatives fighting in the Confederate army: three half brothers, one brother, and three brothers-in-law. This opened her to constant charges of being an enemy sympathizer and even a Southern spy, a bitter dose for one to take whose loyalty to the Union went to the very core of her being. To her and to her sons the South was in rebellion and its soldiers were rebels. While the Reverend Mr. Miner was visiting the Lincolns in April 1862, the battle of Shiloh was in progress, and, as always when a battle was being fought, the tension at the White House tightened to an agonized, sleepless waiting for news. During this period Mrs. Lincoln said bitterly to her old neighbor as they sat in the Red Room, talking of the battle, that she hoped her brothers fighting on the Confederate side would be either killed or taken prisoner. It was a harsh statement and Miner showed his surprise. Mrs. Lincoln explained that "they would kill my husband if they could, and destroy our Government—the dearest of all things to us . . ."

Perhaps in that moment of bitterness she meant what she said; perhaps she wanted to bolster such an attitude in herself by putting it into words. But when the news came that Sam Todd had been killed in that April battle, and when Alexander Todd was killed at Baton Rouge that summer, there was no escape of grief for Mary Lincoln's affectionate heart. It was true she had seen little of these half brothers so much younger than herself, but she had played with them and caressed them on her visits to Kentucky, and they were of her blood. She could not let her sorrow for them be known, lest it be misconstrued as disloyalty to the Union; she must make, she thought, protestations of not caring, and do her weeping privately in her pillow at night. Yet these protestations deeply hurt her Kentucky family, whose loyalty to the cause they believed in was not less than hers to the Union.

Gradually a changed Mary Lincoln took up her altered life. In March one finds her husband acting as her social secretary, writing a note to make an appointment for a friend to see her. She who had so loved to write long flowing letters to her friends found it difficult now, so "Father" did it for her. Mary Owens said of Lincoln that he "was deficient in those little links which make up the great chain of woman's happiness . . ." He was anything but deficient in those little acts which made up the chain of tender care for an ailing wife. One finds those links all through this harrowing year of 1862. When on May 22 he made a secret visit to Aquia, "Mrs. Lincoln alone knew of it." He at all times kept his wife in close touch with what he was doing, how he felt, and what was happening on the field of battle, knowing that she followed the course of the war with life-and-death intensity.

By the latter part of May, Mary was able to write to that dear friend back in Springfield, Mrs. Sprigg. Her words suggest her loneliness in the White House: "What would I give to see you & talk to you, in our crushing bereavement, if any one's presence could afford comfort—it would be yours. . . . Will we ever meet, & talk together as *we have* done. *Time* time how many sad changes it brings." She told Mrs. Sprigg their plans: "The 1st of July, we go out to the 'Soldiers' Home,' a very charming place 2½ miles from the city, several hundred feet, above, our present situation, to pass the summer: I dread that it will be a greater resort [for visitors] than here, *if possible*, when we are in sorrow, quiet is very necessary to us."

Laura Redden, the deaf newspaperwoman, rode out to the Soldiers' Home one day on horseback. As she told the story, Mrs. Lincoln in deep black "entered the room where I awaited her, evidently striving for some composure of manner; but, as I took the hand which she extended to me, she burst into a passion of tears and gave up all effort at self-control." The newspaperwoman continued: "For a moment my feeling of respect for the wife of the President was uppermost; then my sympathies for the bereaved mother got the better of conventionalities, and I put my arm around her and led her to a seat, saying everything I could think of to calm her; but she could neither think nor talk of anything but Willie."

One suspects that Mary Lincoln hated the White House after her son's death. Being at the Soldiers' Home was better, but that involved the President making trips back and forth to his office each day, which created another problem, that of his safety. Mrs. Lincoln worried continually about danger to him and manlike he brushed her off with: "All imagination. What does any one want to harm me for? Don't worry about me, Mother, as if I were a little child . . ." But one August night as he was riding out on horseback to the Soldiers' Home he heard a sudden rifle shot and the whistle of a bullet. He gave a humorous account of the incident to his friend Ward Hill Lamon. His horse (whom Lamon called "Old Abe") gave a sudden bound, and, as Lincoln told it, "unceremoniously separated me from my eight-dollar plughat, with which I parted company without any assent, expressed or implied, upon my part." One may be sure Mrs. Lincoln saw nothing humorous in the incident. Shortly thereafter a newspaper noted that she was insisting to his friend a cavalry escort for her husband. It irked Lincoln to be surrounded by guards as it has irked other Presidents. When a small detail of cavalry accompanied the Presidential couple on a drive he complained that he and his wife "couldn't hear themselves talk" for the clatter of sabers and spurs. As with all couples in the White House, privacy and time for each other seemed almost impossible.

The change which we have noted in Mary Lincoln following Willie's death made a profound difference with regard to her functions as First Lady. She had delighted in parties until the tragedy-shadowed one in February 1862. There were no more such receptions in the house of mourning that year. It was impossible for her to face up to the role of hostess. The concerts on the White House lawn were canceled. Her shattered nerves cried out for quiet. How could she listen to the loud music of the Marine Band reminding her of happy occasions when Willie's eyes brightened at the sound. Yet there was never any way in which Mary could please her public. It had criticized her for festive occasions in wartime; now it began to grumble because it missed the concerts. Secretary Welles finally took the matter up with Lincoln in June of the following year. "The public will not sympathize in sorrows which are obtrusive and assigned as a reason for depriving them of enjoyments to which they have been accustomed," wrote Welles in his diary, "and it is a mistake to persist in it." Lincoln knew how the least noise, the sudden ringing of a bell, the dropping of a book, would make Mary's face go white with panic and her hand fly against her heart to still its wild beating. The matter of the concerts was compromised by the band playing in Lafayette Square across from the White House.

Two things only were of help to Mrs. Lincoln in her depressed state. One was her husband's need of her. "If I had not felt the spur of necessity urging me to cheer Mr. Lincoln, whose grief was as great as my own, I could never have smiled again," she later told her sister Emilie. The second thing was her work among the wounded soldiers in the hospitals; by her own statement that was the only thing that gave her comfort.

Apparently it was June of '62 before she was physically able to make these almost daily visits to the hospitals, where she would pass through the long rows of cots distributing with her own hands fruits, flowers, and delicacies cooked in the White House kitchen. She would talk with the patients, asking in a soft gentle voice questions showing her personal interest, and they knew they had the sympathy of this motherly woman. Some of the pale suffering faces were pitifully young, reminding her of her own sons. She saw injuries that tore at her tender heart. The "hospital gangrene" of that day is no topic for the squeamish. A newspaper mentioned how deeply affected she was by the painful scenes coming beneath her notice but added that it was an impressive sight to see her ministering to the men and to see their response. Possibly it was one way she had of doing penance for her mistakes; certainly no woman devoted only to frivolity would have faced up to the sights, smells and groans she met. She continued her efforts to aid in every way possible from then on. "It may not be known that Mrs. Lincoln has contributed more than any lady in Washington, from her private purse, to alleviate the sufferings of our wounded soldiers," commented one of the newspapers, adding mention of certain risks involved in her constant visiting: "The fear of contagion and the outcries of pestilence fall unheeded upon the ear of those whose missions are mercy."

That newspaper comment was the exception. The young secretary Stoddard saw clearly how in her single-mindedness of purpose to help she was giving no thought to publicity. "She rarely takes outside company with her upon these errands [to the hospitals]," he wrote, "and she thereby loses opportunities. If she were worldly wise she would carry newspaper correspondents, from two to five, of both sexes, every time she went, and she would have them take shorthand notes of what she says to the sick soldiers and of what the sick soldiers say to her. Then she would bring the writers back to the White House, and give them some cake and—coffee, as a rule, and show them the conservatory."

Stoddard was all too right. Two years after Mrs. Lincoln left the White House there appeared this item in a Cleveland paper: "Two calls each week, with a bouquet of flowers, upon any one of the many hospitals that filled Washington, would have made her name immortal." She had fulfilled these terms and far more. There is concrete evidence of her hospital work in Lincoln's telegram to Hiram Barney in August 1862: "Mrs. L. has $1,000.00 for the benefit of the hospitals; and she will be obliged, and send the pay, if you will be so good as to select and send her two hundred dollars worth of good lemmons one hundred dollars worth of good oranges." Husband and wife were working together to aid the wounded soldiers.

But even in her good works Mrs. Lincoln ran into difficulties. The ghastly hospitals of the Civil War had their rules and restrictions and Mrs. Lincoln sometimes found her ministrations "treated by surgeons as impertinent meddling." Speaking to a visitor about her work, she said she was ready and willing to do "anything she could do without incurring the displeasure of the Surgeons and others in authority . . ."

In the heat of July Mrs. Lincoln left Washington and fled north. In August one finds Lincoln answering a telegram to his wife from an old friend and explaining she was "not well." In the fall of 1862 she went to New York and then to Boston, where her eldest son was the special attraction. Travel was the popular panacea of the day and a changing scene was undoubtedly more endurable to Mrs. Lincoln than the tensions and sad associations of the White House. The capable and comforting Elizabeth Keckley went along in the capacity of companion, maid, and sometimes nurse.

The trip served Mrs. Keckley's purposes full well, for she was at that time working in a new organization that wished to help the colored freedmen. On September 22 Lincoln had given out his preliminary proclamation stating that the Emancipation Proclamation would be issued on January 1, 1863. What this meant to those of Negro blood and to all thoughtful people who hated the terrible evil of slavery cannot perhaps now be imagined. Mrs. Keckley, who had been a slave, was fired with enthusiasm. As she said later, "I know what liberty is, because I know what slavery was." It was recognized that the Negroes emerging from bondage without resources and unused to planning for themselves would need help and the "Contraband Relief Association" was formed to aid them. By going with Mrs. Lincoln, Elizabeth Keckley, who was asking contributions for this organization, could reach the philanthropists and abolitionists of the North. No one could help her make these contacts better than the First Lady, who was giving wholehearted support and approval to the project. She headed the list with a donation of $200, and made "frequent contributions, as also did the President." Mrs. Lincoln was beginning to emerge in her little-known but genuine role of abolitionist; this trip doubtless fostered her growing enthusiasm for emancipation.

Two letters which Mrs. Lincoln wrote her husband on this trip have been preserved. Though she does not so state, they were probably written at the Metropolitan Hotel in New York as that is where she and Mrs. Keckley had stayed earlier. They are precious documents in the biography of a marriage, these few letters between husband and wife.

The first was written November 2, and she begins by scolding him gently for not writing. Early November of 1862 was a time of trying decision to the President and his unusual failure to keep in touch with his wife may possibly be explained by this. However, she says, "Strangers come up from W—— & tell me you are well—which satisfies me very much." The letter suggests that she was acting as a sort of ambassador of good will and collector of public opinion. In company with friends she had called on General Scott. "All the distinguished in the land, have tried how polite & attentive, they could be to me, since I came up here. Many say, they would almost worship you, if you would put a fighting General, in the place of Mc-Clellan." She was offering some advice here; whether to remove McClellan was the question with which Lincoln was wrestling at that time. Her reporting of the prevailing opinion in New York had legitimate purpose: "Your name is on every lip and many prayers and good wishes are hourly sent up, for your welfare—and McClellan & his slowness are as vehemently discussed. Allowing this beautiful weather, to pass away, is disheartening the North." One wonders how much these words contributed to Lincoln's removal of McClellan within a week.

"Dear little Taddie," she wrote, "is well & enjoying himself very much." He had evidently lost a tooth, which she intends to send his father. But she herself had not been well. She made the nature of the trouble clear with her italics: "A day or two since, I had one of my severe attacks, if it had not been for Lizzie Keckley, I do not know what I should have done. Some of *these periods,* will launch me away." Mrs. Lincoln evidently was subject to hemorrhages at this stage of her life, in addition to her migraine headaches and chills and fever.

Being a Victorian wife in the first place and Mrs. Lincoln in the second, she asked for money. "I have had two suits of clothes made for Taddie which will come to 26 dollars. Have to get some fur outside wrappings for the coachman's carriage trappings. Lizzie Keckley, wants me to loan her thirty dollars—so I will have to ask for a check of $100 . . ."

In the postscript was a tactful effort to use her influence, probably in regard to some appointment—that habit of hers which was usually based on kindhearted intentions: "I enclose you a note from Mr Stewart, he appears very solicitous about his young friend. Mr S. is so strong a Union man—& asks so few favors—if it came in your way, perhaps it would not be amiss to oblige."

Mary's letter the following day shows how wholeheartedly she was working for the association to help the freed slaves. Mrs. Keckley had been authorized to collect funds but, wrote Mrs. Lincoln to her husband: "She has been very unsuccessful. She says the immense number of Contrabands in W—— are suffering intensely, many without bed covering & having to use any bits of carpeting to cover themselves. Many dying of want." Evidently Lincoln had been receiving funds to relieve suffering, for Mary continued: "Out of the $1000 fund deposited with you by Gen Corcoran, I have given her the privilege of investing $200 her[e], in bed covering." One suspects that Mary as usual was exceeding her authority. Presumably the money deposited with Lincoln had not been designated for the freedmen, as the letter went on: ". . . this sum, I am sure, you will not object to being used in this way. The cause of humanity requires it . . . I am sure, this will meet your approbation. The soldiers are well supplied with comfort." If the Corcoran fund had been given for soldiers, Mary here, with the best of intentions, may have been transferring money provided for one purpose to another use. If so, it was another example of her tendency to do this casually and without understanding what was involved. The letter ended, "Please write by return mail. With much love yours &c."

A few days later we find Lincoln a mere helpless man and husband who did not know what to do about a domestic matter when his wife was away. Evidently the Presidential household was still at the Soldiers' Home and he telegraphed his wife at Boston, where she had gone to see Robert: "Mrs. Cuthbert & Aunt Mary want to move to the White House, because it has grown so cold at Soldiers Home. Shall they?" Mrs. Mary Ann Cuthbert was housekeeper and Aunt Mary a colored servant.

As a final link in the chain of Lincoln's watchful care in that dark year of 1862 we find him telegraphing his wife on December 21: "Do not come on the night train. It is too cold. Come in the morning."

A great sorrow shows up a personality in its true colors. Willie's death made Mary's emotional instability evident as never before. Shock and grief caused further impairment of a neurotic temperament that had already reached abnormality before she entered the White House. But her penitence for her thoughtless frivolity and for all the follies and blunders of that first year shows her fundamentally good heart. Chastened in spirit, she tried in her way to make amends. Her ministering to the sick soldiers in hospitals with its sense of helpfulness and service was the only thing that brought her any release from her sorrow. This is the reaction of a woman with a conscience and a tender heart. As usual we have her acknowledgment of her failings and her expression of deep regret. She had passed, she said, "through the fiery furnace of affliction," and she was not prepared for it. "I had become, so wrapped up in the world, so devoted to our own political advancement that I thought of little else beside. Our Heavenly Father sees fit, oftentimes to visit us, at such times, for our worldliness, how small & insignificant all worldly honors are, when we are *thus* so severely tried."

chapter 24

DARK WHISPERINGS

The fault for which Mary Lincoln reproached herself was "worldliness." Paradoxically, if she had been a little more worldly she would not have made some of the blunders about which she was so regretful. The gardener Watt had pulled the wool over her eyes. Another unprincipled man whose name also began with a *W* did the same thing, one Henry Wikoff, an unsavory adventurer whom the New York *Herald* planted in Washington to serve as their secret reporter. Watt and Wikoff had in common unscrupulousness, love of scheming, and the desire to feather their own nests; these bonds made them act together in at least one notorious incident which flared into the open the very week before Willie died.

Henry Wikoff was a clever villain with great personal charm and the captivating manners of a courtier. His record sounds like something out of a melodrama. He had been acquainted with many notables and even royalty in Europe and had had adventures of a questionable nature in England, France, and Spain. He had even received decorations from Louis Napoleon of France and Queen Isabella of Spain and was called Chevalier Wikoff. Master of intrigue and the art of subtle flattery, he quickly won Mrs. Lincoln's friendship and became in the first year of the Lincoln administration an intimate of the White House and the First Lady's social adviser. For all her pride in her woman's intuition, Mary Lincoln was as a child in the hands of this practiced rascal. The sheltered female training of the eighteen-twenties and thirties, and the life of an Illinois housewife, had given her no prepared defense against the blandishments of this schemer whose surface glamour concealed (for a time) the nature of his machinations. Wikoff undoubtedly knew how to make himself helpful and agreeable on the social front. "No one went so early but this person could be seen cosily seated in a chair as if at home, talking to the ladies of the White House. None called so late but they found him still there." With Mrs. Lincoln so deceived and Wikoff collecting all the inside items possible to be sent to a tricky newspaper, his ubiquitous presence in the White House created a dangerous situation.

In December 1861 a portion of Lincoln's annual message appeared in the New York *Herald* before its presentation to Congress. Someone had got at Lincoln's manuscripts and released a portion of its contents prematurely, a matter with very serious implications. A Congressional investigation was instituted, Wikoff was naturally suspected, and he was subpoenaed to appear before the House Judiciary Committee on February 10, 1862, ten days before Willie Lincoln's death. Thus the whole miserable episode came to a head at a time when the Lincolns were racked with anxiety over their son's illness.

Wikoff admitted he had telegraphed portions of the President's message to the New York *Herald* but refused to tell how he got his information on the ground that he was under a pledge of secrecy. He was arrested for contempt and confined in the guardroom used by the Capitol police beneath Old Capitol Prison. It was probably not a comfortable place and after several nights there he was in a different frame of mind. On February 14 he answered questions and was released. His story was that he got his information from Watt. The gardener then testified to the committee that he saw and read the message in the President's library and repeated portions of it from memory to the chevalier. The impression got abroad, however, that Mrs. Lincoln had permitted Wikoff to copy portions of the message. "Meanwhile," according to Ben: Perley Poore, "Mr. Lincoln had visited the Capitol and urged the Republicans on the Committee to spare him disgrace," so Watt's story, involving no fault on the part of Mrs. Lincoln, was accepted.

Overworked as he was, the President had only recently become aware of Wikoff's character and designs and his role as a familiar in the White House. A few friends of Lincoln's, realizing that the chevalier's presence was part of a plot to strike at Lincoln through his household, had collected information about Wikoff, with clippings from newspapers and the various rumors and gossip bearing upon the whole situation. One evening at the White House two of these friends quietly laid their evidence before the President upstairs behind locked doors. Down-

stairs, unconscious that a reckoning was near, Wikoff
was exercising his charm in entertaining Mrs. Lincoln
and other guests. The President listened to the report of
his two friends, then said grimly: "Give me those papers,
and sit here till I return," and left the room with a determined stride. It is to be regretted that what he said
to the villain is not recorded. It is known that Lincoln
could be mighty in justified wrath and had on one occasion kicked a bad character out of his office. All we have
here is the significant statement: "The scorpion was
driven from the mansion that night . . ."

Thus ended Wikoff's influence and presence in the
White House. With him as with Watt there is a suggestion of a tie-up with the Confederacy. A woman under
arrest as a rebel spy and confined in Old Capitol Prison
wrote a Confederate officer shortly after the Congressional
investigation: "Mrs. Lincoln gave Wycoff the message
you saw when they arrested him to make him tell." How
much of this is gossip which seeped through prison walls,
or how much relates to possible wartime intrigue is not
clear. But that Mrs. Lincoln was the victim of two men
with deep designs is painfully apparent.

Watt of course lost his position on the White House staff
in February of '62. Very shortly a newspaper carried a
notice that "the late gardener at the Executive Mansion"
was rumored to have gone to Scotland. His machinations,
however, continued. He was said to have written a letter
to Lincoln presenting bills for money advanced to Mrs.
Lincoln. According to a gossipy story related to John
Hay, Watt tried to blackmail Lincoln into paying $20,000
for three letters Mrs. Lincoln had written. A prominent
and forceful friend of the President, according to the
account, cleared up this situation by holding over Watt's
head the threat of sending him to Fort Lafayette (where
political prisoners were confined) and finally obtained
the three letters for $1500. The former gardener was said
to have made repeated attempts to sell, for a good consideration, letters and documents and his own account of inside happenings at the White House to newspapers opposed to Lincoln. One gathers that if the fee were large
enough, he would have told almost anything that was
desired.

In spite of the fact that Watt and Wikoff were out of
the White House before the end of Lincoln's first year,

the scandals were not allowed to die: neither the Wikoff imbroglio nor the tales alleging that the gardener had juggled accounts for the benefit of Mrs. Lincoln. The stories made fine material for political mudslinging, a regular mud pile. More than two years after the investigation Attorney General Edward Bates recorded in his diary what a friend told him: "... that a *secret* pamphlet has been gotten up ... levelled agst. Mrs. L. in reference to the infamous *Watt* scandal. He expects to get a copy tomorrow; and if it turn out to be what he supposes, thinks it will produce an explosion." This pamphlet was supposed to be put forth by members of Lincoln's own party who were opposing him.

The truth was that the ailing woman in the White House was from the first a political football to be kicked at from both sides. The extreme or radical element of Lincoln's party fighting him at every turn probably realized that the imprudence and impulsiveness of his wife would furnish a means of striking at him indirectly. Ward Hill Lamon, devoted to Lincoln, wrote a mutual friend of them both on the very day that Wikoff was called before the Judiciary Committee: "There will be open hostility between the President and the abolitionists shortly it is feared—they are now preparing to attack Mrs. Lincoln and it is with great difficulty that the friends of the Administration have kept them still up to this time."

As a matter of fact they had not been "kept still." The evidence of a deliberate launching of a smear campaign against Mrs. Lincoln is abundant. The New York *Herald,* at the time of the Wikoff exposé, assailed "the abolitionists, who have been expending money on certain presses and correspondents to publish and circulate underhanded insinuations and attacks upon ... Mrs. Lincoln, all of which is a part and parcel of a programme marked out at a private gathering of these wise heads ..." The article gives details of the "line of action," involving the circulation of leaflets among members of Congress and soldiers, and newspaper attacks followed by editorials. It tells of later meetings to work out additional details and continues: "The numerous attacks ... and insinuations made against Mrs. Lincoln in certain republican dailies and weeklies, as well as the base falsehoods in certain pretended religious weeklies, published by men who from the pulpit inculcate the doctrine, 'Thou shalt not bear false witness against thy neighbor,' have been the direct fruits of these conspirators..." The article considered the Congressional investigation of the Wikoff-Watt matter (conducted as it was by a committee notably unfriendly to Lincoln) a part of this smear campaign.

A month later the *Herald* was thundering on the same theme. "We might charitably suppose that these Jacobins are as ignorant as they are brutal... but truth forbids such an excuse.... the abolition party, unable to effect the permanent dissolution of the Union, or to mould the President to their detestable purposes, deliberately heaped insults upon the President's wife ..."

It must be remembered that Lincoln came to the Presidency with very low prestige and was unpopular in many quarters, especially with the extremists of his own party. Those who were speaking in belittling terms of Mrs. Lincoln were referring to her husband as "the baboon, the imbecile, the Kentucky mule." The group in Lincoln's party variously called the Radicals, the Vindictives, or the Jacobins considered him hopeless as a President. They disliked and distrusted his tolerant patience, his unwillingness to use the war for partisan gain and for punitive measures against Southerners. Senator Ben Wade sneered at Lincoln as descended from "poor white trash," and said he expected from him a recommendation to give every rebel "a hundred and sixty acres of land." William Lloyd Garrison wrote: "I am growing more and more skeptical of the 'honesty' of Lincoln. He is nothing better than a wet rag ..."

Lincoln caught it from all sides. The New York *Herald*, while not in sympathy with the radical group, alternately patted and stabbed the Lincolns. Few passages could be more belittling than the following, published early in '64: "President Lincoln is a joke incarnated. His election was a very sorry joke. The idea that such a man as he should be the President of such a country as this is a very ridiculous joke.... His title of 'Honest' is a satirical joke. The style in which he winks at frauds ... is a costly joke."

To tear down the wife was to tear down the husband. After Lincoln's death the following statement appeared in the Boston *Journal* (it was written from New York City in January 1866): "The slanders on Mrs. Lincoln, originating with some of the press of this city [New York], are not new. From the moment that she entered the White

House as its mistress till she left it she has been the subject of open or covert attacks. Early in the rule of Mrs. Lincoln a regular conspiracy was formed here . . . to strike her down and strike her husband through her." This article speaks of the planting of Wikoff in Washington as a deliberate part of that plot. Here again one wonders how much of the Wikoff-Watt maneuvering was calculated sabotage of the Lincoln administration.

The effectiveness of the smearing was evident very early. At the end of August 1861 the Chicago *Daily Tribune* published under the caption "HOLD ENOUGH!" the following: ". . . if Mrs. Lincoln were a prizefighter, a foreign danseuse or a condemned convict on the way to execution, she could not be treated more indecently than she is by a portion of the New York press. . . . No lady of the White House has ever been so maltreated by the public press. . . . The sighs and sneers of sensible people all over the land, and the mockery of the comic papers, are the natural consequence."

Almost any act, whether imprudent or not, could be twisted into scandal about Mrs. Lincoln. There was gossip connecting her name with a third man whose name began with a *W*. This gentleman, William S. Wood of New York, had made the journey east with the Lincolns just before the first inauguration and naturally had done his best to be agreeable to the President-elect and his lady. Lincoln soon appointed him Commissioner of Public Buildings and he served in that office a short time pending the confirmation of the appointment by the Senate. Behind the scenes antagonistic political forces were raging. Late in June a letter signed "Union" came to the President saying: "It appears that the appointment of Mr. Wood, as Comr. of P. B. has given great dissatisfactions to the citizens of this District, and some of the dastardly politicians and poltrons are only waiting the action of the Senate, and if Mr. W. is confirmed, they will attempt to stab you in the most vital part, by circulating scandal about your most estimable Lady and Mr. W. They say the papers of this country and europe will teem with it. Human nature is prone to evil I know, but was ever anything so diabolical heard of before?" The writer said with feeling that by his love for his own wife and children he could "form some idea, of the anguish and pain, that such a report might occasion." He was right; a family connection testified later to Lincoln's keen suffering over the newspaper "stabs given to Mary."

When did personal anguish and pain stop a smearing for political purposes? Wood's appointment was not confirmed and B. B. French was appointed in his place. But gossip was soon buzzing about Mrs. Lincoln making a trip to New York with Mr. W. A lady of those days usually traveled under the protection of a male escort; it was proper enough. On May 10, 1861, a newspaper had carried the notice that "Mrs. Lincoln, accompanied by Mrs. Grimsley, and under charge of Mr. Wood" would leave for New York that day. Whether this was the incident the scandalmongers seized on and twisted to their purposes, one cannot say. Possibly it was another journey, a shopping expedition for refurnishing the White House during the brief time Wood was Commissioner of Public Buildings. In his official capacity he could authorize her purchases. Lamon, close friend of the Lincolns, always answered indignantly to the dark insinuations about Mrs. Lincoln in connection with a trip with Mr. W., "No! She was a thoroughly good woman; she was just imprudent." We already know that the First Lady usually gave little thought to possible public misinterpretation of what she did. By September 1861 Mr. Wood, perspicacious at least in this, was charging Watt with dishonesty. Mrs. Lincoln, who was not disillusioned about the gardener at that time, thought Wood was "either deranged or drinking," and wished to have nothing more to do with him.

An obvious point of attack upon a First Lady with relatives fighting on the Confederate side was disloyalty. She was accused of acting as a rebel spy. The Confederacy, of course, had its spy ring in Washington who did the work assigned to them, but when military information leaked through to the Southern forces, Mrs. Lincoln, like as not, got the blame. The accusation of treason was continuous throughout her White House years, and in addition to her other torments Mrs. Lincoln became the target of the kind of hatred that is directed against traitors.

Those close to Mrs. Lincoln knew the charge was absurdity itself. Her loyalty to the Union was deep, whole, and unwavering. Mr. Stoddard, the young secretary who screened her mail, grew sarcastic in his indignation. He ridiculed the gullible public in an absurd account of Confederate spies working their way through the lines, foot after foot, swimming the Potomac, creeping up into the ground "like so many ghosts," climbing a ladder to an upstairs window of the White House through which Mrs. Lincoln would hand out the secret military plans. As a final touch he suggested that they used Jacob's ladder, such an instrument being no more fantastic than the rest of it. There was, as he said "no other way for the alleged treasonable communication to be carried on."

Noah Brooks, who knew the Lincolns intimately, was as indignant as Stoddard at the slanders heaped upon them both. He later made the point that Lincoln by his leadership as President finally neutralized "the wantoness and groundlessness of the tales that related to him," but that Mrs. Lincoln never had the chance to vindicate "by her amiable and dignified life, her own much-misrepresented character." Writing in the eighteen-nineties, Brooks declared that "the slanders of the gossips" survived to that day, that there were still people who believed that Mrs. Lincoln "secretly favored the rebellion which, if successful, would have expelled Lincoln from Washington, if it had spared his life." The accusation of treason implied hostility to her husband. Brooks had firsthand knowledge of the mutual devotion of the Lincolns, he had seen them at home in the White House working together as a married team, he had witnessed the expression in the eyes of each when looking at the other. He answered that implication with a statement in the strongest terms: "The relations of Lincoln and his wife were a model for the married people of the republic of which they were then the foremost pair."

Mrs. Lincoln's intense loyalty to the Union vibrates throughout her letters; the enemy were "degraded rebels," "treason and rebellion, threaten our beloved land, our freedom & rights are invaded..." The greatest force in her life was her love for her husband and he rose or fell by the fate of the Union. So persistent, however, were the distorted accusations picturing her as a Confederate spy that the matter was said to have been taken up by the Committee on the Conduct of the War. This story has come down in a roundabout and unsatisfactory manner. It is alleged to have been told, about twenty years after the event, by an unnamed member of the Committee—a senator—to General Thomas L. James, whose account of it comes secondhand.

The Committee on the Conduct of the War was a joint committee of Senate and House under the leadership of the radicals who were antagonistic to Lincoln. This group, according to the account, proposed one morning to take up for investigation the reports that imputed disloyalty to Mrs. Lincoln. Suddenly in their midst, unannounced, "at the foot of the table, standing solitary, his hat in his hand, his tall form towering above the committee members, Abraham Lincoln stood." His face was filled with "almost unhuman sadness" as he said "slowly, with infinite sorrow" in his tone: "I, Abraham Lincoln, President of the United States, appear of my own volition before this Committee of the Senate to say that, I, of my own knowledge, know that it is untrue that any of my family hold treasonable communication with the enemy." Having said this, he went away "as silently and solitary as he came." By common consent, the group dropped all consideration of the rumors that Mrs. Lincoln was a spy.

The evidence is too vague and in part inaccurate (it was not a committee of the Senate) to justify an established historical conclusion that this incident occurred. One cannot accept Lincoln's words literally from such a long-delayed, indirect account and the dramatization is highly seasoned. The thought comes to mind that this story might be a confused version of Lincoln's interviewing members of the House Judiciary Committee in regard to the Wikoff-Watt imbroglio. But the story points up the ghastly situation created by the idea that Mrs. Lincoln was disloyal. Most people today know how, under the tension of war, rumors fly thicker than bullets. It was even worse in a civil war where brother was turned against brother. For the wife of the Union President to be accused of treason was so startling that the story spread like wildfire and many misguided persons, as Brooks said, sincerely believed it. This gossip flourished throughout the Lincoln administration, growing more bitter as battle followed battle with deaths and suffering. Even after the war was over and Lincoln dead, his widow received many insults accusing her of having been a traitor. Such insults constituted one of the reasons she exiled herself abroad. Another favorite topic in the smear campaign was bribery. Mrs. Lincoln, like her husband and other public officials of the time, received many presents. In some cases it would have been ungracious, not to say impolitic, to decline them. The receiving of a gift raises difficult questions for any Presidential family: is it a gift to the office itself or to the person, and is it given with ulterior motives? A newspaper reported immediately after the first inauguration that Mrs. Lincoln was presented with a fine span of horses. An elegant carriage had been given her even before the inauguration, both presents being bestowed, according to the newspapers, by certain un-named New York gentlemen. If later these gentlemen wanted appointments for themselves or their friends, there was pressure upon Mrs. Lincoln, who tended to view things personally, to say a word in their behalf to Mr. Lincoln.

Just how insidious this giving of presents could be was explained by Mrs. Keckley. At a reception Mrs. Lincoln would be surprised to be asked by a perfect stranger, "*Mrs. President* Lincoln, I hope you admired that set of furs I sent you lately." As a hostess the First Lady must answer graciously: "Oh, was it you sent them, really I am at a loss to thank you for your kindness." Then came this sugared response: "Not at all, madam, it was but a slight and worthless token of the deep esteem I have for the talents of one whose intrinsic merit would, irrespec-tive of your present exalted position, make you an orna-ment in the highest circles of the most civilized society."

According to Mrs. Keckley, when later the politician who had sent the furs would ask a favor, Mrs. Lincoln would find it difficult to refuse. Even if her natural shrewdness had seen through the fulsome flattery, she had already accepted the furs. Mrs. Keckley said this sort of thing went on "for the first few months, but Mr. Lincoln (to use his own phrase) 'shut down on it,' and many scenes, when his wife was goaded on to ask for place by office-seekers, took place." It was doubtless during some of these marital debates that Mary witnessed that firm closing of Lincoln's lips which she herself said meant that he had made up his mind and was not to be moved from his position. It is refreshing to learn also from his wife that Lincoln did not always speak with saintly pa-tience: "Sometimes in Washington," she said, "being worn down, he spoke crabbedly to men, harshly so, and yet it seemed the people understood the conditions around him and forgave."

Mrs. Eunice Tripler, a lady of established position

and decided opinions who had the typical antagonistic attitude of Washington women toward Mrs. Lincoln, obligingly tells (in a quaint little book of recollections) some of the current stories of the first year. To read this account is like listening to chatter at a ladies' tea. They say that Mrs. Lincoln dismissed all the gardeners but one and all the laundresses but one, saving the money to put in her own purse. They say New York merchants sent garments to her asking the privilege of advertising that she would wear these things on certain occasions. They say Mrs. Lincoln wanted the entertainment for the Count de Paris and the Count de Chambord charged to the government and Seward said no. (What was meant here was probably the dinner for Prince Napoleon but that was accurate enough for the gossipers; anyway, weren't they all Frenchmen?) About the time of the entertainment a large amount of manure had been delivered to be spread on the White House grounds, and, according to the story, Mrs. Lincoln sold it and used the money to pay for what was appallingly called "the manure dinner." The number of private and personal items charged to the public "manure fund" was amazing, including, appropriately enough, a couple of private cows.

Mrs. Tripler also heard that Mrs. Lincoln was suspected of sending intelligence to her brother in the Confederate service. President Lincoln "was strangely obtuse to the danger of spies in the White House." The First Lady was, of course, a virago and the story told to substantiate that was amusing both in its inaccuracies and the picture it created. Lincoln was supposed to be starting out in a carriage with Secretary Seward to an important affair of state when Mrs. Lincoln called from an upstairs window, "Stop, Abe, stop. Take these children with you." (Of course, Mrs. Lincoln never called her husband Abe.) Robert and Tad were given as the children, though Robert was a young man at Harvard during the Presidency. Best of all, Seward was quoted as complaining bitterly afterwards that the children kicked the secretarial shins all through the drive. The inaccuracy of one of the circulated stories backfired. According to the following morsel of gossip, Mrs. Lincoln by promises of increased wages persuaded a waiting maid employed by Lady Lyons, wife of the British minister in Washington, to leave her employer and enter service at the White House. In a few days the new maid in the Executive Mansion was most unhappy, because "she was set to making drawers out of the linen sheets of the establishment. This wounded her feelings so much that she soon 'gave notice' to her employer, and when she subsequently spoke of her sorrows to her friends, she said that the extraordinary length of the drawers she was employed on left no doubt on her mind as to the person who was to have the comfort of wearing them." The originator of that story used his inventive powers too far; he created a Lady Lyons who did not exist. Lord Lyons was a bachelor. In the same category belongs the yarn heard by George Bancroft, the historian, to the effect that Mrs. Lincoln wanted a certain rogue made a lieutenant and Lincoln urged the cabinet to approve, telling them that Mrs. Lincoln had for three nights slept in a separate apartment. Bancroft wrote the absurd story to his wife only as a piece of gossip. He had visited with Mrs. Lincoln and found her chatty and gracious and she sent him a bouquet of flowers. In a letter to Mrs. Bancroft shortly afterward the historian commented on the First Lady again: "She is better in manners and in spirit than we have generally heard: is friendly and not in the least arrogant." Lincoln's alleged statement was obviously another product of the rumor factory. Yet to this day one still finds this yarn given as sober fact in biographies of Lincoln.

We have the reaction of that good friend of the Lincolns, Dr. Henry, to the campaign of abuse from factional motives. When Salmon P. Chase, Secretary of the Treasury, was being pushed as Republican candidate for President in 1864, Dr. Henry wrote from the Far West in the spring of that year: ". . . the whole influence of the Treasury Department has been, and still continues to be used to disparage Mr. Lincoln in the public estimation by the circulation of scandalous libels over the Country against him and his accomplished Lady, through the agency of Special Agents." This good friend continued indignantly: "I have known Mrs. Lincoln from her Childhood up, and I can truly say that I have never been acquainted with a kinder and more Estimable woman, and I regard it as an outrage upon all propriety and common decency to continue men in office who use their position and influence continually, to depreciate the President and his family."

In addition to the foes within his own party, the Democrats too struck at Lincoln indirectly through his wife. In the heat of Lincoln's campaign for re-election in 1864 with General George B. McClellan as the Democratic candidate, a New York lady of that party frankly confided her attitude to her diary: "Today I have been writing out all the bad things I have heard of Lincoln and his wife, hoping to get them into the papers. They [the Republicans] so falsely and abominably abuse the Democrats and McClellan that I would like them to have what they deserve." Ironically enough she could get all the "bad things" she wanted from a group of the Republicans themselves.

The lady apparently reflected a certain movement within her party, for in the same month B. B. French in Washington was writing to his brother's wife: "Rumors are about, that the Democrats are getting up something in which they intend to show up Madam Lincoln." Here we have another man who personally knew Mrs. Lincoln well (including her failings) getting indignant at the dirty work that was going on: "I think an appeal to the people, in good set terms, to frown down such ungallant & mean conduct as an attack on a *woman* to injure her husband, would be met, as it should be, with a curse on the movers, & do the getters up of the *vile slander* more harm than their effort would do them good."

An example of the "mean conduct" of an anti-Lincoln newspaper may be taken from *The Crisis* of November 18, 1863. In October a Russian squadron visited the port of New York and much ado was made over entertaining the officers. Mrs. Lincoln was in New York that fall and may well have attended some of the festivities in honor of the visitors. *The Crisis* printed a vile article which pictured her as a depraved woman on board a Russian frigate drinking champagne with Russian officers and offering a toast to "our cousin, Alexander II, Czar of Russia."

Few dark accusations were overlooked by the clacking tongues and avid ears. The smearing, of course, reached friends of the Lincolns. Senator Browning jotted down some of the whisperings in his diary. That journal would one day be edited under the stipulation that nothing reflecting on Mrs. Lincoln should be published. This resulted in the omission of a few passages correctly referred to, in the editorial preface, as "unimportant gossip." A new sidelight on Browning in relation to Mrs. Lincoln has now turned up. He left Washington after Congress ad-

journed in July 1862, and Mrs. Lincoln was quoted by a
close friend as saying "that Browning had gone home, &
she was glad of it—that he became distressingly loving
just before he left." One wonders whether she had aroused
the gentleman's pique by misunderstanding or rebuffing
him. It is possible to collect from newspapers, letters, and
diaries of the time a vast anthology of abuse and form
out of it a terrific indictment of Mrs. Lincoln, and in so
doing not get anywhere near the personality of the injudicious but kind and well-meaning woman in the White
House. For that matter one could make a similar collection of invective against Lincoln and miss his character
by as wide a mark.

The scandalmongers were like a firing line showering
missiles upon a target hidden behind a wall. They could
not see the results of the bombardment in terms of human
hurt. Beyond the wall were aching wounds, shock and
bleeding. There is a world of meaning in two brief sentences which Mrs. Edwards, when she was with Mary
after Willie's death, wrote her daughter: "The *Wikoff
case* has added very much to her unhappiness and to Mr
Ls also— Be careful, to refrain from alluding in an unkind way to her." Added to Mrs. Lincoln's grief was burning humiliation at having been fooled by a cheap adventurer. She was eaten with remorse that her folly had
caused embarrassment to her burdened husband. It
seemed to be her fate to rush headlong into trouble and
pay up for it with tears and penitence.

It had not been easy for Lincoln to face the members
of that unfriendly Judiciary Committee investigating
the Wikoff case, when it was thought that his wife was involved. A man in politics necessarily develops a certain
shrugging off of political mudslinging, but when the blows
hit the wife he loves, whose failings he treats with paternal tenderness, whose defenselessness he knows so
well, the situation becomes well-nigh intolerable.

Here was his cruel dilemma. He knew Mary was the
victim of malicious slander, but he also knew that, because she could not think straight about financial matters, she was an easy victim to schemers and could be influenced by them into action he would not approve. What
can a devoted husband do when he realizes that his wife
is, in certain respects, irrational and irresponsible? We
have traced Lincoln's realization of Mary's mental illness.

In Springfield days he had said, when she had her hysterical seizures, that she was not well. In the White House he had told her plainly that if she did not exercise more self-control she might have to be placed in a sanitarium. But we have a little-known, stronger statement from Lincoln on the subject. A gentleman came to him with a story of how Mrs. Lincoln was being hoodwinked by a designing man into using her influence for transactions from which the villain profited. The visitor and the President talked the matter over for a long while, Lincoln showing deep emotion. Finally—and one can only guess what the statement cost him—Lincoln said, according to the visitor's account given some years later: "The caprices of Mrs. Lincoln, I am satisfied, are the result of partial insanity." The President followed this with the question that must have constantly tortured him in secret: "Is the malady beyond medical remedy to check before it becomes fully developed?" The visitor replied he had little faith in medical remedies, that firmness and kindness were in his opinion the only measures to use.

That was all Lincoln could and did use, firmness and kindness. It was before the days of psychiatry; there was little understanding of mental illness and the word "insane" was used ignorantly and with suggestion of a stigma. In most respects Mrs. Lincoln was not only normal but very intelligent and of course she was unaware of her aberration about money. Such things were a matter of concern as well as of loving understanding to Lincoln. That was why he tried to keep a responsible person with her when he could, watched over her himself, and, when she spent government money in a way he disapproved, offered to make it up out of his own pocket.

Lincoln's increased tenderness toward Mary because of her weakness may be compared to what he said about one of his generals. He told Noah Brooks "that he regarded Hooker very much as a father might regard a son who was lame, or who had some other incurable physical infirmity. His love for his son would be even intensified by the reflection that the lad could never be a strong and successful man."

What was Mary's attitude finally toward the vicious attacks upon her in the newspapers? A patriotic woman, Mrs. H. C. Ingersoll, who, like Mrs. Lincoln herself, gave what help she could in the hospitals, supplies the answer.

In the spring of 1864 Mrs. Ingersoll called upon the First Lady, of whom she had the usual adverse opinion, to enlist her co-operation in a movement to aid the Union cause. The visitor asked her to sign a pledge to purchase no imported goods during the rest of the war. Mrs. Lincoln said she would gladly do so as far as she was concerned but she thought the President should be consulted and give his approval first. (For economic reasons he was not to approve.) While waiting to hear from him in regard to the matter, the two women had a visit of which Mrs. Ingersoll left a full account: "I had an interview of nearly an hour with Mrs. Lincoln,—and I came away from that interview feeling that *never* had I found a person more unlike the newspaper reports of her than she seemed to be."

Both women were mothers who had lost a child; it was easy for them to talk intimately together. The visitor's record continued: "I ventured to allude to the way in which she had been misrepresented by the papers, and that I thought the truth ought to be told about her, particularly that the charges in relation to her rendering 'aid and comfort' to the enemy . . . should be contradicted. 'Oh,' said she, 'it is no use to make any defense; all such efforts would only make me a target for new attacks. I do not belong to the public; my character is wholly domestic, and the public have nothing to do with it. I know it seems hard that I should be maligned, and I used to shed many bitter tears about it, but since I have known real sorrow—since little Willie died,—all these shafts have no power to wound me. If I could lay my head on my pillow at night, and feel that I had wronged no one, that is all I have wished since his death.' " The visitor was deeply moved and left, she said, with her heart "running over with sympathy toward a woman that I had hitherto estimated, to say the least, not highly."

In her indignation at the unjust charges Mrs. Ingersoll wrote an article defending Mrs. Lincoln, planning to publish it in "the little Hospital Gazette" of which she had charge. She read this defense "to a lady friend, not more prejudiced against Mrs. Lincoln than was everybody else." That friend begged her not to publish it, saying "You will only be laughed at for your credulity, no one will believe you, and you will be doing a most unwise thing to put your sentiments in print." Mrs. Ingersoll retorted she would be doing "a *just* thing" and that if she could get Mrs Lincoln's permission she intended to publish it. "Oh," said the other, "she will be only too glad to have anything so complimentary to her published."

Mrs. Ingersoll sent the article to Mrs. Lincoln and received in return an invitation to call. "When I went, she placed the article in my hands, thanked me, and told me she appreciated my motives, and that I was very kind, but she still felt sure that it was best for her that no friend should defend her or say anything about her in print; she had a right to privacy, and she could not allow even her friends to break over the rule she, with her husband's approval, had laid down—which was utter silence in the press on her part." It was ten years after Lincoln's death before Mrs. Ingersoll felt free to publish this story.

Noah Brooks, however, writing from Washington to his California newspaper, the Sacramento *Union*, did not pull his punches. With the competence of a close friend of the Lincolns and an honest reporter, he wrote: "It is not a gracious task to refute these things, but the tales that are told of Mrs. Lincoln's vanity, pride, vulgarity and meanness ought to put any decent man or woman to the blush, when they remember that they do not *know* one particle of that which they repeat, and that they would resent as an insult to their wives, sisters or mothers that which they so glibly repeat concerning the first lady in the land. Shame upon these he-gossips and envious retailers of small slanders. Mrs. Lincoln, I am glad to be able to say from personal knowledge, is a true American woman, and when we have said that we have said enough in praise of the best and truest lady in our beloved land."

Stoddard, Dr. Henry, French, Mrs. Ingersoll and Brooks were able people qualified to answer accusations against Mrs. Lincoln by special personal knowledge. French especially was not apt to be prejudiced in her favor. He knew how difficult she could be; he had to deal with her within the area of the one subject on which she was irrational, and she tried his patience sorely. His indignation at the *"vile slander"* is significant; so is his statement in that connection: "I do not *know* that she has ever done a wrong act ..."

It was French who gave a penetrating evaluation of the gossip about Mary Lincoln: "They tell a great many stories about Mrs. Lincoln, but I do not believe them—indeed I *know* many of them are false—and I am not certain that we may not apply the old law maxim *'falsus in uno, falsus in omnibus.'* She is a very imprudent woman in many things, as I do know, & taking advantage of this the world delights to add in a compound ratio, to the reality."

chapter 25

TELEGRAMS

Mourning or no mourning, public opinion demanded that the everlasting entertainments be resumed. For the chastened woman in the White House, festivities which had been so exhilarating in the first year had become a mockery. *"The world,"* she wrote, "has lost so much, of its charm. My position, requires my presence, where my heart, is *so far* from being." Noah Brooks, seeing the Lincolns almost daily, knew their habits and their wish for the sort of life which most middle-aged unpretentious couples prefer. He wrote to his newspaper: "The President dines at six oclock, and often invites an intimate friend to take pot luck with him, but he and his estimable wife are averse to dinner-giving or party-making, only deviating from their own wishes in such matters for the purpose of gratifying people who expect it of them. They much prefer the same sort of social, unrestrained intercourse with the family that most sensible people do, and have a wholesome horror of state dinners, which are invariably prolific of discord, ill feeling and big expenses."

Mary found out there was no relation between official functions where they were surrounded by a thousand hostile forces and the friendly gatherings of neighbors which she had so enjoyed in Springfield. But there was good sportsmanship in this woman. Young Stoddard, working out with her the final arrangements for a party, noted: "She is entirely willing to do her duty and sit through the evening in her parlor, while her smiling guests pull her in pieces, and she says so, cheerfully, as you chat with her and receive her instructions."

So the year 1863 opened with a huge entertainment on New Year's Day, that same memorable date on which the Emancipation Proclamation was issued. "I stood at Mrs. Lincoln's side during the reception," wrote Mr. French. "It was the first one since we placed little Willie in the tomb. She remarked with a sad sad look, 'Oh Mr. French, how much we have passed through since last we stood here.' She seemed much affected through the first part of the reception and was too much overcome by her feelings to remain until it ended."

In February the newspapers almost forgot the Civil War in giving space to the romance of the dwarfs. General Tom Thumb (born Charles Sherwood Stratton), who at his maximum stood three feet four inches high and weighed seventy pounds, was a favorite exhibit of that aggressive showman, P. T. Barnum. When the little "General" wooed and won a lady about his own size, Miss Lavinia Warren, another of Barnum's dwarfs, people went wild with sentimental interest. Barnum, of course, made the most of it and the wedding was celebrated with great publicity in Grace Episcopal Church, New York, on February 10, 1863.

Several days later the famous pair were in Washington and the First Lady, being convinced by her ever-present advisers that it was her duty to entertain them, hastily arranged a reception. "Mrs. Lincoln, excellent lady that she is, sent & invited us all up . . . to see Tom & his bride, who spent the evening there," wrote Mr. French to his sister-in-law a few days later. Mr. French evidently approved, but Robert Lincoln did not. The Lincolns, as we have seen, had trouble living up to the standards of their eldest son, a not uncommon experience of parents. Robert's mother asked him, if he had no other plans, to dress and come downstairs to the impromptu gathering, and was put in her place by the following lofty reply: "No, mother, I do not propose to assist in entertaining Tom Thumb. My notions of duty, perhaps are somewhat different from yours."

The superior young man from Harvard missed a unique and unforgettable scene: the tall President, his eyes warm with gentle amusement and sympathy, bending down to shake hands with the gorgeously appareled midgets, so quaint and doll-like and yet somehow so pathetic in their human dignity. This small entertainment was on a Friday evening. The regular Saturday reception next day was "a *crusher*," said French: "I never saw such a crowd in the reception room before. When we had got about ½ through Mrs. Lincoln remarked 'I believe these people came expecting to see Tom Thumb & his wife.' I most guess she was right!"

The continual entertaining was a grind, something that had to be done in spite of headaches, chills, fever, worries, sleepless nights and grieving. And the only reward of the effort was faultfinding. The tides of military success advanced and receded but, wrote Stoddard, "There is one tide . . . which never turns, and that is the tide of criticism and advice which sets toward and into the White House." Even Mary's domestic pride in making the mansion lovely with new furnishings had departed, leaving disillusionment behind it because of the all-pervading vandalism. Guests would snip off a yard or two of the lace curtains and damask drapery and "even cut out small bits of the gorgeous carpet, leaving scars on the floor as large as a man's hand." This was hard on Mary, who had loved the beautiful articles she had selected with a fresh enthusiasm which must later have seemed to her naïve.

Nothing was safe. Pilfering was in the air. Parson William G. Brownlow said that after being in Washington a few days he felt an almost irresistible desire to pick somebody's pocket. One day a man was caught in the White House skinning off the damask cover of a sofa. Noah Brooks wrote an account of the incident to his paper ending with a comment which is like a grimace: "Mine Gott, vat a Peoples!"

Occasionally friends and relatives from Springfield would turn up in Washington. Mary's cousin and Lincoln's former law partner, John Todd Stuart, was elected to Congress as a Democrat in 1862 and, though that was the party opposed to Lincoln's, relations between him and the First Family were cordial. Mr. Stuart attended a White House reception with a couple of visiting cousins, Charles and Sue Craig, and wrote his wife an account of the affair that has interesting overtones. Mrs. Lincoln showed every thoughtfulness to Cousin John and his guests, asked them all to remain after the reception for a private visit, and arranged to send her carriage to Willard's next day for Sue and Charles to accompany her to church and then to dinner at the White House. But even so delightful a person as Mr. Stuart shows a certain touchiness in his letter because Cousin Mary in her high position was not as available as she had been in the home on Eighth Street; the relatives could not run in to see the First Lady on a moment's notice; she had a social schedule.

There was no quarter in which Mary was free from criticism. Mrs. Conkling, once "dear Merce," wrote her son and told him how "exceedingly kind and attentive" Mrs. Lincoln had been to Mr. Conkling when he was in Washington, inviting him to dinner and the Tom Thumb reception, and planning to send a gift back with him to Springfield for her, yet the letter has its suggestion of the Springfield attitude: "Only think of me writing to her *royal highness*."

In the spring of 1863 Dr. A. G. Henry came to Washington. So welcome was this old and intimate friend that when he came to say good-by, Lincoln would not have it so, but insisted that he move to the White House. The President also proposed that the good doctor join a Presidential party for a trip to the army front. He could not say no, so when on April 4 a little steamer, the *Carrie Martin*, pushed out of the Washington navy yard, Dr. Henry was aboard with President and Mrs. Lincoln, Tad, and Noah Brooks. The weather had been bad for several days, so that the starting of the trip had been delayed, and, soon after the vessel got in motion, snow began to fall furiously. Navigation in a blinding snowstorm was too hazardous, and the little steamer was forced to anchor for the night in a cove in the Potomac. Noah Brooks had some grim reflections on what would happen if the rebels chanced to make a raid on the Potomac during those hours of dark and storm, but he probably kept these thoughts to himself as he, Lincoln, and Dr. Henry sat up long after midnight telling stories and discussing the state of affairs. The rest of the party had retired to whatever type of bunk the little craft afforded.

Mary needed her good sportsmanship on this journey, for the next method of transportation after they landed at Aquia Creek was "an ordinary freight-car fitted up with rough plank benches," whose discomfort could hardly have been dispelled by the car's profuse decorations of flags and bunting. At Falmouth station "two ambulances and an escort of cavalry received the party," to take them to their destination, Hooker's headquarters of the Army of the Potomac.

It was Mary who had advised this expedition. Noah Brooks reported to his California newspaper about a week later: "The thoughtful wife of the President, an able and a noble woman, ought to have the credit of originating the plan of a tour through the Army by the President, as she saw what an excellent effect would be given to the troops, now in good condition and ready to march, by coming in contact with their Commander-in-Chief and his family." One suspects she also saw what a relief it would be to Mr. Lincoln to get out of Washington for a while with two comfortable and favorite companions like Dr. Henry and Noah Brooks.

At General Hooker's headquarters the Presidential party was assigned to three large hospital tents which had the luxury of floors and were furnished with camp bedsteads. Then began a series of colorful reviews of the various branches of the army. Noah Brooks described the cavalcade from headquarters to the reviewing stand: "The President, wearing a high hat and riding like a veteran, with General Hooker by his side, headed the flying column," while on the skirts of the procession rode Tad, "his gray cloak flying in the gusty wind like the plume of Henry of Navarre." It was a grand spectacle they had come to see, "this immense body of cavalry, with banners waving, music crashing, and horses prancing, as the vast column came winding like a huge serpent over the hills past the reviewing party, and then stretching far away out of sight." It was noticed that Lincoln merely touched his hat in return salute to the officers but uncovered to the men in ranks.

There was pageantry, color, and excitement. Once Lincoln remarked at the end of a strenuous day of reviewing, "It is a great relief to get away from Washington and the politicians. But nothing touches the tired spot." It could not have rested him to go through the hospital tents, as he did, but the sympathy of his compassionate heart brightened the pale suffering faces on the cots as he went by.

Once, as the Presidential party drove around the encampments, they came upon a queer little settlement of tents and shanties. It was a camp of colored refugees who flocked out eagerly to yell, "Hurrah for Massa Linkum." Mrs. Lincoln, with a warm friendly glance at the numerous children, asked her husband how many of them he supposed were named Abraham Lincoln. The President answered, "Let's see; this is April, 1863. I should say that of all of those babies under two years of age, perhaps two thirds have been named for me."

Not all the hazards of the trip were of a military nature. One day as Lincoln entered General Sickles's headquarters, where he was to have luncheon, he received a "bouncing kiss" from a dashing lady of fantastic career, the Princess Salm-Salm. Lincoln was so taken aback and discomposed that someone explained very quickly that the lady had kissed him on a wager. In her bold and adventurous existence the kissing of a President was a minor episode. Mary presumably knew of the incident, perhaps saw it, and it undoubtedly increased the jealous little lady's conviction that it was not safe to let other women get too near her husband, blameless as he was, when things like this could happen to him.

In the summer of 1863 the Lincolns, as usual, moved out to the Soldiers' Home. Mrs. Lincoln and Tad took a trip in June, the former evidently leaving behind some wifely instructions as to getting recreation and fresh air, for we find the dutiful husband reporting to her by telegram on June 15: "Tolerably well—have not rode out much yet, but have at last got new tires on the carriage wheels, & perhaps, shall ride out soon." He had acknowledged by wire on June 11 the three dispatches she had sent him and reassured her on the matter about which she was always anxious when absent from him: "I am very well; and am glad to know that you & 'Tad' are so." We have reached that revealing body of evidence, the notable exchange of telegrams between the Lincolns in 1863.

It was unfortunate Mrs. Lincoln did not stay away longer, for she returned to receive an injury. On the morning of July 2, while driving in from the Soldiers' Home to the White House, she had a serious carriage accident. The driver's seat became detached from the rest of the carriage with the result that the driver was thrown out and the frightened horses ran away.

It was figured out later that the screws which held the driver's seat had been removed by hostile hands in an attempt to injure the President. Mrs. Lincoln, who was alone in the carriage, was thrown violently to the ground and struck the back of her head on a sharp rock, that head already subject to so much agonizing pain. She was carried to the nearest hospital, where her wounds were dressed, and then removed to the Soldiers' Home.

There was no question this time as to the nurse the Lincolns wanted; the much-loved Mrs. Pomroy was sent for at once, and took charge. The papers at first announced that the injury was not serious and Lincoln telegraphed Robert the following day: "Don't be uneasy. Your mother very slightly hurt by her fall." The full effect of the shock and injury was not immediately understood. Mrs. Pomroy soon found that the wound was "dangerous" and that she had a very ill woman to take care of. The wound became infected and suppurated, so that it had to be opened. For three weeks the nurse tended her patient night and day; at the end of the period she was completely exhausted.

The accident occurred while the battle of Gettysburg was raging. It was a time of double strain and anxiety for Lincoln. He was always worried and unhappy when his wife was ill, and even though, after three days of terrific fighting, the Union was victorious at Gettysburg, he was painfully disappointed that the Confederate forces were not pursued and captured. Always when battles were going on he remembered that men were being mutilated or were dying. Mrs. Pomroy, to whom he bared his troubles, recalled him walking the floor in an agony of distress.

On July 11 Lincoln sent a three-word telegram to Robert, who was in New York. "Come to Washington." Robert apparently neither came nor answered. On July 14, his father again wired him: "Why do I hear no more of you?" It took considerable statesmanship just to deal with his eldest son. It is possible that Robert was slow to realize his mother's injury but in time he came to understand the truth. Two years later he said to his Aunt Emilie, "I think mother has never quite recovered from the effects of her fall," and in this connection he paid tribute to her pluck in rising above her pain to show a cheerful and optimistic face, a quality that meant everything to her husband, who was so inclined to gloom.

At the end of the three weeks Mrs. Lincoln was recovered enough to go on a journey. She wanted Mrs. Pomroy to go with her, but that faithful friend was worn out. Lincoln thanked the nurse over and over again for saving "Mother's life." His gratitude knew no bounds; he was ready to grant any request she saw fit to make, and he himself took her back to the hospital, their laps and the carriage piled high with flowers for her wounded soldiers. In Lincoln's own words, she was "one of the best women I ever knew."

Mary seemed destined to carriage accidents. Another was to shake her emotionally before the year was out. Still later in the Presidency, on an occasion when she and Lincoln were riding together, an iron hoop was caught under the carriage and pierced through the back seat between them. These accidents were like hammers beating upon Mary's sick nerves.

Practically everyone in Washington was neurotic in the summer of 1863. The cost of living was soaring as happens in wartime, military matters were in a critical state, and in the hot weather the capital became what someone inelegantly but expressively called "the City of stink." Mr. French, self-possessed gentleman though he was, became so alarmed at the flying rumors that he decided "to provision my house for about three months, so as not to starve." There was the constant rumble of war equipment along the streets and an "Engineer corps with a pontoon train" sounded so ominous one day that it threw the French household into a small panic; "there was a *darn sight* of rumpus, and a stranger would have rather thought Washington just going to be 'tuck,'" wrote Mr. French to his brother a few days later, adding with a faint twinkle, "but I, being used to such things believed no such thing and I don't believe it now!"

On August 5, the summer of '63, Noah Brooks wrote to his newspaper: "The past three or four days have been the very hottest of the season, the mercury going up to 104 degrees in the shade in some parts of the city . . ." He had described the heat as "truly awful" on July 28. It was essential that Mrs. Lincoln go where it was cooler. John Hay wrote early in August: "Bob and his mother have gone to the white mountains," adding the interesting sidelight, "Bob is so shattered by the wedding" of a much-admired lady "that he rushed madly off to sympathize with nature in her sternest aspects."

At times the President would proclaim a day for giving thanks for military successes; such a national thanksgiving day was celebrated while the President's wife was on Mount Washington. A newspaper correspondent who spoke with the First Lady there left a description which brings into sharp focus a pleasant, companionable personality. She was "fleshy," he wrote, but she "has a very fair, cheerful, smiling face, which does one good to look upon." The word "cheerful" is applied to Mary as inevitably as the word "sad" is to Lincoln. "She is quite light complexioned, has blue eyes and dark auburn hair, and on the whole, as might be hoped and expected of a President's wife, has a very easy, agreeable way." Her hair usually described as brown was so rich in color that this reporter thought of it as auburn.

His account enables one to see the lady in speech and action: "She came up to the desk, and with a cheerful smile said, 'I presume you did not expect to see me again so soon.' . . . 'Please let me have paper and I will write home; and I want a piece of rock to carry.' I offered to send the specimen she chose down by her driver; she said, 'No every lady should have a great pocket.' I speak of these remarks showing her easy, unassuming way. For the last ten minutes I have waited, that Mrs. L. add a postscript to a letter I now hold directed to A. Lincoln, President U.S., Washington, D. C. . . . as the fair lady hands back my pen she adds, 'I am sorry to trouble you, but you know a woman's letter is incomplete without a postscript.' "

Mary all her life loved the grandeur of mountains and their bracing air. This visit to Mount Washington at a time when the military outlook was brighter lingered happily in her memory, so much so that sixteen years later, when she had only one young person on whom to lavish her motherly affection (and that person tragically enough not her one remaining son), she wrote her grandnephew from France offering to finance a vacation for him. She had celebrated a patriotic day on that high mountaintop; she wanted the young relative to have that thrill. "I wish you to pass your *fourth* of July, at the *Tip Top House* on the White Mountains." So much had occurred in those sixteen years that she was not sure that she remembered the hotel correctly: "Do I give it the right name?" she added doubtfully. The newspaper account at the time shows her recollection was correct.

There was an unusual amount of sickness at Washington that summer and fall. The Lincolns thought that Tad too should get away as much as possible. The boy's frequent illnesses and frail health were a constant worry to his parents and after Willie's death they were doubly anxious about him. The tension of war and death had its effect also upon this sympathetic and nervous child. These factors explain why Mrs. Lincoln and Tad were away from Washington so much in the latter half of 1863. Fortunately for the record messages passed back and forth, sometimes several a day, between the traveling wife and the husband who could not leave his duties in that storm center, the White House.

If there were no evidence except the flood of telegrams the Lincolns exchanged in 1863, we would still have a complete picture of a devoted man and wife, neither of whom, when they were separated, could be satisfied without constant assurance that all was well with the other. Each showed thoughtfulness based on a deep understanding of the way the other felt, something that comes only with years of a close-knit marriage. He knew that to her his well-being was the most important thing, so he dutifully reported on the state of his health. One catches a glimpse of her life-and-death intensity about the success of the Union in his detailed accounts to her of all that was happening on the military front. His wording indicates her competent knowledge of these events. Lincoln's complete unselfishness was apparent in the messages; he missed his wife and son but he wanted them to have what was best and pleasantest to them.

One can follow the exchange day by day. On September 20 he wired her at New York: "I neither see or hear anything of sickness here now; though there may be much without my knowing it. I wish you to stay, or come just as is most agreeable to yourself." Next day he put it a little stronger: "The air is so clear and cool, and apparently healthy, that I would be glad for you to come. Nothing very particular, but I would be glad to see you and Tad." "Father" was plainly homesick for his family.

"Mother" was just as anxious to get home as "Father" was to have her come. But at this point a contretemps seems to have been caused by the housekeeper, Mrs. Cuthbert. All we know is that Mrs. Lincoln received from her a message that caused some misunderstanding, for on the following day, September 22, Lincoln wired his wife: "Did you receive my dispatch of yesterday? Mrs. Cuthbert did not correctly understand me—I wanted her to tell you to use your own pleasure whether to stay or come; . . . and I really wish to see you— Answer this on receipt."

The answer was forthcoming on that same day: "Your telegram received. Did you not receive my reply? I have telegraphed . . . to have the car [railroad car] ready at the earliest possible moment. Have a very bad cold, and am anxious to return home, as you may suppose. Taddie is well."

Perhaps her cold was the cause of delay, for she was still in New York two days later. On September 24 Lincoln wired his wife a long message containing six words that were like a dagger stab to them both. The President had to tell Mary of the death of one they both loved, but because that person was a Confederate, he must be guarded and refrain from an expression of sorrow. In the middle of a telegram of many lines telling of the battle of Chickamauga appeared the following: "Of the killed, one Major Genl. and five Brigadiers, including your brother-in-law, Helm . . ." So much for a record that must go through the War Department, but when the news had reached Lincoln he had cried out to a friend in his grief: "I feel as David did of old when he was told of the death of Absalom. 'Would to God that I had died for thee! Oh, Absalom, my son, my son.'" The death was not less an agony to Mary, picturing the grief of the "Little Sister" she loved with maternal love.

Parental anxiety with watchfulness over their sons was always with the Lincolns. In October the President wired Robert: "Your letter makes us a little uneasy about your health. Telegraph us how you are. If you think it would help you, make us a visit." A little over a month later Tad was ill again. It was hard for the father to go out of town under the circumstances but he was scheduled to speak at the dedication of a soldier's cemetery at Gettysburg, Pennsylvania. He had been asked, as an afterthought, to say a few appropriate words after the brilliant orator of the day, Edward Everett, had delivered his two-hour oration. Everett had been invited on September 23 and the date of the dedication, November 19, was set to suit his convenience. Lincoln did not receive his invitation to speak until November 2, and it is not recorded that anything was said about making the arrangements and the date convenient for him.

Mary delighted to go places with her husband and he liked to have her with him; it was doubtless due to Tad's illness that she did not go to Gettysburg. She missed hearing him utter his immortal words there, but she did not fail to contribute to his peace of mind as much assurance as she could. Her telegram of November 18 read: "The Dr. has just left. We hope dear Taddie is slightly better. Will send you a telegram in the morning." That Lincoln spoke of his anxiety while at Gettysburg appears in his own letter to Edward Everett written November 20, the day he returned to Washington: "Our sick boy, for whom you kindly enquired, we hope is past the worst."

As always in family life, as one worry disappeared another loomed up. The President himself was not well when he returned. Young Stoddard was shortly greeted with an ominous question from Lincoln's own doctor: "Have you been vaccinated?" As the young man bared his arm, not knowing what it was all about, the physician said quietly: "Mr. Lincoln's case is not fully developed yet. Varioloid." The White House had been turned into a smallpox hospital. Stoddard reported that the whole country was nervous about the case and was beginning to eye the qualifications of Vice-President Hannibal Hamlin. What of the worry of the wife always subject to panic at any threat to her loved ones? Her husband was the foundation of her life; she was dependent as a child upon his calmness and strength. Now she saw him sick and suffering from almost intolerable irritation. It was an unhappy time and Mary's nervous apprehension doubtless made it more so to Lincoln, who, manlike and husbandlike, did not want to be a cause of worry to her. Fortunately the illness was a mild one. Out of it came a touch of Lincoln's humor. A lady once questioned him in regard to some of the witticisms attributed to him, mentioning a few of the stock stories. "He laughed, and said, 'The papers make me smarter than I am; I have said none of these things with one exception. I did say, when I had the small pox, "Now let the office-seekers come, for at last I have something I can give all of them." ' "

Early December found the First Lady once more on a trip. Often there was special reason for her going away; she sometimes participated in Sanitary Fairs, or made an appearance at some public patriotic function. Again we can take up the chronicle by telegrams. On Friday, December 4, she wired her husband from New York: "Reached here last evening; very tired and severe headache. Hope to hear you are doing well. Expect a telegraph to-day." Perhaps this crossed one the faithful husband sent that same day saying "All going well," and he followed this up by writing on the two succeeding days, December 5 and 6, "All doing well."

Tad had remained with his father, and on December 6 the worried wife and mother sent this wire: "Do let me know immediately how Taddie and yourself are. I will be home Tuesday without fail; sooner if needed." Not content with this and fearing perhaps that to spare her anxiety Lincoln was giving her an overly optimistic report, she checked up on him by telegraphing a member of the White House staff, Edward McManus, on the same day: "Let me know immediately exactly how Mr. Lincoln and Taddie are."

Three telegrams of the next day, December 7, epitomize family affection and the wish to be together. The husband sent this at 10:30 A.M.: "All doing well. Tad confidently expects you to-night. When will you come?" The wife's answer came promptly: "Will leave here positively at 8 A.M. Tuesday morning. Have carriage waiting at depot in Washington at 6 P.M. Did Tad receive his book? Please answer." Lincoln sent the desired reply at seven that evening: "Tad has received his book. The carriage shall be ready at 6 P.M. to-morrow." Few husbands burdened as Lincoln was with a thousand matters to look after would have done so well.

The White House about this time had a dear but surprising visitor. Emilie Todd Helm, left a widow with three small children dependent upon her, wished to come from the deep South to Kentucky to join her mother, Mary's stepmother, at Lexington. Almost penniless after her husband's death, there was no place else for her to go. General Grant was asked for the necessary pass but she waited for it in vain. Finally she started anyway and with her little daughter Katherine got as far as Fort Monroe. There Federal officers told her she could not go farther without taking the oath of allegiance to the United States. It was a cruel dilemma for the young widow, alone and not knowing which way to turn, yet she refused to do what she considered treason to her dead husband and the South. The officers in perplexity wired the situation to Lincoln, and promptly got the brief but dramatic reply: "Send her to me." Thus Emilie was brought to the White House.

It was hard to connect the pale, black-clad widow who arrived with the beautiful "Little Sister" whom Lincoln had lifted in his arms at Lexington or with the glowing young girl for whom Mary at Springfield had planned a "white velvet bonnet smothered in lovely white plumes." Civil War had made youth and joyousness of life seem like something in another and remote existence. Emilie recorded in her diary: "Mr. Lincoln and my sister met me with the warmest affection, we were all too grief-stricken at first for speech. . . . We could only embrace each other in silence and tears." The two sisters dined alone together, selecting safe topics such as old friends in Kentucky and Springfield. They could not mention the vital things filling their minds: the death of Emilie's husband, of Willie and of the three brothers of them both. "Allusion to the present is like tearing open a fresh and bleeding wound and the pain is too great for self-control," ran Emilie's diary. "And the future, alas, the future seems empty, of everything but despair." The deep affection was intact, warm and fresh from renewed touching of hands and lips, but there was a great restraint. "This frightful war comes between us like a barrier of granite closing our lips but not our hearts, for though our tongues are tied, we weep over our dead together and express through our clasped hands the sympathy we feel for each other in our mutual grief."

The softhearted parental couple in the White House did just what could have been predicted: "She and Brother Lincoln pet me as if I were a child, and, without words, try to comfort me." One suspects that it was partly for this that Lincoln had caused Emilie to be sent to the White House. Mary tried to distract her mind from its overwhelming grief. Perhaps it was as a part of this effort that a ride in the state carriage was planned and, with the usual ill-fortune that dogged the First Lady, the ride too ended in disaster. The carriage ran over a little boy, breaking his leg. Emilie said truthfully that "Mary mothers all children." To her the sight of the hurt little figure on the ground was distress beyond words; she jumped out of the carriage crying, "Oh, the poor baby! Who is he, where does he live? I will take him to his mother." Fortunately a doctor took charge and removed the boy to his home, where Mary went at once to tell the mother how distressed she was about the accident and to assure her that she wanted to help in every way possible. The First Lady sent fruit and flowers and promised the little boy some toys, a promise that was richly fulfilled the next day when she and Emilie called and made the eyes of the invalid sparkle with an array of gifts glamorous to children.

It was another nerve-racking experience to a woman whose impairment was becoming more and more evident.

Emilie's diary takes us inside the White House walls to a close-up focus on Mary as she was at the end of 1863. The younger sister came upon her one day reading a newspaper. Having examined some of the newspaper smearing which Mary was constantly receiving, we can understand why she dropped the sheets, held out her arms and said, "Kiss me, Emilie, and tell me that you love me! I seem to be the scape-goat for both North and South!" It was an apt and accurate statement. At that moment the two women heard Lincoln's voice as he approached and Emilie marveled at the change in her sister; she threw off her despondent attitude, lifted her shoulders and smiled. She must not let her husband, still run-down from his illness, suspect her depression. She questioned Emilie anxiously later that day: "Emilie, what do you think of Mr. Lincoln, do you think he is well?" Lincoln had scarcely recovered from his varioloid at this time and Emilie thought he looked very ill but she merely replied, "He seems thinner than I ever saw him." "Oh, Emilie," exclaimed Mary, "will we ever awake from this hideous nightmare?"

Emilie's diary pictures in unforgettable words the worry of Lincoln and Mary about each other. Again we find the husband begging a sister to stay with his wife to help and comfort her. He had not been fooled by Mary's assumed cheerfulness when he joined the two women, though he played the game too and lightly remarked, "I hope you two are planning some mischief." Later he said to Emilie when Mary was not present: "Little Sister, I hope you can come up and spend the summer with us at the Soldiers' Home, you and Mary love each other—it is good for her to have you with her—I feel worried about Mary, her nerves have gone to pieces; she cannot hide from me that the strain she has been under has been too much for her mental as well as her physical health." Again we have Lincoln's recognition that mental illness was involved in his wife's case. He asked Emilie what she thought about Mary's condition and Emilie answered frankly: "She seems very nervous and excitable and once or twice when I have come into the room suddenly the frightened look in her eyes has appalled me. . . . I believe if anything should happen to you or Robert or Tad it would kill her." The worn man shook his head sadly, and made his pathetic plea: "Stay with her as long as you can." Lincoln knew that having an "enemy," the widow of a Confederate officer, in the White

House was causing all kinds of criticism, but Mary's need here carried more weight with him than political expediency.

Emilie had an experience one night that made her realize more than ever her sister's nervous condition. After good night had been said, Mary came to Emilie's room with tear-stained face, quivering smile, and a strange shining in her eyes which frightened the younger sister. Out of longing, sick nerves, perhaps thoughts so vivid that they seemed to take visual shape or perhaps out of dreams, there had come to Mary experiences that brought her momentary solace, a solace she wanted to share with Emilie, who was also in deep bereavement. "I want to tell you, Emilie, that one may not be wholly without comfort when our loved ones leave us." Speaking of the "deep pit of gloom and despair" into which her little son's death had plunged her, she continued, ". . . if Willie did not come to comfort me I would still be drowned in tears, and while I long inexpressibly to touch him, to hold him in my arms, and still grieve that he has no future in this world that I might watch with a proud mother's heart—he lives, Emilie!" said Mary with a thrill that gave her sister a shuddering awe. "He comes to me every night, and stands at the foot of my bed with the same sweet, adorable smile he has always had; he does not always come alone; little Eddie is sometimes with him and twice he has come with our brother Alec . . . You cannot dream of the comfort this gives me."

Emilie was a well-balanced woman. She wrote in her diary: "It *is* unnatural and abnormal, it frightens me. It does not seem like Sister Mary to be so nervous and wrought up. She is on a terrible strain and her smiles seem forced. She is frightened about Robert going into the Army."

That was another dread preying on Mary's mind. As so often with her she could view the subject only as a matter of personal feeling and this involved conflict both with her husband and her eldest son. She would say to Lincoln, who thought it Robert's duty to go: "Of course, Mr. Lincoln, I know that Robert's plea to go into the Army is manly and noble and I want him to go, but oh, I am so frightened he may never come back to us!" Lincoln would sadly remind her that mothers all over the country were making this sacrifice, but Mary would urge her own fears and one suspects the conversation ended with her in tears and hysterics. Lincoln was in a cruel dilemma. He knew he was being severely criticized because his son was safe when other men's sons were dying on the battlefields, yet he feared that Robert's leaving might be the final strain that would topple Mary's unbalance into complete break-down. In a way he had to choose between consideration to his wife and to his son. Robert felt he should join the army and was doubtless resentful that his mother put him in a humiliating position by opposing it. In yielding as long as he did to his wife's wishes, Lincoln put himself in conflict with his son. It is another case where he continued in a course of action which was not expedient politically in order to avoid putting pressure on her.

While Emilie was at the White House an incident oc-curred which brought the painful situation into sharp focus. General Sickles and Senator Harris were calling one day when the latter, turning to Mrs. Lincoln, said sternly, "Why isn't Robert in the Army? He is old enough and strong enough to serve his country. He should have gone to the front some time ago." Mary's face turned white as death, but biting her lip and fighting for self-control she said quietly: "Robert is making his preparations now to enter the Army, Senator Harris; he is not a shirker as you seem to imply for he has been anxious to go for a long time." She defended her son fairly and took the blame her-self. "If fault there be, it is mine, I have insisted that he should stay in college a little longer as I think an educated man can serve his country with more intelligent purpose than an ignoramus." Senator Harris arose and said pointedly, "I have only one son and he is fighting for his country." Then he turned to Emilie, whose presence he evidently resented, and making an ironic bow flung at her the provocative remark, "And, Madam, if I had twenty sons they should all be fighting the rebels." Emilie was a Todd and the senator got as good as he sent. "And if I had twenty sons," she promptly answered, "they should all be opposing yours." Emilie then left the room to hide her tears. Mary followed, put her arms around her sister, and the two wept wordlessly together.

General Sickles took it upon himself to go upstairs in the White House and report the whole conversation to Lincoln, who was still feeling so unwell that he was lying down. The President's eyes twinkled at the quickness of Emilie's retort. But when Sickles angrily pounded the table and shouted, "You should not have that rebel in your house," Lincoln asserted that great inner dignity of his which kept others in their places. "Excuse me, General Sickles, my wife and I are in the habit of choosing our own guests. We do not need from our friends either advice or assistance in the matter." He maintained Mary's dignity here as well as his own. In justice to Emilie he added, "Besides, the little 'rebel' came because I ordered her to come, it was not of her volition."

Divided loyalties even complicated relations between Tad and his little cousin Katherine Helm. The two children were seated on a rug in front of the fire one evening, Tad entertaining his guest by the good old-fashioned method of showing photographs. Holding up one of his father he said with great pride, "This is the President." Katherine shook her head in emphatic denial: "No, that is not the President, Mr. Davis is President." Tad was outraged and shouted furiously, "Hurrah for Abe Lincoln." Small Katherine had just the same amount of Todd blood as Tad, so she promptly yelled, "Hurrah for Jeff Davis." Tad as usual appealed to his father, who, with twinkling eyes, drew the two belligerents to his lap, one on each knee, and exercised his statesmanship by saying: "Well, Tad, you know who is your President, and I am your little cousin's Uncle Lincoln."

Little Katherine found in the White House an object to which she took a great fancy. It was a small china inkwell, just the thing to please a little girl, with dainty china rosebuds climbing all over it and an alluring red blossom on the top to lift it by. Mary saw the longing in the child's eyes, and promptly gave her the bright little object. Katherine treasured it all her life. One finds it today at Helm Place near Lexington, Kentucky, and, touching it gently, one is reminded of that sweet quality of Mary Lincoln: her understanding love of children.

Emilie was sensitive to the embarrassment her presence caused the Lincolns, and wished to continue her journey to Kentucky. They begged her to stay longer and wanted her to plan a long visit with them when they moved to the Soldiers' Home the following summer. There were fewer visitors and no entertainments at this quiet retreat, hence less chance of incidents like the encounters with Senator Harris and General Sickles. Emilie did return for a definite purpose in the fall of '64 and the visit resulted in a conflict of loyalties that seared everyone concerned. In spite of unchanged family affection the fact remained that she and Mary each thought the other had been a traitor to the cause that was right and patriotic.

On December 14 of '63 Lincoln gave Emilie a pass for her journey to Kentucky. He also wrote out the oath of allegiance for her and a special Presidential pardon conditional upon her taking it, but she would not take the oath; her code of honor would not permit it. The President knew, however, he could trust that same code to keep her from doing anything to embarrass him. At the time of parting he and Emilie talked together of the misfortunes of the Todd family and of Emilie's young husband Ben, who had so recently been killed in battle. Part of Lincoln's great burden was the realization that the people of the South (that South in which he himself had been born) blamed him for their sufferings. "You know, Little Sister," he reminded Emilie, "I tried to have Ben come with me. I hope you do not feel any bitterness or that I am in any way to blame for all this sorrow." He put his arms around her and they both wept.

Civil war! A friend commented on the lines in Lincoln's face. He answered simply: "I feel as though I shall never be glad any more." Mary could have said the same.

chapter 26

"IF HE IS RE-ELECTED"

The year 1864 opened as usual with a huge New Year's reception. These functions always required painstaking planning and consultation with one or more of the White House secretaries. From a cryptic entry in John Hay's diary on January 1, one suspects that there had been friction between him and Mrs. Lincoln, possibly about the arrangements for the party. "I did not attend the reception today, laboring all the morning under a great disgust," wrote the young man who seems to have been in "a state of mind," to use the expression he once applied to Mrs. Lincoln. It was perhaps as well that next day he went away on a mission. A secretary who could not get along with Lincoln's wife, and who gave a "disgusted snort" when the President stopped work to listen to Tad's whims, had his drawbacks.

The social program at the White House seems to have been accelerated during the first four months of 1864. It was election year and Mary was entertaining as many people as possible. Life had been complicated to the breaking point up to this time; now Lincoln, trying to run the war (using such faulty material, human and otherwise, as was available) and weighed down with a thousand cruel perplexities, had to stand for re-election. The vast flood of criticism from all sides threatened to engulf him until, in the fall of the year, it receded. At times he had little hope of winning and Mary too was racked with doubt. But she had always supported him on the social front; if standing in line and being gracious to the public would win votes, she would do it.

Our chatty source of information, Commissioner French, described the vast crowd at the reception of April 9. "It has either rained, or snowed, or done something it ought not to, out of doors, at *every* reception for the past 2 months," he wrote. "Yesterday the rain descended in torrents, still *they came* & would come if a

Sodomitic shower were in full progress." French went early and, as he said, had "a cosy talk" with "my good friend Madam L.," who apologized "for not sending me a release for the day—said she did not believe any body would come . . ." French mentioned that Senator Sumner dropped in. "Then the President joined us, and was as pleasant & funny as could be . . . Edward came & told us that the hall was filled with people; 'open the doors' said the President, and behold a crowd equal almost to a New Year's reception . . . they kept coming in a steady stream, till almost 3. Then the show was over."

A familiar figure, missing around the White House since Willie's death, appeared at a Saturday reception during this year, Julia Taft, who had been away at school. Mrs. Lincoln greeted Julia with all the old affection, but when Tad came in and saw her, he threw himself down on the floor and kicked and screamed until he had to be carried out. Mrs. Lincoln said, "You must excuse him, Julia. You know what he remembers." Julia, like Willie's toys, recalled to Tad a happiness that had turned to intolerable pain.

February of this year was a time of ups and downs. Early in the month the artist F. B. Carpenter began his six months' stay at the White House for the purpose of painting the Emancipation Proclamation scene, the picture which now hangs in our Capitol. Carpenter left a restrained account of the dreadful night of February 10, when the White House stables burned to the ground. Two ponies, Tad's and the one cherished because it had been Willie's, were burned to death. A fire against the blackness of night with the cries of helpless animals caught in the blaze is a horrible thing. The tender hearts of the three Lincolns had no defense against the pain of this disaster. Fortunately Tad did not hear of it until it was over; when he learned what had happened to the pets, he threw himself on the floor and could not be comforted.

Shortly thereafter Lincoln was ill. On the 20th Mrs. Lincoln wrote General Sickles: "The President, is a little better to day, was able to visit the 'blue room;' to night, I will try & persuade him to take some medicine & rest a little on the morrow." Apparently she was not too sure her advice would be followed.

His irregular eating and lack of appetite worried her. Even when she sent or took a tray of food to his office "he was often too busy or too abstracted to touch it." The wife was always trying to think up a scheme to make her husband eat. One such pleasant conspiracy involved the help of a young woman named Alice whom the Lincolns had taken into their service because she had been ill and was badly in need of employment. Alice Johnstone proved helpful, understanding, and the very sort of person Mrs. Lincoln could depend upon.

One day the First Lady, worried over the gaunt, hollow-eyed face of her husband, had an inspiration. "Alice," she said, "do you know how to make a dish of fricasseed chicken and small biscuits with thick cream gravy poured over it, all on one platter?" "I'll try," answered Alice entering wholeheartedly into the plan. "It would be so good to see Mr. Lincoln eat something."

The conspirators worked out the details carefully. The meal was to be served in the small dining room with no servants, only the family present. Tad, of course, was the only messenger who could be depended upon to fetch his father. When Lincoln entered the room, saw the homelike setup and the menu, he exclaimed, "Oh, Mary, this is good. It seems like old times come back!" The worn face and homesick voice so touched Alice she had to leave the room to hide her emotion. When she returned, she heard Lincoln laughing and Tad announced joyfully, "Oh, Alice, he ate three helps and more gravy than you and me and mother could [together]!"

In this year again one can follow the doings of the Lincolns in telegrams. Lincoln wired General Butler on April 7 that he and Mrs. Lincoln would visit Fort Monroe the following week, but four days later he canceled the plan because Mary was ill. It seemed as if she could not stay long at the White House without getting sick. What she called "bilious attacks" came all too frequently and drained her of qualities she needed in her position: patience, clear thinking, and endurance. We have Mary's own description of this illness. Finding that she had to break an engagement to visit hospitals with Mrs. Welles, she wrote her telling of the prolonged pain and dreadful nausea of what is now called migraine headache.

The only solution was for her to get away from the

storm center as much as possible. We find her telegraphing her husband from New York on April 28 telling him that she and Tad had arrived safely, asking that a draft be sent to her (she must have gone shopping), and ending: "Tad says are the goats well?" Lincoln replied on the same day: "The draft will go to you. Tell Tad the goats and father are very well—especially the goats."

In June Mrs. Lincoln went to Boston but Tad remained behind. Perhaps the prospect of visiting the army, with all the thrills that reviews, bright uniforms, band music and soldier life could give a boy, had something to do with it; at all events he and his father visited General Grant's army while his mother was away. On June 24 the President reported by wire to his wife that they had returned "safe and sound." From her husband's various telegrams we learn Mrs. Lincoln and Tad were at Manchester, Vermont, by the last of August, remaining until about September 8, for on that date Lincoln's message assured her that all was well "including Tad's pony and the goats."

The First Lady traveled much that year but one could always count on her being with her husband when danger threatened. And danger emphatically did threaten Washington the second week in July, when the Confederates under General Early got so close that the cannonading at Fort Stevens was distinctly heard at the White House. For three days, July 10, 11, and 12, it was touch and go as to whether the capital would not be entered by the enemy. Fort Stevens, poorly manned, was its slender defense, and there the Commander in Chief of the Army went and became a target for enemy fire as he exposed his tall form on the parapet.

Mary went with her husband to Fort Stevens and was present when an event took place that must have made her heart stand still with terror. One of the soldiers in the fort wrote his wife what happened. He explained that a Confederate sharpshooter got up in the top of a house and "thought he would kill some of our men that was on the parapets." "Old Abe and his wife was in the Fort at the time," he continued, "and Old Abe and his doctor was standing up on the parapets and the sharpshooter that I speak of shot the doctor through the left thigh, and Old Abe ordered our men to fall back." Lincoln was slow to get down from the parapet and the story goes that a young officer, Oliver Wendell Holmes (later to become justice of the Supreme Court), seeing the President's danger and exasperated at his deliberation, said to him, "Get down, you fool."

Another soldier reported that Mrs. Lincoln stood beside Lincoln on the parapet with rifle bullets flying around them. Whether that happened the same day on which the doctor was shot (July 12) is not clear, but she was there at that time and after the incident was in great anxiety and begged Lincoln to leave the fort, which he refused to do. It was a terrific ordeal for Mary but in none of the accounts is there any mention of hysteria on her part. On the contrary, her fighting blood was up, as a wife's always is when there is menace to her husband.

What hurt her was just what bothered Lincoln—that the enemy got away. Two or three weeks later when the crisis was over Secretary Stanton called upon the Lincolns at the Soldiers' Home and Stanton said playfully to the First Lady, "Mrs. Lincoln, I intend to have a full-length portrait of you painted, standing on the ramparts at Fort Stevens overlooking the fight."

"That is very well," was the prompt retort, "and I can assure you of one thing, Mr. Secretary, if I had had a few *ladies* with me the Rebels would not have been permitted to get away as they did!" The implication was that he, as Secretary of War, should have managed the matter more successfully.

Both the Lincolns showed courage and forgetfulness of self at Fort Stevens. Yet there the President saw war in terms of blood, bullets piercing live flesh, and men crumpling to the earth. There is a vast difference of realization between viewing a statistic and seeing a bloody figure convulsed in agony. Afterwards when battles raged there might be a mental picture. Early's raid and the experience at Fort Stevens were part of the war attrition that was wearing both the Lincolns down.

They had some lighter hours and a few moments of genuine uplift. Perhaps the crowning of the Capitol dome toward the end of 1863 had given them such a feeling. Julia Taft was in the Capitol grounds on the day when a huge crane lifted and swung the great statue of Armed Freedom into its place on top of the dome. As the fastenings were pulled away a white dove first circled the mighty head against the sky and then alighted on it. In an awed hush the spectators whispered, ". . . a sign of peace."

Julia's father said to her, "You must tell the President." The unfinished dome had seemed so symbolic of the broken Union that work on it had been pushed forward at all costs. When Freedom was unveiled in May of '64 and took up her endless survey of Washington, it was like an augury of coming victory.

One evening the Lincolns had a bit of comedy. On June 6 a now-forgotten humorist, Stephen Massett, had written the President asking him to set "an hour any evening this week" when the writer could present to him and Mrs. Lincoln "a few sketches that may possibly interest and amuse you." The letter was accompanied by a quaint poster advertising a reading called "Drifting About" by Jeems Pipes of Pipesville, Massett's stage name. The flavor of wisecracking in the eighteen-sixties appears in one of the topics: "Eating Roast Pig with the King of the Cannibal Islands (my only Essay on Bacon in foreign parts)."

Anything dramatic appealed to Mary and her husband. The appointment was made and a few evenings later Carpenter heard "the voice and ringing laugh of the President" issuing from the Red Room, where Jeems was putting on his show. After Jeems imitated a stammering man, Lincoln said: "I want to offer a suggestion. I once knew a man who invariably *'whistled'* with his stammering . . . if you could get in a touch of nature like that it would be irresistibly ludicrous." With the President showing him how, Pipes went through several rehearsals until he had mastered the technique to Lincoln's satisfaction.

One catches a glimpse of the Presidential couple this year of '64 through a distinguished pair of eyes. Walt Whitman lived on the route Lincoln took as he came into town each day that summer from the Soldiers' Home. The poet and the President got so they would always "exchange bows, and very cordial ones," as the President rode by about eight-thirty with the escort of cavalry upon which Mary had insisted. Occasionally the poet would see the Lincolns riding together in an equipage "of the plainest kind," Mary "in complete black, with a long crape veil," a symbol of her sorrow. Whitman noted the sadness deep in Lincoln's eyes.

Tad was their one pleasure and means of relaxation. But anxiety entered even into their enjoyment of their whimsical son, because he was frequently ill. John Todd

Stuart, calling on the President one morning, found that he was not available. Lincoln had been up all the night before with Tad, who was ailing. The fact that the President needed his sleep meant nothing if the sick boy wanted his father with him.

The two were so close to each other. Lincoln had moments of escape from care when he took his youngest by the hand and walked over to Joseph Stuntz's little toy shop on New York Avenue near the White House. Joseph Stuntz was an old soldier of France who could carve the most wonderful wooden soldiers and other irresistible toys. To go into the Christmasy atmosphere of his shop was to enter a child's world of enchantment. Some have conjectured rather absurdly that Lincoln worked out military problems with the toy soldiers as he played with them. It was enough that the shop was a good place to forget about the war and problems and join Tad in a little boy's delight in Toyland.

There was apparently no year in which the Lincolns did not have in-law worries but the war created problems of special difficulty. Throughout the Presidency the Coles County relatives were writing labored and misspelled letters to the White House, asking for contributions and giving conflicting accounts as to the care of Lincoln's stepmother. Lincoln was deeply concerned about the welfare of Sarah Lincoln, a solicitude in which Mary fully joined him, but he could not go to Illinois to see how she was and which of the conflicting stories was correct. That was the in-law worry on his side of the house.

One of Mary's half sisters, Martha Todd White of Selma, Alabama, caused a furor of adverse publicity to the Lincolns early in 1864. Emilie had awakened their loving concern, but Martha with a very different personality was a source of embarrassment and exasperation. A letter written by Mrs. White to the President on December 19, 1863, perhaps gives the beginning of the story. In this letter she asked permission to replenish her wardrobe with articles not obtainable in the South and the papers that would enable her to take this merchandise through the lines.

The lady did return South around early March 1864. Shortly after her departure the newspapers were breaking out in a rash over a story that Mrs. Lincoln's half sister, a rebel, on a pass from the President, had taken through the lines three large trunks of medicine and much merchandise, including a rebel uniform with buttons of pure gold. Details varied and of course grew in the telling; those gold buttons were worth from four thousand to forty thousand dollars depending upon the newspaper or gossiper.

Fortunately Lincoln himself made, to his Secretary of the Navy, Gideon Welles, a careful statement of what happened, and Welles wrote it down in his diary the same day. This is historical evidence that can be trusted. By this account Mrs. White when in Washington tried a number of times to see the President and Mrs. Lincoln but both refused to see her. Lincoln, however, sent her a pass to enable her to return South, and the aggressive lady "sent it back with a request that she might take trunks without being examined." When the President refused this, she "then showed her pass and talked 'secesh' at the hotel," making herself so obnoxious that Lincoln said if she "did not leave forthwith she might expect to find herself within twenty-four hours in the Old Capitol Prison." Welles thought the story in connection with Mrs. White "a subject of scandal and abuse." Just what the lady smuggled through the lines is difficult to determine. Mrs. Grimsley thought she carried through almost her weight in quinine and that Mrs. White subsequently boasted how she had outwitted her too credulous "brother Lincoln."

Mary, of course, received her special smearing in the stories which were being mouthed around. She was accused of sending information to the enemy by Martha White. By her own statement Mrs. Lincoln repeatedly refused to see her half sister in spite of the latter's persistent attempts and pressure brought to bear by various people. The call of her own blood was always subordinate to her loyalty to her husband and the Union.

Martha White turned up in Washington again in March 1865, and wrote from Willard's Hotel a peremptory letter to the President asking him for a permit to get her cotton out of the South. He must act quickly, she told him, and the "permit will have to be irrespective of all military authority . . ." She complained of being treated badly by officers at Fort Monroe. Getting cotton out where it could be sold was a matter of livelihood to many Southerners, but one gathers between the cold lines of this letter the writer's scorn for anything Yankee, especially the Yankee President. An endorsement on this letter in Lincoln's hand says he gave her a pass South. This would enable her to get home, but it was not a permit in regard to the cotton. It would not be surprising if Martha White caused Mary Lincoln to have one or more of her severe headaches.

Another in-law very difficult to deal with was Mary's brother Levi O. Todd. He was an exception to the relatives in Kentucky in being a Unionist. In September 1864 he wrote the President telling him he had been working for his re-election. After this preamble he asked Lincoln to lend him from "$150 to $200" which he would use, as he said, "to your advantage and my own as I stand in great need of things." His plea is pitiful, but Lincoln knew Levi for the undesirable character he was, a man whose wife had had to being him, alleging habitual drunkenness, cruel and inhuman manner, and failure to support her and the children. The President evidently did not respond to the request for money, and his failure to do so brought bitter reproaches from one he cared for dearly.

For here Emilie Todd Helm comes again into the story. The Lincolns had invited her to visit them in the summer of 1864 but her coming meant only heartache for all concerned. She came to plead for something that Lincoln had the power to give her, but would not as a matter of principle. She too wanted him to make it possible for her to get her cotton out of the South in order to sell it. Of the tenderhearted President's many dilemmas, few were more bitter than this. Emilie, the loved little sister, widowed and with three little children dependent upon her, needed the money desperately. How could Lincoln refuse her in her grief and want? Yet the matter of getting cotton through the lines was a public issue, a burning question with far-reaching complications. He could have done it if she had been willing to take the oath of allegiance. When she had departed from Washington the year before, he had written out a document specifying that she was to be permitted to get her cotton after she had taken that oath. As we have seen he had even written out the oath itself, but she would not take it. She remained one of the enemy. What would have been the repercussions if the President had given a widely sought-for privilege to the widow of a Confederate officer and his own wife's half sister? He could not in loyalty to the Union yield to her pleading, yet who can measure the pain that this refusal cost him?

Disappointed and desperate, Emilie left to take the long journey back to Lexington. When she arrived there she found that Levi Todd had died. If he could have had medical treatment and the right kind of food and care, perhaps he might have lived; he had said to Lincoln in his letter that he was "in *actual necessity*" of food and clothing. Emilie found her mother ill in bed following the shock of Levi's death. The remnant of the Todd family in Kentucky was in want and sorrow; their way of life was being destroyed.

Emilie sat down and wrote a letter to the man in the White House that is the tragic essence of civil war. It began coldly, "Mr. Lincoln." She told him what she found after her "long tedious unproductive and sorrowful visit" to him. "Levi Todd . . . died from utter want and destitution . . . another sad victim to the powers of more favored relatives. . . . I again beg and plead attention & consideration to my petition to be permitted to ship my cotton & be allowed a pass to go South to attend to it— My necessities are such I am compelled to urge it— The last money I have in the world I used to make the unfruitful appeal to you. You cannot urge that you do not *know them* for I have told you of them. I have been a quiet citizen and request only *the right* which humanity and justice always gives to widows and orphans. I also would remind you that your *minnie bullets* have made us what we are . . ."

At this point some glimmer of how her words would hurt may have cut through her desperation, or perhaps it was only a valiant woman's defense for laying her heart bare. She ended: "If you think I give way to excess of feeling, I beg you will make some excuse for a woman almost crazed with misfortune." She could see the situation only in terms of her suffering and her belief that the Confederacy was the cause which was just. She and Lincoln were both adhering to what they believed was right and patriotic; it is a case study or epitome of what the Civil War meant.

The pain of Mary, the loving older sister, torn two ways in that struggle between Emilie's pleading and Lincoln's refusal, necessarily cut deep. This was probably one case where she could see both sides, but the rule with her in a choice between Lincoln and her family was that her husband came first. She thought of herself as Mary Lincoln, not Mary Todd Lincoln.

In the summer of 1864 the chances of Lincoln's re-election looked darker than ever. The war was going badly for the Union and criticism was pouring over Lincoln in a hot thick stream. He was doubtful whether he would win and Mary's nervous condition was worse than ever. Increasingly irrational in regard to money, she was getting more and more deeply in debt. Her urge to buy was psychopathic but it was given justification in her mind by an incident in the spring of that year.

Some patriotic ladies started a movement to buy no foreign goods, such as laces, dress goods, or ornaments during the war. One of them, as we have seen, called on Mrs. Lincoln to ask her to sign such a pledge. Mrs. Lincoln very properly waited to get the President's approval before doing so. When the matter was presented to them Lincoln and the Secretary of the Treasury explained that the government needed the revenue that came from the importation of luxuries. This planted in Mrs. Lincoln's mind the idea that wearing costly clothing was a patriotic duty. It was a most welcome thought to her tastes. Continuing public criticism added to the impulse. "I must dress in costly materials," she told Mrs. Keckley. "The people scrutinize every article that I wear with critical curiosity. The very fact of having grown up in the West, subjects me to more searching observation." And there was another angle to the matter. With her ever-present sense of insecurity, she thought these expensive clothes might serve as a sort of insurance, that she could sell them if she were ever in want. She used her credit as the President's wife to buy clothes, jewels and furs, and now her debts had accumulated to an enormous extent.

She became hysterical as she explained the situation to Mrs. Keckley shortly before the election. Reaching out for reassurance she asked her colored friend if she thought Mr. Lincoln would be re-elected. He must be, the distracted woman said, he did not know of her debts and if he were defeated he could not pay them. "If he is re-elected," she went on, "I can keep him in ignorance of my affairs; but if he is defeated, then the bills will be sent in, and he will know all." This was followed by a hysterical sob.

Mrs. Lincoln also confided her troubles about her debts to Isaac Newton, Commissioner of Agriculture. John Hay several years later called on "Father Newton," as he called him, and the gossipy old fellow began to talk about Mrs. Lincoln. "Oh," he said (according to Hay), "that lady has set here on this here sofy & shed tears by the pint a begging me to pay her debts which was unbeknown to the President."

Her irrationality had woven a snare about her. There was a flaw in her reasoning and judgment, but the suffering of her affectionate heart was whole, normal, and agonizing. During the election campaign she was haunted by the dread that the opposing party would find out how much she owed and use that fact against her husband. This possibility made her beside herself with anxiety and fear. Out of that frenzy she grasped a twisted notion that was later to bear bitter fruit: "The Republican politicians must pay my debts. Hundreds of them are getting immensely rich off the patronage of my husband, and it is but fair that they should help me out of my embarrassment."

This perverted logic became fixed in her mind. Politics had become connected with her streak of irrationality; it had gotten into the area where she was abnormal and irresponsible. The many facets and tremendous importance of Lincoln's campaign for re-election had stimulated her interest in a subject for which she had always had a taste, political maneuvering. All along she had been helping her husband in various ways, such as writing letters to convey certain information and sending bouquets or photographs to the right person at the right time. Lincoln, because of her great interest, had accepted these little services and had kept her informed on political matters.

A letter from a politician to a general gives a perfect picture of the First Lady acting as a go-between for her husband. George Ashmun, politician, deep in a move against Secretary Chase (who was willing to be nominated for President in 1864), wrote General Nathaniel P. Banks: "There can be no doubt but that Mr. C[hase] is desperately bent on supplanting the President. . . . I have had but little conversation with him [Lincoln] *directly* on the subject, but Mrs. L—— keeps me thoroughly informed of everything,—& you may rely upon the existence of the ripest state of inflammation between Mr. L and Mr. C."

The trouble was that Mrs. Lincoln, never too discreet and now irresponsible in regard to money, was keeping entirely too many people "informed of everything." She was writing generals, politicians, prominent men of all kinds many letters that were like a safety valve for her overwrought nerves, but were anything but safe in other respects. She liked to treat small details of appointments or politics as important secrets, throwing in a confidential *"entre nous"* or "just between us," and giving only a mysterious initial instead of a full name. The tangles of political interplay had for her something of the interest of a plot or drama.

A perfect example of this type of letter is one Mrs. Lincoln wrote Abram Wakeman early in 1865. He was a New York politician whom Lincoln appointed postmaster in 1862 and surveyor of the port of New York in 1864, both positions having what might be called possibilities for politicians. He worked earnestly for Lincoln's re-election and a number of letters passed between him and the President directly. His effort in her husband's behalf and the fact that he was a man of charming personality made him a valued friend of Mrs. Lincoln.

Secretary Welles wrote a description of Wakeman in his diary: ". . . he is affable, insinuating, and pleasant, though not profound nor reliable . . . Wakeman believes that all is fair and proper in party operations which can secure by any means certain success, and supposes that every one else is the same."

On March 20, 1865, Mrs. Lincoln wrote this politician a letter worthy of examination. Beginning "Hon. Mr. Wakeman. My Dear Sir," she told him she was sending him a picture of little Taddie, adding that "it may interest your children." She continued: "We are having charming weather & I am most happy to say, that my blessed Husband's health has much improved." Lincoln was in poor health at this time and much depressed, and Mary was worried about him. The letter told of their going to the opera with Mr. Sumner, where they "had a very gay little time," and Mr. Lincoln, throwing off his heavy manner, made himself "very, very agreeable." She and her husband were going down to the front that week; that was *"entre nous,"* she said and added: "I gladly seize on any change that will benefit him."

She made mysterious reference to an offer Mr. L. made to Mr. B. Mr. Wakeman must give W. to understand that she regretted that Mr. B. did not accept the offer. Without going into the personnel and tangled intrigues of those who were playing the political game in New York, it may be mentioned that W. could possibly have been Thurlow Weed, a powerful New York politician of whom Wakeman was a devoted follower. It has been suggested that Mr. B. was James Gordon Bennett, editor of the New York *Herald*, who had recently declined Lincoln's offer of a ministry to France.

In March 1951 six more letters of Mrs. Lincoln to Abram Wakeman came to light. They are apparently similar to the letter just mentioned. As this is being written they are not yet available to investigators. But we know from Mrs. Lincoln's own words that she considered Wakeman one of the politicians who, according to her twisted notion, ought to help her pay her debts. She wrote later mentioning the "lucrative office" he had received from Lincoln, and expressing the idea that he should in return give financial assistance to her.

Mrs. Lincoln's idea that thriving politicians should help her pay her debts stemmed from her irrationality about money but it was simple and logical to her. Certain New York politicians had been delighted to give expensive presents to her, such as the handsome carriage and span of horses she had received from some of them early in the Presidency. There are indications that politicians did help her pay her debts. The newspaper of which Thurlow Weed was editor stated later that she had received large sums of money from contributors in New York even *"before"* Lincoln's death, and probably without his knowledge." These politicians did not know that Mrs. Lincoln was mentally ill but they did know that she had a considerable and dangerous knowledge of what they had been doing politically.

It is a painful fact that Mrs. Lincoln's obsessions had entangled her in a wretched situation in 1864. According to Mrs. Keckley the deluded First Lady even deliberately planned to "be clever" to unscrupulous men in order to get their influence for Lincoln's re-election. Then she meant to drop them. It was a game Lincoln would never have sanctioned but he did not know of it, and she did not intend to tell him until the election was over. She had always felt that his goodness and honesty were taken advantage of by unprincipled men and that she had to look out for him.

Time, as always, would make her realize her folly. As usual we have her own acknowledgment of her fault and her regret. Five years after Lincoln's re-election, when she was living in desolation, she was to write her dear friend, Mrs. Orne: "If I had not formerly ... allowed my thoughts to dwell so much upon that *sea of trouble,* (politics) perhaps such *perfect solitude* unattended by even a *menial,* would not now be mine. All that I ever did was actuated by the purest motives, but where there are designing wicked men & I *truly* may say women—such acts are so often misinterpreted— A deep interest in my idolized husband & Country alone caused me—ever to trouble myself, about other than, womanly matters."

Mary Lincoln was playing with fire in 1864. Her nerves had "gone to pieces," as Lincoln had realized. She was subject to "wayward impulsive moods" in which she "was apt to say and do things that wounded him deeply," said Mrs. Keckley, who recognized how "very tenderly" Lincoln loved his wife. After the outbursts were over, Mary as always was deeply sorry. It was her old failing of Springfield days but in the White House the hysterics seem to have been better kept behind the scenes.

There is a remote story that once when Lincoln made an impromptu speech, Mary expressed her strong disapproval of it afterwards in the hearing of Governor Richard Oglesby. This was not so much a loss of self-control as a habit of speaking her mind in emphatic terms. The tale was said to have been told by Governor Oglesby to an Illinois crony "with whom he sometimes talked and drank all night." Drinking all night is a better basis for croniness than for accuracy of statement. Also Governor Oglesby had a dispute with Mrs. Lincoln in June 1865 in which he failed to have his way; did his telling of the incident follow that date when he had a grievance? The account came through Oglesby's crony; it is indirect but the point of it, that Mrs. Lincoln would at times blurt out her feelings in extreme terms, is indisputable. Lincoln's speech was really a brief declination to make a speech. She was possibly disappointed that he really said nothing at all. She always wanted him to appear at his best. This outburst is one of the few, if not the only one, semi-public enough to leave some sort of record until we come to March 1865.

When Election Day, November 8, finally came, it was dark and stormy as the fears in Mary Lincolns' heart. Noah Brooks, going to the White House in the afternoon, found it almost deserted and the President alone. Lincoln was worried and anxious about the outcome and "entreated" Brooks to stay with him all afternoon. With this understanding friend he was able to relax and he told Brooks an incident involving Tad and a turkey which happened earlier in the day. The original destination of the turkey when brought to the White House had been a platter but this became impossible when Tad made a pet of him and named him Jack. On Election Day Jack, revealing a taste for politics, had strolled over to a nearby camp where the soldiers were casting their votes. Tad, bursting into his father's office, dragged him to the window to see the soldiers "voting for Lincoln and Johnson." Lincoln noticed the turkey stalking about the polls and asked whether Jack was voting. "No," answered Tad quickly, "he is not of age."

About seven in the evening the President splashed through rain and mud to the War Department to get the election returns by telegraph. Mary remained in the White House, her nerves tense with anxiety. When encouraging news began to trickle over the wires her husband promptly sent a report to her, remarking to those gathered there with him, "She is more anxious than I." About midnight it was possible for her to relax, for it was clearly indicated that Lincoln had been re-elected. About two in the morning a crowd came to serenade Lincoln's empty chamber at the White House and a messenger was sent to fetch him from the telegraph office. He made a graceful speech from a White House window saying he had no sense of personal triumph but gave "thanks to the Almighty for this evidence of the people's resolution to stand by free government and the rights of humanity."

The day after the election Lincoln told Brooks of a strange experience he had had four years earlier. According to the President's words as promptly recorded by Brooks, the incident had occurred just after his election in 1860. Returning home weary late in the day he had thrown himself on a lounge in his chamber. He could see himself reflected in a mirror opposite and then he noticed his reflection had two faces, one paler than the other. The incident made him feel uncomfortable. He told his wife about it and she was worried, for the dark thought came to her that this might be a sign that he would be twice elected and the paleness of the second face an indication he would not live through the second term. When Lincoln had strange dreams, usually she expressed the opinion that there was nothing in dreams, but this incident was different. It gave her the unhappy impression that it was a warning of disaster. When Brooks mentioned the matter to her, she was greatly surprised that the President had told the story. Seeing that it was a distressing subject Brooks said no more about it. Mary did not like to bring the chilling augury to the surface of her mind; she preferred to leave it in the depths of her consiousness along with all the other dark fears that constantly lurked there.

Now that the excitement and elation of the election was over, she was as worried as ever. When Mrs. Keckley congratulated her, she answered with a sigh: "Thank you, Elizabeth; but now that we have won the position, I almost wish it were otherwise. Poor Mr. Lincoln is looking so broken-hearted, so completely worn out, I fear he will not get through the next four years."

The day after the election Lincoln said to Noah Brooks: "I should be the veriest shallow and self-conceited blockhead upon the footstool, if in my discharge of the duties that are put upon me in this place, I should hope to get along without the wisdom that comes from God, and not from men." The election brought forth fresh expressions of his deepening religious faith. To Mrs. Keckley he said when she congratulated him: "Madam Elizabeth I don't know whether I should feel thankful or not. The position brings with it many trials. We do not know what we are destined to pass through But God will be with us all. I put my trust in God."

He had let himself be guided by that divine power in regard to the issuing of the Emancipation Proclamation. At the meeting of his cabinet to discuss that momentous

question in September 1862 he had told them, somewhat
hesitatingly, that shortly before, when the military situation was critical, he had made a promise to himself and
his Maker that if the rebel army was driven out of Maryland, he would issue the Proclamation. "The rebel army
is now driven out," he said, "and I am going to fulfill
that promise." It was almost as if he had asked a question as to the divine will. With conflicting advice being
forced upon him from all sides and a hundred facets to
every move he must make, decision was difficult. "I
know that the Lord is always on the side of the right," he
had said in the early days of the war; "but it is my constant anxiety and prayer that I and this nation may be on
the Lord's side."

Lincoln talked much to Noah Brooks about his religion
and several times mentioned "the change which had
come upon him." An incident in 1864 offers a sharp
focus on that change. That summer the loved old friend
of his youth, Joshua Speed, came to Washington and
the Lincolns invited him out to spend the night at the
Soldiers' Home. Joshua remembered Lincoln in early life
as "a skeptic"—that is, as one who raised questions
about religion and tried to reason things out. He found
that the youthful inquirer had come a long way.

Arriving at the Soldiers' Home toward evening, Speed
found the President sitting near a window intently reading his Bible. As Speed told it: "Approaching him I said,
'I am glad to see you so profitably engaged.' 'Yes' said
he, 'I am profitably engaged.' 'Well,' said I, 'if you have
recovered from your skepticism, I am sorry to say that
I have not.' Looking me earnestly in the face, and placing
his hand on my shoulder, he said, 'You are wrong Speed,
take all of this book upon reason that you can, and the
balance on faith, and you will live and die a happier
and better man.'"

Perhaps the two old friends felt a slight constraint
that the years had brought a difference of opinion where
once they had held the same views. Lincoln had confided
his early gropings to Joshua, but it was to Noah Brooks
that he spoke fully about his matured religious beliefs.
"His language seemed not that of an inquirer," wrote
Brooks, "but of one who had a prior settled belief in the
fundamental doctrines of the Christian religion. . . . He
said, too, that after he went to the White House he kept

up the habit of daily prayer. . . . In many conversations with him, I absorbed the firm conviction that Mr. Lincoln was at heart a Christian man, believed in the Saviour, and was seriously considering the step which would formally connect him with the visible Church on earth."

Did Mary urge him to join the church? That must be a matter of conjecture. But it is known that she loved her church, that the narrow uncomfortable pew at Springfield had deep, sweet associations for her, that she turned to her religion for strength and comfort. It is reasonable to suppose that she wanted her husband united with herself in church membership as they were united in other matters. Later, when explaining her husband's Christianity and defending it against attack, it will be found that the wife's testimony as to her husband's religion was to prove the most poignant of all.

chapter 27

"AS ARDENT AN ABOLITIONIST"

Both Lincoln's religion and statesmanship had ripened
during the first four years in the White House. Had similar changes been taking place in any of Mary's views?
After Willie's death she was impaired and her obsession about money grew constantly worse. In most matters, however, her quick mind remained normal but
some of her attitudes had undergone transformation.
She was by 1864 a very different woman from the lighthearted housewife who had come to Washington. The
influence of certain personalities, momentous events, and
the all-pervading tragedy of war and death had affected
her, even as, in a different sense, they had molded an
Illinois lawyer into a great statesman. Both she and her
husband had undergone a shifting in their attitude toward slavery. We have come to the amazing and hitherto
neglected story of Mrs. Lincoln as abolitionist.

The warmhearted young girl in Kentucky had loved
the colored house servants and had abhorred the cruelties
of slavery. She had grown up under the influence of those
who believed in compensated emancipation and she married a man who believed in this method of gradually abol-
ishing slavery.

But there were in the country many humanitarian people whose indignation at the moral evil of slavery burned
like a flame. They wanted quick action. Some of these
abolitionists had become martyrs to the cause. Theodore
Weld faced hostile mobs so often it became almost routine; Elijah Lovejoy was shot by antiabolitionists. It has
been noted that Mary in 1856 took care to say that her
husband was not an abolitionist. It was a group that was
hated and reviled. To belong to it would have been detri-
mental to Lincoln's political plans. As so often there were
high-minded men who were selflessly fighting for an
ideal they believed in, and not-so-high-minded politicians using the cause for political manipulation. In 1864

we find the same Mrs. Lincoln who eight years before had been so careful to keep her husband's name clear of the hated term saying: "Mr. Sumner says he wishes my husband was as ardent an abolitionist as I am."

Charles Sumner had a great deal to do with the change. This outstanding senator from Massachusetts had become an intimate at the White House, and a warm congenial friendship had developed between him and the First Lady. His appearance and personality were both constructed along striking lines. He had the polish of an excellent Boston background and education. The Emily Posts of that era could hardly have found a single fault in his courtly manners and his knowledge of dress and etiquette. His mind was saturated with literary erudition and the culture that comes from extensive travel, qualities much appreciated and enjoyed by Mrs. Lincoln. He was a handsome, impressive, and to many people an irritating man.

Lincoln was said to have remarked that Sumner was just his idea of a bishop, but he liked him and perhaps got out of him that special amusement which a person with a sense of humor gets from one who has none. Sumner had rendered statesmanlike aid in avoiding war with England in 1861 and the Lincolns had that reason to be grateful to him.

The Boston senator's dignity was so important to him that he once remarked that he never allowed himself, "even in the privacy of his own chamber, to fall into a position which he would not take in his chair in the Senate." He carefully rehearsed his speeches with gestures in front of a pier glass in his room, before their impressive and pompous delivery in public. He was a stuffy man in a stuffy age. Sandburg describes him on the Senate floor: "Sumner rose to heights of stubborn granite and grandeur; also he sprawled in puddles of the ridiculous and the asinine." But his convictions, irritating in their self-righteous expression, were sincere. He believed profoundly in the abolition of slavery and the betterment of the Negro.

Sumner visited with the Lincolns almost constantly. He attended their receptions, he went to the opera with them, he accompanied them on a trip. Mrs. Lincoln, always ready to indulge her love of literary expression in letters, wrote to him frequently. The closeness of the

friendship appears in her own words when she was looking back later to the days "When good Senator Harris would
come in our drawing room so frequently in the W.[hite]
H.[ouse] & finding Mr. S. would say in his cheerful way
— 'Ah Sumner we are sure of finding you here.' And S.
would often laugh & reply— 'This is the first administration in which I have ever felt disposed to visit *the house*
and I consider it a *privilege.*'" Mrs. Lincoln was flattered
that so important a man found her entertaining and
sought her out: "And *I* was pleased, knowing he visited
no other lady. His time was so immersed in his business. And that cold & haughty looking man to the world
would insist upon my telling him all the news & we
would have such frequent & delightful conversations &
often late in the evening— My darling husband would
join us & they would laugh together, like *two* school
boys."

Mary Lincoln's many letters to Charles Sumner suggest the topics discussed in these friendly and informal
chats; the letters deal with books, operas, poems and
poets, political and military news, and the great cause of
abolition. She wrote a letter of introduction for two colored people, "very genteel & intelligent persons," who
would call to see him as one whom all their race had "so
much cause, to honor . . ." The same letter contains her
expression of sorrow over the death of an outstanding
abolitionist, Owen Lovejoy; she felt he could ill be spared
from the crusade. "Our friend, whom we all *so* loved &
esteemed, has so suddenly & unexpectedly passed away—
Mr. Lovejoy! An all wise power, directs these dispensa-
tions, yet it appears to our weak & oftentimes erring
judgments, '*He* should have died *hereafter.*'" An outline
of the personality of Lincoln's wife may be drawn from
her letters to Sumner; they show her graciousness, her
animation, her intelligent interests, her profound beliefs, her gift of literary expression. Even her shortcom-
ing of hasty word and action crops out in two letters of
apology: "Words, are scarcely an atonement, for the inadvertent manner, in which I addressed you on yesterday,
therefore, I pray you, accept this little peace offering, for
your table, a few fresh flowers, brought up, by the gardener."

She never learned what her husband knew so well:
that it is sometimes advisable to hold back a letter for

second judgment. Once she had to apologize to Sumner "for having written you so candid & as it *now* appears, so unnecessary a letter, as I did, a few days since. I regretted writing you, immediately after the note was sent..." The amende honorable was gracefully expressed. The letter dealt with rumors of a possible appointment which she opposed and against which she wanted Sumner to use his influence. She thought there was a chance that certain men were seeking to have General N. P. Banks put into the cabinet. The rumor was thin and the appointment most unlikely, but because Banks was not ardent for abolition and because *"true* friends" were writing her "frequently" to "deplore such a prospect," she wanted Sumner's help in preventing such an appointment. She felt the matter so intensely that she wrote the senator, though aware that she may have been going beyond her province and doing something "unbecoming in *me*." Her zeal for abolitionism is unmistakably evident in this correspondence.

An observing reporter justly remarked that Mrs. Lincoln's long and close friendship with Sumner was in itself an answer to the slander that she was in sympathy with the South and slavery.   •

Friendship with another outstanding personality had much effect on Mrs. Lincoln's abolitionism. Sumner was in close touch with various people who were working for abolition. Probably he was the one who told the First Lady about an ardent champion of the cause, a fiery little woman journalist and platform speaker named Jane Grey Swisshelm. She had been editor of several papers advocating abolition, and Sumner had been her personal friend and a faithful subscriber to her Pittsburgh *Saturday Visiter*. Mrs. Swisshelm abhorred slavery with all her heart and fought it aggressively with a trenchant pen. Her literary output, her crusade for abolition, and her work in hospitals were all factors to engage Mrs. Lincoln's interest and she was anxious to meet the plucky little woman who had done so much in the antislavery movement.

But Jane, owing to the prevailing unfavorable impression about the First Lady, had no wish whatever to meet Mrs. Lincoln. The journalist had gone early in 1863 to Washington, where, like certain other patriotic women, she gave what aid she could to the wounded soldiers. She presents a fearful picture of conditions in Washington hospitals in her autobiography and she also tells therein of her first meeting with Mrs. Lincoln.

Some of Mrs. Swisshelm's friends wanted her to go to a White House reception but she protested that she did not want to meet the President, for she had no respect for him and considered him an obstructionist to abolition. He was not radical or precipitate enough to suit a firebrand like herself. She also objected to meeting Mrs. Lincoln, whom she despised as a Southerner and had heard spoken of as a Confederate spy. Jane was finally persuaded to attend the reception but as a gesture of contempt she refrained from dressing up, went in her old clothes and kept her coat over her arm. She tells what followed: "I watched the President and Mrs. Lincoln receive. His sad, earnest, honest face was irresistible in its plea for confidence, and Mrs. Lincoln's manner was so simple and motherly, so unlike that of all Southern women I had seen, that I doubted the tales I had heard."

Mrs. Swisshelm had had a hard life and had rubbed up against all kinds of people. Experience had taught her how to size a person up. Here is her first judgment about Mrs. Lincoln: "Her head was not that of a conspirator. She would be incapable of a successful deceit, and whatever her purposes were, they must be known to all who knew her."

It had been Jane's intention merely to watch at the reception and not to meet the Presidential couple; it tells quite a bit about the personality of both that she suddenly changed her mind. She was horrified at Lincoln's ordeal of handshaking: "I could not resist going to him with the rest of the crowd, and when he took my hand I said: 'May the Lord have mercy on you, poor man, for the people have none.'" Lincoln laughed heartily at this frank sympathy. "When I came to Mrs. Lincoln, she did not catch the name at first, and asked to hear it again, and a sudden glow of pleasure lit her face, as she held out her hand, and said how very glad she was to see me. I objected to giving her my hand because my black glove would soil her white one; but she said: 'Then I shall preserve the glove to remember a great pleasure, for I have long wished to see you.'"

Jane was completely won over. "I understood at once I had met one with whom I was in sympathy. No polite-

ness could have summoned that sudden flash of pleasure.
Her manner was too simple and natural to have any art
in it; and why should she have pretended a friendship
she did not feel? Abolitionists were at a discount. . . . I
recognized Mrs. Lincoln as a loyal, liberty-loving woman,
more staunch even than her husband in opposition to
the Rebellion and its cause, and as my very dear friend
for life."

Dear friends they were as long as Mary Lincoln lived.
Both were ardent in their affections and dislikes and
in their loyalties; both hated cruelty and injustice. At the
reception Jane had wondered what caused Mrs. Lincoln
"to give one of her brightest smiles of the evening to a
little, old woman, noted for nothing but abolitionism . . ."
On further acquaintance with the wife of the President
she came to the conclusion that abolitionism was the
answer; "it was simply as an Abolitionist that she hon-
oured me with her friendship and confidence at a time
when she held the proudest social position in the world,
and I had not the means to get a second dress. She must
have known I was poor; but nothing in our intercourse
ever reminded me that my $10 must go as far as her
$1,000; and the ground of her friendship was my sym-
pathy with her husband. I never knew a woman who
more completely merged herself in her husband. Whatever aid or counsel she gave him, in her eyes his acts
were his own, and she never sought any of the credit due
to them."

In her work in Washington Jane Swisshelm frequently
conferred with and appealed to Mrs. Lincoln. When a
little group of patriotic women wished to organize a society to furnish the army with female nurses, Jane, who
knew firsthand the neglect in the ghastly wards of the
wounded, went to the First Lady. "She was willing to
coöperate, and I went to Secretary Stanton, who heard
me," but he explained the complications that would
arise with thousands of untrained women pressing their
services upon the government.

Jane's strong-minded individualism tended to be impatient with the rules and regulations, especially if the
suffering of a patient in the hospital was involved. She
clashed with Dorothea Dix, superintendent of nurses
in Washington, who threatened to have the outspoken
little reformer arrested. Jane gave her the lofty reply:

"I shall not be sorry Miss Dix, if you do; for then I shall apply to my friends, Mrs. Abraham Lincoln and Secretary Stanton, and have your authority tested." No more was said of arrest, probably to Jane's disappointment.

Mrs. Swisshelm was a friend and fellow worker of Mrs. H. C. Ingersoll, who, as has been related, called upon a Mrs. Lincoln she despised from hearsay and, like Jane herself, was completely won over by personal contact with the First Lady. Mrs. Ingersoll shared Jane's antislavery sentiments, and she too found Mrs. Lincoln's views on the subject congenial. "Of slavery, and her own experience of it, while she lived in a slave state," wrote Mrs. Ingersoll, "she gave me some very interesting recitals, and her expressions were strong enough to satisfy any abolitionist." Both women were delighted with Mrs. Lincoln's devotion to the cause. Mrs. Swisshelm summed it up that "she was more radically opposed to slavery" than her husband and she "urged him to Emancipation, as a matter of right, long before he saw it as a matter of necessity." One gathers that Lincoln's wife would have had him issue the proclamation earlier. The radical element of Lincoln's party, with whom Mrs. Swisshelm was in sympathy, was impatient at his deliberation and his waiting until military victory and other factors made the time ripe for the event.

Mrs. Swisshelm's mention of Secretary Stanton brings up a most unexpected friendship. That she should be allied with Stanton, who belonged to the radical wing of the Republican party, was logical, as that group advocated abolition; but that Mrs. Lincoln should become a friend of Stanton, the pepper pot of Lincoln's cabinet table, is surprising. Offhand it would have been supposed that Stanton's record and characteristics would have made this impossible. He had been a Democrat and antagonistic to Lincoln before he became Secretary and he often failed to treat Lincoln with the respect due to a President. Stanton personally was irascible, rude, and contentious, dictatorial, capable at times of intrigue and cruelty, an unpredictable man whom many people cordially detested and avoided at all costs. It follows that there were numerous pungent descriptions of him. A mild one with considerable flavor was given by Lincoln's country cousin, Dennis Hanks, who visited the White House in 1863. Stanton, said Dennis, was "a frisky little

Yankee with a short coat-tail... too fresh altogether."

Stanton and Mrs. Lincoln had their clashes at first. We have seen that she needled him with a sharp reference to the rebels getting away at Fort Stevens; she laid the responsibility for this on him as Secretary of War. It has been said that she sent him books and clippings describing such an exacting and disagreeable person as he was. But Stanton himself, in all friendliness toward her, told the incident that won her over and created a certain understanding between them.

An individual whom he designated as "one of those indescribable half loafers, half gentlemen" came to Stanton's office with a card from Mrs. Lincoln requesting that the bearer be made a commissary. Stanton snapped out: "There is no place for you, and if there were, the fact that you bring me such a card would prevent my giving it to you"; with this he tore the card up. The next day the same individual appeared with a formal letter from Mrs. Lincoln making the same request. Again the visitor was rebuffed in harsh terms and the letter also was torn up, one suspects with considerable violence.

Stanton then betook himself to see the First Lady and told her he had called in regard to the card and letter she had sent him. She replied: "Yes, Mr. Secretary, I thought that as wife of the President I was entitled to ask for so small a favor." Stanton replied: "Madam, we are in the midst of a great war for national existence. Our success depends upon the people. My first duty is to the people of the United States; my next duty to protect your husband's honor, and your own. If I should make such appointments, I should strike at the very root of all confidence of the people in the government, in your husband, and you and me." Her answer came quickly: "Mr. Stanton, you are right, and I will never ask you for anything again," and, said Stanton, "she never did."

It is a little-known story and one to ponder in what it shows: Mrs. Lincoln's reasonableness, and her instant surrender when she was convinced that Stanton was trying to save the Union and protect her husband. She gave Stanton her confidence henceforth and years later one finds her grieving over his death, and writing to a friend: "I, too, dearly loved Mr Stanton & greatly appreciated the services he rendered his country, our loved, bleeding land, during the trying rebellion." Her favor-

able opinion may throw new light on Lincoln's tolerance
of that irritating individual.

Mrs. Lincoln's many trips to New York and especially
Boston, where she met antislavery people, undoubtedly
contributed to her changing attitude. This was especially true of her visit to those cities in the fall of 1862
when Mrs. Keckley was with her trying to raise funds
for refugees from slavery. This remarkable colored
woman herself probably played her part in molding Mrs.
Lincoln into an abolitionist. As a slave Mrs. Keckley
had been shamefully mistreated. If she related her sufferings to the First Lady, who loved her and depended
upon her, the natural result would have been an intense
resentment against an institution which made such cruelties possible. At all events Mrs. Lincoln gave her sympathetic help to Mrs. Keckley's effort in raising funds for
the Negroes and that itself led to abolitionist contacts.

The greatest influence upon Mary's changed views was
her husband's deliberately worked-out decision to free
the slaves. As Mrs. Swisshelm said, Lincoln's wife fundamentally merged her life in his. She could become impatient, scold him and argue with him, but in the end his
considered action was the most important thing with
her. As the stirring events of the war moved forward and
Lincoln first announced to his cabinet, and then, with
careful timing, issued the Emancipation Proclamation,
Mary's spirit was caught, like that of other abolitionists,
in a great moral surge for justice to what she called "all
the oppressed colored race." Two letters give something
of the enthusiasm and sense of gathering drama as the
date for the definitive proclamation approached. Two
days before that event Mrs. Lincoln wrote Sumner asking for the address of the aged, distinguished Josiah
Quincy in Boston. Sumner was the best person possible
to put her in touch with antislavery Bostonians. The
wife wanted to send a picture of her husband, about to
become the Great Emancipator, to Mr. Quincy, a little
gesture in public relations. On January 2, 1863, the day
after the great event, Eliza S. Quincy, daughter of Josiah,
wrote Mrs. Lincoln telling her of the thrill and exultation when the news that the slaves were to be freed arrived. A vast audience was assembled to greet the proclamation when it first came over the wires. "It was a sublime moment," wrote Miss Quincy—"the thought of the

millions upon millions of human beings whose happiness was to be affected by the words of President Lincoln, was almost overwhelming. . . . It was a day & an occasion never to be forgotten.—I wish you & the President could have enjoyed it with us here."

There was a great uplift to thousands of liberty-loving minds on January 1; preachers, orators, poets raised their voices in rejoicing over the triumph of human freedom. Eliza Quincy thought that the "'Declaration of Emancipation' . . . must rank in the future with that of Independence,—& the 1st of January 1863 with the 4th of July 1776."

Few expressed what that day meant to them more feelingly than Lincoln's wife: "How admirable, is Whittier's, description of the thraldom of Slavery and the emancipation, from the great evil, that has been so long allowed, to curse the land. The decree, has gone forth, that 'all men are free,' and all the perfidious acts . . . cannot eradicate, the seal, that has been placed on the 'Emancipation Proclamation.' It is a rich & precious legacy, for my sons & one for which, I am sure, and *believe*, they will always bless God & their father."

An understanding friendship with the colored people themselves had been the cornerstone on which Mary Lincoln's abolitionism had been built. The little girl of Lexington, Kentucky, whose tender heart had been horrified at cruelty to slaves, had come a long way. Throughout that way her considerate affection for colored people had been unbroken. It had that special quality which comes to those fortunate ones whose early memories include the ministering of gentle brown hands and the looking up trustfully into benevolent, dark-skinned faces. Item by item one can trace Mary Lincoln's consideration for the Negro. It was revolutionary to many minds at the time that the President and Mrs. Lincoln should open the White House grounds to a Negro Sunday school festival, making every possible arrangement for the enjoyment of the visitors, or that they should together graciously receive a colored nurse who brought a gift as a testimonial of the appreciation of her race.

The colored people in Washington knew they had genuine friends in President and Mrs. Lincoln. Perhaps that knowledge was what gave some of them courage to linger outside when the New Year's reception of '65 was taking place. When the visitors of pomp and circumstance had departed, the group of Negroes timidly pressed forward and entered the White House to greet their President. Lincoln's spirit rose to meet the occasion with such a hearty welcome that the brown faces shone both with laughter and tears. The Lincolns had the courage and conviction to do these things and Mary Lincoln gave her husband full co-operation. Their attitude was one and the same.

The friendship of the Lincolns with that notable Negro orator Frederick Douglass makes a heart-warming story. Douglass left a record of an incident which occurred on the evening of Lincoln's second inauguration. In his own words: "For the first time in my life, and I suppose the first time in any colored man's life, I attended the reception of President Lincoln . . ." As Douglass approached the White House entrance, he was seized by two policemen and forbidden to enter. He told them that the President would want to see him, "bolted" by them and so got inside, where he was promptly seized by two other policemen. They were conducting him to a window which had a plank that led outside, when he called to a friend to appeal to the President.

Douglass was sure of his welcome by Lincoln. A few months before the President had invited him to "come up and take a cup of tea" with him and had sent the Executive carriage to bring the Negro to the White House, an amazing procedure to many minds of 1864. Douglass later said that Lincoln was one of the few white men with whom he ever passed an hour that failed to remind him in some way, before the interview was over, that he was a Negro.

The result of the quick appeal to the President at the inauguration reception was an invitation to come at once to the East Room. The splendor of the scene there—"A perfect sea of beauty and elegance"—was deeply impressive to the colored man's unaccustomed eyes. When Lincoln saw him approaching, his face lighted up and he called out, "Here comes my friend Douglass." As the President shook his hand cordially he said: "Douglass, I saw you in the crowd to-day listening to my inaugural address. There is no man's opinion that I value more than yours: what do you think of it?" The colored man, conscious of the thousands waiting to shake hands with the President, had to be brief: "Mr. Lincoln, it was a sacred effort." Lincoln answered, "I am glad you liked it."

Some there were at the reception who would have admired, while others would have despised, the President for thus greeting a Negro. By none, however, least of all by the distinguished colored leader, could it have been forgotten. It was a momentary meeting, this last occasion when Douglass saw the President to speak to him, but it was a significant incident in both their lives.

In the confusion of the crowd, for it was one of the largest receptions the Lincolns held, Douglass was not presented to Mrs. Lincoln. She asked her husband about this omission later and he explained that he thought Mr. Douglass had been introduced to her. Both regretted the oversight. But she came later to know Douglass well. Theirs was a lasting friendship and he left eloquent testimony in her behalf. Naturally, in the political smearing directed against Lincoln's wife, along with the vicious accusation that she was in sympathy with the rebels, went the story that she was opposed to emancipation. Twice in printed statements Frederick Douglass set right this "great injustice" to her. The time was to come in Mary Lincoln's widowhood when she gave treasured mementos to certain colored friends who had loved her husband. To Frederick Douglass she sent a favorite walking stick of the President, saying that no one would appreciate it more than he would. In that time of her desolation he was to prove himself a true friend.

Lincoln's friendship to the colored race has been well fixed in the public mind. That his wife was at one with him in this matter needs emphasis. The colored people themselves knew it. A member of that race collecting in recent times the folklore of his people from his "interviews with the old folk" wrote: "I learned that no colored servant who knew her ever thought her actions crazy or that she had a mean disposition. . . . The old folks loved Mary Lincoln with a love that went with them to the tomb, and they thought of her as second only to the Emancipator."

Lincoln's two great services to his country were preserving the Union and freeing the slaves. Overwhelming evidence shows that in both vast endeavors and achievements his wife gave him her wholehearted and passionate support. It was not necessary that Mary Lincoln should have the philosophical insight of a statesman. Seldom indeed has that been expected of a President's wife. She had faith in the man she loved and championed his causes as her own. He stated that his paramount object was to save the Union. Throughout the war that saving of the Union was a life-and-death matter to her patriotic spirit. The letters of her widowhood are starred with her tributes to him for this achievement; always to her he was "the great & good man, who *so* faithfully served his bleeding country, & saved it from its rebel foes."

Her moving tribute to emancipation has been given. There is an appreciation of Lincoln's wider service to mankind in her beautifully worded letter of acknowledgment to a committee of French citizens who presented her a gold medal "in honor of the great man whose name you bear." The committee, which included Victor Hugo and other notables, offered the medal, as they wrote, "at the desire of upward of 40,000 French citizens." In a ceremony in Paris, December 1, 1866, the medal was received in Mrs. Lincoln's behalf by John Bigelow. Mrs. Lincoln wrote in answer: "I cannot express to you the emotions with which I receive this manifestation of the feelings of so many thousands of your fellow Countrymen. So grand a testimonial to the memory of my husband, given in honor of his services in the cause of liberty, by those who labor in the same great Cause in another land, is deeply affecting . . ." This is Lincoln the great exponent of democracy.

One does not claim for Victorian Mary Lincoln a wisdom that went down the long reach of history. She took, womanlike, a short cut by her faith in the man she loved, and touched the verdict of the years.

chapter 28

CITY POINT

The year 1865 opened with a series of White House entertainments. The newspapers extended themselves in describing the brilliance of the receptions and the illustriousness of such guests as cabinet members, ambassadors, and generals. Mrs. Lincoln's costumes were described in minute detail: "heavy brocade purple silk, very richly trimmed with black velvet, over which was thrown a rich and exquisitely wrought black lace shawl," or "rich dress of pearl color, heavily trimmed with the richest black lace, with a neat head-dress composed of a coronet of exquisite flowers." Such accounts furnished further incentive to the First Lady in her extravagant buying.

But apparently some economies had been introduced. Senator Chandler, one of the radical group who constantly opposed Lincoln, wrote his wife his opinion about being all dressed up with nothing to eat. The expense of feeding the masses who came to the White House must have grown to enormous proportions, but Chandler blamed Mrs. Lincoln: "If she will prepare refreshments I have no objection to a dress parade, but to fix up for nothing is in my judgment a humbug." He concluded that "of all Stupid things White House receptions are the most so." This "Xanthippe in pants," as he was called, was hardly one to bring sweetness and light to a party himself.

In the ordeal of handshaking Lincoln remained his unaffected self. Sometimes he was almost boyish. He was overheard saying to Judge David Davis between handshakes: "I never knew until the other day how to spell the word 'maintenance.'" And syllable by syllable he spelled it to the judge between greetings to the long line of people passing by.

Among those who passed may have been some who had attended the first receptions of the Lincolns. They could have noted a great change in the faces of the Presidential pair. Behind the momentary social warmth of expression were two sad faces filled with weariness. The vigorous countenance of the fifty-two-year-old President who had assumed office in 1861 now had deep lines of sadness and strain; it had become thin, sick, and old. Yet behind the eyes shone a steady and unconquered spirit. The pictures of Mary up to 1862 had shown a woman with keen interest in living and a buoyant lift of the head. When she was photographed clad in mourning for Willie, her face had a stunned look; the buoyancy was gone; her spirit had not, like his, come through its ordeals untouched.

For them both, worry piled upon worry. There was the question of Robert's entering the army upon which they had not agreed. It will be remembered that Mrs. Lincoln had urged that their eldest son finish college before enlisting. That excuse for delay no longer existed; Robert had graduated. On January 19, 1865, Lincoln wrote an embarrassed letter to General Grant. He asked that the general read and answer it as though the writer were not the President but only a friend. Of Robert, he wrote: "I do not wish to put him in the ranks, nor yet to give him a commission, to which those who have already served long are better entitled, and better qualified to hold. Could he, without embarrassment to you, or detriment to the service, go into your military family with some nominal rank, I, and not the public, furnishing his necessary means?"

Again Lincoln was caught on the horns of a cruel dilemma. He was fully aware that it was not fair or democratic to put his son in a safe berth when other men's sons were fighting and dying. Yet he had seen how Willie's death had impaired his wife. Knowing Mary's shattered state Emilie Helm had said that she believed if anything should happen to Lincoln, Robert, or Tad, it would kill her. Lincoln feared Mary's worry over danger to Robert might cause her further or complete breakdown.

He tried to be fair to General Grant as party to the action. If Grant found the request embarrassing, Lincoln wrote, he must say no without the least hesitation. The result was that Robert joined Grant's staff with the rank of captain. It was not a dangerous position but in his mother's emotions it was; the long-dreaded situation had come, Robert was in the army and that meant to her, as she wrote Charles Sumner, "our own Son, is daily participating or exposed to the battles..." It was another anxiety added to the many that were breaking her down physically and nervously.

To Robert, her first-born now grown to manhood, Mary was drawn more closely at this time because a romance was in the making for him. Mrs. Lincoln with her unfailing love for young people had taken a great liking to Senator Harlan's attractive daughter Mary. Lincoln was said to have told Stanton that he thought Mrs. Lincoln had picked out Mary Harlan for a daughter-in-law. There was certainly much that a sentimental mother could do in the way of inviting the Harlans (complete with daughter) to join a party or go on a trip, and Mrs. Lincoln did it. It was a good choice. The marriage, destined to take place three years later, was a devoted one and Mary was to give a mother's loving heart to Robert's wife.

In February the lovable and fatherly physician, Dr. Anson G. Henry, came to Washington to see Lincoln about an appointment. Mrs. Lincoln hoped passionately that their old friends, the Henrys, could be located near them. "Dr," she said to him, "Why cant you come to Washington with Mrs Henry, *we* would like very much to have you here, but I suppose I would be troubling you a good Deal." Her headaches and other ailments were so many now; what a comfort it would be to have the understanding physician who had known her since she was a girl. Dr. Henry replied it all depended upon the President and Lincoln's wife answered confidently: "Mr Lincoln wont refuse you any thing you ask him for I *know*."

She had been so glad to see Dr. Henry on his arrival that he had kissed her. He wrote his wife about it in playful and appealing fashion: "I wont tell you what I done when I first met Mrs. Lincoln, but you may *guess*. ... You will not I know get jealous of me. When you come to see Mr Lincoln, you will get even with me for he likes you quite as well if not better than I do his Wife." Tactful man!

Dr. Henry was older than the Lincolns but he felt a boyish thrill when he escorted Mrs. Lincoln to the Capitol to attend a joint meeting of both houses of Congress. The galleries were crowded and ladies were even sitting on the steps in the aisles. In the congestion at the door Dr. Henry became separated from the First Lady and was stopped by the doorkeeper. He explained that he was Mrs. Lincoln's escort, but doorkeepers are suspicious people and that did no good until an Illinois friend chanced by and vouched for him. Then, to use his own words, "The Door opened quickly, and the Door Keeper sung out at the top of his voice, 'Ladies make way for Doct. Henry,' and I clambered down and over them as best I could & took my seat by side of Mrs President with thousands of eyes turned upon me, No doubt asking themselves the question 'Who is Dr Henry?'" He wrote all this to his wife, "the one I love dearer than all on earth beside." Well might Mrs. Lincoln in writing to Mrs. Henry describe Lincoln and Dr. Henry as "two of the best men & the most devoted husbands" that two women ever possessed.

A letter of Dr. Henry's in March reveals that a change was in prospect as to Lincoln's private secretary. Noah Brooks, who had the best of intellectual and personal qualifications for the position, had become so loved and trusted a friend of both the Lincolns that the President was anxious to have him "take the place near him." Nicolay and Hay—the two went together—had failed to get along with a number of people, including the President's wife. Nicolay had maintained a distant but correct relationship with her; Hay's expressions indicate a more hotheaded attitude. Brooks gave Mrs. Lincoln respect, liking, and understanding; naturally she responded to this approach with her best self.

It happened that Noah Brooks was a good friend of Dr. Henry's. The latter wrote his wife: "I have been working ever since I have been here with Mrs. Lincoln to get Nickolay out as private Secretary and Mr. Brooks in his place." Lincoln of course appreciated the undoubted efficiency and devotion of Nicolay and Hay. He offered the former the post of consul at Paris but there was a period when, as Brooks said, "it appeared doubtful if Nicolay could be induced to go abroad ..." Lincoln wanted Brooks so much that he made every possible concession, even offering to let him continue his newspaper correspondence which paid as much as the position of secretary. This Brooks declined to do. The President felt that Brooks in taking the secretaryship would be making a financial sacrifice but Brooks expressed his own feeling to a friend: "I would have made myself poor for the sake of serving a man so dear to me . . ."

Finally Nicolay accepted the consulship, Hay was appointed secretary of the legation at Paris, and Brooks was to take up his duties as Lincoln's private secretary shortly after the inauguration.

That great event of March 4, 1865, was swiftly approaching. A platform had been erected on the east front of the Capitol as it had four years before. The city of Washington was preparing herself for her high moment just as hundreds of men and women were planning what they would wear to the historic revelries. Mrs. Lincoln was doubtless having fittings of her costume for the grand Inaugural Ball, a white satin trimmed in deep and priceless lace, with a point lace shawl to cover the white and shapely shoulders. Though the glow and thrill of the first inauguration were gone, she would play her part in the drama in queenly fashion.

March 4 dawned dark and rainy. The brilliant costumes of the spectators soon hung limp and bedraggled above wet and muddy feet. The difficulty of managing the crowds and the parade to the Capitol was greatly increased by the weather.

For the preliminary ceremony of the Vice-President taking the oath Mrs. Lincoln sat in the diplomatic gallery of the Senate. It proved to be a painful event, as Andrew Johnson, weak from recent illness, had bolstered his strength by alcoholic stimulant. The combination of weakness and drink resulted in his making something of a spectacle of himself, and Mrs. Lincoln ever after regarded him with intense dislike and suspicion.

After this painful scene the President, notables, and audience removed to the platform outside for the supreme event. As Lincoln stepped forward to deliver his inaugural address, the dark clouds broke and sudden brilliant sunshine illumined his face. Many of the crowd, interpreting this as an omen of peace and prosperity after four dark years of war, were profoundly stirred. That sudden illumination might also be taken as symbolic of the shining words Lincoln then spoke: "With malice toward none; with charity for all; with firmness in the right, as God gives us to see the right, let us strive on to finish the work we are in; to bind up the nation's wounds; to care for him who shall have borne the battle, and for his widow, and his orphan—to do all which may achieve and cherish a just and a lasting peace, among ourselves, and with all nations."

The usual crowded and exhausting reception at the White House took place that evening and the Inaugural Ball two days later. Noah Brooks noted that it "was a very handsome affair; but its beauty was marred by an extraordinary rush of hungry people, who fairly mobbed the supper-tables, and enacted a scene of confusion whose wildness was similar to some of the antics of the Paris Commune." There seems to have been good reason for Mrs. Lincoln to discontinue refreshments at her receptions.

Chief Justice Chase wrote to Mrs. Lincoln on Inauguration Day and sent her the Bible upon which Lincoln had taken the oath. Both the book itself and the association would be sacred to her. Chase marked the page the President's lips had pressed, the twenty-seventh and twenty-eighth verses of the fifth chapter of Isaiah, beginning: "None shall be weary nor stumble among them; none shall slumber nor sleep . . ." The sleeplessness applied to Lincoln in the White House, but not the freedom from weariness; he was tired to the bone and far from well. Like Mary herself he now had severe headaches.

He had said to Joshua Speed about ten days before the inauguration: "I ought not to undergo what I so often do. I am very unwell now; my feet and hands of late seem to be always cold, and I ought perhaps to be in bed . . ." To Mrs. Harriet Beecher Stowe he had made a stronger statement: "I shall never live to see peace; this war is killing me." His depression was hard on Mary, who depended on him as a child does on a parent. Her worry ran through the letters she was writing at the time. Her dread of losing her husband combined with her unreasoning urge to buy, led to a strange act. About the early part of March she bought a thousand dollars' worth of mourning goods, perhaps a twisted kind of preparedness born of her sense of insecurity. It was a deed that indicated clearly both her anxiety and the degree to which her irrationality had progressed.

She thought a trip and change might help him. On March 19 she had mentioned in a letter to Sumner how she liked to get Lincoln away from his work when possible, so it seemed providential that about that time an invitation came from General Grant to visit his headquarters at City Point, Virginia. The war was drawing to a close with victory for the Union; it was an exhilarating moment to visit the front. Besides, Captain Robert Lincoln was there. His father wired him they were coming but to keep quiet about it. Mary wrote to Sumner on March 23: "The President & myself are about leaving for 'City Point,' and we cannot but devoutly hope, that change of air & rest, may have a beneficial effect on my good Husband's health."

Her anxiety fluctuated according to Lincoln's feelings day by day. "I am happy to say, that Mr Lincoln, is feeling much better to day," she wrote early in April, but she added a word showing how quickly he became exhausted; a trip through the hospitals a few days before, "although a labor of love, to him, fatigued him very much." Lincoln's face undoubtedly had at this time the sick and worn expression of his last photographs. Husband and wife, planning to go on that journey to City Point, were both breaking down; he physically, she physically and mentally. Her uneasiness about him added to her extreme nervousness.

Father, mother, and Tad left on the *River Queen* on March 23, 1865, as scheduled. During their stay at City Point they slept on the boat, anchored in the James River under the bluff on which Grant's headquarters were established, and ate their meals aboard except when they were guests of the general. Several days after their arrival a distressing episode occurred, one which has become widely known because of the accounts left by several officers who knew of it. Their stories differ somewhat. General Adam Badeau, whose record is perhaps the best known, even places the incident in the wrong year, saying it happened in 1864; he also indicates that it occurred on one day of the month while General Sherman places it on another. Checking these recollections against each other, one gets the following story.

On March 26 (to use Sherman's date) the Lincolns were to go to a grand review of a part of the Army of the James then commanded by Major General Edward O. C. Ord. Lincoln rode out from City Point to the review ground on horseback but Mrs. Lincoln, accompanied by Mrs. Grant, followed in an "ambulance," a half-open carriage with two seats besides that of the driver. This conveyance had to pass through swampy terrain over corduroy roads—that is, roads made up of the trunks of small trees. To make matters worse the tree trunks were of uneven size. Progress was slow and very bumpy. Mrs. Lincoln, fearing they would be late for the review, expressed a wish to go faster and General Horace Porter (then Colonel), one of her escorts, reluctantly gave the order to the driver. As General Porter tells it: "We were still on a corduroyed portion of the road, and when the horses trotted the mud flew in all directions, and a sudden jolt lifted the party clear off the seats, jammed the ladies' hats against the top of the wagon, and bumped their heads as well. Mrs. Lincoln now insisted on getting out and walking; but as the mud was nearly hub-deep, Mrs. Grant and I persuaded her we had better stick to the wagon as our only ark of refuge."

What that blow on the head did to Mrs. Lincoln cannot now be determined. We know that she suffered intensely from migraine headaches and had injured her head cruelly in her carriage accident less than two years before. General Porter noticed that she "had suffered so much from the fatigue and annoyances of her overland trip that she was not in a mood to derive much pleasure from the occasion." The blow possibly started one of her headaches; at least we know that two days later she was ill.

With all this unfortunate attempt at haste the review had started by the time the ambulance arrived. Mrs. Ord, wife of the General, was strikingly handsome and a beautiful figure on horseback, "riding with extreme grace a spirited bay horse." Mrs. Lincoln found out that this attractive woman had ridden side by side with the President in the procession that went ahead of her. Many of the troops she thought had taken Mrs. Ord for the First Lady. Circumstances that day all conspired toward Mrs. Lincoln's exasperation; it was more than the ailing woman could take.

She had always been jealous, perhaps because at times she realized her own failings. Her jealousy had been aroused the day before by the mention that the President had given the wife of General Charles Griffin special permission to remain at the front. Perhaps that meant Lincoln had seen her alone; Mrs. Lincoln flared at the thought. She did not intend that her husband should see any woman alone. That idea had set her wild the day before; now when she found the beautiful Mrs. Ord had ridden beside the President in her place, Mrs. Lincoln went berserk.

It was all the officers who were escorting the carriage could do to keep the frenzied woman from jumping out of it. Mrs. Grant tried to pacify her and received some stinging remarks in return. At this point there was a halt and a young officer rode up and innocently tried to say something gay and cheerful. "The President's horse is very gallant, Mrs. Lincoln," he remarked brightly, "he insists on riding by the side of Mrs. Ord." Noticing that he had made a huge mistake, the young man speedily dropped behind.

When the ambulance arrived at its destination Mrs. Ord naturally came up to pay her respects, upon which Mrs. Lincoln loosed upon her such a flood of insulting language that she burst into tears. It was a distressing scene.

The First Lady remained in this abnormal and frenzied state of mind the rest of the day, berating Lincoln in the presence of others, creating scenes and acting like what she was, a woman temporarily out of her mind. Badeau with the perspective of later years referred to her as one "not knowing the purport of her own words or the result of her own deeds, or perhaps vainly struggling to restrain them both, and regretting in her saner intervals the very acts she was at other times unable to control." Lincoln, his eyes filled with pain, tried to quiet her, calling her "Mother" and speaking gently.

He knew she was a sick woman, at times not responsible for what she did; he knew also what her own agony would be when she recovered her balance and realized the painful spectacle she had made of herself. Not once before in the four years in the White House had she made a public outburst of this kind. She had those four years to her credit, but all the effort this unstable woman had put forth to make that record would be lost in this one incident. In the future if a person were to know only one thing about Mary Lincoln in the period of the Presidency it would in all likelihood be this incident.

What the sick and weary couple who had gone through so much together in mutual loyalty said to each other in the privacy of their stateroom is not known. One has no word of Mary's shame, her tears, her pain. When Grant and Sherman called on Lincoln on the *River Queen* next day, Mrs. Lincoln was not to be seen. When they called again the following day and inquired after her as a matter of courtesy, in the words of General Sherman, "the President went to her stateroom, returned, and begged us to excuse her, as she was not well." That was all he could ever in loyalty say and it was the simple comprehensive truth.

Leaving her husband and Tad at City Point, Mary went back to Washington for a brief stay. As to the reason for this return, she was said to have stated later: "Mr. Lincoln had a dream when down the river at City Point ... that the White House had burned up. Sent me up the river to see." There are details hidden here but there is no doubt that it was better for the overwrought woman to get away from the center of publicity at this time. Lincoln wired Secretary Stanton to have the coachman meet her at the wharf in Washington at eight o'clock on Sunday morning, April 2.

An old friend was on the boat. Carl Schurz wrote his wife on that very Sunday: "The first lady [*Landesmutter* in his German] was overwhelmingly charming to me [*über alle Massen liebenswürdig mit mir*]; she chided me for not visiting her, overpowered me with invitations, and finally had me driven to my hotel in her own state carriage. I learned more state secrets in a few hours than I could otherwise in a year. I wish I could tell them to you. She is an astounding [*erstaunliche*] person."

On arrival, Mary at once got off a message to her husband telling him she had landed safely and all was well, concluding: "Miss, Taddie & yourself very much— Perhaps, may return with a little party on Wednesday—give me all the news." The last was an unnecessary request because Lincoln sent her on that day two long telegrams giving all details of military developments, even copying into the first one a telegram he had received from Grant. His second wire contained the glorious news that Petersburg was completely enveloped by Union forces; the long war was drawing to a close. He did not fail to tell her that he and Tad were well and would be glad to see her and her party when she returned.

Mrs. Lincoln at once passed on the good news to Sumner, even enclosing in her letter the telegram she had just received from her husband. She invited Sumner to be one of the party when she went back. Her spirits were soaring with joy over the turn of events: "We have been within six miles of Richmond, *the promised land,* from which a proclamation *may* be issued, within the next two weeks, 'there is no such word as fail' *now!*".

She was joyfully assembling various friends to join her triumphal party. Mrs. Keckley asked to go along, as Petersburg was her old home, and of course Mrs. Lincoln said she would be delighted to have her. Senator Sumner and the Harlans (it was important to Robert to bring Mary Harlan) were in the group which left Washington by boat on Wednesday April 5. Mrs. Lincoln was very anxious to rejoin Lincoln at City Point; she sent a message en route to Secretary Stanton from Fort Monroe asking him if the President could not remain there "until we arrive." In the original manuscript her usually smooth handwriting shows nervousness and agitation. But alas for her high hopes, Lincoln with Tad had made the dramatic entry into Richmond by the time she and her party arrived, a great disappointment.

To console her the entire party of the *River Queen,* according to Mrs. Keckley, went to Richmond, and Mary had the exultation of visiting the Jefferson Davis mansion. But the fact that Lincoln had entered first without her remained a sore point. With considerable temper she squelched a young officer who was so untactful as to tell her how "pretty young ladies" had made a great ado over the President on that first entry.

The party also visited Petersburg, where Lincoln went through the hospitals. It was noticed how "infinitely tender" he was with the wounded soldiers but the experience left him tired and shaken.

On the way back to City Point by train Lincoln noticed a terrapin sunning himself by the roadside. He asked to have the train stopped and the terrapin brought in, whereupon he and Tad had a happy time watching the creature's ungainly movements. Mrs. Keckley's account leaves one a little in doubt as to which boyish observer enjoyed the performance more. Perhaps it was Lincoln's way of forgetting those hospital scenes.

chapter 29

LAST RIDE TOGETHER

In early April every effort seemed to exhaust the President. The day before the *River Queen* started back to Washington there was a review. Afterwards Lincoln said to his wife: "Mother, I have shaken so many hands to-day that my arms ache to-night. I almost wish I could go to bed now." Many a wife can guess how Mary's nerves tightened at his repeated signs of fatigue and illness.

But there was no rest for him. A few hours before the boat left, a military band came on board to serenade the President and his party. The Marquis de Chambrun had come to the *River Queen* as Lincoln's guest on April 6, so in his honor Lincoln suggested that the band play the "Marseillaise." They played it twice. To use the Frenchman's own words: "He then asked me if I had ever heard 'Dixie' . . . As I answered in the negative, he added: 'That tune is now Federal property; it belongs to us, and, at any rate, it is good to show the rebels that with us they will be free to hear it again.' He then ordered the somewhat surprised musicians to play it for us."

The Marquis de Chambrun made the trip back to Washington with the Lincolns. The *River Queen* docked at its Potomac wharf on the evening of April 9. The marquis, Senator Sumner, and the Lincolns drove home in the same carriage. Mrs. Lincoln was in a nervous, foreboding mood; she was strangely silent as they approached Washington. That underlying dread of assassination or harm to Lincoln could not be shaken off. Stanton had been very apprehensive about the President going to Richmond, where embittered foes could still lurk with vengeful purposes. Mary undoubtedly shared this anxiety and scenes of war and destruction had not served to diminish the feeling. Nor had that apprehension been relieved by an incident which occurred during their stay at City Point.

While driving along the James River the Lincolns had

come to an old country graveyard, quiet and lovely with the early flowers and tender green of springtime. Husband and wife got out of the carriage and walked together among the graves; and Lincoln, weary and feeling the sense of peace in such a resting place, said: "Mary, you are younger than I. You will survive me. When I am gone, lay my remains in some quiet place like this." How the words must have chilled her heart, which was always now afraid. She would remember his wish and see that it was carried out, even though it would bring down public vituperation upon her.

Her mood was dark with fears as the carriage from the wharf neared Washington. Suddenly she broke her silence by saying to the marquis, "That city is filled with our enemies." When the President heard this he "raised his arm and somewhat impatiently retorted: 'Enemies! We must never speak of that.'" But next day a great victory sent her spirits soaring. She wrote Sumner a letter that sang with joy and thankfulness: "In honor of this great & glorious day perhaps, the gardener has sent up to my rooms, an unusual supply of flowers & I have concluded to exercise my *rejoicing* spirit of the 'Consummation, so devoutly to be wished,' by having a bouquet left on the tables of yourself & the Marquis. Mr L—— told me the news, last night at ten oclock, that Lee & his Army, were in our hands & it would have been my delight, to have been able to send the communication to all of our recent travelling companions, well knowing how much sweeter your dreams would have been."

She gave a glimpse of the rejoicing citizens of Washington: "If possible, this is a happier day, than last Monday, the crowds around the house have been immense, in the midst of the bands playing, they break forth into singing." But there are certain sad thoughts that come with the rejoicing at the end of any war. Mary coninued: "If the close of this terrible war, has left, some of our hearthstones, *very, very* desolate, God, has been as ever kind & merciful, in the midst of our heavy afflictions as nations, & as individuals."

The following day, Tuesday, April 11, she wrote again to Sumner. It was another invitation. There was to be a great celebration of victory that evening. Would Senator Sumner come to the White House "about 8½ o'clock" to see the great crowd that would assemble with music in front of the mansion and hear the President make a little speech? She was also inviting the Marquis de Chambrun and had "had the *moral courage,* to write him a note in French." The whole city was to be illuminated and she was anxious to get a good view of it. Perhaps Sumner, the marquis, and herself, "accompanied by some other lady of course," could drive around for about half an hour to see the illumination. "It does not appear to me, that this *womanly* curiosity, will be undignified or indiscreet, qu'en pensez vous?"

It was well worth seeing, that illumination. The night was misty and "The reflection of the illuminated dome of the Capitol on the moist air above" was seen many miles away. "Arlington House, across the river, the old home of Lee, was brilliantly lighted, and rockets and colored lights blazed on the lawn, where ex-slaves by the thousand sang 'The Year of Jubilee.' "

Lincoln made the promised speech to the assembled thousands. Out of his magnanimity and understanding he expressed the wish to receive the South back into the Union without vindictiveness. On the day before, when a crowd had assembled and called for him, he had asked the band to play "Dixie," just as he had at City Point. His speech of Tuesday showed the great statesman at his zenith, in spite of his weary body.

Worn out as he was, Lincoln's troubled sleep of late had been broken by strange dreams. A recent dream had left him under the shadow of such deep melancholy that he finally sought relief by telling it. He said that falling asleep from extreme weariness in his White House chamber, he dreamed he heard the sound of weeping throughout the house. He thought he rose and went downstairs and wandered to the sound of sobbing through the vacant rooms until he came to the great East Room, where he saw "a catafalque, on which rested a corpse wrapped in funeral vestments." There were soldiers on guard and people weeping. In his dream Lincoln asked one of the soldiers who was dead. "The President," came the answer, "he was killed by an assassin!" The shock of this and a burst of grief from the crowd awakened the sleeper, who slept no more that night.

Thus Lincoln told it to his wife and Ward Hill Lamon. Mary was chilled and frightened but tried to brush it off for the sake of them both. "That is horrid!" she exclaimed. "I wish you had not told it. I am glad I don't believe in dreams, or I would be in terror from this time forth."

Lincoln by this time had noticed how much the story was affecting her. In his turn he tried to make light of the matter: "Well, it is only a dream, Mary. Let us say no more about it, and try to forget it." But Mary did not forget.

On Wednesday Lincoln in his office wrote a little note to his wife, a loverlike note from a man long married, "playfully & tenderly, worded," she said, "notifying, the hour, of the day, he would drive with me." She put it away to treasure with others she was keeping, "dear, loving letters to me, many of them written to me, in the 'long ago,' and quite yellow with age." Before the year was out she would pore over that precious package, rereading the letters as best she could for tears.

Thursday night Lincoln had another dream, weird but not unhappy. He had had the same dream several times before just prior to certain momentous battles; he was convinced, as he told his cabinet on Friday morning, that it was the forerunner of some significant event. In this dream he said "that he seemed to be in some singular, indescribable vessel, and that he was moving with great rapidity towards an indefinite shore . . ."

Lincoln's spirits had lifted during this week of rejoicing. He and Mary with the Harlans had taken a long drive together across the Potomac into Virginia, where war had ceased and springtime had come. Senator Harlan noticed how the President's whole appearance had become "transfigured," the sad look had vanished from his eyes to be replaced by an "indescribable expression of serene joy . . . His countenance had become radiant . . ."

He turned this relaxed and happy face to Robert on Friday morning when the eldest son came into his room to show him a picture of General Robert E. Lee. The President looked at it thoughtfully and said: "It is a good face; it is the face of a noble, noble, brave man. I am glad that the war is over at last." That reminded him that now Robert could lay aside his uniform, so he began to talk to him about his continuing his study at law. At last one could plan the future in a world at peace. Just to think in terms of normal living seemed a blessing too great to realize.

Lincoln was happy that day. "Dear husband, you almost startle me, by your great cheerfulness," Mary said to him that afternoon when they went for their drive. There were just the Lincolns in the carriage because he had wished it so. When she had asked him whether she should invite someone to go with them he had answered, "No, I prefer to ride by ourselves to day." He wanted to talk to her about the future, the happy unstrained days ahead. They could settle back now into the old familiar companionship of their marriage. That companionship was like an old coat, stretched and frayed by long use but all the more comfortable for that reason. It did not matter that the coat had never been a perfect fit; it was the coat he had selected from all others because it was the one he liked; habit had adjusted it to his needs and he felt at home in it.

He was supremely happy on that last ride together; "... well I may feel so, Mary," he said, "I consider *this day*, the war has come to a close— We must *both*, be more cheerful in the future—between the war & the loss of our darling Willie—we have both, been very miserable."

Mrs. Lincoln later told some of the plans for that cheerful future. "My husband intended, when he was through with his presidential terms, to take me and the family to Europe." Before their revived spirits was the lure and joy of travel and seeing new things. When they returned from abroad they would "go to California over the Rocky mountains, and see the prospects [prospectors' claims] of the soldiers, etc., digging out gold to pay the national debt." In this connection she mentioned again how "cheery" and "funny" he was. According to her understanding, Lincoln's intention up to 1865 had been ultimately to return to Springfield to live, but in that year he "Changed his opinion" though he had not "settled on any place particularly." Ahead of them stretched four peaceful years in Washington before that decision had to be made.

As they returned from the drive two friends were just leaving the White House. Friendships too could be on a relaxed basis now; the President called to the dignified gentlemen, "Come back, boys, come back." He visited with them, laughing and jesting, until he was late for dinner. Dinner must not be delayed too long as they were going to Ford's Theater that evening.

But with all his lightness of spirit, Lincoln was still tired and worn-out. He complained of it at the table but thought a good laugh at the comedy might help. Mary did not want to go; her head was aching, as usual, but Lincoln said if he stayed at home he would have no rest, as he would be obliged to see company all evening. Mary of course decided then to go with him, headache or no headache. The talk that afternoon had made them feel so close; never had she felt "so unwilling to be away from him."

They had invited various friends to accompany them but for one reason or another the invitations had been declined. When they learned that General and Mrs. Grant would be unable to join them, Lincoln "felt inclined to give up the whole thing," but their attendance had been announced and Mrs. Lincoln felt (and her husband agreed with her) that they ought not to disappoint the people who had gone to the theater to see them. How many times in spite of fatigue and illness they had yielded to the pressure of the public wish.

It was about eight-thirty when the Lincolns with their last-minute guests, Miss Clara Harris and her fiancé, Major Henry R. Rathbone, seated themselves in the flag-draped box at Ford's Theater. Mary sat next to her husband, who was in a large rocking chair, and one observer noted that she liked to point out this or that bright spot in the play and "seemed to take great pleasure in witnessing his enjoyment." It was drafty in the box and Lincoln, at a look from his wife, got up and put on his overcoat.

As they sat in the box, conversation reverted to the topic of their afternoon drive, the future plans of the Lincolns. Long afterwards Mrs. Lincoln was said to have repeated to a relative her husband's seemingly fateful words as they spoke of their future travels: "There is no city I desire to see so much as Jerusalem."

During the third act Mary found that she was nestled against her husband and was looking up into his face. It was an instinctive expression of that feeling of closeness, but she realized how it would look to others and said to him softly: "What will Miss Harris think of my hanging on to you so[?]" "She wont think any thing about it," he answered, giving her an affectionate smile. They were his last words and fittingly enough they embodied his loving reassurance to her.

Her hand was held close in his. When a pistol shot rang out a moment later perhaps it was the convulsive jerk of those gentle fingers that made her realize before anyone else that the President had been shot. Or her eyes could still have been upon his face. It was her agonized screams that first told the audience what had happened. Then she fainted. It had come at last, the calamity she had lived in terror of so long, had come just when she was beginning to think the danger was over. What followed—the escape of John Wilkes Booth, the assassin, the pandemonium in the audience, the coming of doctors, the search for the wound—was a confused horror to a woman beside herself with panic and grief.

When the unconscious form of the President was carried out of the theater, across the street and up the curving steps of the Peterson house, the distracted wife followed crying and wringing her hands. As he was borne through the narrow hall into a back bedroom, in the crowding and confusion she momentarily lost sight of him and cried frantically, "Where is my husband? Where is my husband?" She was guided into the chamber where the dying President had been laid on the bed. Bending over him, she covered the unconscious face with kisses, calling him every endearing name, and begging him to speak just one word to her. He had never failed to respond to her need and tenderness before; she could not believe, could not accept it, that he would not do so now. Once in her unreasoning agony she wanted Tad sent for; "she knew he would speak to him because he loved him so well."

The little room gradually became crowded with doctors, members of the cabinet, and other prominent men. Robert was soon there to weep at intervals upon the shoulder of Senator Sumner through a night that to him seemed endless. It is doubtful whether Mary Lincoln was aware of their presence. As the hours dragged on she realized there was no hope and she then began to beg her dying husband to take her with him.

The constant sound of Lincoln's labored breathing

drove her into such convulsions of grief that at intervals she had to be led away from the bedside and be taken in a front room, from which her heartbroken sobs and exclamations could be heard. Once she remembered Lincoln's strange dream of people weeping over a dead body in the White House and cried out, "His dream was prophetic." In her agony she prayed that night that she too might die. At intervals she would return to the bedside, again to kiss him, to call him by the tender names used in intimacy through all their years together, to beseech him to take her with him.

About six in the morning it began to rain heavily as it had on their wedding day almost twenty-three years before. As the grayness of dawn appeared in the windows about seven, Mary visited her husband for the last time. The beloved face on the bed, which in the first hours of the night had appeared calm and natural, had undergone a change. The right eye, behind which lodged the fatal bullet, had become swollen and discolored. The wife took one look and fell fainting to the floor. A woman friend, summoned during the night, caught her in her arms as she fell and held her to the open window, beyond which the rain was falling fast.

When she revived Mary once more went to the bedside. For the last time she kissed the dear face and sobbed her words of love. As she passed through the hall back to the parlor a young reporter heard her moan, "Oh, My God, and have I given my husband to die." Never had he heard, as he said, "so much agony in so few words." At seven-twenty-two Lincoln breathed his last.

Throughout the city began the tolling of bells. It was nine in the morning when they took Mary Lincoln back to the mansion which she had left so happily with her husband a little over twelve hours before. The doctor said she must go to bed immediately and those in attendance started to take her to her usual bedroom. But she drew back: "not there! oh not there," she said. Not there in the room still warm with his living breath and sweet feeling of special closeness which had been between them the evening before. So they took her to a room she had not formerly used.

Elizabeth Keckley came that Saturday morning, April 15, to the great white mansion where everyone spoke in subdued tones and moved with muffled tread. She entered the room where the body lay, the same room where she had once seen the President weep over the boyish face of his little dead son. Now he lay in death where Willie had been. Mrs. Keckley in her tears said truly that the whole world was in grief when Abraham Lincoln died.

But the distilled essence of the great agony which was surging over the country was in the heart of the sick and broken widow. She too had received a wound that was fatal, though it would be long years before she could die. Two lives had crashed that day. Lincoln's struggle was soon over; his mystic ship was safe in harbor; it was Mary's ship, crippled, that must sail on and on into mist, darkness, and storm.

chapter 30

"WITHOUT HIM"

"Mrs. Lincoln still remains at the White House, more dead than alive, shattered and broken by the horrors of that dreadful night, as well as worn down by bodily sickness," wrote Noah Brooks on May 10. Mrs. Keckley stayed beside her bed in the darkened chamber, ministering to her in the terrible convulsions of grief that alternated with periods of complete prostration. Robert hovered over his mother with tender affection. When she gave way to cries and hysterical shrieks, Tad would crouch at the foot of her bed "with a world of agony in his young face." Often at night the boy would hear her sobbing and would get up to go to her with wise little words of comfort: "Don't cry, Mamma; I cannot sleep if you cry! Papa was good, and he has gone to heaven. He is happy there. He is with God and my brother Willie. Don't cry, Mamma, or I will cry, too." Tad could help; his mother would clasp him in her arms and try to calm herself.

She denied admittance to most of her friends. The understanding and faithful Mrs. Gideon Welles visited her and it was the son Edgar T. Welles who wrote a note to the one in charge not to tear down the framework which had been erected in the East Room for the White House services. He explained: "Mrs. Lincoln is very much disturbed by noise. The other night when putting them up, every plank that dropped gave her a spasm and every nail that was driven seemed to her like a pistol shot."

There were so many sounds to stab her grief: the distant footsteps of the thousands of people who came to file by the coffin in the East Room with tear-stained faces, the tolling of church bells when the body of Abraham Lincoln was finally carried out of the White House. When the funeral train bore him home to Illinois through a sorrowing country, the widow remained bedridden in her chamber to picture that black-draped return journey against the bright memory of their coming East together.

That faithful friend, Dr. Henry, was in Richmond at the time of the assassination. He could not believe the news until he reached the White House and saw the loved face of the President still and cold in death. "Then the terrible truth flashed upon me," he wrote his wife, ". . . and I wept like a child refusing to be comforted . . ." When he regained his self-control, he went to "poor heart broken Mrs. Lincoln." Along with her overwhelming grief Mary had the widow's feeling that the very foundations of her life had been swept away, that she had no one to turn to for support and protection. Here was a man strong, tender, and good, qualities of the husband she had lost; she clung to him and "wept most hysterically" on his shoulder.

Dr. Henry remained in attendance upon Mrs. Lincoln during the rest of her stay in Washington. "I am the best comforter she finds," he wrote Mrs. Henry, "and I spend several hours a day with her. . . . I believe our departed friend[s] hover over and around us, and we are fully cognizant of all that transpires, while we are not sensible of their presence." That he made Mrs. Lincoln "a convert to this doctrine" and that it was a great "comfort and consolation to her," as he claimed, is evident throughout her letters. They abound in expressions like this: "My belief, is so assured, that *Death,* is only a blessed translation, to the 'pure in heart,' that a very slight veil separates us, from the 'loved & lost,' and to me, there is comfort, in the thought, that though unseen by us, they are very near."

Out of his great understanding Dr. Henry explained to his wife that "Poor Mrs. Lincoln was not only proud of her Husband"; she loved him with an intensity possible only to such a high-strung, passionate temperament.

Mary told Mr. Miner later that she had no recollection of the days that followed the murder of the President. The minister's perception equaled the doctor's: "When her husband was shot down by her side her nervous system was completely shattered and her mind was unhinged by the shock." She was in no condition to make important decisions but, as with a widow always, such unaccustomed decisions crowded upon her. She was forced to make an effort to take up her changed life.

To carry out the wishes of her dead husband was a sacred obligation to her. Lincoln had intended to give a young man a certain appointment. As early as May 3, the day before Lincoln was laid to rest in Oak Ridge Cemetery at Springfield, Mary summoned strength to sign a recommendation that the appointment be carried out, according to her husband's wishes.

Lincoln had expressed his wish to Mary in regard to another matter and her determination that this wish should be respected was bringing bitter denunciation upon the widow even before her husband was buried. Without consulting her, a local committee in Springfield had bought six acres of the Mather grounds in the heart of the city for a burial place for Lincoln, paying $5300 for it. A vault was nearly completed before Mrs. Lincoln telegraphed her refusal to have him buried there. He had told her he wanted to be buried in a quiet country cemetery and there was the added factor that she feared she could not be buried beside him in the public location in Springfield. From the moment of his death one supremely wished-for destination found expression in her letters: "to rest, by the side of my darling husband."

But, perhaps because some local pocketbooks were involved, Springfield was in a fury over her refusal. "The people are in a rage about it and all the hard stories that ever were told about her are told over again," ran a letter written in that city on April 30; "She has no friends here . . ." The matter was taken up in the newspapers with the usual antagonistic misrepresentation; the papers gave the impression that there was bitterness between Mrs. Lincoln and Mrs. Mather. This was not true, wrote Mary; she had selected Oak Ridge because she knew "that the beauty & retirement of the spot" would have been her husband's choice.

Even after Lincoln was buried controversy and denunciation went on. The Springfield Monument Association wanted to erect the monument to Lincoln in the center of the city instead of placing it over his remains. Mary threatened if they did so to have her husband's body removed to Washington and deposited in a vault under the Capitol.

A decision had to be made as to where Mrs. Lincoln would go to live. Robert, in consultation with O. H. Browning and David Davis, who had come to Washington to take charge of Lincoln's estate, had decided it was best for her to return to Springfield, where the old home was still owned by the family. Mary was of another mind. Added bitterness between her sisters and herself had accumulated during the war. In the background had always been the fact that they had looked down on Lincoln and had hurt him cruelly by opposition to his marrying into the family. The grief which permeated all her letters as a widow was combined with a passionate reverence for the greatness and goodness of the husband she had lost, yet there were those in Springfield who still felt she had married beneath her. The decision also had to be made at the very time when public abuse of her was raging in Springfield; and "all the hard stories" about her were being repeated, because she would not let a few of its citizens dictate where her husband should be buried.

Most intolerable of all was the idea of going back into that home on Eighth Street where every room would stab with its memories of past happiness. Mary shunned objects with associations that had turned to pain. When she was able to be out of bed and start the dreary process of packing to leave the White House, she gave away many articles intimately associated with Lincoln. These things were presented as mementos to those who had revered her husband. The colored people, whose love for the Emancipator had a special reverential quality, received much. Yet Mary treasured other keepsakes, most of all certain letters Lincoln had written her through the years which were especially expressive of his love for her.

The widow finally decided to go to Chicago. Mrs. Keckley helped the weak and sobbing woman pack "fifty or sixty boxes" in addition to many trunks. With her ever-present feeling of being poor and insecure, Mrs. Lincoln had saved everything, even to the bonnets she had brought from Springfield. Robert begged her to burn up her old stuff, which was good advice, for those boxes were the starting point of a public furor.

A smear campaign, once launched, is like a snowball rolling down an endless hill, accumulating increased weight and momentum as it rolls. Stories were soon being briskly circulated that Mrs. Lincoln had carried off a great amount of the White House furnishings. The number and size of the boxes constantly increased. The newspapers, conditioned to abuse of her, took up the accusation, especially when the question arose, toward the end of 1865, of a new appropriation to refurnish the White House for the Johnson administration. It was the first item in a long series of public attacks which were to beat upon Abraham Lincoln's widow as long as she lived. In her bereavement she remained what she had been during her husband's Presidency, a football of politics to be kicked at from both sides.

Mary Lincoln in letters to her friends indignantly denied that she had taken any of the White House belongings. She gave a detailed list of the contents of the boxes: "Wax work—Country quilts—made by old women, who bowed the knee in reverence to the good & great man. Old rude chairs—made by veteran hands. These things coming from such patriotic persons—were more precious than gold to my darling husband." There is no doubt the many presents received by the Lincolns brought up the question as to which were personal gifts and which were essentially gifts to the nation to be left in public custody. Other Presidential families have had to recognize that the person and the office are not easily separable. One small article of furniture, a dressing stand which Lincoln had used and liked, was taken with the permission of the Commissioner of Public Buildings and another stand equally good was procured and left to replace it. Many of the objects in the boxes were given by Mrs. Lincoln later in Chicago for the benefit of charity fairs.

It has been seen that vandalism in the White House was rampant during Lincoln's occupation. In the five weeks following his death when Mrs. Lincoln was confined to her chamber there was lack of responsible supervision, and Mrs. Keckley, who was in the White House at the time, said that a great deal of the furniture was stolen. There is no reason to doubt Mrs. Lincoln's statement of her innocence of the charge of taking White House property, but the accusation was to follow her and have practical effects in the treatment she received in regard to a pension.

On May 22 a feeble, black-clad Mary Lincoln walked for the last time down the White House stairs of stately memories and was driven to the station to take the train to Chicago. Mrs. Keckley and Dr. Henry as well as her two sons accompanied her on the journey. The silence of the departure was painful; there was scarcely a friend to tell her good-by. In her wish for rigid seclusion she had refused to see the many ladies who had called upon her during those five agonizing weeks; now they did not come to be turned away again. They doubtless interpreted as snobbishness what was really the prostration of grief.

The trip to Chicago was an agony of migraine headache. After a brief stay at the Tremont House she removed to a less expensive location in Hyde Park with Robert, Tad, and Mrs. Keckley. Their quarters were small and unattractive and Robert said he "would almost as soon be dead as be compelled to remain three months in this dreary house." Mrs. Keckley shortly returned to Washington.

Thus Mrs. Lincoln began her unfortunate policy of seclusion, shunning contact with relatives and old friends whose faces she said would bring back memories she wished to avoid. This not only shut her off from the advice and guidance of those with balanced judgment, which she sorely needed, but it also deprived her of companionships that would have drawn her back into normal life and interests.

"I still remain closeted in my rooms, take an occasional walk, in the park & as usual see no one," she wrote Dr. Henry in July, yet apparently she did not connect this self-imposed seclusion with her statement in the same letter: "I cannot express how lonely & desolate we are."

Her one outlet was letter writing. Shut up with nothing to do, she lived in letters to her friends and from this time on one can almost write her life and thoughts in her own words. A series of dramatic events, any one of which could well be the theme of an Ibsen drama, was destined to involve this ill-fated woman and it is possible to get her own expression of the anguish and grief and in some cases intolerable outrage which these fearful incidents were to cause her.

Her letters contain an anthology of a widow's pain. There is no aspect of the agony of loss which she has not put into unforgettable phrasing. "Day by day, I miss, my beloved husband, more & more," she wrote Mrs. Welles three months after Lincoln's death. "How, I am, to pass through life, without *him* who loved us so dearly, it is impossible for me to say. . . . I must patiently await, the hour, when, 'God's Love,' shall place me, by *his* side again. Where there are no more partings & *no more* tears shed. For I have almost become blind, with weeping . . ."

It was an age that made a ceremony of bereavement. Mary's expressions of grief bear a striking resemblance to those of the little widowed queen who sat on the throne of England at this time. Queen Victoria was pouring out her sorrow in passionate underlined phrases that could easily be interchanged with those in Mary Lincoln's letters. "Oh! my fate is *too too dreadful!*" wrote Victoria. "If I *could* but go soon to him, and be at rest! Day and night I have no rest or peace. God's will be done." Both women sought seclusion and found it painful to see those who reminded them of the happy past. The basic thing with each was a great, single, unending love for her husband, and a reverent devotion to his memory.

Mary regretted her own failings. Self-reproach appears in her letters and torturing thoughts of what might have been. "If . . . even with trembling anxiety, I had been permitted to watch over and minister, to my idolized husband, through an illness, and receiving his loving farewell and in return, I could have thanked him for his lifelong . . . devotion to me & mine, and I could have asked forgiveness, for any inadvertent moment of pain, I may have caused him, perhaps, *time,* could partially assuage my grief, and leave me, to perform more calmly, the life duties, that remain to me." This she wrote to that lasting friend, Charles Sumner, and in the same letter she gave haunting expression to her appreciation of Lincoln's achievement. She was enclosing to Sumner, the letters she had received from Queen Victoria and the Empress Eugénie of France and telling him of the "innumerable letters and resolutions, from distinguished persons, in all portions of the habitable globe" which had come to her. A large scrapbook made up of the speeches and resolutions passed in England after the President's death had been sent to her, she said. It was filled with signal tribute by the English, yet Mary sensed that it would be years before Lincoln's full measure could be taken. "*Their* eyes," she wrote, "were only beginning to comprehend the nature and nobility of the great, good man, who had accomplished his work, and before *his Judge,* it was pronounced complete."

Love, grief, and reverence for her dead husband constitute one of the two main topics in the black-bordered

letters of widowed Mary Lincoln. The other principal subject was centered in the area in which she was mentally
ill, in her irrationality about money and in her obsession
that she was in dire poverty. In view of the enormous
debts she had contracted in her psychopathic urge to buy,
her financial condition was enough to frighten any widow.
With the passing of her prestige as the wife of the President, bills began to pour in upon this sick and frantic
woman. She did not dodge the responsibility of paying her
debts.

Lincoln left an estate of more than eighty-three thousand dollars, which, under the expert handling of David
Davis as administrator, increased to over one hundred
and ten thousand by the time his final report was filed in
1868. Since Lincoln left no will, Mary and her two sons
each received a third, nearly thirty-seven thousand dollars apiece in the final settlement. In the three years before the estate was settled, cash, as often happens, was
scarce and prices after the war were soaring. Mary was
uncertain as to what she could count on. She variously reported the annual income of herself and her sons as from
fifteen hundred to eighteen hundred apiece. (With the
high interest rates of the time this works out correctly.
Her irrationality was not a matter of arithmetic.) With
her constant feeling that the foundations of her life had
crumbled, leaving her broken and unprotected in the
ruins, and with her inability to think rationally about
money, she lay awake at night wondering how she would
provide for herself and her two sons.

In her mind—frantic with the knowledge of those awful
debts—ideas, worries, and fears revolved ceaselessly.
David Davis must not know of the debts, she reasoned; he
might pay them out of the estate, thus leaving her and her
sons penniless. It is significant that no claims to cover
debts incurred by Mrs. Lincoln were filed against the
estate. She must contrive somehow to pay those debts
privately.

Living in Chicago, Mrs. Lincoln needed someone she
could trust to attend secretly to the settlement of her debts
in the East. She selected Alexander Williamson, the sympathetic young Scotsman who had been the loved tutor of
Willie and Tad in the White House. From June 1865 until
toward the end of 1867, she wrote him frequent letters
about her financial worries. They reveal her nervous con-

dition and the pitiful state to which her irrationality had progressed. Dealing with the topic on which she was unbalanced, they are like a hospital chart recording the fever of her mental illness. A good number of them have been preserved. To judge Mrs. Lincoln by these letters alone would be like focusing on a wound or abscess and accepting the result as a picture of the whole person.

The letters deal mostly with ways and means to get her debts paid. Mr. Williamson must see this or that person in high place and exert pressure to have money contributed for her benefit. It was common at the time to raise money by popular subscription for those who had served their country well or to bestow the gift of a house upon a public hero. Here is Mary's statement of the way she looked at the matter: "Notwithstanding my great & good husband's life, was sacrificed for his country, we are left to struggle, in a manner entirely new to us—and a noble people would pronounce our manner of life, *undeserved*. Roving Generals have elegant mansions showered upon them, and the American people—leave the family of the Martyred President, to struggle as best they may! Strange justice this." She resented having to room and board without the means for a home where she could grieve in private. But in the long run her accusations that the public was unjust and ungrateful added to her unpopularity.

There was good reason for her as Lincoln's widow to expect subscription funds and a home. Even before she left the White House a movement had been started to raise a fund for her by one-dollar subscriptions. In the end something over ten thousand dollars thus raised was given her. Likewise there was newspaper mention early in May of the possibility of presenting a homestead to her. Her tortured mind seized on these hopes as a way out of her tangled finances. It should be noted that Congress at the end of 1865 did vote the widow one year's Presidential salary, which after various deductions came to something over twenty-two thousand dollars. The sum was used to buy a home which, on her limited income, she could not keep up. It was to be five years after Lincoln's death before Congress voted her an annual pension which relieved her financial stringency but not her sense of it.

In her letters to Alexander Williamson Mrs. Lincoln poured out her grief, her fears, her schemes thought out in the dark hours of sleepless nights, her suspicions and denunciations of those who were not helping her, her sense of injustice at the treatment she was receiving, her resentment at public misrepresentation and accusations. She enclosed to the kind young Scotsman careful lists of what she had bought at certain stores in Washington and instructed him to plead with those stores to take the goods back.

Some of the abuse of her came from the fact that the public did not know about her debts and that it was her frantic effort to pay them that was causing her such embarrassment. The size of Lincoln's estate was soon public knowledge. Why, reasoned people, with such an estate, should she be in actual want, as she said she was? They did not know that poverty with her was an obsession, beating upon a mind that at the same time honestly acknowledged the obligation of the debts. Added to this was her feeling that she must live with a dignity befitting the widow of Abraham Lincoln.

In July of '65 the beloved Dr. Henry, en route by ship to Olympia, Washington, was lost at sea. It was another heavy blow; Mary considered him her "best friend." She wrote Mrs. Henry a letter remarkable for its expression of sorrow and heartfelt sympathy. She and Mrs. Henry, she said, had lost "two of the best men & the most devoted husbands" that ever lived. In the following year Mary tried to sell certain stocks in order to give some of the proceeds to her friend, widowed like herself.

"We are boarding & as every thing is so enormously high here . . . our means, only allow us, to board genteely, and with this, I suppose, we must *just now*, be content," ran Mary's letter to Mrs. Welles in the fall of '65. But that was not an important matter beside her great loss and grief: "With my darling husband any lot, would have been cheerfully borne." She and her sons were then staying at the Clifton House in Chicago. Having her goods in storage was an additional worry to her, especially as a bad fire occurred in December just one block from the warehouse where they were stored. "The precious relics, belonging to my husband, are a continual source of anxiety to me."

She wrote these words to Mrs. Welles when she was sitting up for the first time in a week after returning from a harrowing trip. Shortly before Christmas she and Robert had gone to Springfield for the occasion when Lincoln's body was transferred from the public receiving vault in which it had been placed into a new one. The experience had made Mary ill. At best now she was incapacitated for almost three days out of each week with her agonizing headaches. She wrote Mrs. Welles about the new vault "containing places for my husband, myself & 4 sons." Eddie and Willie now lay with their father. "When my good cousin—Mr John Stuart, pointed to the vacant niche, by my beloved husband's side which he said, was reserved for me, . . . I prayed, that my own appointed time, would not, be far distant."

When the New Year 1866 came in, Mary had nothing joyous to look forward to but she probably thought that every possible hurt had already been inflicted on her. Yet fate was contriving incredible new happenings to cause her anguish. Such an incident was to take place in this new year through the agency of that self-designated psychoanalyst, William H. Herndon.

chapter 31

HERNDON LECTURES ON ANN RUTLEDGE

"Lincoln's death was the most important event in Herndon's life," says Herndon's biographer. With the immediate demand for details of the martyred President's career, the man who had been his law partner for sixteen years suddenly became important and was quoted over the country. This turning to him as an authority soon launched him into collecting material for a life of Lincoln which he proposed to write. He began assiduously to send letters of inquiry and to seek interviews.

As a part of this effort he wrote Robert Lincoln in the summer of 1866 asking if he might have an interview with Mrs. Lincoln. Mary graciously answered him herself: "The recollection of my beloved husband's, *truly,* affectionate regard for *you* & the knowledge, of your great love & reverence, for the best man, that ever lived, would of *itself,* cause you, to be cherished, with the sincerest regard, by my sons & myself." The widow continued: "In my overwhelming bereavement, those who loved my idolized husband . . . are very precious to me & mine." She was planning to come to Springfield soon to visit the tomb "which contains my All, in life" and she made an appointment with Herndon to see him at the St. Nicholas Hotel.

When they met early in September 1866, Herndon seated himself with pen and paper at a table and prepared to take down, as he said later, "as well as I could, the *substance* of what she said." He had been drinking and she was revolted at the smell of liquor on his breath. Some of her statements on that occasion have already been quoted in these pages, her loving description of Lincoln and details of life in Washington. She understood that Herndon had never known Lincoln the President, only Lincoln the Springfield lawyer, and she tried to tell him how magnificently her husband had risen to meet the nation's crisis, how "he rose grandly with the circumstances of the case, and men soon learned that he was above them all." She continued proudly: "I never saw a man's mind develop itself so finely." She made that statement of infinite understanding: "Mr. Lincoln had a kind of poetry in his nature."

Herndon, to use his own word, "examined" her on Lincoln's religion. Had Lincoln joined a church? Mary answered honestly that he had not. One conjectures that Herndon then pointed out that this meant Lincoln was not "a technical Christian," a phrase and a bit of reasoning he was to use later in a lecture. At all events Herndon's record of the interview reads: "Mr. Lincoln was not a technical Christian," which was a term Mary would hardly have thought of using. It must be remembered that Herndon was careful to state that he did not take down her statements word for word, but "the *substance* of what she said." When he later quoted her as saying her husband had not been a technical Christian, she was horrified.

It was useless for Mary to tell Herndon, as she did, how loving a husband Lincoln had been to her; the words fell on deaf ears. Herndon for over a year had been riding the theory that Lincoln had not loved the woman he married. He had heard that Lincoln in New Salem had grieved over the death of a friend, a girl named Ann Rutledge, and some had supposed that if he grieved so much he must have been in love with the girl. Here was a clue he would follow. He was preparing to write a book. In the literary climate of the age, when novels dripped with sentiment over the sorrows and joys of true lovers, the hero of every book needed a satisfactory romance. Herndon was antagonistic to Mrs. Lincoln. An early sweetheart for Lincoln would serve his purpose beautifully.

Working on this clue, he sought out the people who had been around New Salem thirty or more years before, when Lincoln and Ann Rutledge lived there. Herndon was a shrewd lawyer who had practiced how to sway juries to his way of thinking. When he descended upon these country people with questions as to whether young Lincoln had been in love with Ann Rutledge, using a lawyer's tricks of suggestion as to what he wished said, he began to collect all kinds of reminiscences. Herndon himself in another connection said: "Men and women are inquisitive and hint a thing to them only and they will flesh the story falsely seen to suit the demands of the mind." If these people could help Herndon make out his case, there would be the reward of reflected importance for themselves and their vanished village. He jotted down their statements in hurried, staccato notes which are preserved in the Herndon-Weik manuscripts, which were not available to the public until 1942.

All the statements collected by Herndon were efforts to recall what had happened thirty or more years before, given largely under his prodding or suggestion. No contemporary evidence as to the romance exists. In the years between the eighteen-thirties and the eighteen-sixties no mention of it is recorded. When a full examination and critical analysis of Herndon's material about Ann Rutledge was made in the nineteen-forties, it was found to be a mass of vague and contradictory statements, some pro, some con, no two of them agreeing in every particular. The statements were consistent on two items only: that Ann was engaged to John McNamar (who was using the name McNeil while building up his fortune at New Salem) and that Lincoln grieved when she died.

Lincoln had boarded at Ann's home, the Rutledge Tavern, early in his stay in New Salem, and the Rutledge family had his intimate friendship and affection. Ann's fiancé was also a friend of his; he called him "Mack." Of course Lincoln grieved and so did the whole community when the young girl died. The death of a friend was always taken hard by Lincoln; we have seen how in the White House he wept and gave extreme expression to his grief over the loss of Elmer Ellsworth, Edward D. Baker, and Ben Hardin Helm, all this when he had twice the years and maturity that he had had when Ann was buried. He was deeply depressed for a time after Ann's death but was soon attending to business as usual. Herndon was to "psychoanalyze" this grief into actual insanity.

There was a significant difference between what people knew while Ann lived and what they later "supposed." This is illustrated by the testimony of James Short, one of Lincoln's closest friends, whom he called "as honorable a man as there is in the world." Jimmy Short lived half a mile from the Rutledges after they in 1833 moved about seven miles north of New Salem to a farm owned by Ann's fiancé, John McNamar, evidently a family arrangement. If Lincoln ever courted Ann, the courtship took place there. Short, with whom Lincoln stayed when he went out that way, said that while Ann was living he "did not know of any engagement or tender passages" between her and Lincoln but after her death he "then supposed" that if Lincoln grieved so much "there must have been ... something of the kind."

One naturally is curious to know what John McNamar, a respected man in the community who was known to be engaged to Ann, had to say. He returned from a long absence shortly after her death, expecting to marry her. This acknowledged fiancé told how he carved Ann's initials on a board at her grave. In reading this statement from the man himself one gets a direct picture of a lover grieving over Ann, not a posthumous conjecture. McNamar also wrote: "I never heard ... [any] person say that Mr Lincoln addressed Miss Ann Rutledge in terms of courtship neither her own family nor my acquaintances otherwise." If Lincoln had courted Ann as Herndon said while "all New Salem encouraged his suit," it is strange that her acknowledged fiancé got no inkling of that courtship when he returned.

McNamar also had never heard of Lincoln having a "crazy spell." His statement suggests that Lincoln's depression over Ann's death got mixed up with his melancholia later over the broken engagement with Mary Todd, both events being far back in the mist of years and memories. Writing Herndon and mentioning the "crazy spell" of which he had never heard before, McNamar said that his brother-in-law, James Short, "informs me that there was such a report though not very publick and at a later period than you supposed and from a different source namely a lover's disappointment with regard to the lady whom he afterwards married."

One aspect of the evidence is full of meaning: Those people who were closest to Lincoln and Ann "knew" least about any "romance." The letters of Ann's brother, R. B. Rutledge, the main spokesman for the family, reveal that he thought Herndon, not himself, was the authority on the subject. If the Rutledges supposed, as people often do today, that Lincoln had told his law partner about the love story, they were in error. Herndon never said Lincoln told him anything about Ann but stated repeatedly that Lincoln did not make a confidant of him and that he had to read his secrets in his face and actions. There is no verified utterance by Lincoln, either oral or in writing, that mentions Ann's name. We find R. B. Rutledge writing

Herndon that he trusted to his "honesty and integrity as a historian" to go over his (Rutledge's) statements and correct them. Though this brother of Ann was seventeen when she died, his evidence is confused and contradictory; he confesses uncertainty and says he had to compare notes with others. In other words, the Rutledges did not rely on their own knowledge but had to build up and harmonize their testimony and have it checked for presumed correctness by Herndon, who, they apparently thought, knew more of the matter than they did.

There are amusing touches in the scattered pieces of "evidence" in the Herndon-Weik manuscripts in addition to some highly original spelling. When Herndon asked about one sweetheart for Lincoln, three extras were offered: a Miss Short and a Miss Berry without substantiation, and Miss Owens, as we have seen, quite correctly. The year following Ann's death Lincoln was busily courting Mary Owens. In fact, he said of Miss Owens that he "saw no good objection to plodding life through hand in hand with her." Though he wrote this in 1838 referring to a conversation he had had with Miss Owens's sister in 1836, he was basing this statement on his impression of the lady three years earlier—in 1833, when Ann was very much alive.

An obliging witness named Cogdal even resurrected Ann and had her living in Iowa and Lincoln still in love with her, twenty-five years after she was buried. One old settler thought another old settler had "*lied* like *hell*." The accusation of prevarication appears also in a pertinent letter which is not in the Herndon-Weik manuscripts. When Herndon's book was finally published, R. J. Onstott, a native of New Salem, was highly indignant. As to Ann being the sweetheart of Lincoln, he wrote, "the Story is a lie out of Whole Cloth." He gave a simple explanation of a much overworked incident: his father, he said, had gone to see Ann and her family in her final illness. "I know," he added, "that Lincoln did go to see her once at her reques[t] as others did." It was the way of neighbors in time of trouble.

For a further examination of Herndon's material on Ann Rutledge the reader is referred to the critical historical study entitled "Sifting the Ann Rutledge Evidence" which was published in *Lincoln the President* in 1945. One can accept the two items on which there is consistent testimony: that Ann was engaged to John McNamar and that Lincoln grieved about her death. But the story of a romance between Lincoln and Ann (which Lincoln's close friend called a mere conjecture after Ann's death) is not substantiated by any reliable evidence, only long-delayed reminiscence which is so contradictory as to cancel itself out. Inasmuch as the romance was a supposition after Ann died, and was not known to the world at large until after Lincoln died, it is doubly posthumous. It is not authentic history.

But what Herndon collected was manna for his sentimentalizing and psychoanalyzing mind. A supposed grief over a dead sweetheart would in Herndon's psychoanalysis explain everything about Lincoln which he had not understood and fit right into the sweetly sorrowful atmosphere of Victorian literature. As a result of his investigations he had no hesitation in proclaiming in a public lecture at Springfield on November 16, 1866, that "Abraham Lincoln loved Miss Ann Rutledge with all his soul, mind, and strength," that she "loved him as dearly," that Ann was "honestly engaged" to two men at the same time, that the lovely maiden sickened and died under the conflict of emotion and duty (à la Victorian novel), that Lincoln's heart was buried in her grave, and that he went out of his mind as the result of her death. In soaring rhetoric the lecturer gave his imagined description of Lincoln's condition: "His mind wandered from its throne . . . walked out of itself along the uncolumned air, and kissed and embraced the shadows and illusions of the heated brain." As his biographer has remarked: "By rights Herndon should have been a writer of romantic novels."

Few if any in Springfield had heard of Ann Rutledge before the lecture. Joshua Speed in Kentucky, the one person to whom Lincoln had poured out his intimate confidences in regard to affairs of the heart, said it was all news to him. What of the effect on Mary Lincoln living in overwhelming grief in Chicago at the time? Her one comfort was the memory of her husband's devotion and her feeling that he was watching and waiting for their reunion on the other side. To this broken woman there came the news that Herndon was publicly proclaiming that her husband had never loved her, that his heart had been buried in another woman's grave. It has been well said that in her mind it was "a stunning blow of vindictive cruelty."

Mary had never heard of Ann Rutledge. She wrote
David Davis asking him to see Herndon and "direct his
wandering mind" to the falseness of certain of his statements. It is rather ironic that she apparently thought
Herndon, who was so prone to describe other people
as crazy, was somewhat unbalanced himself. Had there
actually been such an episode of early love, years before
she met Lincoln, she would not have had reason to resent it. (She was quite sensible about that). Herndon's
far-fetched deductions and distortion of Lincoln's character were another matter. It is a distinction which we must
make today. "As you justly remark," she wrote David
Davis, "each & every one has had a little romance in their
early days—but as my husband was *truth itself*, and as he
always assured me, he had cared for no one but myself, . . . I shall assuredly remain firm in my conviction
that *Ann Rutledge,* is a myth—for in all his confidential
communications, such a romantic name, was never
breathed . . ." She had the memory of all their intimate
and devoted years together as she continued: "Nor did his
life or his joyous laugh, lead one to suppose his heart,
was in any unfortunate woman's grave—but in the proper
place with his loved wife & children."

Seeing the anguish and humiliation which the lecture
caused his mother, Robert Lincoln came to Springfield to
ask Herndon to desist. His letters to Herndon were scrupulously courteous. Just after his visit to Springfield and
conversation with Herndon, he wrote to him: "As I said
then, I have never had any doubt of your good intentions . . ." He pointed out to Herndon the way in which
people were talking about his lecture and continued: "All
I ask is that nothing may be published by you, which after
careful consideration will seem apt to cause pain to my
father's family, which I am sure you do not wish to do."
Robert achieved nothing except that Herndon subsequently called him some uncomplimentary names.

But Robert doubted Herndon's "good intentions" in another matter which came up around this time; he became
convinced that Herndon told a falsehood in order to get
the property which Lincoln had left in the law office. As
Robert related it, when David Davis as administrator of
Lincoln's estate asked Herndon about the office property,
Herndon told him, "falsely as we both believed, that my
father had made him a present of all the contents of the

office, as he was starting for Washington." Robert explained that "the pecuniary value was small; Justice Davis shrugged his shoulders and with my assent dropped the matter." It is not the purpose here to question Herndon's sincerity. But it is part of the story to show that Robert, Mrs. Lincoln, and Judge Davis believed him capable of telling falsehoods. The incident helps explain Mrs. Lincoln's subsequent description of Herndon: "a drunkard, an outrageous story-teller—to use a mild term and as he stole my husband's law books & our own private library, *we* may *safely* call him thief."

Of course the Ann Rutledge story spread like wildfire. It came to the ears of Mary's beloved former pastor, James Smith, in Scotland. About that time Mr. Smith received from Herndon a letter of studied insolence inquiring about Lincoln's religion. Smith considered Lincoln a Christian and to Herndon, proud of his infidelity, the word "Christian" was like a red flag to a bull. He demanded of the minister if he had any "written evidence" that Lincoln had accepted Christianity. If no written evidence, what had Lincoln said to him on the subject: "Give me his exact *words,* and not your understanding of them by any kind of implication. . . . As you were a gentleman before you were a Christian, I ask you in that capacity *first* to answer these questions . . ."

Smith answered both this insulting epistle and Herndon's lecture in an open letter to the Chicago *Tribune.* In his lecture Herndon had suggested (falsely and irresponsibly) that after Ann's death Lincoln "*never* addressed another woman . . . 'yours affectionately'; and . . . abstained from the use of the word '*love.*' . . . He never ended his letters with 'yours affectionately' . . ." We have already read various letters which Lincoln wrote his wife that are thus signed.

Smith properly took issue with this statement and with Herndon's theory that Lincoln had never loved the woman to whom he had "solemnly promised before God and man to be a faithful, loving, and affectionate husband . . ." If Herndon's statements were true, wrote Mr. Smith, they made Lincoln "worse than a dishonest man." The minister also reminded Herndon that a law office was not "the best field" for judging character. "It is in the family circle the man exhibits himself as he really is . . ." That statement hit Herndon in a vulnerable spot. He had not been a

familiar at the Lincoln fireside where the pastor had been
so welcome a guest and where he had noted, as he said,
the "heart overflowing with love and affection" which
Lincoln gave his wife. Smith's answer was a strong one
and Mary's beaten spirit rose with the feeling she had a
champion. After reading Herndon's insolent letter which
Mr. Smith also had printed in the *Tribune* along with his
answer, Mary called Herndon "a dirty dog."

The tracing of the development of the Ann Rutledge
legend and its results is necessary because of their tremendous bearing on present-day opinion of Mrs. Lincoln.
The biographer who writes about her and about the personal life of Lincoln is in a position analogous to playing
against loaded dice. The idea is firmly fixed in the public
mind that Lincoln romantically loved Ann Rutledge
(which is unsupported by any reliable evidence) and that
he never loved his wife, which is unanimously contradicted by the whole volume of contemporary evidence, including his own letters to her as well as the testimony of
those around them. There is no reason to doubt Mary Lincoln's statement that Lincoln often told her she was the
only one he had ever really loved. He said himself that he
was only "a little in love" with Miss Owens and that it was
a great relief to him when she declined his proposal of
marriage. This relief can be contrasted with his terrible
depression when his engagement with Mary Todd was for
a time broken.

Mrs. Lincoln apparently believed that Herndon had invented the love story of Lincoln and Ann. If she did, that
was an injustice. Herndon with all his queer mental proc-
esses had his own type of honesty; he required some clue
or shred of what he considered evidence before setting his
psychoanalysis in motion. His starting point may well
have been a short article published during the second
year of Lincoln's Presidency in the *Menard Axis*, a weekly
newspaper in Petersburg, Illinois. A clipping of this is to
be found today in the Herndon-Weik manuscripts.
Written by an anti-Lincoln man, the article is a belittling
sketch of Lincoln at New Salem. Along with several
proved falsehoods the writer tells how this rough uncouth
youth fell in love with an unnamed girl who sickened and
died, whereupon he became so melancholy and unbalanced that his friends "placed him under guard for fear
of his committing suicide." This last sentence again sug-

gests a confusing of Lincoln's sadness over Ann's death with the stories of his terrible depression after his broken engagement with Mary Todd. Mrs. Bennett Abell, at whose cabin Lincoln was staying at the time of Ann's death, put his grief in the right perspective when she said "he was not crazy but he was very disponding . . ."

The writer of the article in the *Menard Axis,* John Hill (son of Sam Hill of New Salem), later admitted that at the time of Lincoln's stay in New Salem: "I knew no more as to who he was than I did of the inhabitants of the Fegee Islands." It has been suggested that since this article appeared in Lincoln's lifetime (1862) he would have denied it if it had not been true. But Lincoln made a point of not reading hostile newspaper articles; that fact is trebly documented. Even if the unimportant little newspaper had ever reached Washington and Lincoln had read it—a remote possibility—it would have been folly for the President to confer publicity by needlessly answering a piece which at the time was virtually unnoticed. If one were to incorporate into the Lincoln story all the false statements which were not denied by the President, the result would be a huge volume of spurious Lincolniana.

Herndon did not invent the idea of a romance between Lincoln and Ann but he did, out of his psychoanalysis and his conviction that he knew truth by intuition, invent the results of the supposed romance. As his biographer, David Davis, has summed it up: "Whether Lincoln and Ann were in love, whether they were engaged . . . are conjectures on which Herndon's own witnesses differed sharply. His further inferences that Lincoln's entire life was shaped by this romance, that Ann's death caused Lincoln to throw himself into politics, and that Lincoln never loved another woman rest upon no particle of proof; they are examples of Herndon's historical intuition."

With Herndon, at the very start of his collecting biographical material on Lincoln, accepting these baseless assumptions as true, the natural result was that in the following years, as he built up the Lincoln-Rutledge romance for his biography on the one hand, he tore down Mrs. Lincoln and the Lincoln marriage on the other. A whole bill of goods as to the "unhappy" marriage went along with the conjectured love story. Of a piece with the high coloring of the Ann Rutledge tale was Herndon's fabrication of a wedding occasion at which Lincoln as bridegroom failed to appear, his further "historical intuitions" that Mary Todd's love for Lincoln was canceled by this wedding default (which never occurred), and the bizarre theory that she married him for "revenge."

Herndon hated Mrs. Lincoln, but in his own self-justifying mind he considered that, in bringing out his deductions from the supposed romance to explain the "unhappy" marriage, he was doing justice to her. In 1873, however, he was to have a public quarrel with Lincoln's widow, and after that there was no question of even this upside-down justice; his hatred of her became fanatical. As his biographer has pointed out, after 1874 Herndon "believed anything about Lincoln's wife that was bad. Some of his comments were unprintable."

One can trace this increasing hatred in Herndon's letters to his literary collaborator, Jesse Weik, up to the time the Herndon life of Lincoln appeared in 1889. Herndon poured out his thoughts and conclusions to Weik in a tumbling stream. Weik was to use what he thought best. One gets a glimpse into the casual genesis of statements that have since been taken as literal truth: "Draw on your imagination and fill up," wrote Herndon: "it will please the people . . ." One finds Herndon's own wavering cogitations as to certain aspects of the Lincoln-Rutledge romance. It bothered him greatly that he could not get around the fact of Ann's engagement to McNamar. He perhaps realized that the rigidly honorable Lincoln would not have made love to his friend's fiancée while the latter was absent. Even when his biography of Lincoln was in printer's proof, that book which was to stamp the legend indelibly upon the public mind, one finds Herndon writing Weik: "Again the more I think of the Ann Rutledge story the more do I think that the girl had two engagements . . . I shall change my opinion of events & things on the coming of new facts and on more mature reflection in all cases—and so excuse me for 'sorter' wabbling around." He quickly added, however, that he did not want the text of the book changed.

All the vast literature about the Lincoln-Rutledge romance stems from Herndon. For decades the story rode along on his authority, his eccentricities not being fully understood. His material or "evidence" on the subject was not thoroughly studied with due skepticism and critical analysis until after 1942. Meanwhile the legend, which is composed of a supposition of the love affair plus Herndon's fabricated deductions from that supposition, had taken hold. The poetic tale had become embedded in books honestly intended as authentic history, while its popular embellishments in novels, radio scripts, and dramas had sometimes out-Herndoned Herndon. It has been taken to the hearts of the public with some very practical results. In 1919 the sister of Ann Rutledge, Sarah Rutledge Saunders, then about ninety, read one of the popular effusions on the romance published in that year. Mrs. Saunders pointed out various elements in the volume that were "not *true at all*" and gave it as her opinion that someone "wanted to get off a Book" to make money.

The aged lady spoke words of wisdom. There is pressure upon publishers and authors to play up the legend to please the popular taste. This has continued to be true after the publication (in 1945) of the analysis which has been referred to by one scholar as "completely pulverizing the Ann Rutledge myth." The public wants to believe the romantic tale. Herndon had followed his own advice: he had drawn on his imagination and pleased the people.

Herndon's contribution of pseudoanalysis has perpetrated a vast hoax. It takes away Lincoln's real love and substitutes a bogus love. It presents him as mooning over John McNamar's fiancée during the years he was a loving, indulgent husband whose merry laugh was famous among his friends. It is tied up with picturing a loving wife as a cold and heartless shrew, taking from Mary Lincoln that which was her greatest glory—her full unwavering love and devotion for her husband. The fictitious role as Lincoln's one love makes Ann a usurper who robs Lincoln's wife of the thought and consideration normally directed toward the woman who has shared a great man's life.

The legend launched by Herndon has not only warped the characters of the Lincolns in the public mind; it has also warped Lincoln literature. In biography and drama it has tended to crowd out the true and significant things about Lincoln in the manner of the cowbird fledging, also an overgrown impostor, which pushes out the rightful inhabitants of the nest it has invaded.

Herndon's trumped-up notion as to the lasting effect of the conjectured romance on Lincoln's life reaches the zenith of absurdity in the poem by Edgar Lee Masters which is inscribed on Ann's tombstone. In lines whose

poetic power is almost hypnotic, Lincoln's magnanimity
and service to mankind are presented as deriving from the
girl who, if she had lived a little longer, would in all likelihood have become Mrs. John McNamar. Ann's tombstone
reads:

> *Out of me unworthy and unknown*
> *The vibrations of deathless music!*
> *"With malice toward none, with charity for all."*
> *Out of me forgiveness of millions toward millions,*
> *And the beneficent face of a nation*
> *Shining with justice and truth.*
> *I am Ann Rutledge, who sleep beneath these weeds,*
> *Beloved of Abraham Lincoln,*
> *Wedded to him, not through union*
> *But through separation.*
> *Bloom forever, O Republic,*
> *From the dust of my bosom.*

Ann even gets credit for the state of the Union. There
are those who have difficulty understanding the meaning,
and some low-minded individuals, it is said, give an improper interpretation to that ambiguous wedding.

Masters's poem soars to rare literary heights but the
following brutal parody gets down to the prosaic facts:

> *Out of Herndon's spite and mental ramblings*
> *The vibrations of a deathless legend,*
> *With malice toward Mary, wife of Lincoln.*
>
> *Out of this legend millions upon millions*
> *Of readers, listeners, audiences at plays,*
> *Erase the love that Lincoln bore his wife,*
> *His many tender years of full devotion,*
> *And give that love to Ann, innocent usurper.*
>
> *This is Ann Rutledge who sleeps beneath these weeds,*
> *Beloved of and betrothed to John McNamar.*
> *Lincoln, the friend of both, grieved when she died;*
> *That tells the story; but the legend blooms forever*
> *Out of the quirks and hate in Herndon's bosom.*

chapter 32

THE OLD-CLOTHES SCANDAL

The early months of 1867 found Mrs. Lincoln in an agony of mortification over the Ann Rutledge lecture. Yet the blow that ill fortune had in store for her the autumn of that year was to prove even more humiliating and to attract a great deal more public attention.

Her stream of letters continued to deal with her financial worries. We have a description of her about this time: all her natural sprightliness and gaiety gone, a sad sedate woman sitting in her lonely room, trying to focus her attention upon some book while her fingers ran nervously through her hair; then suddenly, because she must take some action, seizing a pen and dashing off a letter which she was apt to regret as soon as it was mailed. Many of these letters she asked to have burned, which seemed to insure their preservation. This was the year that Robert despairingly wrote his fiancée that nothing he could say or do would convince his mother that she was not in actual want. Her financial condition was truly difficult but her statements and actions in regard to it were not in reason.

She had used most of the twenty-two thousand dollars which Congress had given her out of a year's Presidential salary to purchase and furnish a house at 375 West Washington Street, Chicago. According to her later account she was saving every penny she could at this time in order to pay those terrible debts. The purchase of the house resulted in further worry and frustration. By September of '67 she was writing a friend in defeat: "With the most rigid economy, which I am compelled to practise, I find it will be absolutely impossible to continue housekeeping on my present means. . . ." Yet she so wanted a home, she said, in which to retire in her sorrow. The letter is splotched, as with tears.

What to do? She had shut herself off from relatives and friends who could give her sound advice. She would sell some of her expensive clothes and jewels. In her seclusion and mourning, she reasoned, she would have no more use for them. Even in the White House she had, in foreboding, considered them a sort of insurance against a time when she might be in want. She could think of no other way of raising money. According to a newspaper account in '67 the distracted woman for more than a year had been pawning some of her articles, incognito, at a dingy little pawnshop.

The only place with a market for such an elaborate wardrobe as hers would be in New York. She wrote Mrs. Keckley to meet her in that city about the middle of September. She failed to give the colored woman adequate directions as to the time and place of meeting, with the result that when the exhausted Mrs. Lincoln arrived on September 16 and went to the St. Denis Hotel, there was no one to welcome and comfort her. Nothing reveals Mary's Victorian timidity and dependence on others more than the frantic note she wrote Mrs. Keckley the following morning: "I arrived *here* last evening in utter despair *at not* finding you. I am frightened to death, being here alone."

She had registered as Mrs. Clarke; in selling her goods, she was extremely anxious to avoid publicity. When the faithful Mrs. Keckley finally arrived, Mrs. Lincoln had already visited the firm of W. H. Brady, commission broker, at 609 Broadway, and tried to sell some of her jewelry. It would have been impossible for one of her qualities to conceal her identity long, even though she wore a heavy veil, but after presenting herself as Mrs. Clarke, she handed over a ring with her name inscribed in it, a fact which Mr. Keyes of the firm promptly discovered. Mrs. Lincoln left Brady & Company, in some haste, but when Mr. Keyes called on her at her hotel, she confessed her identity.

Once Brady and Keyes found out they were dealing with the much-talked-of Mrs. Lincoln, they were full of suggestions, all of which would result in much advertising for their firm. They assured her if she would place her affairs in their hands that they would raise "at least $100,000 in a few weeks." Some days passed in negotiations. Mrs. Lincoln and Mrs. Keckley made several unsuccessful attempts to sell the clothes to secondhand dealers. Meanwhile they were forced to move from lodging to lodging to conceal Mrs. Lincoln's identity. "Keyes and Brady called often," said Mrs. Keckley, "and they made Mrs. Lincoln believe that, if she would write certain letters for them to show to prominent politicians, they could raise a large sum of money for her."

Mrs. Lincoln finally followed their directions and supplied the letters. Though written in New York, they were dated Chicago and disclosed a plan for having the Brady firm sell her clothes because she was "pressed in a most startling manner for means of common subsistence..." One letter contained a barbed reference to the men of the Republican party "for whom my noble husband did so much" who have "unhesitatingly deprived me of all means of support and left me in a pitiless condition." According to Mrs. Keckley, "Mr. Brady proposed to show the letters to certain politicians, and ask for money on a threat to publish them if his demands, as Mrs. Lincoln's agent, were not complied with." The Republicans, especially with a Presidential election coming up the following year, could not afford to have it said they were leaving the widow of their martyred President in want.

It was the old story of Mrs. Lincoln being taken advantage of by shrewd men for their own purposes. The Brady firm was, of course, entitled to a commission on sales or collections; in the end, when the whole unhappy plan fell through, they presented a bill of about eight hundred dollars to Mrs. Lincoln. Horace Greeley, according to Mrs. Keckley, expressed distrust of Brady and Keyes and apparently with reason.

When no results were forthcoming from the scheme, Mrs. Lincoln finally gave Brady permission to place her wardrobe on exhibition for sale and decided to return to Chicago. On the train she saw a gentleman reading a copy of the New York *World* in which Brady had published the letters she had given him, and overheard humiliating comment on the subject.

Mrs. Keckley said that Mrs. Lincoln had given Brady permission to publish her letters. Brady may have been justified in believing this, as one of her letters specifically stated that she left everything to his "good judgment and excellent sense," and put all into his hands. But Mary said later that the publication came as a surprise to her. The New York *World* was a wicked choice, being aggressively Democratic and bound to play up the whole affair to the embarrassment of the Republican party. Moreover the *World* quoted Mrs. Lincoln as saying that while she was attached to that party, "such men as Weed, Raymond, and Seward . . . to accomplish their purposes would drag it down to the lowest depths of degradation." She was said to have added this intriguing statement: "The late President thoroughly tested these men, and had become fully aware before his death of their treachery and falseness." The whole affair had been thrown into the boiling pot of politics.

Mrs. Keckley had remained in New York to look after further details of the clothes selling. Back in Chicago Mrs. Lincoln wrote her on October 6: "I am writing this morning with a broken heart after a sleepless night of great mental suffering. R[obert] came up last evening like a maniac, and almost threatening his life, looking like death, because the letters of the *World* were published in yesterday's paper. . . . I pray for death this morning. Only my darling Taddie prevents my taking my life. . . . Tell Mr. Brady and Keyes not to have a line of mine once more in print. I am nearly losing my reason."

The following day the *World* printed another letter of Mrs. Lincoln, one that set forth fully her distorted idea that those politicians who had fared well in the Lincoln administration should help her financially. It concerned Mr. Wakeman, surveyor of the port of New York, whom we have met in an earlier chapter.

W. H. BRADY, ESQ.

My Dear Sir:
Please call and see Hon. Abram Wakeman. He was largely indebted to me for obtaining the lucrative office which he has held for several years, and from which he has amassed a very large fortune. He will assist me in my painful and humiliating situation, scarcely removed from want. He would scarcely hesitate to return, in a small manner, the many favors my husband and myself always showered upon him. Mr. Wakeman many times excited my sympathies in his urgent appeals for office, as well for himself as others. Therefore he will only be too happy to relieve me by purchasing one or more of the articles you will please place before him.

Five days later it was mentioned in the *World* that Mr. Wakeman when approached by "Mrs. Lincoln's agent" was "affable" and "profuse of promises" of help which he failed to keep. After the publication of Mrs. Lincoln's letters, it was insinuated that he had gone to Chicago because ". . . it was evident that Mr. Wakeman is not desirous of having any more letters published, and would seem to be desirous of creeping out of the 'unpleasant affair' by having an interview with Mrs. Lincoln." One newspaper mentioned that Mrs. Lincoln had denounced Wakeman as one of the ungrateful Republicans.

With the affair breaking thus into print, curiosity seekers flocked to Brady's at 609 Broadway to look at and finger the items for sale but not to buy. Newspapers rocked with articles and editorials on the old-clothes scandal. Some said Mrs. Lincoln was blackmailing certain politicians to give her money or else she would make public shady transactions in which they had taken part. The resultant shaking in their boots of those particular politicians who could not afford to be investigated furnishes the one comic element in the grim story. Their safeguard against what Mrs. Lincoln might say was to put into circulation every possible story to discredit her. Thurlow Weed, in a strategic position as editor of the New York *Commercial Advertiser*, printed in that paper a long smearing article reviving in detail the old story that Mrs. Lincoln had padded the bill for the Napoleon dinner, suggesting that her presents were bribes, and stating that Congress and the people would have provided for her, if she had not forfeited their respect. This article was widely reprinted. The New York *Herald* promptly slapped back at this attack by "the old lobby king, Thurlow Weed," defended Mrs. Lincoln's right to sell her clothes, and added: "The fact is, these old Republican politicians have always persecuted Mrs. Lincoln."

All the scandalous rumors of the smear campaign during Lincoln's Presidency were blown into the open again, plus the accusation that Mrs. Lincoln had carted off the White House furnishings. Someone added an ingenious trimming to the last: she had prolonged her stay in the White House by pretending she was about to become a mother, so as to give herself more time to pack up the spoons and other articles.

The *Southern Opinion* of Richmond suggested Mrs. Lincoln was getting ready to marry again. It also published a belittling parody-poem stressing the accusation that she was trying to sell articles she had received as bribes:

What Cabinet member (now hid in the dark)
Bought his seat by his gifts to you, fair Mrs. Clarke?
What opulent presents were made in advance
By seekers of missions to Russia and France?

The most resentment-arousing of all the accusations, that she was a traitor to the Union, was well aired again. Robert Lincoln, abnormally sensitive to publicity, was frantic. He was quoted as saying that his only explanation of his mother's clothes selling was that she was insane. A number of newspapers suggested that Mrs. Lincoln was a monomaniac on the subject of money. The accusation filled her with horror and resentment. One gets her reaction in a letter she wrote to Mrs. Keckley: "A piece in the morning *Tribune* . . . says there is no doubt Mrs. L.—— *is deranged*—has been for years past, and will end her life in a lunatic asylum. They would doubtless like me to begin it *now*."

She had mentioned, more than a year and a half before, that she was receiving letters on the subject of her taking the White House furnishings. Undoubtedly at this time letters of abuse were pouring in upon this sick and nervous woman and there was no kind Mr. Stoddard to screen them. Newspapers with denunciatory articles about her were thrown upon her doorstep. She wrote Mrs. Keckley: "If I had committed murder in every city in this *blessed Union,* I could not be more traduced." "I suppose I would be *mobbed* if I ventured out," ran another letter. "You would not recognize me now. The glass shows me a pale, wretched, haggard face, and my dresses are like bags on me. And all because I was doing what I felt to be my duty." An added element of her suffering was the realization that all this public furor would make getting a pension from Congress more difficult than ever.

"Never was an act committed with a more innocent intention than mine was," Mary wrote on October 18. "Having no further use for the articles proposed to be sold —and really requiring the proceeds—I deposited them with an agent & I presumed no publicity would result

from it. I was not more astonished than *you* would have
been to see my letters in print." She poured out her brood-
ing bitterness to her friend: the Republican politicians had
not helped her with a pension, and when she tried to help
herself she was persecuted. She soon lost faith in Brady
and Keyes: "I begin to think they are making a political
business of *my clothes,* and not for *my* benefit either."

By the end of 1867 Mrs. Lincoln was trying desperately
to halt the forces she had set in motion. She was writing
Mrs. Keckley, who was still looking after her interests in
New York: "I believe any more newspaper attacks would
lay me low. . . . I tremble at the bill that B. & K. [Brady &
Keyes] may send me, I am so illy prepared to meet any
expense." By January 12, 1868, she was doing her best to
get her clothes out of their hands: "For heaven's sake see
K. & B. when you receive this," ran her letter, "and have
them immediately returned to me, *with their bill.* I am so
miserable I feel like taking my own life." A proposal that
certain clothes she had given Mrs. Keckley be paraded
in Europe had almost turned her wild; she continued, "R.
[obert] would go *raving distracted* if such a thing was
done." Anything was better than more publicity.

A new accusation appeared in the fall of '67. It was suggested that Mrs. Lincoln was writing a book on her experiences in the White House and that the radicals were
loudly announcing that she was of unsound mind in their
fear of exposures to come. One paper stated that Mrs. Lincoln denied the accusation. There were many rumors
afloat about some such book.

A small volume called *Behind the Scenes,* giving an intimate account of the Lincolns in the White House, was
published in the spring of 1868 over the name of Elizabeth Keckley. Mrs. Keckley was intelligent and literate but
she undoubtedly had the help of a ghost writer or ghost
writers. In her old age she said, according to a newspaper
interview, that she told her story to two newspapermen
who employed stenographers, got what she said down in
writing, and published it. Thus it would seem that a number of people had a hand in the book, especially as it was
made the vehicle of the views of a special group, the
abolitionists, who were earnestly working for the betterment of the Negro against antagonistic forces. The very
fact that it was put out over the name of a mulatto was
significant of this. So once more a matter concerning Mrs.

Lincoln was involved in one of the bitter public questions of the day.

The preface, over Mrs. Keckley's signature, stated that the purpose of the book was to make people understand Mrs. Lincoln and her good intentions. "If I have betrayed confidence in anything I have published," ran this foreword, "it has been to place Mrs. Lincoln in a better light before the world." There is no reason to doubt that Mrs. Keckley told the story with the idea of helping Mrs. Lincoln, and told it with what appears to be, with the testing of modern research, a high degree of accuracy. But the publication of the book, which stepped on a lot of prominent toes which were very much alive, resulted in another furor. A viciously clever parody *Behind the Seams* by "Betsey Kickley," who was represented as a Negro woman who could sign her name only by making an X for her mark, was rushed into print the same year.

Mrs. Lincoln's humiliation and resentment about the Keckley book apparently ended her friendship with the faithful colored woman whose record is one of loving devotion. The widow was thus deprived of one of the few remaining persons who could comfort her. This estrangement was one of the miserable chain of events resulting from the clothes-selling fiasco. Early in 1868 the bulk of the garments were returned to Mrs. Lincoln and she paid over eight hundred dollars to Brady and Keyes.

With the newspapers hurling accusations, with abusive letters pouring in upon her, Mary was afraid to venture out for fear of insult. She saw only one solution to her situation; she must leave the country. To avoid "persecution, from the vampyre press," she later wrote Mrs. Orne, ". . . I had to flee to a land of strangers for refuge." She had determined to do this shortly after the Keckley book appeared; the humiliation of a Victorian woman at having her intimate life exposed can hardly be imagined. Her resentment flashed out in a letter to Mrs. White in May of '68, in which she mentioned her proposed plan to go abroad. "This proposition from me," she wrote with vehemence, "does not argue *a debt of $70,000!!* as *the colored* historian asserts." Mary then added: "It is my comfort to know, that I do not owe, a dollar in the world . . ." Later she told how she and Robert collected and paid all debts, thereby enduring considerable privation. "It was our pride to have it said," she wrote James H. Orne, husband of her beloved friend—"that there were no debts against the estate—but I can assure you—in perfect truth that *many dinnerless* days, have fallen to *my* position in consequence of *all this*." She apologized to him for the tear-stained paper.

There is reason to believe that certain Republician politicians helped Mrs. Lincoln secretly in paying her personal debts incurred by her extravagance during Lincoln's Presidency. Gossiping Isaac Newton talked to John Hay about it. "There was one big bill for furs which give her a sight of trouble," Hay quoted Newton as saying—"she got it paid at last by some of her friends—I don't know who for certain—not Sim Draper [a New York Republican politician] for he promised to pay it ... but after Lincoln's death he wouldn't do it."

There is always danger, when treating Mrs. Lincoln's actions within the area of her irrationality, of forgetting that in most respects her mind and personality remained normal. In the midst of the old-clothes scandal Robert made a statement which a biographer of Mrs. Lincoln might well repeat today: ". . . it is very hard to deal with one who is sane on all subjects but one." To balance the picture it must be remembered that in these early years of her widowhood she was writing fine and appealing letters untouched by her obsessions. A blind girl had written her a letter of sympathy. Mary was deeply touched and answered: "My dear young friend, although unknown to me, I love you, for being able, so thoroughly to appreciate the noble character of my idolized husband." Mindful of the girl's misfortune, for which she was most sympathetic, the widow continued: "My . . . husband, was the *light* of our eyes—we never felt . . . that we could love him sufficiently. . . . life is *all darkness*, the sun is a mockery to me, in my great sorrow."

In the summer of '67 she had gone to Racine, Wisconsin. She was considering placing Tad in a school there, but when she visited it she said "there was an air of *restraint* which I did not exactly like." Her maternal tenderness was repelled by the institutional aspect of the school. "My feelings were specially *shocked*," she wrote, "by seeing the little white cots of the boys, where they are wont, to repose so far away, from the loving Mothers, who would at any moment, give almost their life to see them."

It was at the beginning of the year of the old-clothes

scandal that she wrote her superb letter to the French citizens who had sent a gold medal, the letter in which she recognized Lincoln's role in world democracy. At the end of that tormented year, hagridden as she was by fear of want, she sent goods and money to the stepmother Lincoln had loved, with a letter of infinite tenderness and an offer to help her in any way she could.

By the summer of 1868 Mary's plan to go abroad had taken definite shape. The date of sailing, however, had complications. As she wrote Mrs. White: ". . . you are aware I am peculiarly situated, being exceedingly anxious to witness the marriage of my son—with a young lady, who is so charming & whom I love so much. The terror of having to proceed to *Washington* to witness it, almost overpowers me. My little son is so anxious to remain, until that event takes place & perhaps the regret I may also feel in the future that I had not gratified them all by remaining, has quite determined me."

After Robert's wedding in September 1868, Mrs. Lincoln and Tad set sail on October 1 on the *City of Baltimore* and ultimately arrived in Frankfort on the Main in Germany. There Tad was placed in the " 'Institute' of Dr. Hohagen," where he studied "with a number of well behaved German and English boys." A kindly gentleman, F. W. Bogen, formerly an army chaplain, noticing on shipboard the "quiet and throughout dignified deportment" of the black-clad widow, offered his friendship and assistance in travel, as he also was going to Frankfort. He wrote Charles Sumner how she was situated: "She lives very retiredly in the Hotel d'Angleterre, occupies only one room, sees few friends, yet her daily necessary Hotel expenses (she takes her meals in her room, in order not to be exposed to the gaze of the curious) are nearly 9 florins [something over four dollars], the lowest rate at which she could reduce them." Mr. Bogen explained that owing to the high rank her husband had held, and the impression that she was receiving a pension from the United States government, she was charged extra-high prices on all sides.

Thus began the pattern of her years abroad, wandering from place to place, taking cheap, cold lodgings, suffering continually from prostrating headaches, rheumatic pain and respiratory infections, obsessed with poverty. She was now clinging desperately to the hope that in America a pension would be given her. One follows her flittings by her many letters.

During Tad's vacation in the summer of '69 he and his mother visited Scotland for seven weeks, traveling, as she said, "incog—Mrs. Lincoln's name, was never breathed." In the beauty of majestic scenery and in the thoughts of beloved poems suggested by visiting Burns's birthplace, Mary's natural responsiveness rose momentarily above her sorrow and once more her spirit felt a thrill. That summer she had the comfort of seeing beloved old friends. She visited her former pastor, James Smith, in Scotland; she feared his days were numbered and made a special effort to take the trip. Mrs. James H. Orne and her family were happily making a prolonged stay abroad at that time. Mary had some precious visits with her. On September 12, 1869, that compassionate friend poured out Mary's situation in a long letter to Charles Sumner.

Arriving at Frankfort, Mrs. Orne had called upon Mrs. Lincoln late one evening. In her own words: "I followed the waiter to the *fourth story* and the back part of it too—and there in a small cheerless desolate looking room with but one window—two chairs and a wooden table with a solitary candle—I found *the wife the petted indulged wife* of my *noble* hearted just good *murdered* President Abraham Lincoln—the 'Justinian'—can you believe it?—it would be hard to say which overcame me most the painful meeting or *the place*— My very blood boiled within my veins and I almost *cried out—shame on my countrymen*— Mrs. Lincoln was completely overwhelmed with grief—her sobs and tears wrung my own heart and I thought at the moment if her *tormentors* and *slanderers* could see her—they surely *might be satisfied*."

It had been so long since Mary had had someone to whom she could unburden her heart. Mrs. Orne sat listening until dawn began to outline the solitary window. She explained in her letter to Sumner that Mrs. Lincoln could not afford a maid and when she was ill in bed Tad stayed away from his school to care for her. The letter continued: ". . . to say *she lives retired* does not express her manner of life—she lives *alone*. I never knew what the word *Alone* meant before."

Mrs. Orne told Sumner of the rumors circulating abroad: that Mrs. Lincoln had been accessory to the assassination of her husband and that the American officials had sent her in exile abroad as punishment. The result was that even the servants in the hotel treated her with rudeness and scorn. Mrs. Orne was aghast at such cruelty and injustice: ". . . it seems to me Abraham Lincoln might call for vengeance from the ground—and yet his *loving gentle big* heart—with all *his sensitiveness*—whilst breaking over the cruelties practised upon the wife of his bosom —would in his agony cry out 'Father forgive them.' "

The reason Mrs. Orne wrote to Senator Sumner was that he was fighting in Washington to procure a pension for Mrs. Lincoln. On January 14, 1869, a bill had been introduced in the Senate that would have given Mrs. Lincoln a pension for life, the amount left blank. In February a letter from her asking for a pension had been read in the Senate. Sumner proposed the amount of $5000 for the pension. The bill failed to pass the Fortieth Congress, which adjourned on March 3, a cruel dashing of Mrs. Lincoln's hopes. From the first days of her widowhood she had hoped for, and felt that she was entitled to a pension. Mr. Bogen had explained her reasoning in his letter to Sumner: "Her husband, the Constitutional commander-in-chief of the Army and Navy of the U. S., fell by the ball of an assassin, during the war. The widow of a private even who . . . died in the service of the U. S. receives a pension." To Mary it seemed a slight to Lincoln's memory that provision was not made for his wife and children.

When the Senate of the Forty-first Congress met in special session, Sumner promptly introduced on March 5, 1869, a pension bill for Mrs. Lincoln in the amount of $5000. Over a year later a bill making the pension $3000 was introduced in the House of Representatives. The effort to have a pension voted for Mrs. Lincoln went through all the vicissitudes and delaying tactics that a bitter opposition could achieve. Meanwhile there were many months of anxious waiting on the part of the widow living abroad. News of some of the setbacks would reach her. In May she was living just outside of Frankfort and one day she went into the city to get Tad some needed schoolbooks, to see her doctor, and above all to examine the newspapers which she constantly hungered for and saw so seldom. "I went to the Eng—reading room—" she wrote Mrs. Orne, "and there met my *terrible fate. . . .* an Eng. paper said that the Senate com. had decided against on the ground, that I had property to the amount of $60,000! ! !" She collapsed and her physician had to be called to attend her. Doctors then seem to have had a neat system for disposing of patients they could not help: they sent them some place else. Mrs. Lincoln was hustled off to Bohemia within twelve hours, where she lodged in a third-floor room without even a serving woman to help her. Arriving exhausted, she longed for death.

One terrible feature of the pension fight was that it revived public abuse of Mrs. Lincoln. Some thought that the anticipation of this had been a factor in her going abroad. "I dread to have my name again before the people—" she wrote in January 1870, ". . . my nerves could scarcely stand many more attacks." The bitter debate in the Senate had aired all the old accusations. Personal attacks on her by the opponents of the bill knew no restraint. Richard Yates of Illinois, vaunting his friendship for Abraham Lincoln, made this deadly insinuation about the widow of his friend: "There are recollections and memories . . . that I will not recall publicly . . . a woman should be true to her husband . . . I shall not . . . go into details . . . God Almighty bless the name and fame of Abraham Lincoln."

Lyman Trumbull supported the bill. Simon Cameron pointed out that Mrs. Lincoln had been the victim of deliberate slander, that those opposed to Lincoln had done "all they could to make a bad reputation for Mrs. Lincoln" and had succeeded.

Finally on July 14, 1870, more than five years after her husband's death, an annual pension of $3000 was voted for Lincoln's widow, passing by a narrow margin 28 to 20 with 24 absent. Less than half of the Republican senators voted yea; many of them had wanted the bill killed by inaction. The present bill had already passed the House of Representatives, 85 to 65, with 77 not voting. This action put Mrs. Lincoln in a much better financial position but nothing could remove her obsession of poverty. That reduction of two thousand dollars was a burning humiliation; from then on her efforts were concerned with having the amount increased.

The pension news was possibly late in reaching Mary for the onset of the Franco-Prussian war was disrupting her plans around that time. She and Tad had gone to Innsbruck, Tirol, Austria, for a brief holiday when they were notified "that the French were on the Rhine" and they must return to Frankfort and settle their affairs in Germany. The emergency, which caught Mary short of money, was a harrowing experience. "My heart has been made sick the past summer, by being *almost* in the midst of the fearful war, which has convulsed the Continent," she wrote Charles Sumner in September from England, to which she and Tad had fled.

In the unhappy autumn of '69 Mary had had one fundamental source of joy: a child had been born to Robert and his wife. Nothing could have rejoiced her maternal heart more. Another Lincoln baby and a little girl! The new grandmother wrote Mrs. Orne about the event and between the lines one reads her longing that the baby be named for her. But "as *the other Grandmama presided* with the Dr & nurse over the advent of the darling child perhaps *she* may consider *herself* entitled to the name—surely myself, as *one Grandmother* (how very queer that sounds *to me*) being named Mary, the mother of the child *Mary,* the child being called so too, would be rather too much in the beginning." "Mary Lincoln" happily became the baby's name. Her adoring grandmother called her "Little Mamie" and was quite sure she was the perfection of babyhood.

Mrs. Lincoln's affection poured out in her letter to her daughter-in-law: "That blessed baby, how dearly I would love to look upon her sweet young face. . . . I do so trust that Bob will come over with you if it is only for three months . . . He loves you so *very dearly* . . . I was such an excessively indulged wife—my darling husband was so gentle and easy. You know you will always be *First Love* of daughters-in-law."

She delighted to send gifts to Robert's wife: "I never see anything particularly pretty—that I do not wish it was yours." She worried about her daughter-in-law's health and hoped she would not have another baby too soon: "I hope you will have a good rest and enjoy yourself *free* for a year or more to come. . . . You should go out *every day* and enjoy yourself—you are so *very young* and should be as gay as a lark. Trouble comes soon enough, my dear child, and you must enjoy life, whenever you can."

Mrs. Lincoln felt that Tad's English education was being neglected. By September 10, 1870, she found a desirable English tutor for him: "The gentleman . . . is very highly educated—very quiet and gentlemanly and patience itself." But her seventeen-year-old son was continually homesick: "Tad is almost wild to see Bob, you and the baby," she wrote Robert's wife; "he thinks the latter must be a rare young lady, I am also of his opinion."

In her letters to her daughter-in-law one finds the normal Mrs. Lincoln. A gentleman who saw much of her in England gave a description of her at this time: "bright," "sympathetic, cordial, sensible . . . with no trace of eccentricity in conduct or manner." He added: "I could not for the life of me recognize the Mrs. Lincoln of the newspapers in the Mrs. Lincoln I saw." Mrs. Orne had the same experience. Hearing reports that Mrs. Lincoln was deranged, this good friend reported to Charles Sumner: "I have watched her closely—by day and by night—for weeks—and fail to discover any evidence of abberration of mind in her."

Benjamin Moran of the American legation in London wrote in his journal on September 4, 1870, of meeting "the wife of ex-President Lincoln" and being "agreeably surprised to find her an unpretending woman of excellent manners, much intelligence and very lady like appearance." He had a long talk with her, noting her "expressive face," "very decided Southern accent," deep black dress and widow's cap. Her height, he thought, was "about 5 feet 3 inches." "After seeing her," he concluded, "I am prepared to believe that all the attacks upon her in the newspapers were sheer scandal and falsehoods." This is the more remarkable as the critical Mr. Moran was not given to any amiable habit of thinking well of the people he met.

Because of a bad cough and much pain of rheumatism, she went to Italy early in 1871, leaving Tad in an English school until spring. Then mother and son started home to America, home to see Robert, "who is all that is noble and good and his lovely little wife," home to the magnet of a grandchild. That voyage, though a rough one, undoubtedly had its sweet anticipations for her. In Chicago they found Robert, his wife, and child well and rejoicing over their arrival. At last Mary Lincoln held her little namesake in her arms. She had that brief moment of respite and uplift, but fate was preparing for this ill-starred woman two final and terrible tragedies.

chapter 33

"WITHOUT TADDIE": INSANITY?

What changes had the years abroad wrought in Tad? The New York *Tribune,* noting the arrival in the city of Mrs. Lincoln and her youngest son, answered this question: "He has grown up a tall, fine-looking lad of 18, who bears a faint resemblance to the tricksy little sprite whom visitors to the White House remember. . . ." Looking at him people noticed a very different resemblance, one that drew their hearts to him. His mother had repeatedly mentioned in her letters that he reminded her so much of his father. Mrs. Orne, visiting them in Frankfort, had been struck with this likeness, both in looks and traits of character.

After a brief and welcome stay at Robert's home, Mrs. Lincoln and Tad removed to the Clifton House. One who was there remembered that Tad "was a very lovable boy, quiet, gentle mannered and good-natured, nothing loud or boisterous about him, and he was quite a favorite in the house."

The change had begun when the tearful twelve-year-old after his father's death faced up to the truth: "I am not a President's son now. I won't have many presents any more. Well, I will try and be a good boy . . ." As a practical start he began to dress himself without help in the mornings.

From the beginning of his mother's widowhood his tender spirit rose to her need of him. When he heard her sobbing in the depths of night, he went to her bedside to comfort her. When she returned to Chicago from the humiliating clothes-selling trip to New York, "At the depot," she said, "my darling little Taddie was waiting for me, and his voice never sounded so sweet."

During her severe illnesses abroad he was her nurse. She found his ministering as gentle as a woman's and the tenderness in his eyes watching over her was like that she had seen in the eyes of his father. Once in Frankfort when she was recovering from a sharp illness she wrote that the physician "has directed me to wear flannel next my skin—and dear careful Taddie has just brought me in, some soft *woollen ones.*"

He knew the value to her battered spirit of a pleasant compliment. "My Mother, is a great woman," he would say to her playfully. Through affection he could influence her where others failed. Once she laid aside her mourning garments, because it was Tad's birthday and he wished it.

It was a difficult role for a boy in his teens, to be all in all in a foreign land to a mother who was sick in body and mind. Nor was study involving a foreign language easy, especially to one with a speech defect. This Tad finally overcame completely by reading aloud as a regular exercise. Robert added interesting details: ". . . as it was done mainly while he was in Germany & under a German (English speaking) tutor, he came home . . . articulating perfectly, but with deliberation—speaking German perfectly but in English owing to his practice in reading he had a slight German accent." In England he studied with his tutor seven hours a day. It was not the life or the climate for a youth who was probably tubercular.

Tad was ill with a severe cold shortly after he and his mother arrived in Chicago in May of '71. He evidently improved for a while, then relapsed into a long illness. On June 8 his mother wrote Mrs. White: "My dear boy has been *very, very* dangerously ill . . . I have been sitting up . . . constantly for the last ten nights . . ." It was a "torturing illness"; owing to a dropsical condition in the chest Tad could not lie down but must sit up in a chair. Robert had never witnessed "Such suffering," and it lasted six weeks. Mary, hovering over her son, grasping at every straw for hope, daily saw the thin young face etched with pain.

Early in the second week of July Tad seemed better and his mother's tension eased slightly. With the hope of recovery in their hearts, she and Robert could jest tenderly with the invalid. On Friday that week a picture of Robert's little daughter, Mary Lincoln, was brought to the sick boy and he brightened as he looked delightedly at the loved baby face. But at half past four the next morning, July 15, Robert was hastily summoned to the side of his dying brother. There were several hours of agonizing distress; then Mary saw her youngest son fall forward in his chair, and the light went out of the dear eyes that had looked at her with Lincoln's own understanding love.

The exhausted mother was in a state of collapse. She was too ill to make the journey to Springfield when Tad was placed in the tomb beside his father. For the fourth time in her life Mary lay utterly prostrated with the grief of an irreparable loss. Her agony was like that which had followed the death of Willie but then she had had a gentle husband to sit by her bedside. When that husband was taken away, Tad had stood by to comfort her. Now she was almost alone. "I feel that there is no life to me, without my idolized Taddie," she wrote. "One by one I have consigned to their resting place, my idolized ones, & now, in *this* world, there is nothing left me, but the deepest anguish & desolation."

It is possible that Mrs. Lincoln had intended to make a home for herself and Tad in Chicago. Her pension had eased her financial stringency. Tad's death left her shattered and unable to plan. Her nervousness and melancholia were overwhelming. Robert employed Mrs. Richard Fitzgerald, mother of Eddie Foy, the actor, to be nurse, guard, and traveling companion, a most difficult position to fill. Mrs. Lincoln went back to her old restless flitting from place to place, trying to get away from the grief in her own heart.

In the summer of 1872 she visited Wisconsin seeking help for increased physical discomfort in waters that were thought to be medicinal. It was said that a dropsical condition had developed. She later referred to trouble from bloating. Wherever she went she sought seclusion. But even the privilege of being unnoticed was denied her. A fresh spurt of tongue-wagging about the widow was taking place that summer, owing to the publication of a most sensational book.

Ward Hill Lamon, aspiring to be the author of a life of Lincoln by a method that involved little effort on his part, had bought copies of all the Lincoln material (letters, interviews, records, and other documents) which Herndon had collected up to September 1869. Herndon, of course, would not have parted with copies of his cherished documents if he had not needed money badly, but neglect of his law practice, drink, and a financial depression were ruining him. Lamon then arranged for Chauncey Black, a man unfriendly to Lincoln, to write the book from Herndon's records. It was a deadly combination. The resulting *Life of Abraham Lincoln* "by Ward H. Lamon" was published in late May 1872.

Mary Lincoln was not to live to see the publication of Herndon's biography of her husband, but in the Lamon volume were set forth the features of it most calculated to fill her with horror: the illegitimacy of Lincoln's mother, Lincoln as defaulting bridegroom (Mary of all people knew that story was poppycock), the Ann Rutledge tale tied up with Herndon's theory that the Lincoln marriage was unhappy, the accusation that Lincoln was not a Christian, insinuations that he was illegitimate. To Mary the publication was another in the long list of betrayals by those she had counted as friends.

She poured out her vigorously worded indignation in a letter, paying her respects to the "debased character of the author" who had written "sensational falsehoods & base calumnies, wherewith he may . . . enrich *his* coffers." She had not read the book, she said, she would not allow it to be brought into her presence.

Finally, with the public buzzing about the question of Lincoln's illegitimacy and his supposed love for Ann Rutledge and unhappy marriage, Mary again fled the borders of her own country, this time into Canada. She returned from an absence of some months to find that Lamon's book had launched a controversy over Lincoln's religion.

On December 12, 1873, Herndon delivered in Springfield a lecture with the thesis that Lincoln, like Herndon himself, was an infidel. In substantiation of this, he quoted Mrs. Lincoln as having said to him during their interview in 1866 that Lincoln was not a "technical Christian." To use the devout wife's testimony to brand her beloved husband with a term she abhorred seemed the final stab. The lecture also contained much discussion of Lincoln's insinuated illegitimacy. It referred to Mary's beloved former pastor James Smith as "a great old rascal" and made him out as a liar. Mary was devoted to James Smith; he had championed her against Herndon after the Ann Rutledge lecture and she had gone to Scotland to see him in the summer of 1869 because she feared his days were numbered. The result of the lecture was a quarrel between Herndon and Mrs. Lincoln that got into the newspapers and swept the country.

It has long been known that Mary wrote her cousin John Todd Stuart about Herndon's lecture. On December 19, 1873, the *Illinois State Journal* announced on the first page that Mrs. Lincoln "denies unequivocally that she had the conversation with Mr. Herndon, as stated by him." This statement was ambiguous, and many failed to take in the qualifying phrase "as stated by him," so that the impression got out that Mrs. Lincoln had denied having had the interview itself. This impression too went over the country and stung Herndon to the quick.

As his biographer has said: "It was the signal for Herndon to loose all his long stored-up hatred for Mary Lincoln." He wrote an open letter giving full details of the interview, presenting Mrs. Lincoln as a liar and referring to her "spasmodic madness." It was printed as a broadside called "Mrs. Lincoln's Denial and What She Says," as well as being published in newspapers over the country.

It has been accepted that Mrs. Lincoln did deny the interview. Now at last, with the unfolding of new evidence, her own voice can be heard to say that the charge is not true. Her letters to John Todd Stuart, here used for the first time, show that she not only did not deny the interview but also specifically told her cousin not to deny it. What she denied was Herndon's use of her conversation; it was, she said, "utterly false" and "entirely perverted." It is well to emphasize that she now stands clear of having made a false denial. With Herndon's broadside capturing widespread attention and Mrs. Lincoln's own statement on the subject not available until the present, too much has been made of this untrue accusation against Mary Lincoln.

Her letters bring to light some close-up details of the interview: "When Herndon, presented his disagreeable self to me, at the time, he mentions, his appearance & the *air* he brought with him, were so revolting, that I could scarcely ask him to be seated. . . . The flowing bowl, must have been *entirely* exhausted—when he wrote that intellectual production [the lecture]." A friend had said to her, she continued: "Certainly, my dear Mrs. Lincoln, your thoughts rise above such 'small barking dogs' as this creature Herndon & Lamon." She would not dignify them by shedding tears over what they had done. "I have no tears *left,* for those, for whom my beloved husband, did *so much* and have vilified *his* memory, and those of his sorrowing family."

This small-barking-dog attitude toward Herndon was to prove a great mistake in the long run. Mary and her relatives felt that it was perhaps best to ignore a man of such poor standing in the community. In 1873, with little law practice left, Herndon was living in poverty on a farm six miles north of Springfield. One may have a genuine pity for the man in those pinched and frustrated years. He made a pathetic picture when he walked the weary miles into town, so unkempt that little boys were told there was a bird's nest in his shaggy beard. One of them remembered years later how he tried, somewhat fearfully, to get close enough to investigate the truth of this statement. Neighbors had seen Herndon, dead drunk, "hauled home from town just like you would haul a hog on hay in the back end of the wagon . . ." Mary and her relatives did not realize that in time Herndon's printed word would reach a public which did not, like themselves, know him and his failings and limitations.

In one of her letters to John Todd Stuart at this time Lincoln's widow rose to a heart-warming defense of her husband's living Christianity. Very soon, after Herndon met her for the interview in 1866, she remembered well, she said, that he "branched off" on the question of Mr. Lincoln's religious beliefs. "I told him in positive words," wrote Mary, "that my husband's heart, was naturally religious—he had often desribed to me, his noble mother, . . . the prayers she offered up for him, that he should become a pious boy & man. And then I told Mr. Herndon, what an acceptable book, *that* Great Book [the Bible], was always to him. In our family bereavements, it was *there,* he first turned for comfort. Sabbath mornings he accompanied me to hear dear good old Dr. Smith, preach & moreover, I reminded Mr. Herndon, that his last words, to his dear friends on leaving for Washington, with an impending Rebellion before the country were words uttered in great a[n]xiety & sadness 'Pray for me!' "

In closing she expressed her utter frustration in combating Herndon's misrepresentations: "What more can I say in answer to this man, who when my heart was broken with anguish, issued falsehoods, against me & mine, which were enough to make the Heaven's blush."

In her letters to Cousin John, Mary revealed the deadly hurt of Herndon's insinuation that Lincoln was not legitimate. If that were true she and her sons were not even entitled to the name of Lincoln; they were Hankses. After Lamon's book (which contained the first published suggestion that Lincoln might have been illegitimate) appeared, Robert Lincoln, smarting with humiliation, began a frantic search for the facts about the marriage of Thomas Lincoln and Nancy Hanks.

Abraham Lincoln himself had written the date of his parents' marriage in the family Bible in Coles County, along with the other marriages, births and deaths. After Lincoln was assassinated Dennis Hanks removed the page and folded it so that it became worn in the creases and fell into fragments, with the result that the upper-right-hand corner with that marriage date was lost. Fortunately one of the relatives, John J. Hall, had copied the full page before Dennis removed it from the Bible, but Herndon evidently did not know of this full copy. As he related in his lecture on Lincoln's religion: when he visited Coles County he saw the page which Dennis Hanks had torn out of the Bible and it was "broken up into squares of about two inches." Herndon put the pieces together, found there was no marriage date for Lincoln's parents, and jumped to the conclusion that this was evidence of Lincoln's illegitimacy. Robert Lincoln, however, had evidently obtained a transcript of the complete record that had been copied by Hall, which showed Lincoln's parents had been married over two and a half years before he was born. Herndon mentioned in his lecture that Robert claimed to have proof of the marriage date, but, said Herndon: "I aver there is no such record."

All this explains Mary's remark in her letter to her Cousin John: "... the *missing page*—which you know will *once more safe & sure* make us Lincoln's *once more* ... is deposited in my son's vault."

Herndon's utterly false insinuation that Lincoln was illegitimate was based on his own groundless inference and fragments of gossip as thin as wisps of smoke. He himself with his usual vacillation wavered in his belief of them from day to day. As his biographer has said:

"Had Herndon published his 'evidences,' he would have been revealed as the irrational and speculative man he was." But he gave out the insinuation that Lincoln was illegitimate (wagging tongues would do the rest) and thereby caused Lincoln's widow a world of humiliation. To be helpless to stop Herndon's publicizing of untruths about her husband and herself caused in Mary a torturing frustration which Dr. Evans thought contributed to her psychopathic condition which followed.

Again Mrs. Lincoln went traveling. March 1875 found her in Florida. From testimony given two months later one gets a picture of what these final blows had done to her. It was said that now she had delusions of persecution. But when in history has a woman had greater justification for believing herself persecuted? Sick and nervous as she was, her life had become a nightmare of fear. She walked the floor through sleepless nights, keeping the gas turned high against the threat of the dark, eyeing her windows with dread of the nameless terror that might enter through them.

In the daytime the smoke from a neighboring chimney might suggest to her that the city was about to burn. Her personal pride was drowned in fear; the habit of a lifetime was neglected and she at times failed to give thought to neatness in dress. If food tasted strange, she was sure she was being poisoned. When she entered a public dining room, she whispered: "I am afraid; I am afraid."

She had no one left now to depend on and love except Robert. What if something should happen to him as it had to all the others? She was having hallucinations now and she became convinced that Robert was ill. Perhaps there was a starting point of the idea, such as a delayed letter; at all events she telegraphed Robert's physician in Chicago on March 12: "My belief is my son is ill; telegraph. I start for Chicago to-morrow." The doctor got in touch with Robert, who telegraphed his mother that he was quite well and that she should remain in Florida. She probably did not receive his wire before she sent her second telegram, which arrived an hour and a half after her first. It was to Robert himself and it gave a glimpse into her tortured mind: "My dearly beloved son, Robert T. Lincoln—Rouse yourself and live for your mother;

you are all I have; from this hour all I have is yours. I pray every night that you may be spared to your mother."

She arrived on March 15 in Chicago, where she went to the Grand Pacific Hotel, in spite of Robert's wish to take her to his home. The son faithfully stayed at the hotel with her, in a room adjoining hers, getting little sleep because of her restlessness and fears at night. At times she acted in irresponsible fashion and once left her room without being properly dressed. When Robert put his arm around her to lead her back and, assisted by a hotel employee, forced her into her room, she screamed: "You are going to murder me."

She was carrying in her pocket securities for fifty-seven thousand dollars. Her buying mania persisted. She left the hotel to make wild purchases, spending large sums of money. Robert naturally was fearful she would dissipate her estate; yet the only way he could get the control of it out of her hands in order to protect her interests was to have her declared legally insane. He called for an insanity hearing.

On May 19, 1875, the Cook County Court in Chicago witnessed a poignant scene. Mrs. Lincoln, "gentle looking and modestly attired," sat quietly and intelligently listening while various physicians and witnesses recited incidents of her hysterical behavior and gave their united opinion that she was insane. Robert wept as he told of his efforts to take care of her and how kind she had always been to him. The eyes of his mother rested upon his tears benignly and with loving sympathy.

What was the testimony Mary Lincoln heard as she sat in quiet dignity in that courtroom? That she thought a man had taken her pocketbook and when she was asked who he was, she had answered (because she thought she had seen him in Florida) that he was a Wandering Jew. Did they not understand that all she meant by that was that the man traveled from place to place; had she not written Mrs. Orne with the same usage, ". . . you are such a wandering *Jewess*."

A doctor testified that in one of her agonizing headaches she had told him an Indian was removing the bones of her face and pulling wires out of her eyes. Perhaps this was, as the doctor called it, a hallucination; perhaps it was only her graphic attempt to tell him what the pain was like. There is no doubt that Mrs. Lincoln had strange imaginings born out of the great shocks that had beaten upon her. There is also no doubt she acted in hysterical fashion when her fears overwhelmed her. But the real cause of that trial was, of course, her unmistakable irrationality in regard to money.

The jury returned a verdict of insanity. The proud name "Mary Lincoln" was then written in the "Lunatic Record" of the Cook County Court, page 596. The words "does not manifest homicidal or suicidal tendencies" were inserted in handwriting and the words "free from vermin or any infectious disease" were crossed out of the printed form. The court ordered that she "be committed to a State hospital for the Insane."

After the verdict Robert with pale, tear-stained face went to his mother and tenderly took her hand. Mary had understood fully all that went on, yet she said to Robert in stunned unbelief: "O Robert, to think that my son would ever have done this." She permitted herself no other evidence of emotion; it was her last public appearance and she met it with dignity and composure.

By evening the numbing effect of the blow had worn off and Mary had come to a full realization that her one remaining son was getting ready to shut her up in an institution. She, of course, had no awareness of her irrationality in regard to money; to her the trial was a final catastrophic betrayal. She had gone through all her other sorrows without attempting to take her own life; always before she had someone left to love and live for; now she had no one. She tried to commit suicide that evening and even in this it was the old story of her being frustrated. The papers later described how she eluded her attendants at the hotel, asked at several drugstores for laudanum and camphor, was finally given a harmless mixture with that label. But she drank it believing it would mean a welcome death. The next day she was taken to a private sanitarium at Batavia, Illinois, superintended by Dr. R. J. Patterson and known as Bellevue Place.

For the first time Mary was under the care of a doctor who specialized in nervous and mental illness. The treatment, or perhaps the rest, apparently did her good, as from this time on the mention of hysteria fades from her record. Also when she reached the sanitarium her aimlessness was replaced by a purpose; she began to plan how she could regain her liberty. She could not turn to Robert; he had become the enemy who had had her locked up. Dr. Evans, who made so excellent a study of the insanity subject, gave out this significant statement: "It was said that Mrs. Lincoln, writing from the sanitarium, charged her son with putting her there—which was true—and for improper motives—which was not true." Robert was naturally appointed conservator of his mother's estate. In her mind, apparently, the fact that he obtained control of her money by having her declared insane furnished his motive.

The evidence of the trial showed that Robert had done everything possible to care for and protect his mother. For three weeks before the hearing he had paid a man to guard her without her knowledge when she went on the streets. She would not come to his house because of a misunderstanding with his wife. He had consulted Judge David Davis, who had administered Lincoln's estate, and Mary's loved cousin John Todd Stuart, and obtained their approval before he called for the sanity trial. His mother's interpretation as to his motive was without foundation; yet, since it related to the subject on which she was irrational, money, she believed it.

Of course the news that Mrs. Lincoln had been adjudged insane flashed all over the country. Mrs. Orne in distress wrote to Robert asking questions. Robert's answer indicates that he, as he said, had done his duty as he saw it. Six physicians had advised the step. The law made a jury verdict of insanity necessary before he could deprive his mother of her liberty in putting her where she would be cared for. She was in the private part of the house of Dr. Patterson, taking drives and walks with members of his family and her meals with them or in her room as she pleased. A carriage was at her disposal and she could receive calls and return them if accompanied by some suitable person.

Robert's letter to Mrs. Orne continued: ". . . we are on the best of terms. . . . So far as I can see she does not realize her situation at all." He believed this but it was far from the truth. Mary Lincoln was not revealing her thoughts to the son who in her mind had betrayed her for money. She was outraged at being shut up behind barred windows and deprived of her liberty and she was making very intelligent efforts to be released.

She enlisted the help of two good friends of happier days, Judge and Mrs. James B. Bradwell. Here were two influential people with legal training (Mrs. Bradwell was the first woman lawyer of Illinois) who were convinced by Mrs. Lincoln that she was sane and had been cruelly wronged. That fact itself shows how small a part of her whole personality her streak of irrationality was. Judge and Mrs. Bradwell set to work. In Mary's own words: "When all others, among them my husband's supposed friends, failed me in the most bitter hours of my life, these loyal hearts, Myra Bradwell and her husband, came to my assistance and rescued me, and under great difficulty secured my release from confinement in an insane asylum."

It was probably due to their efforts that talk arose about Mrs. Lincoln being "virtually imprisoned behind grates and bars" and "locked by her jailer as a prisoner." Dr. Patterson issued a public letter in reply stating that her release would only lead to "extended rambles," and to a renewal "of her purchasing mania and other morbid mental manifestations." He stressed the considerate treatment she was undoubtedly receiving and continued somewhat indignantly: "She has had, until the 16th inst., private unrestricted personal intercourse with Judge Bradwell, who, in a threatening and insulting letter to me, calls himself 'her legal adviser and friend.'" "The wife of Judge Bradwell," wrote Dr. Patterson, "until the date above named, has been permitted to visit Mrs. Lincoln, write her numerous letters, bear messages and packages of letters from her, and lodge over night with her in her room."

Dr. Patterson mentioned efforts to have Mrs. Lincoln transferred to Springfield to live with Mr. and Mrs. Ninian W. Edwards. They were standing by Mary in her fight to regain her liberty. In September, after a little less than four months in the sanitarium, she was removed to the Edwards home though still under judgment of insanity. She remained quietly there for nine months, until a second sanity trial was held in Chicago on June 15, 1876. The jury reversed the former verdict and found that "the said Mary Lincoln is restored to reason and is capable to manage and control her estate."

Returning to Springfield, Mrs. Lincoln on June 19 wrote Robert a letter in which she poured out the furious resentment that had seethed within her for the last thirteen months. Reading it, one can pity the sensitive man who had done his uninspired but conscientious best. The letter began abruptly: "Robert T. Lincoln." His mother demanded immediate return of all her goods in his possession, listing them in detail and indicating they had been appropriated. "I am now in constant receipt of letters, from my friends denouncing you in the bitterest terms," wrote Mary Lincoln, "six letters from prominent, *respectable* Chicago people such as you do not associate with." Two clergymen, she said, had written her that they would offer up prayers for Robert on account of his wickedness against his mother.

One infers that Mrs. Edwards too resented the stigma of insanity which the son had placed upon his mother. Mary's letter went on: "Trust not to the belief, that Mrs Edward's tongue, has not been *rancorous* against you all winter & she has maintained to the very last, that you dared not venture into her house & our presence." The letter ended in a last stabbing sentence: "Send me all that I have written for, you have tried your game of robbery long enough."

It is understandable why the shrinking Robert Lincoln made an effort to collect and destroy those letters of Mrs. Lincoln, which, to use his own words, revealed "the distressing mental disorder of my mother." Her letters written to the Bradwells have vanished. But other letters have been preserved (though not all of them can be quoted here) enough to tell the story of Mary Lincoln's resentment toward her son on account of the insanity trial, and the pitiful estrangement that resulted from it.

Just how far did Mary Lincoln's mental illness go? Because of that verdict of "insanity," which was a legal term, not a psychological one, many people have taken it for granted that she "lost her mind." One piece of evidence at the trial has rarely been quoted: that on general topics her conversation was rational and normal. She was irrational within a limited area and it is well to note what Dr. Evans says about that: "This complex of mania for money, extravagance, and miserliness—paradoxical as it appears to laymen—is well known to psychiatrists. *It is present in many people who are accepted as normal*" (Italics are the author's.) Dr. Evans also stated that Mrs.

Lincoln when she was declared "sane" at the second trial had just the same degree of irrationality as she had when the jury had found her insane.

Newly available letters written by her after the sanity trials show that her mind was not only clear but highly intelligent and that beneath the bruising of grief and public abuse, her affectionate nature remained basically the same. At the time when Dr. Evans made his valuable study he concluded that Mrs. Lincoln wrote few letters in this later period; he did not know of one after the middle of 1878. The next chapter will tell of one hundred letters which she wrote between 1876 and 1880 and we will find that they appear as the product of a keen and normal mind. It seems a vast pity that a legal process for appointing a conservator of her estate and arranging for her medical care had to brand as a lunatic a neurotic, grief-shocked woman who was rational on all subjects but one.

chapter 34

"DEAR LEWIS"

After her release from the decree of insanity in June
1876, Mary stayed with Mr. and Mrs. Ninian W. Edwards
in Springfield until fall. Their loyalty in helping her get
out of the sanitarium and in taking her into their home
had buried the bitterness between them. From then on
Mary's letters overflow with love and gratitude toward
her oldest sister and her family. But sadly she had lost
faith in John Todd Stuart, the cousin she had so loved
and trusted; in court she had heard that he had advised
Robert to have the insanity trial.

Mrs. Edwards had a grandson, Edward Lewis Baker
Jr., the son of Julia Edwards Baker. Born in 1858, he
was seventeen or eighteen during the year Mary was with
the Edwardses. At a time when this maternal woman
was filled with bitterness toward her one remaining son,
this lovable youth who reminded her, as she said, of
Willie and Tad, came into her life. The result was inevitable; she gave him her whole motherly heart. He had,
like Tad, a sunny nature and a sympathetic understanding that could make a battered, aging little woman feel
protected, valued, and feminine again.

Mary herself described Lewis in the letter she wrote
him upon receiving his photograph: " 'Love crowned you
at your birth,' . . . I remember, whilst in Washington in
the summer of *1861*—I sent your mother a bottle of
Jordan water, which had been sent me from Palestine, as
she had mentioned that she was going to have her children christened. I believe that face of yours, loved by
so many persons, *so* abounding in intelligence, good looks,
& sweet sympathy, was watered by this same Jordan
water. Yet, it required, my dear Lewis, nothing of the
kind, to beautify that nature of yours, that gladdens so
many hearts."

Mary had been branded as insane in a day far less understanding of mental illness than our own. The shame

of it overwhelmed her. "I cannot endure to meet my former friends, Lizzie," she told Mrs. Edwards bitterly, "they will never cease to regard me as a lunatic, I feel it in their soothing manner. If I should say the moon is made of green cheese they would heartily and smilingly agree with me. I love you, but I cannot stay. I would be much less unhappy in the midst of strangers."

Once more she fled into what she herself called "an *exile*." Young Lewis was her escort on the trip to New York where she embarked for France. During the next four years she wrote to him giving intimate details of what she was doing and, as her thoughts were much in the past, of what she remembered. These letters, here used for the first time, fill in a gap which has been largely a blank. They destroy the accepted picture of Mary Lincoln in those years as a distracted woman with a greatly disordered mind. There is not a trace of abnormality in these letters. Her personality emerges from them in a sort of Indian summer in which her natural qualities of sympathy, affection, and responsiveness have their last shining before pain and disease darkened them toward her final illness.

Her headquarters were at Pau, France, but there are letters from Havre, Avignon, and Bordeaux with mention of trips to Naples, Marseilles and Biarritz. In her flitting about, her Victorian conscience would not permit her to travel on Sunday.

The first letter to Lewis, written from Havre on October 17, 1876, shows a calmer Mary Lincoln than the fear-haunted woman of a year and a half before. She was in deeply appreciative mood of all that the Edwards family had done for her and of her pleasant treatment in Havre. "Such kindness, deference & attention, as I met with on my arrival here, it is impossible for me to describe to you." Then followed a delightful acknowledgment of her mistake in keeping herself secluded: "It is pleasant to be *thus* received, although of course, I am aware it is entirely my own fault, as in N. Y. & Phil, in keeping myself aloof from dear friends, who love me well. I propose to act in a more *civilized* manner in the future, which conclusion will greatly please your *very dear* Grandma."

Her thoughts centered on Lewis. She refused to have communication with Robert. By his own statement he did not even know where his mother was in Europe. But to Lewis she wrote: *"Words,* are impossible to express, *how* near you are to my heart." She planned vacations for him; he must visit places she had loved, Niagara Falls, Mount Washington. He must enjoy his youth; it did not last always. She wanted to finance a trip abroad for him: "I shall never feel satisfied until you see the beautiful Pyrenees, & have a four or five months journey, on *this* side of the water." She advised him to go to college but not to go into politics.

She talked much of the past and of her lost sons. She told Lewis what had not been known before, that Lincoln was holding her hand when the fatal shot was fired. When death took Lewis's two little sisters she wrote tenderly and understandingly of his sorrow: "We are never prepared for these things ... God, gives us our beloved ones, we make them our idols, they are removed from us & we have patiently to await the time, when *He* reunites us to them." Then followed perhaps the most poignant sentence in all her expression of her own grief: "And the *waiting,* is so long!"

One day she received a thrill that sent her spirits soaring. She did not receive American papers, a constant regret to one who was interested in all that was going on. But there was a weekly paper called the *American Register* published at Paris, and, as she was reading it casually in June 1879, her eyes fell on a short article suggesting that Robert Lincoln would be a likely candidate for the Presidency. In spite of her bitterness toward him, he was still her son. To think of a Lincoln in the White House again! All the old glory and honor, and her precious granddaughter the child of the White House! "*Little Mamie* with her charming manners & presence, in the event of *success,* will grace the place." In her elation there was a flash back to the optimism and impetuosity of Mary Lincoln in her prime. Her thoughts leaped ahead to what would happen if Robert became President. She even began to speculate about his cabinet.

She felt "so isolated from the world." On June 12, 1880, she complained she did not know who was nominated. When political news came she did not always approve of it. When President Hayes had placed in his cabinet David M. Key, "a man, who served in the Confederate Army, during the War," she was indignant. "We have too many other men in our country, with talents & patriotism, to the *true cause,* not to reward a Secessionist." Her indignation at the secession movement and intense devotion to "the *true cause,*" so vital and fundamental to Lincoln, remained as stanch as during the war.

There is some mention of the financial complications arising from living in a foreign country. Mails were uncertain. Sometimes a "pension paper" did not come and once the form was not filled out to the satisfaction of the consul with whom she had to deal. In her management of matters like this she gives one a surprise.

She had left her financial affairs at home in charge of Mr. Jacob Bunn in Springfield. Eighty-nine business letters she wrote Mr. Bunn have been preserved. They show an intelligent woman dealing competently with financial transactions, watching the fluctuations of gold, following the intricacies of exchange and interest rates, and managing to get these matters straightened out—all this in a country where she was using a foreign language.

Homesickness runs through the letters to Lewis. She so longed to see them all, to be in the home circle, to know all the news. "It needs no assurance of mine, to convince you, that a long period of absence from America . . . is simply an *exile.*"

Mary Lincoln had gone to Pau perhaps because it was considered a health resort. Disease was rapidly overtaking her now. There is good reason to believe she had diabetes. She is quoted as referring to "continual running waters," she was subject to boils, was losing weight, and having trouble with her vision. Before she lost weight she had a condition which caused bloating of her tissues. She had for years suffered from some form of rheumatism, especially in her back. She probably had high blood pressure.

In December 1879, while hanging a picture over the mantel, she fell from a stepladder and seriously injured her spine, causing partial paralysis of the lower part of her body. By January 16 her weight was down to one hundred pounds and she was writing of "my poor broken back, with its *three* plasters & my left side always in pain."

The letters after her fall trace continued suffering and an increasing conviction that she must come home. Early in June 1880, when she attempted with the help of a *bonne* to make arrangements to remove from a fourth floor, the torturing left side gave way and she collapsed.

She apologizes for telling about this: "This is a weary recital to you, dear Lewis, but with your great, good heart perhaps it will not be amiss, to write you the exact truth."

The letter of October 7, giving the date of her sailing (October 16) has a note of desperation: "I cannot trust myself, *any longer* away from you all—I am too ill & feeble in health . . . I entreat you, by all that is merciful, dear Lewis, to meet me on the steamer."

That steamer was *l'Amérique* and Sarah Bernhardt was also aboard. The great French actress tells in *Memories of My Life* how she noticed on deck "a lady dressed in black with a sad, resigned face." At a sudden lurch of the ship, both were thrown, and it was only Sarah's seizing of the lady's skirt that prevented the latter from falling head first down a stairway. The actress's account continues: "Very much hurt, though, she was, and a trifle confused; she thanked me in such a gentle, dreamy voice that my heart began to beat with emotion.

"'You might have been killed, madame,' I said, 'down that horrible staircase.'

"'Yes,' she answered, with a sigh of regret, 'but it was not God's will.'"

Sarah Bernhardt revealed her name, and the lady, very pale, said in a voice scarcely audible, "I am the widow of President Lincoln." With dramatic interpretation the actress said she felt: "I had just done this unhappy woman the only service that I ought not to have done her—I had saved her from death."

Lewis met his aunt on the boat as requested. There was much ado over Sarah's arrival. The little gray-haired woman had to stand back at the disembarking to make a pathway for the great actress. People have read humiliation into her mind on that occasion, but Lewis reported it otherwise to his family. He was amused at the fanfare, and his aunt appreciated his gay attitude but was only too glad to pass unnoticed. She wanted no gaze of strangers; she had learned that "In ill health & sadness quietude & loved faces, are far best." When Lewis took her to a hotel, he registered by her wish as "Edward Lewis Baker and Aunt."

Lewis took her back to Springfield to the Edwards home. There Robert came to see his mother in May 1881. This is evidently the visit mentioned by Dr. Evans when

Robert asked her forgiveness and love. He took with him that most effective of all advocates, his little daughter, Mary Lincoln. His mother's affectionate heart could not hold out against her son and grandchild; she promised to forgive and forget. Dr. Evans doubted whether she ever completely did so, but we will find that she did establish close relations with Robert and his family again. Because he was her son she could forgive him much.

But he was still Robert the uncomprehending. On returning to Washington from Springfield he wrote Mrs. Orne concerning his mother: "The reports you have seen about her are exaggerated very much. She is undoubtedly far from well & has not been out of her room for more than six months and she thinks she is very ill. My own judgment is that some part of her trouble is imaginary."

In the fall of that year, 1881, the pain and illness which Robert could not comprehend caused Mrs. Lincoln to seek in New York the medical attention of Dr. Lewis A. Sayre, the leading orthopedic surgeon of his day. He was said to have known her when both were young in Lexington, Kentucky.

That fall, owing to agitation about raising the amount of Mrs. Lincoln's pension, her name was again appearing in the newspapers. Reporters came to interview the invalid, who was living at Dr. E. P. Miller's medical baths establishment on West 26th Street, in New York. A newspaperman in November found her propped up with pillows on a sofa and unable to move without assistance as the result of the spinal injury received in her fall. "She is, in fact, deserted and next to friendless," ran his pitying account, "with the exception of her son Robert and his wife, Mary, who visit her at intervals of two or three weeks."

We know then that affectionate relations had been resumed and we find her defending Robert from criticism. She was, of course, still irrationally convinced of her poverty and dire need of the increased pension, but Robert must not be blamed for not taking care of her. "His kind heart had urged this many times," she was quoted as saying, "and also his wife had done the same . . ." But his mother said she "did not desire to have him do so, for he had his own brood to look after and had his hands full." The reporter who wrote this had spent two hours with her and found that "Mentally Mrs. Lincoln is active and clear, talks with great rapidity, and is pleased to meet her friends who may call to visit her."

In pouring out her obsession as to her poverty she chanced to give a rare bit of description of Abraham Lincoln. "Her eyes suffused with tears as she related instances of her husband's generosity during the war, and said that she had remonstrated with him, fearing that he would go out of office in debt. He said, 'Never mind, Mary, I'll go back to law, and with hard work, I think I can get together enough to make us comfortable enough for life.'" He would have done it too, added Mrs. Lincoln. "My husband could not have lived and not worked."

Two dear friends of former days, Mr. and Mrs. N. W. Miner, came to see her. They found her in a poorly furnished back room at Dr. Miller's, gray-haired, "almost blind," "partially paralyzed," helpless, with no one to wait upon her. Filled with compassion and indignation, Mr. Miner shortly thereafter delivered before a pastor's conference in New York a stirring vindication of Mrs. Lincoln. This received much publicity and set in motion additional forces toward the increasing of her pension. In January 1882 her pension of $3000 annually was raised to $5000 and Congress at the same time voted her a donation of $15,000.

But the movement had stirred up the old unfavorable stories about her. A poignant statement which Mrs. Lincoln made to Mr. Miner applied to all the cruel publicity of her widowhood: "Mr. Miner, what have I done, that I am so persecuted by the press? I am a poor, lonely woman; my husband is dead, and two of my sons are dead; my health is shattered, and I am almost blind from constant weeping. I try to keep myself secluded from the world, but I cannot escape them; they will follow me, and say hard and cruel things about me. I long to leave the world and be at rest."

On March 21, 1882, his Aunt Mary wrote from New York her last letter to "My dear Lewis." The writing is large and uneven; she could no longer see to pen her flowing script. She was returning to Springfield, she said, giving him the hour at which to meet her and asking him to look after the invalid's chair which she was sending.

With invalid chair Mary Lincoln came back to her room at the Edwards home. The shades of that room were kept drawn, shutting out a view of the streets where she had once walked lightly, joyous with life. The shadows in her mind were deepening. She seemed closer to those who had "gone before." Once, after a severe illness abroad, she had written Mrs. Orne: "I have been so near my husband—there were days of delirium—when I can quite recall—that my dearly loved ones—were hanging over me . . ." Her long habit of wifely devotion was now outlasting crippled body and clouded mind: she told one who was ministering to her that the place beside her on the bed was the President's place. Her love for him was greater than her life.

No sunlight was permitted to come into her darkened room; it was lighted dimly with candles. Perhaps the light hurt her half-blinded eyes. In the storeroom the floor sagged beneath the accumulations of her shopping, concrete evidence of that streak of mental illness which had caused such havoc in her record. On the street outside little boys scurried in fright past the house with the shade-drawn room where people said there was "a crazy woman."

In July she was suffering from an attack of boils. One Saturday she walked across her room with someone to help her but it was her last effort. That evening the frail little body became paralyzed and she passed into unconsciousness. At 8:15 on Sunday evening, July 16, 1882, her labored breathing ceased.

The news of Mary Lincoln's death flashed over the country. It came to that stanch little woman, Jane Swisshelm, who found it "sad, glad tidings," because, as she said: "I have mourned with her often, and why should I not rejoice with her now?" She remembered what Mrs. Lincoln had told her: "Ah, my dear friend, you will rejoice when you know that I have gone to my husband and children!"

Jane started to write a tribute to Lincoln's widow but for once her vigorous pen faltered: "I want to write of her as a historical character—as one to whom the people of this country owe a great reparation," were her words, "but can only think of her as a most affectionate, faithful friend."

Mary's friends came to the Edwards home on the hill to look down at her as she lay in her casket in the same room and almost the same place where forty years before she had stood as a bride. They noticed that the thin, worn face was calm and peaceful, with the faint suggestion of a smile. The hands were folded across her breast; on her finger was a wedding ring inscribed, "Love is eternal."

The funeral service was held in the First Presbyterian Church, successor to the one where, on quiet and neighborly Sundays, she used to sit beside Mr. Lincoln in "our particular pew." It was a fitting funeral for the widow of a President. The flower designs were many, costly, and elaborate; the pallbearers included the governor of Illinois and Springfield's leading dignitaries. In the list was the Honorable James C. Conkling, once a member of the lighthearted coterie, who had described young Mary Todd as "the very creature of excitement." Among the banked-up floral tributes was a large design in the form of a book, "made of carnations with the words 'Mary Lincoln' in forget-me-nots, on the open pages, . . . the loving offering of the people" of Springfield.

In his sermon the Reverend James A. Reed presented a moving analogy. He spoke of two stately pine trees he had seen growing on a high ledge so close together that their branches and roots were intertwined. One was struck down by lightning. The other was seemingly unhurt at first, but the blow that had destroyed its mate was fatal to it also: "Its after subsistence was merely a living death. Similar was the course of life with the illustrious Lincoln and his mate . . ."

A long procession of carriages followed the casket of Abraham Lincoln's widow as it was borne to Oak Ridge cemetery, quiet and beautiful as the little graveyard in Virginia where she and her husband had once walked together. A great crowd of people stood by as she was laid where she had longed to be. "When I again rest by *his* side, I will be comforted," she had said. "And the *waiting,* is so long!"

The cruel years were ended. Mary Lincoln was at peace.